Rethinking National Identity in the Age of Migration

*Bertelsmann Stiftung, Migration Policy Institute (eds.)*

# Rethinking National Identity in the Age of Migration

The Transatlantic Council on Migration

| Verlag Bertelsmann**Stiftung**

Bibliographic information published by the Deutsche Nationalbibliothek

The Deutsche Nationalbibliothek lists this publication in the
Deutsche Nationalbibliografie; detailed bibliographic data
is available on the Internet at http://dnb.d-nb.de.

© 2012 Verlag Bertelsmann Stiftung, Gütersloh
*Responsible:* Dr. Christal Morehouse, Michelle Mittelstadt
*Copy editor:* Fayre Makeig
*Production editor:* Christiane Raffel
*Cover design:* Elisabeth Menke
*Cover illustration:* Hill Street Studios/Getty Images
*Typesetting and Printing:* Hans Kock Buch- und Offsetdruck GmbH, Bielefeld
ISBN 978-3-86793-427-5

*www.bertelsmann-stiftung.org/publications*

# Contents

# Introduction

*Demetrios G. Papademetriou, Jörg Dräger*

Globalization has been rewriting more than just the rules of economic behavior among nations. It has also created and nurtured the conditions for greater human mobility, with unprecedented levels of diversity transforming communities and challenging closely held notions of national identity. The Transatlantic Council on Migration, an initiative of the Migration Policy Institute with policy support from the Bertelsmann Stiftung, convened in Berlin on November 16–18, 2011 to examine the role migration plays in the social unrest seen in societies on both sides of the Atlantic. The Council's goal: help shape a new vision for social cohesion that harnesses diversity's potential benefits for all elements of society.

While a consensus may be emerging as to what has *not* worked well in the realm of immigrant integration (albeit with some misunderstanding, such as the role of multiculturalist policies), less thought has been given to proactively articulating a new "social contract" to bring immigrants and natives together in pursuit of shared goals. This volume – the Council's sixth edited volume – contributes to the debate by offering ideas for the next generation of policies that can build more inclusive civic identities. The book, which contains in-depth analyses and policy recommendations, builds on the Council's prior volumes: *Delivering Citizenship* (November 2008); *Talent, Competitiveness and Migration* (April 2009); *Migration, Public Opinion and Politics* (November 2009); *Prioritizing Integration* (April 2010); and *Improving the Governance of International Migration* (November 2011). The resulting collection deepens the evidence base on the complex migration and integration issues that challenge transatlantic societies.

The volume opens in Section One with the Council's statement on "Rethinking National Identity in the Age of Migration." Demetrios G. Papademetriou and Ulrich Kober distill the main themes and recommendations that emerged from the Transatlantic Council's meeting in Berlin on how to mitigate the disorienting effects of rapid societal change. The authors dissect the roots of society's anxiety about immigration and put forward ten innovative policy ideas that can help create the conditions for cohesive societies. They argue that the key to fostering greater cohesiveness is to involve *all* citizens in the process of shaping the new "we."

Section Two, "Managing Diversity in Challenging Times," offers in three chapters three perspectives on the perceived "failure" of integration models in many Western democracies. Will Kymlicka begins this section with his chapter on "Multiculturalism: Success, Failure, and the Future." His analysis challenges four powerful myths about multiculturalism and discusses the factors that can either facilitate or impede its successful implementation.

In Chapter Two, Cas Mudde focuses on the complex relationship between migration and the rise of radical-right political parties in three industrialized regions: North America, Western Europe, and Central and Eastern Europe. Titled "The Relationship Between Immigration and Nativism in Europe and North America," this chapter charts the uneven success of far-right parties in these regions and analyzes the diverse state responses. The author shows that the relationship between immigration and extremism is not as clear-cut as is often assumed.

Christian Joppke is the author of Chapter Three, "The Role of the State in Cultural Integration: Trends, Challenges, and Ways Ahead," which examines how different European approaches to cultural integration have converged in important ways. Many liberal states have constitutional restrictions on state intervention in sensitive identity issues, which are for the individual and not the state to decide. A second commonality, for over a decade now, is "civic integration" policies that seek to bind newcomers to majority institutions and culture by requiring them to learn the host-society language and acknowledge basic host-society norms and values. This chapter concludes with recommendations on how governments may achieve a mode of civic integration that is restrained enough to respect the moral autonomy of immigrants and aggressive enough to further a more cohesive and integrated host society.

Section Three, "Country Perspectives," contains eight case studies on national identity in the age of migration. It examines the lessons that can be drawn from different approaches to immigrant integration and diversity in North America and Europe, looking specifically at Canada, France, the United States, Germany, the Netherlands, the United Kingdom, Spain, and Norway.

In Chapter Four, Irene Bloemraad takes an in-depth look at the Canadian approach to pluralism. She asks whether Canada is truly an outlier in terms of being able to deflect anti-immigrant sentiment and opposition to multicultural policies directed at immigrants and settled minority groups. In her piece on "Understanding 'Canadian Exceptionalism' in Immigration and Pluralism Policy," Bloemraad concludes that immigrant selection policy and geography are not sufficient to explain why Canada is more open to and optimistic about immigration: The Canadian view of immigration as a nation-building exercise is also a key factor.

Patrick Simon examines France's controversial public debates on national identity in Chapter Five, "French National Identity and Integration: Who Belongs to the National Community?". Concerns that the split allegiances of "foreigners" might weaken social cohesion in France are examined systematically using the findings of the "Trajectories and Origins: a Survey on Population Diversity in France" (TeO) study. The author strongly challenges the perception that ties to another country automatically undermine individuals' commitment to France and argues that restrictive definitions of national identity can be counterproductive.

Chapter Six, "Contested Ground: Immigration in the United States," is by Michael Jones-Correa. As immigration to the United

States has increased and spread to new regions, there have been growing concerns that it has negatively impacted the US economy and altered the social fabric of society. This chapter analyzes the roots of American anxiety about immigration – particularly illegal immigration – and the policy responses implemented over the past 50 years.

Naika Foroutan is the author of Chapter Seven on "Identity and (Muslim) Immigration in Germany." Germany is already a diverse country and will become increasingly so over time. One-fifth of the population is comprised of immigrants or the children of immigrants and, in many of Germany's largest cities, a majority of children under the age of 6 have a so-called migration background. However, while Germany has become a country of immigration during recent decades, a still dominant perception in media and public discourse is that of a homogenous German society in which those with a migration background cannot fully belong. Muslims have become a focus of public debate despite comprising only 5 percent of the population, and German public opinion contains some of the strongest anti-Muslim sentiments in Western Europe. This chapter concludes with recommendations on how policymakers can combat negative stereotypes and develop a new national narrative reflective of Germany's demographic reality.

In Chapter Eight, "The Netherlands: From National Identity to Plural Identifications," Monique Kremer analyzes the highly politicized issue of what it means to be "Dutch." A new dialogue in the Netherlands has marked a departure from multiculturalism and a turn toward "culturalized citizenship" – the idea that being Dutch means adhering to a certain set of cultural and social norms and practices. Immigrants now have to "become Dutch," not only through language acquisition, but also in a cultural and moral sense. Kremer concludes that accepting the existence of plural national identities can be beneficial for social cohesion.

Shamit Saggar and Will Somerville are coauthors of Chapter Nine titled, "Building a British Model of Integration in an Era of Immigration: Policy Lessons for Government." This chapter analyzes developments in integration policy over the past 15 years in the United Kingdom, dating from the election of the Labour government in May 1997 until the present day. The analysis focuses on whether policy has influenced (or has been perceived to influence) national identity, immigrant integration outcomes, and neighborhood cohesion. The chapter draws conclusions about the future direction of integration policy in the United Kingdom.

Chapter Ten, authored by Joaquín Arango, is titled "Exceptional in Europe? Spain's Experience with Immigration and Integration." In just a decade, Spain's foreign-born population increased from less than 4 percent of the total population to almost 14 percent. Fewer than 1.5 million immigrants resided in Spain in 2000, compared to 6.5 million in 2009. But, unlike other European countries, Spain has not seen a significant backlash against immigration, even amid an economic crisis that has hit the country hard and led to extremely high levels of unemployment – especially among immigrants. There is evidence, however, that this could be changing. This chapter concludes that Spain's exceptionalism is in danger and that economic stresses will be a key determinant of social cohesion in Spain. Yet, given the influence that politicians have on societal attitudes, the new government would be well advised to continue with policies that foster integration and promote the idea that immigration benefits society.

"Immigration and National Identity in Norway" is authored by Thomas Hylland Eriksen and comprises Chapter Eleven of this volume. Debates about integration, immigration policy, multiculturalism, and national identity have flourished in Norway in recent years – particularly in light of the atrocities of July 22, 2011. Although less than one-third of immigrants in Norway are from predominantly Muslim countries, it is Muslim immigrants who are the object of the greatest political and social debates. Looking ahead, Eriksen finds that a society that has historically been very ethnically and culturally homogenous faces a key challenge: adjusting to its increasing diversity. In order for the nation to instill solidarity and cohesion, a number of steps need to be taken, including strengthening unity and citizenship, promoting diversity within a framework of Norwegian values, and ensuring representation of diversity in the public and private sectors.

The appendix of this volume includes a resource section, information about the Transatlantic Council on Migration, biographies of the authors, and acknowledgments.

With this book, the Transatlantic Council on Migration – together with MPI and the Bertelsmann Stiftung – hopes to deepen the level of knowledge and policy deliberations on migration on both sides of the Atlantic.

# Section I:
# The Transatlantic Council on Migration

# Council Statement: Rethinking National Identity in the Age of Migration

## The seventh plenary meeting of the Transatlantic Council on Migration

*Demetrios G. Papademetriou, Ulrich Kober*

### Introduction: The Roots of Society's Anxiety over Immigration

Large-scale immigration has led to unprecedented levels of diversity around the globe, transforming communities in fundamental ways and challenging long and closely held notions of national identity. In recent years, this rapid demographic transformation has coincided with a set of deeper challenges – first and foremost among them the most severe economic downturn in decades. Political leaders thus find themselves having to navigate a tangled web of complex policy dilemmas – from how to respond to economic insecurity to how to continue to draw benefits from (and make the political case for) globalization, to coming to terms with hybrid identities – all challenges that have caused enormous anxiety and even social unrest.

In the last few years, the backlash against immigration has manifested itself in increasingly vocal criticisms of "multiculturalism." A chorus of European leaders has claimed that the very policies that aimed to weave societies together have instead split them apart, emphasizing difference rather than building community. And as people fear that the social fabric of their communities may be fraying, they have tightened their grip on the things they hold most dear – their identity, language, culture, and values. In response, many countries have narrowed the rights to residence and citizenship and attempted to more rigidly enforce cultural conformity, taking steps whose (predictable) effect has been to isolate – or, in some cases, penalize – those who fall outside these norms.

The seventh plenary meeting of the Transatlantic Council on Migration brought together high-level officials from Europe and North America in Berlin in November 2011. The Council meeting focused on what policymakers can do to mitigate the disorienting effects of rapid societal change – especially change tied or *perceived to be tied* to immigration – in order to create stronger and more cohesive societies. For governments, both the challenge and opportunity has become to create a new definition of "we" based on a more inclusive idea of national identity and belonging, and to convince the broader society that investing in integration is an investment in shared futures.

Skepticism about immigration – and, in particular, negative public reactions to it – does not always dovetail with the arc of large-scale immigration: Extreme reactions have occurred in places *without* large or sudden increases in the immigrant population. The opposite is also true: Not all places with sizeable or unexpected inflows of immigrants have experienced social disorder. Nor is illegal immigration the main culprit across societies. In fact, anti-immigrant expressions in some countries (e.g., the United States) continue to flourish even in the face of evidence of 40-year lows in illegal flows.

For example, the foreign-born population in the Netherlands has increased by less than 2 percentage points in the past decade, yet the Party for Freedom and Democracy (VVD) has become the third-largest in the country while campaigning on an anti-Muslim platform.[1] In the same vein, the Swiss referendum to ban minarets passed by over 50 percent in a country with a Muslim population of less than 6 percent (Pew Forum on Religion and Public Life 2010). And, in the United States, the state of Alabama, whose immigrant population hovers under 4 percent,[2] recently passed one of the country's most

---

1  See Eurostat 2011. Muslims make up 5.5 percent of the Dutch population. See Pew Forum on Religion and Public Life 2010.
2  Alabama's foreign-born population increased from 43,533 in 1990 (1.1 percent of the population) to 168,596 in 2010 (3.5 percent of the population). See Migration Policy Institute Data Hub 2011a.

restrictive immigration laws. This may be evidence of the fact that it is the pace of change and composition of a flow, not the magnitude, which has the greatest effect. Though the state's immigrant population of 168,596 ranked it 33rd among US states in 2010, Alabama experienced the fastest rate of growth in its foreign-born population in the United States between 2000 and 2010 – with 92.1 percent growth compared to the national average of 28.4 percent. More than half of the state's immigrant population is Hispanic, with a sizeable number undoubtedly illegally present.[3]

Elsewhere, however, unprecedented rates of growth in immigration have not given rise to the kinds of anti-immigration reactions one might have expected. In Spain, the foreign-born share of the population soared from 3.6 percent in 2000 to 14 percent in 2010 (Migration Policy Institute Data Hub n.d.; Papademetriou, Sumption, and Terrazas 2011); and, in Ireland, it increased from 7 percent in 1995 to 12.8 percent in 2010 (ibid.). Yet, despite rising, if isolated popular reaction to immigration, neither country has produced a political party with an anti-immigrant platform on the national stage.

Finally, immigration itself is typically not the only, or even the most prominent, driver of the anxiety, social unease, and occasional unrest in our societies today, although it is often a contributing factor. More properly, immigration's effects on society are best understood as they interact with several different frames at once:

– *A cultural frame:* the sense of loss of control of the markers of one's identity, namely language, cultural norms, and a basic societal ethos
– *A social frame:* the relative costs to social "constancy" and familiarity that large influxes of newcomers – especially the visibly differ-

---

3 Migratio Policy Institute Data Hub 2011b. Measuring the unauthorized migrant population is an inexact science, especially at the state level. Jeffrey Passel estimates that, in 2010, there were between 75,000 and 160,000 immigrants illegally resident in Alabama. With such a broad range, combined with a high margin of error, we cannot be sure what percentage of the foreign born in the state is illegally resident. See Passel 2011.

ent – entail and fears that neighborhoods cannot quickly adapt to new needs

- *An economic frame:* concerns over the redistribution of public goods and resources, and over the high perceived costs of immigration and integration
- *A political frame:* the public's loss of confidence in the political classes as well as the sense of loss of sovereignty to supranational bodies, such as the World Trade Organization (WTO) or the European Union (EU)
- *A security frame:* the fear that society's newest members are not committed to their new country and might contribute to social unrest, illegality, crime, and even terrorism.

It is how these different concerns interact with one another – and become *activated* in specific national contexts – that fuels the anxiety that often surrounds immigration and contributes to extremist political views. In this context, immigration has become a visible target over which to exercise control in a time of great uncertainty.

**The Five Principal Drivers of Anxiety**

*1. Culture and Loss of Identity*

Many fear that the shared norms and values that bind societies together are weakened when newcomers do not adapt to the host-country language, culture, and identity – and, worse, if they harbor and practice illiberal cultural practices. On both sides of the Atlantic, the perceived cultural and/or linguistic homogeneity of "newcomers" (e.g., Muslims in Europe or Latinos in the United States) are seen as more of a challenge – and more likely to result in emphasis of a subculture rather than integration into the mainstream – than would be the case with a genuinely multiethnic wave of immigrants. Visibly and religiously different newcomers are thus thought to undermine closely held notions of who the "we" is in society, even when they comprise small portions of the foreign-born population.[4]


## 2. Rapid Pace of Social Change

Many feel that too much change has occurred too fast, with negative consequences for neighborhoods and entire cities, especially for their overburdened education, health, transportation, and public-safety systems. Countries that had very small foreign-born populations two decades ago (e.g., Spain, Ireland, or Greece) became massive immigration destinations seemingly overnight, with inadequate and/or uneven legal and institutional preparation. And even in countries more accustomed to immigration, workers settled in areas that had not experienced much new immigration for many decades. As suggested earlier, anxiety about immigration is typically associated less with the *absolute numbers* of newcomers than with the *speed of change* and its geographic concentration. As the second generation comes of age in these societies, the question of *who gets to define* societal norms is paramount. While certain mechanisms exist to compel the newly arrived to adapt to the host-country culture and identity (e.g., civic integration and citizenship tests), the ability of the second and third generations to "redefine" the national ethos cannot be impeded.


## 3. Economics and Inequality

Unease over the unequal distribution of public goods and resources – especially in the face of sometimes grossly uneven outcomes between the "winners" and "losers" of globalization – have placed new

---

4 Some recent legislation governing Muslim cultural practices, for example, reflects this: The 2011 ban on wearing burqas that went into effect in Belgium is estimated to apply to as few as 30 women; and even in France, with a Muslim population of approximately 4.7 million, the ban on burqas and niqabs is estimated to apply to 300–2,000 people. See BBC News 2010; *Le Parisien* 2011; and *The Guardian* 2011.

strains on communities, particularly those unaccustomed to accommodating immigrants and minorities. A critical driver of public opinion about immigration is whether immigrants are seen as economic assets or liabilities. But while it is almost impossible to quantify all the economic contributions of immigrants, fiscal costs can be counted more easily – and they frequently tend to be confused with economic effects. Immigrants are often depicted as a financial burden on the host society, contributing to greater unemployment and wage depression, and straining the welfare state – in other words, taking more out of the system than they are contributing to it. Further, publics feel they shoulder not only the short-term costs of immigration, but also the long-term costs of *integration* – and lose sight of the totality of long-term benefits, which are almost always very significant.

Policymakers thus find themselves straddling two contradictory and highly emotive migration debates. One revolves around the economic importance of labor migration – which for countries with long-term low fertility is often stark – and the other around the cultural "costs" of past migration. While little can be done about the latter (other than focusing strongly on education, training, and investment in the civic engagement of the progeny of earlier immigrant waves), the former goes to the core of economic growth and competitiveness, especially in terms of creating a "welcoming culture" that can attract the better-skilled immigrants that competitive economies require.

### 4. Politics: Low Confidence in Government and Loss of Sovereignty

With hardly any exceptions, there is extraordinary dissatisfaction with the government elites on both sides of the Atlantic. Even publics with favorable views of immigration in general have negative views about those in charge of managing it, who are seen as either unaware of or indifferent to the effects of immigration on local communities – and on those who globalization leaves behind. The fact that, as a rule, politicians are deeply reticent to hold regular conversations with their publics about immigration – only engaging the issue when things go wrong – leaves the impression that no one is in control. Finally, the steady loss of sovereign control over the issue to seemingly "unaccountable" supranational bodies with a growing reach on immigration decisions further fuels popular distrust, at least in some quarters.

*5. Security and Social Unrest*

Publics want to believe there is a steady hand holding the reins of the immigration system. What is most destabilizing is when public expectations of how much – and what kind – of immigration to expect diverge from reality, which in turn leads people to perceive the immigration system as "out of control." Highly publicized and often inflated accounts of illegality are brandished by opportunistic politicians, especially on the far right. Meanwhile, hard data demonstrating the success of enforcement efforts tend to fall on deaf ears. Immigration's perceived link to crime – and, even more worrisome, to terrorism – completes the circle of fear and anxiety. Trust in the system can only be restored if everyone in society can see and understand the rules governing immigration *and* be confident that they will be enforced.

## Conclusions: Creating the Conditions for Cohesive Societies

Integration will have "succeeded" when immigrants and their children have equal opportunities to compete for the same economic outcomes and can participate in civic and political life on the same basis as their native counterparts. To achieve this, states must invest in both targeted and mainstream policies in the two most important loci of integration: workplaces and schools. But there is also an intangible factor in all this: the *feeling* of belonging. States, working closely with civil society, have the responsibility to lay the foundation for immigrants to be seen as important contributors to society and to consistently and systematically reinforce this message; to create level playing fields in which everyone is treated equally and no one faces barriers to school or work; and to identify and reinforce shared values and norms.

21

In pursuing these ends, states must think and act strategically, using a surgeon's scalpel rather than a butcher's cleaver: Efforts to legislate cultural practices or suppress objectionable views often backfire,
further triggering the impulse to reject mainstream values. States
should instead strive to be active facilitators, providing factual information and resources to create the virtuous cycles of desirable behavior.
When tensions in society inevitably erupt, the state must protect free
speech and encourage a robust debate: Efforts to suppress people's ability to voice their real fears and anxieties will only foment extremism.

### Ten Steps for Fostering Greater Cohesiveness

*1. Leaders must listen to and demonstrate that they understand the
concerns of their electorate*

Policymakers and politicians must listen carefully to the legitimate
concerns and fears of their electorate. While some apprehensions
about migration – particularly those concerning jobs and loss of national identity – may be overstated, policymakers will only work to
further entrench these anxieties by ignoring or dismissing them.
Governments have to take anxiety about immigration seriously and
communicate thoughtfully and on an ongoing basis with their publics
– in an honest, direct, and fact-supported manner – about how immigration is affecting everyone's lives – and what policymakers are doing to address its downsides. At the same time, however, leaders must
actively engage the public and lead the discourse about the value of a
well-conceived and -executed immigration policy.

*2. Build a sense of "ownership" in the integration process*

Rapid change can be destabilizing for communities, especially when
people feel they have little control over things that greatly influence (or
are *perceived* to greatly influence) their daily lives. Chief among these

is the fear that large-scale immigration, and the resulting expansion of who the "we" is in society, are chipping away at the markers of national identity to which people have become accustomed. One way of assuaging this concern is to involve *all* citizens in shaping the next generation of cultural norms and values, giving them a sense of ownership over the integration process. This will become ever more important as the second generation comes of age in new countries of immigration, yielding a new pool of citizens who will contribute to molding and redefining social and political life.

### 3. National identity is now more than ever about becoming rather than being

Countries, such as Canada and the United States, that emphasize a process of belonging and "becoming," rather than a static sense of "being," are better able to embrace, "digest," and benefit from diversity than societies whose very actions betray a fear that newcomers will dilute a nation's core identity. In a world that is changing as fast as it is, such fears – whether openly expressed or clearly implied through governments' public policy choices – foster the very forces of "exclusivity" that undermine social cohesion and prevent newcomers from being accepted by the host community. Such forces, in turn, become the real barrier to immigrants' social and political participation, especially for the visibly different and those who practice certain minority religions.

Immigrant integration cannot succeed unless national identity is redefined in an inclusive way, focusing on shared values and on experiences that bind people together – including work – rather than on exclusive characteristics (e.g., shared ancestry) that newcomers cannot possibly acquire. Articulating a dynamic nation-building narrative – and an inclusive national identity – that incorporates immigrants is critical to creating a pragmatic definition of "we." This should be reinforced in the public square, through school curricula (telling the story of minority contributions, as in Canada), and in the narratives of leaders of public and private institutions so that immigrants see themselves as accepted by the society's institutions and those who lead them.

*4. Acknowledge the reality of and eliminate barriers to the coexistence of multiple identities*

Efforts to restrict plural identities are counterproductive. Empirical studies in Canada, France, and the Netherlands show that strong ethnic ties and national pride are not mutually exclusive: 47 percent of immigrants to France, for example, say they "feel French" despite maintaining ties (and even citizenship) to their country of origin (Simon 2012). This indicates that the choice to have dual citizenship is more of a practical consideration than evidence of split loyalties. The same French study finds that 90 percent of those found to have a "minority identity" (that is, who say their ethnicity is an important feature of their identity) say they "feel at home in France," pointing to a robust new generation with "hyphenated" identities. Evidence further shows that policies circumscribing the expression of these identities produce the opposite effect: "Symbolic" ethnic ties become more salient precisely *because* they are restricted. The conclusion of this and similar studies makes the compelling case that immigrants integrate most smoothly when they are able to *combine* their ethnic identity with a new national identity (as opposed to having to choose between them).

*5. Create clear pathways to permanent residence and citizenship –
and implement them impartially*

The existence of a clear *pathway to permanent residence and citizenship* that is applied dispassionately is critical. Even if not all immigrants will become citizens, the fact that they are viewed as *potential* permanent members of society after an initial (but finite) period in the migration process can serve as a powerful incentive for greater engagement in community life on the part of both natives and newcomers alike. The government should also find ways to encourage publics to picture a shared future with their neighbors. Doing so successfully will make both parties more likely to make long-term investments in building community.

### 6. *Offer practical, nonpunitive integration assistance*

States should provide robust, subsidized integration mechanisms (e.g., language classes) to help newcomers negotiate their new environment more effectively and develop a stake in the future of the community in which they settle. Canada's successes on this front make a strong case that language and civics courses that are voluntary, free, and not punitive in intent (i.e., not tied to continuing access to residency or social benefits) are most successful. However, this does not mean that there are "no strings attached" in terms of the host society's expectations of newcomers. Both Canada and Australia have insisted on shared liberal values by formally defining the range of "legitimate cultural traditions" in their constitutions. Moreover, ensuring that integration and naturalization processes are meaningful (e.g., by asking immigrants to demonstrate their knowledge of host-country language, civics, and values) exist alongside efforts to assist applicants in successfully meeting these requirements. Governments must thus strike an often delicate balance between requirements that are so lenient as to become meaningless and those that are so stringent as to be exclusionary.

### 7. *Focus integration efforts on the places where integration takes place most naturally: workplaces and schools*

While some immigrant groups seem to succeed everywhere they go (e.g., university-educated Asian immigrants often outperform natives on both sides of the Atlantic), far too often the story is one of integration failures. Many immigrants (and their children), as well as long-standing minorities, lag behind their peers in educational and labor-market attainment. In several countries, immigrant unemployment rates are close to double those of natives, and the poor outcomes of some groups (e.g., certain Turkish, North African, Caribbean, or Southeast Asian immigrants) stubbornly persist across generations. Even though some of the "fault lines" of the identity crisis may point to cultural differences, the *solution* may not be cultural. At the core of most failures in integration lie social and economic breakdowns. It is thus more useful (and less controversial) to emphasize investment in practical areas, such as employment or education, than to legislate norms and values. And for programs in these areas to succeed, immigrants themselves will have to believe that education is the basis of their future success.

The benefits of emphasizing *work* amount to much more than earning a living: Employment is a vehicle for contributing to society and, thus, a way of belonging. And it can help change the perceptions of the receiving community about various immigrant groups and thus, by extension, about immigration itself. Moreover, there is a "culture of work" that is itself a critical form of participation in society and can build a shared identity – and common cause – that does not pivot around ethnicity. Moreover, as integration efforts take hold and mature, politicians should gradually break the habit of structuring their relationships with immigrants and their children on the basis of their ethnicity or religion. It may, in fact, be more productive to engage with individuals based on their economic contributions – often the glue that binds them to the entire community – rather than on their ethnicity, which sets them apart.


*8. Focus on all disadvantaged populations, not just immigrants*

As both great affluence and great poverty continue to grow, the question of how increasingly scarce public resources are distributed will divide societies. When a state's own citizens are suffering, it may be difficult to argue for investments in policies seen as disproportionately benefiting newcomers. This will become ever more problematic as resources become scarcer. Instead, governments should consider gradually honing in on *sets of circumstances* that apply to broader swaths of society (particularly poverty and lack of education) as a means of building larger coalitions of support. In the United States, for example, the gap in educational outcomes between poor and rich children is now twice as large as the gap between black and white children. In these circumstances, it may be both politically smart and wise in policy terms for investments in integration to be reframed so as to apply to all disadvantaged populations in society, rather than focusing exclusively on the newest arrivals (or those perceived as "newcomers"). Further, since different immigrant groups (and subgroups within them) have widely different outcomes, designing policies for immigrants *as a group* is unlikely to be effective and alienates natives.

### 9. Legislating cultural practices should be a last resort, not a first impulse

The state's responsibility is to create incentives for society to move toward certain goals. However, it should do this with a soft touch. States should focus on encouraging *and enabling* the kinds of measures discussed here – not *requiring* them unless strictly necessary (e.g., for public safety reasons). In other words, states should be facilitating and encouraging good practice, and creating alternatives, rather than using coercive means to stop unwanted (but otherwise not illegal) practices. For instance, states can foster dialogue and support institutions through which groups can negotiate their differences, rather than attempting to curb practices through coercive means, which can backfire. In a small minority of cases involving violence toward others, stronger action will be necessary (e.g., stopping practices of genital mutilation, spousal abuse, or honor killings), but these interventions should be very narrowly targeted.

10. *States should set the tone about immigration, both through measured*
   *political language and body language*

Government officials should signal to their citizen constituents that immigrants and their families *belong*, and policies should aim to help them become fully engaged members of society. At the same time, they need to signal to immigrants that they *can* belong. "Body language" – or things that are expressed through action rather than political language – is often more important than words. Importantly, the government's narrative must *match* its actions on the ground to be believable (e.g., telling people they belong equally in society will lose its meaning if immigrant-dense neighborhoods have chronically inferior access to quality services). The manner in which this vision is communicated is critical. Countries, such as Spain, that weave anti-discrimination into their national identity and public discourse are better equipped to combat emerging anti-immigrant political groups than Greece, where the gap between political rhetoric and practice is at times impossible to bridge.

At base, achieving an effective mode of civic integration requires a delicate balancing act: Governments must enact policies and messaging narratives that are restrained enough to respect the moral autonomy of immigrants yet are aggressive enough to further integrated, more cohesive host societies.

## Works Cited

BBC News. Belgian lawmakers pass burka ban. April 30, 2010. http://news.bbc.co.uk/2/hi/8652861.stm.

Eurostat. *Migrants in Europe: A Statistical Portrait of the First and Second Generation.* Brussels: European Commission, 2011. http://epp.eurostat.ec.europa.eu/cache/ITY_OFFPUB/KS-31-10-539/EN/KS-31-10-539-EN.PDF.

*Le Parisien*. Le voile intégral banni de la rue. April 11, 2011. www.leparisien.fr/societe/le-voile-integral-banni-de-la-rue-11-04-2011-1402496.php.

Migration Policy Institute (MPI) Data Hub. Spain Country Profile. n.d. www.migrationinformation.org/datahub/countrydata/country.cfm.

Migration Policy Institute (MPI) Data Hub. 2010 American Community Survey and Census Data on the Foreign Born by State. 2011a. www.migrationinformation.org/datahub/acscensus.cfm.

Migration Policy Institute (MPI) Data Hub. States Ranked by Percent Change in the Foreign-Born Population: 1990, 2000, and 2010. 2011b. www.migrationinformation.org/datahub/files/MPIData Hub_ACS_2010-NumbericDifferenceForeignBorn.xlsx.

Papademetriou, Demetrios G., Madeleine Sumption, and Aaron Terrazas (eds.). *Migration and the Great Recession: The Transatlantic Experience*. Washington, DC: MPI, 2011.

Passel, Jeffrey S. *Unauthorized Immigrant Population: National and State Trends, 2010*. Washington, DC: Pew Hispanic Center, 2011. www.pewhispanic.org/files/reports/133.pdf.

Pew Forum on Religion and Public Life. *Muslim Networks and Movements in Western Europe*. Washington, DC: Pew Research Center, 2010. http://features.pewforum.org/muslim/number-of-muslims-in-western-europe.html.

Simon, Patrick. *French National Identity and Integration: Who Belongs to the National Community?* Washington, DC: MPI, 2012. http://migrationpolicy.org/pubs/frenchidentity.pdf.

*The Guardian*. France's burqa ban: women are 'effectively under house arrest'. September 19, 2011. www.guardian.co.uk/world/2011/sep/19/battle-for-the-burqa?intcmp=239.

# Section II:
# Managing Diversity in Challenging Times

# Multiculturalism:
# Success, Failure, and the Future

*Will Kymlicka*

## Introduction

Ideas about the legal and political accommodation of ethnic diversity have been in a state of flux around the world for the past 40 years. One hears much about the "rise and fall of multiculturalism." Indeed, this has become a kind of master narrative, widely invoked by scholars, journalists, and policymakers alike, to explain the evolution of contemporary debates about diversity. Although people disagree about what comes after multiculturalism, there is a surprising consensus that we are in a post-multicultural era.

This chapter contends that this master narrative obscures as much as it reveals, and that we need an alternative framework for thinking about the choices we face. Multiculturalism's successes and failures, as well as its level of public acceptance, have depended on the nature of the issues at stake and the countries involved, and we need to understand these variations if we are to identify a more sustainable model for accommodating diversity.

This chapter will argue that the master narrative 1) mischaracterizes the nature of the experiments in multiculturalism that have been undertaken, 2) exaggerates the extent to which they have been abandoned, and 3) misidentifies the genuine difficulties and limitations they have encountered and the options for addressing these problems.

Before we can decide whether to celebrate or lament the fall of multiculturalism, we need first to make sure we know what multiculturalism has meant both in theory and in practice, where it has succeeded or failed to meet its objectives, and under what conditions it is likely to thrive in the future.


## The Rise and Fall of Multiculturalism

The master narrative of the "rise and fall of multiculturalism" helpfully captures important features of our current debates. Yet, in some respects, it is misleading and may obscure the real challenges and opportunities we face. In its simplest form, the master narrative goes like this:[5]

From the 1970s to mid-1990s, there was a clear trend across Western democracies toward the increased recognition and accommodation of diversity through a range of multiculturalism policies (MCPs) and minority rights. These policies were endorsed both at the domestic level in some states and by international organizations, and involved a rejection of earlier ideas of unitary and homogeneous nationhood.

Since the mid-1990s, however, we have seen a backlash and retreat from multiculturalism, and a reassertion of ideas of nation building, common values and identity, and unitary citizenship – even a call for the "return of assimilation."

This retreat is partly driven by fears among the majority group that the accommodation of diversity has "gone too far" and is threatening their way of life. This fear often expresses itself in the rise of nativist and populist right-wing political movements, such as the Danish People's Party, defending old ideas of "Denmark for the Danish." But the retreat also reflects a belief among the center-left that multiculturalism has failed to help the intended beneficiaries – namely, minorities themselves – because it has failed to address the underlying sources of their social, economic, and political exclusion and may have uninten-

---

5　Joppke and Morawska 2003; Koopmans 2006. For Britain, see Hansen 2007; Back et al. 2002; Vertovec 2010. For Australia, see Ang and Stratton 2001. For Canada, see Wong, Garcea, and Kirova 2005. For a good overview of the backlash discourse in various countries, see Vertovec and Wessendorf 2010.

tionally contributed to their social isolation. As a result, even the center-left political movements that initially championed multiculturalism, such as the social democratic parties in Europe, have backed away from it and shifted to a discourse that emphasizes "civic integration," "social cohesion," "common values," and "shared citizenship."[6]

The social democratic discourse of civic integration differs from the radical-right discourse in emphasizing the need to develop a more inclusive national identity and to fight racism and discrimination, but it nonetheless distances itself from the rhetoric and policies of multiculturalism. The term post-multiculturalism has often been invoked to signal this new approach, which seeks to overcome the limits of a naïve or misguided multiculturalism while avoiding the oppressive reassertion of homogenizing nationalist ideologies.[7]

## What Is Multiculturalism?

### A Misleading Model

In much of the post-multiculturalist literature, multiculturalism is characterized as a feel-good celebration of ethnocultural diversity, encouraging citizens to acknowledge and embrace the panoply of customs, traditions, music, and cuisine that exist in a multiethnic society. Yasmin Alibhai-Brown calls this the "3S" model of multiculturalism in Britain – saris, samosas, and steel drums (Alibhai-Brown 2000).

Multiculturalism takes these familiar cultural markers of ethnic groups – clothing, cuisine, and music – and treats them as authentic practices to be preserved by their members and safely consumed by

---

6   For an overview of the attitudes of European social democratic parties to these issues, see Cuperus, Duffek, and Kandel 2003.
7   For references to "post-multiculturalism" by progressive intellectuals, who distinguish it from the radical right's "anti-multiculturalism," see, regarding the United Kingdom, Alibhai-Brown 2000 and 2004; regarding Australia, Jupp 2007; and regarding the United States, King 2004 and Hollinger 2006.

others. Under the banner of multiculturalism, they are taught in school, performed in festivals, displayed in media and museums, and so on. This celebratory model of multiculturalism has been the focus of many critiques, including the following:

- It ignores issues of economic and political inequality. Even if all Britons come to enjoy Jamaican steel-drum music or Indian samosas, this would do nothing to address the real problems facing Caribbean and South Asian communities in Britain – problems of unemployment, poor educational outcomes, residential segregation, poor English language skills, and political marginalization. These economic and political issues cannot be solved simply by celebrating cultural differences.

- Even with respect to the (legitimate) goal of promoting greater understanding of cultural differences, the focus on celebrating "authentic" cultural practices that are "unique" to each group is potentially dangerous. First, not all customs that may be traditionally practiced within a particular group are worthy of being celebrated or even of being legally tolerated, such as forced marriage. To avoid stirring up controversy, there's a tendency to choose as the focus of multicultural celebrations safely inoffensive practices (e.g., cuisine or music) that can be enjoyably consumed by members of the larger society. But this runs the opposite risk, of the trivialization or Disney-fication of cultural differences (Bissoondath 1994), ignoring the real challenges that differences in cultural and religious values can raise.

- Third, the 3S model of multiculturalism can encourage a conception of groups as hermetically sealed and static, each reproducing its own distinct practices. Multiculturalism may be intended to encourage people to share their customs, but the assumption that each group has its own distinctive customs ignores processes of cultural adaptation, mixing, and mélange, as well as emerging cultural commonalities, thereby potentially reinforcing perceptions of minorities as eternally "other." This, in turn, can lead to the strengthening of prejudice and stereotyping, and, more generally, to the polarization of ethnic relations.

- Fourth, this model can end up reinforcing power inequalities and cultural restrictions within minority groups. In deciding which traditions are "authentic," and how to interpret and display them, the state generally consults the traditional elites within the group – typically older males – while ignoring the way these traditional practices (and traditional elites) are often challenged by internal reformers who have different views about how, say, a "good Muslim" should act. It can therefore imprison people in "cultural scripts" that they are not allowed to question or dispute.

According to post-multiculturalists, the growing recognition of these flaws underlies the retreat from multiculturalism and signals the search for new models of citizenship that emphasize 1) political participation and economic opportunities over the symbolic politics of cultural recognition, 2) human rights and individual freedom over respect for cultural traditions, 3) the building of inclusive national identities over the recognition of ancestral cultural identities, and 4) cultural change and cultural mixing over the reification of static cultural differences.

This narrative about the rise and fall of 3S multiculturalism will no doubt be familiar to many readers. In my view, however, it is inaccurate. Not only is it a caricature of the reality of multiculturalism as it has developed over the past 40 years in the Western democracies, but it is a distraction from the real issues that we need to face. The 3S model captures something important about natural human tendencies to simplify ethnic differences and about the logic of global capitalism to sell cosmopolitan cultural products. But it does not capture the nature of post-1960s government MCPs, which have had more complex historical sources and political goals.

## Multiculturalism in Context

It is important to put multiculturalism in its historical context. In one sense, it is as old as humanity – different cultures have always found ways of coexisting, and respect for diversity was a familiar feature of many historic empires, such as the Ottoman Empire. But the sort of multiculturalism that is said to have had a "rise and fall" is a more specific historic phenomenon, emerging first in the Western democracies in the late 1960s. This timing is important, for it helps us situate multiculturalism in relation to larger social transformations of the postwar era.

More specifically, multiculturalism is part of a larger human-rights revolution involving ethnic and racial diversity. Prior to World War II, ethnocultural and religious diversity in the West was characterized by a range of illiberal and undemocratic relationships of hierarchy,[8] justified by racialist ideologies that explicitly propounded the superiority of some peoples and cultures and their right to rule over others. These ideologies were widely accepted throughout the Western world and underpinned both domestic laws (e.g., racially biased immigration and citizenship policies) and foreign policies (e.g., in relation to overseas colonies).

After World War II, however, the world recoiled against Hitler's fanatical and murderous use of such ideologies, and the United Nations decisively repudiated them in favor of a new ideology of the equality of races and peoples. And this new assumption of human equality generated a series of political movements designed to contest the lingering presence or enduring effects of older hierarchies. We can distinguish three "waves" of such movements: 1) the struggle for decolonization, concentrated in the period 1948–1965; 2) the struggle against racial segregation and discrimination, initiated and exemplified by the African-American civil-rights movement from 1955 to 1965; and 3) the struggle for multiculturalism and minority rights that emerged in the late 1960s.

Each of these movements draws upon the human-rights revolution, and its foundational ideology of the equality of races and peoples,

---

8   Including relations of conqueror and conquered, colonizer and colonized, master and slave, settler and indigenous, racialized and unmarked, normalized and deviant, orthodox and heretic, civilized and primitive, and ally and enemy.

to challenge the legacies of earlier ethnic and racial hierarchies. Indeed, the human-rights revolution plays a double role here, not just as the inspiration for a struggle, but also as a constraint on the permissible goals and means of that struggle. Insofar as historically excluded or stigmatized groups struggle against earlier hierarchies in the name of equality, they too have to renounce their own traditions of exclusion or oppression in the treatment of, say, women, gays, people of mixed race, religious dissenters, and so on. Human rights, and liberal-democratic constitutionalism more generally, provide the overarching framework within which these struggles are debated and addressed.

Each of these movements, therefore, can be seen as contributing to a process of democratic "citizenization" – that is, turning the earlier catalog of hierarchical relations into relationships of liberal-democratic citizenship. This entails transforming both the vertical relationships between minorities and the state and the horizontal relationships among the members of different groups. In the past, it was often assumed that the only way to engage in this process of citizenization was to impose a single undifferentiated model of citizenship on all individuals. But the ideas and policies of multiculturalism that emerged from the 1960s start from the assumption that this complex history inevitably and appropriately generates group-differentiated ethnopolitical claims. The key to citizenization is not to suppress these differential claims but to filter them through and frame them within the language of human rights, civil liberties, and democratic accountability. And this is what multiculturalist movements have aimed to do.

The precise character of the resulting multicultural reforms varies from group to group, as befits the distinctive history that each has faced. They all start from the antidiscrimination principle that underpinned the second wave but go beyond it to challenge other forms of exclusion or stigmatization. In most Western countries, explicit state-sponsored discrimination against ethnic, racial, or religious minorities had largely ceased by the 1960s and 1970s, under the influence of the second wave of human-rights struggles. Yet ethnic and racial hierarchies persist in many societies, whether measured in terms of economic inequalities, political underrepresentation, social stigmatization, or cultural invisibility. Various forms of multiculturalism have been developed to help overcome these lingering inequalities.

The focus in this report is on multiculturalism as it pertains to (permanently settled) immigrant groups,[9] but it is worth noting that struggles for multicultural citizenship have also emerged in relation to historic minorities and indigenous peoples.[10]

## The Evolution of Multiculturalism Policies

The case of immigrant multiculturalism is just one aspect of a larger "ethnic revival" across the Western democracies (Smith 1981) in which different types of minorities have struggled for new forms of multicultural citizenship that combine both antidiscrimination measures and positive forms of recognition and accommodation. Multicul-

---

9   There was briefly in some European countries a form of "multiculturalism" that was not aimed at the inclusion of permanent immigrants but, rather, at ensuring that temporary migrants would return to their country of origin. For example, mother-tongue education in Germany was not initially introduced "as a minority right but in order to enable guest-worker children to reintegrate in their countries of origin" (Schönwälder 2010: 160). Needless to say, this sort of "returnist" multiculturalism – premised on the idea that migrants are foreigners who should return to their real home – has nothing to do with multiculturalism policies (MCPs) premised on the idea that immigrants belong in their host countries, and which aim to make immigrants feel more at home where they are. The focus of this paper is on the latter type of multiculturalism, which is centrally concerned with constructing new relations of citizenship.

10  In relation to indigenous peoples, for example – such as the Maori in New Zealand, Aboriginal peoples in Canada and Australia, American Indians, the Sami in Scandinavia, and the Inuit of Greenland – new models of multicultural citizenship have emerged since the late 1960s that include policies such as land rights, self-government rights, recognition of customary laws, and guarantees of political consultation. And in relation to substate national groups – such as the Basques and Catalans in Spain, Flemish and Walloons in Belgium, Scots and Welsh in Britain, Quebecois in Canada, Germans in South Tyrol, Swedish in Finland – we see new models of multicultural citizenship that include policies such as federal or quasi-federal territorial autonomy; official language status, either in the region or nationally; and guarantees of representation in the central government or on constitutional courts.

tural citizenship for immigrant groups clearly does not involve the same types of claims as for indigenous peoples or national minorities: Immigrant groups do not typically seek land rights, territorial autonomy, or official language status. What, then, is the substance of multicultural citizenship in relation to immigrant groups?

The Multiculturalism Policy Index is one attempt to measure the evolution of MCPs in a standardized format that enables comparative research.[11] The index takes the following eight policies as the most common or emblematic forms of immigrant MCPs:[12]

- Constitutional, legislative, or parliamentary affirmation of multiculturalism at the central and/or regional and municipal levels
- The adoption of multiculturalism in school curricula
- The inclusion of ethnic representation/sensitivity in the mandate of public media or media licensing
- Exemptions from dress codes, either by statute or court cases
- Allowing dual citizenship
- The funding of ethnic group organizations to support cultural activities
- The funding of bilingual education or mother-tongue instruction
- Affirmative action for disadvantaged immigrant groups.[13]

Other policies could be added (or subtracted) from the index, but there was a recognizable "multiculturalist turn" across Western democra-

---

11 Keith Banting and I developed this index, first published in Banting and Kymlicka 2006. Many of the ideas discussed in this chapter are the result of our collaboration.

12 As with all cross-national indices, there is a trade-off between standardization and sensitivity to local nuances. There is no universally accepted definition of multiculturalism policies and no hard and fast line that would sharply distinguish MCPs from closely related policy fields, such as antidiscrimination policies, citizenship policies, and integration policies. Different countries (or, indeed, different actors within a single country) are likely to draw this line in different places, and any list is therefore likely to be controversial.

13 For a fuller description of these policies, and the justification for including them in the Multiculturalism Policy Index, see the index website, www.queensu.ca/mcp. The site also includes our separate index of MCPs for indigenous peoples and for national minorities.

cies in the last few decades of the 20th century, and we can identify a range of public policies that are seen, by both critics and defenders, as emblematic of this turn. Each of the eight policy indicators listed above is intended to capture a policy dimension where liberal-democratic states faced a choice about whether or not to take a multicultural turn and to develop more multicultural forms of citizenship in relation to immigrant groups.

While multiculturalism for immigrant groups clearly differs in substance from that for indigenous peoples or national minorities, each policy has been defended as a means to overcome the legacies of earlier hierarchies and to help build fairer and more inclusive democratic societies.

Therefore, multiculturalism is first and foremost about developing new models of democratic citizenship, grounded in human-rights ideals, to replace earlier uncivil and undemocratic relations of hierarchy and exclusion. Needless to say, this account of multiculturalism-as-citizenization differs dramatically from the 3S account of multiculturalism as the celebration of static cultural differences. Whereas the 3S account says that multiculturalism is about displaying and consuming differences in cuisine, clothing, and music, while neglecting issues of political and economic inequality, the citizenization account says that multiculturalism is precisely about constructing new civic and political relations to overcome the deeply entrenched inequalities that have persisted after the abolition of formal discrimination.

It is important to determine which of these accounts more accurately describes the Western experience with multiculturalism. Before we can decide whether to celebrate or lament the fall of multiculturalism, we first need to make sure we know what multiculturalism has in fact been. The 3S account is misleading for three principal reasons.[14]

First, the claim that multiculturalism is solely or primarily about symbolic cultural politics depends on a misreading of the actual policies. Whether we look at indigenous peoples, national minorities, or

---

14 For a more detailed defense of this account, see Kymlicka 2007, chapters 3–5.

immigrant groups, it is immediately apparent that MCPs combine economic, political, social, and cultural dimensions. While minorities are (rightly) concerned to contest the historical stigmatization of their cultures, immigrant multiculturalism also includes policies that are concerned with access to political power and economic opportunities – for example, policies of affirmative action, mechanisms of political consultation, funding for ethnic self-organization, and facilitated access to citizenship. In relation to all three types of groups, MCPs combine cultural recognition, economic redistribution, and political participation.

Second, the claim that multiculturalism ignores the importance of universal human rights is equally misplaced. On the contrary, as we've seen, multiculturalism is itself a human-rights-based movement inspired and constrained by principles of human rights and liberal-democratic constitutionalism. Its goal is to challenge the traditional ethnic and racial hierarchies that have been discredited by the postwar human-rights revolution. Understood in this way, multiculturalism-as-citizenization offers no support for accommodating the illiberal cultural practices within minority groups that have also been discredited by this human-rights revolution. The same human-rights-based reasons we have for endorsing multiculturalism-as-citizenization are also reasons for rejecting cultural practices that violate human rights. And, indeed, this is what we see throughout the Western democracies. Wherever multiculturalism has been adopted, it has been tied to larger human-rights norms and has been subject to the overarching principles of the liberal-democratic constitutional order. No Western democracy has exempted immigrant groups from constitutional norms of human rights in order to maintain practices such as forced marriage, criminalization of apostasy, or clitoridectomy.

And this, in turn, points out the flaws in the claim that multiculturalism denies the reality of cultural change. On the contrary, multiculturalism-as-citizenization is a deeply (and intentionally) transformative project, both for minorities and majorities. It requires both dominant and historically subordinated groups to engage in new practices, to enter new relationships, and to embrace new concepts and discourses – all of which profoundly transform people's identities.[15]

One way to think of this is to recognize that the human-rights revolution is a two-edged sword. It has created political space for ethnocultural groups to contest inherited hierarchies. But it also requires groups to advance their claims in a very specific language – namely, the language of human rights, civil-rights liberalism, and democratic constitutionalism.

This is obvious in the case of the historically dominant majority group in each country, which is required to renounce fantasies of racial superiority, to relinquish claims to exclusive ownership of the state, and to abandon attempts to fashion public institutions solely in its own (typically white/Christian) image. In fact, much of multiculturalism's "long march through the institutions" consists precisely in identifying and attacking those deeply rooted traditions, customs, and symbols that have excluded or stigmatized minorities. Much has been written about this process, not only about the transformations in majority identities and practices it requires, but also about the backlash it can create.[16]

But MCPs are equally transformative of the identities and practices of subordinated groups. Many of these groups have their own histories of ethnic and racial prejudice, anti-Semitism, caste and gender exclusion, religious triumphalism, and political authoritarianism – all of which are delegitimized by the norms of liberal-democratic multiculturalism.[17]

---

15  "Nothing has changed more over thirty years of identity politics than the identities of men and women, immigrants and old-timers, indigenous and non-indigenous persons, Muslims and Christians, Arabs and Westerners, Europeans and non-Europeans, cultural minorities and majorities, heterosexuals and homosexuals" (Tully 2000: 231).

16  For a discussion of "white backlash" against multiculturalism in Britain and Canada, see Hewitt 2005 and Hansen 2007.

17  There are groups that wish to contest their subordinate status vis-à-vis the dominant group while still asserting superiority over other groups. Some East Asian groups in Canada, for example, vocally protest against any racism they suffer, yet they show higher levels of racism than white Canadians in relation to Aboriginal Canadians. Some upper-caste Hindu immigrants from India decry the fact that whites have not fully accepted them, yet they try to avoid contact with lower-caste immigrants from their home country. Some North African men object to discrimination in the job market, yet they refuse to hire women or to work for women. One could extend this list indefinitely.

For all such people, multiculturalism offers both opportunities and challenges. These policies provide clear access points and legal tools for nondominant groups to challenge their status. But there is a price for this access, namely, accepting the principles of human rights and civil liberties, and the procedures of liberal-democratic constitutionalism, with their guarantees of gender equality, religious freedom, racial nondiscrimination, gay rights, due process, and so on. In other words, subordinated groups can appeal to MCPs to challenge their illiberal exclusion, but those very policies also impose the duty on them to be inclusive.

## Multiculturalism in Practice

So far, this chapter has focused on multiculturalism's aspirations. But are MCPs working in practice? Have they, in fact, successfully contested ethnic and racial hierarchies and created more democratic relations of citizenship? One safe, if unsatisfying, answer is to say that we don't yet have enough evidence.[18] This partly reflects the difficulty of disentangling the effect of MCPs from other causal factors, such as changes in immigrant selection rules or labor market regulations.[19] Still, while recognizing the incompleteness of the evidence, we can point to some intriguing results from recent research.

### The Canadian Success Story

One of the few studies that has tried to isolate the effect of MCPs was conducted by Irene Bloemraad (2006), who compared the integration of Vietnamese immigrants in Boston and Toronto (Bloemraad 2006).

18  This, indeed, is the conclusion reached by several recent reviews, which insist that the effects of MCPs remain largely unknown. See Marc 2009.
19  As Jeffrey Reitz puts it, while academic discussions of multiculturalism have been extensive, "there is no real evaluation. The information base for such an evaluation is simply not there" (Reitz 2009: 13).

An interesting feature of this comparison is that the two groups are essentially similar in their pre-arrival characteristics – they arrived at the same time with roughly the same levels of education, wealth, language skills, and so on. And yet the Vietnamese have integrated into the political sphere more effectively in Toronto than in Boston, and Bloemraad argues that Canadian multiculturalism is a central part of the explanation. Canada's proactive MCPs have sent a clear message that Vietnamese political participation is welcome, and have also provided material and logistical support for the self-organization and political representation of the community. Bloemraad's study also showed a similar result for the Portuguese community in the two cities: Here again, the Portuguese are more politically integrated in Toronto than in Boston despite arriving with similar characteristics.

This is one example of a more general finding that we might label the Canadian comparative success story. Canada was the first Western country to adopt an official multiculturalism policy toward immigrant-origin ethnic groups, and it remains the only country in which multiculturalism is enshrined in the constitution. If MCPs have perverse or unintended effects, they should therefore show up first and most clearly in Canada. And yet studies have shown otherwise:

– Immigrants in Canada are more likely to become citizens (ibid.), to vote and to run for office (Howe 2007), and to be elected to office than immigrants in other Western democracies (Adams 2007), in part because voters in Canada do not discriminate against such candidates (Black and Erickson 2006; Bird 2009).

– Compared to their counterparts in other Western democracies, the children of immigrants have better educational outcomes (OECD 2006), and while immigrants in all Western societies suffer from an "ethnic penalty" in translating their skills into jobs, the size of this ethnic penalty is lowest in Canada (Heath 2007).

– Compared to residents of other Western democracies, Canadians are more likely to say that immigration is beneficial (Focus Canada 2002) and less likely to have prejudiced views of Muslims (Focus Canada 2006). And whereas ethnic diversity has been shown to erode levels of trust and social capital in other countries, there appears to be a "Canadian exceptionalism" in this regard (Kazemi-pur 2009; Harell 2009).

While Canada's comparative success in these fields is widely recognized, skeptics question whether multiculturalism plays any significant role in it. Critics sometimes argue that Canada's record of integration is explained by other factors, such as the fact that Canada's immigrants tend to be more highly skilled than immigrants in other countries and that there is a relatively open labor market. In other words, immigrants bring with them higher levels of human capital and can more easily employ that human capital in the labor market in Canada than they can in other countries. In this view, the presence of MCPs contributes nothing to the successful integration of immigrants in Canada, and may in fact impede it (see, e.g., Goodhart 2008).

While the selectivity of Canada's immigration policy is important, it's worth noting that many of the studies cited – including Bloemraad's – control for the skill level of the immigrants. In her study, the Vietnamese integrate better in Toronto than in Boston despite having identical pre-arrival skill levels. Indeed, Canada's comparative success is not primarily at the level of the most highly skilled immigrants, who are likely to do well wherever they land. Rather, it is in relation to less-skilled immigrants that the "citizenship gap" emerges most clearly between Canada and the United States.

Moreover, a number of recent studies have helped clarify the positive role that MCPs can play within broader processes of immigrant integration. This research suggests that MCPs operate at two broad levels: individual identity and institutional design.

At the individual level, surveys indicate that multiculturalism provides a locus for the high level of mutual identification among native-born citizens and immigrants in Canada. In most countries, native-born citizens with a strong sense of national identity or national pride tend to be distrusting of immigrants, who are seen as a threat (Sides and Citrin 2007). But, in Canada, which has officially defined itself as a multicultural nation, multiculturalism serves as a source of shared national identity and pride for native-born citizens and immigrants alike. Studies show that, in the absence of multiculturalism, national identity is more likely to lead to intolerance and xenophobia.[20] Indeed, Canada may be the only Western country where strength of national identity is positively correlated with support for immigration, a finding that is difficult to explain except by reference to multiculturalism (Johnston et al. 2010; Laczko 2007).

A similar dynamic has been found in studies of trust and social capital. Whereas Robert Putnam has found that social capital declines as ethnic and racial diversity increases in the United States (Putnam 2007), the same pattern has not been observed in Canada (Kazemipur 2009), particularly among the younger generations who were raised under the multiculturalism policy (Harell 2009). For them, diversity has been normalized.

A recent international study has also confirmed the constructive role that multiculturalism plays in enabling healthy processes of individual acculturation (Berry et al. 2006). Many studies have shown that immigrants do best, both in terms of psychological well-being and sociocultural outcomes, when they are able to combine their ethnic identity with a new national identity. Scholars often call this an "integration orientation," as opposed to either an "assimilation orientation" (in which immigrants abandon their ethnic identity to adopt a new national identity) or a "separation orientation" (in which immigrants renounce the new national identity to maintain their ethnic identity). Defenders of multiculturalism have long asserted that MCPs can encourage and enable an integration orientation – indeed, this is known as the "multiculturalism hypothesis" (Berry, Kalin, and Taylor 1977). Members of immigrant minorities will be more likely to identify with a new national identity if they feel their ethnic identity is publicly respected.[21]

---

20  For further discussion of the way multiculturalism facilitates rather than impedes mutual identification in Canada, see Uberoi 2008 and Esses et al. 2006.

21  The International Comparative Study of Ethnocultural Youth, studying over 5,000 youth in 13 countries, has confirmed that countries with MCPs encourage the development of this integration orientation, with better resulting outcomes. See Berry et al. 2006.

At the institutional level, we also have evidence of the role that multiculturalism plays in creating more inclusive and equitable public institutions. For example, the Organization for Economic Cooperation and Development (OECD) study that established Canada's comparative advantage in educating immigrant students emphasized that a crucial factor in this success was the presence of specific policies to address issues of cultural and linguistic diversity in the school population – policies that, in the Canadian context, have emerged under the rubric of multiculturalism (OECD 2006). These policies help to explain why the children of immigrants do better in Canada than in other Western democracies even when controlling for the skills, education, and income of their parents.

Similarly, multiculturalism has been shown to play an important role in making Canada's political process more inclusive. As Bloemraad's study shows, MCPs have encouraged and enabled the Vietnamese community to participate more quickly and more effectively in mainstream Canadian institutions. In particular, the MCPs have facilitated the self-organization of the community and created 1) new cadres of community leaders who are familiar with Canadian institutions and practices, 2) new mechanisms of consultation and participation, and 3) a more welcoming environment.

In short, it appears that Canada's comparative success is not entirely attributable to the selectivity of its immigration intake. Several recent studies suggest that Canada's MCPs also play a positive role in promoting integration, participation, and social cohesion, both through individual-level effects on attitudes, self-understandings, and identities, and through society-level effects on institutions.

### The European Experience

Whether similar positive results have been achieved – or could be achieved – in other countries is more difficult to determine. We do not have many reliable cross-national studies that attempt to isolate the effects of MCPs. However, it's worth noting that Bloemraad herself has attempted to test the effects of MCPs internationally, and her study of diversity and social capital in 19 countries shows that MCPs have a positive impact on political participation and social capital (Kesler and Bloemraad 2010). Even if we exclude Canada from the sample, MCPs remain positively associated with participation and social cohesion. Earlier cross-national studies show that multiculturalism has a positive effect on reducing prejudice (Weldon 2006), that children are psychologically better adapted in countries with MCPs (Berry et al. 2006), and that MCPs may strengthen rather than weaken redistributive solidarity (Banting and Kymlicka 2006; Crepaz 2006).

It should be emphasized again how fragmentary this evidence is: Future research is almost certainly going to qualify the conclusions. And this evidence is only about general trends, not universal laws. Even if MCPs are associated with better outcomes internationally, they still may have had perverse effects in particular countries, on particular issues. This, indeed, is the view of Ruud Koopmans, who has argued that MCPs in the Netherlands have had detrimental effects on the integration of immigrants in that country.[22] This claim is intensely disputed by a number of other Dutch scholars, who think that Koopmans is blaming multiculturalism for ills that are, in fact, due to other policies entirely (e.g., labor market policies).[23] But even if it is true, as Koopmans argues, that MCPs have had perverse unintended effects in the Netherlands, the cross-national evidence sug-

22  Koopmans 2010; Ersanilli and Koopmans 2011. Another work that blames MCPs for poor integration outcomes in the Netherlands is Sniderman and Hagendoorn 2007.
23  In the Dutch case, immigrants have in the past had relatively open access to a generous welfare state, yet faced a relatively closed labor market. In any country, this combination is likely to create a perception amongst some native-born citizens that immigrants are a burden, are undeserving and lazy, and take more from society than they give. Multiculturalism is not the cause of this problem, which rather lies in the structures of the welfare state and the labor market, but Koopmans argues that under these circumstances, MCPs can exacerbate the problem, reinforcing an "us" versus "them" mentality and discouraging the sorts of measures that are needed for more effective integration. Bloemraad expresses doubt that MCPs are really an exacerbating factor in this causal story; see Bloemraad 2011. For related doubts about Koopmans' analysis, see Duyvendak and Scholten 2011.

gests that this is a Dutch anomaly and not the general trend regarding the effects of MCPs. If we cannot conclude from the Canadian case that MCPs are always and everywhere a success, we equally cannot conclude from the Dutch case that MCPs are always and everywhere a failure. The evidence to date suggests a general, though not universal, positive effect.[24]

In short, multiculturalism in the West emerged as a vehicle for replacing older forms of ethnic and racial hierarchy with new relations of democratic citizenship, and there is some significant, if not yet conclusive, evidence that it is making progress toward that goal.

## The Retreat from Multiculturalism

But this raises a puzzle. If post-multiculturalist claims about the flaws of multiculturalism are largely misguided, then what explains the fall of multiculturalism? If multiculturalism is inspired by human-rights norms and seeks to deepen relations of democratic citizenship, and if there is some evidence that it is working, then why has there been such a retreat from it?

### Rhetoric versus Reality

Part of the answer is that reports of the death of multiculturalism are exaggerated. The Multiculturalism Policy Index ranks the strength of immigrant MCPs across 21 OECD countries at three points in time – 1980, 2000, and 2010 – and the clear trend has been toward the expansion of MCPs over the past 30 years, including in the last ten (see Appendix 1). There are some high-profile exceptions: There has been a significant reduction in the Netherlands, and modest ones (from a low base) in Denmark and Italy. But the last decade has also seen a

---

24 It is worth noting that there is also growing evidence for the positive impact of MCPs for indigenous peoples and substate national groups; see Kymlicka 2007.

strengthening of MCPs in a number of countries, including Belgium, Finland, Greece, Ireland, Norway, Portugal, Spain, and Sweden. In other countries, the scores have increased marginally or remained stable. Overall, the record of multicultural policies in Europe is one of modest strengthening. As Appendix 1 indicates, the average score for European countries rose from 0.7 in 1980 to 2.1 in 2000 and 3.1 in 2010. Other independent efforts to measure the strength of MCPs in Europe have arrived at the same conclusion.[25]

This may surprise many readers, given that talk of multiculturalism is so unfashionable in political circles. But the retreat may indeed be more a matter of talk than of actual policies. Certain politicians in Britain and Australia, for example, have decided not to use the "m word" – instead favoring terms like diversity, pluralism, intercultural dialogue, or community cohesion – but these changes in wording have not necessarily affected actual policies and programs on the ground. In Derek McGhee's words, speaking of Britain, "In many ways this retreat from an open hostility to multiculturalism is, on examination, an exercise in avoiding the term multiculturalism rather than moving away from the principles of multiculturalism altogether" (McGhee 2008: 85). In their recent overview of the situation across Europe, Steven Vertovec and Susan Wessendorf similarly conclude that while the word multiculturalism "has mostly disappeared from political rhetoric," replaced with a "pervasive emphasis on so-called integration," this "has not emerged with the eradication, nor even much to the detriment, of actual measures, institutions, and frameworks of minority cultural recognition ... Policies and programs once deemed 'multicultural' continue everywhere" (Vertovec and Wessendorf 2010: 18, 21).

---

25 Koopmans' index of Indicators of Citizenship Rights for Immigrants (ICRI) includes both an individual equality/nondiscrimination dimension and a multiculturalism dimension, with 23 different indicators for the multiculturalism dimension. Developed independently, the consistency between his ICRI results and the MCP results helps confirm the trend we both observe. Koopmans, Michalowski, and Waibal 2011.

Our data strongly confirm this analysis.[26] The data also demonstrate that the rhetorical backlash is not limited to countries that have practiced an active multicultural strategy. Chancellor Angela Merkel's announcement that multiculturalism has "utterly failed" is puzzling, since the approach has not actually been tried in a significant way in Germany. Official policy at the national level has been hostile to institutionalized pluralism, and multicultural initiatives have emerged primarily in cities with large immigrant populations. Merkel's critique of multiculturalism is therefore a red herring, but as Karen Schönwälder notes, it serves a political purpose: "By creating an imaginary picture of a multicultural past," conservative political leaders "can present their own policies as innovative" (Schönwälder 2010: 162).

There are no doubt many reasons why political leaders in Europe have chosen to rhetorically portray themselves as opponents of a "tired" and "naïve" multiculturalism, and as champions of a more "innovative" and "realistic" approach. But we must not confuse rhetoric and reality, and our index reveals that the retreat from multiculturalist rhetoric is not matched by any comparable retreat from multiculturalist policies. Talk of a "wholesale retreat" (Joppke 2004: 244) from MCPs is, therefore, misleading.

---

26  It is worth noting that there has been no retreat from the commitment to multicultural citizenship for either indigenous peoples or national minorities. On the contrary, the trend toward enhanced land rights, self-government powers, and customary laws for indigenous peoples remains fully in place across the Western democracies and has been reaffirmed by the UN General Assembly through the adoption of the Declaration of the Rights of Indigenous Peoples, in 2007. Similarly, the trend toward enhanced language rights and regional autonomy for substate national groups remains fully in place in the Western democracies. These two trends are increasingly entrenched in law and public opinion, backed by growing evidence that they have contributed to building relations of democratic freedom and equality. Few people today would deny that regional autonomy for Catalonia has contributed to the democratic consolidation of Spain, or that indigenous rights are helping to deepen democratic citizenship in Latin America.

Yet something clearly has changed at the level of public policies. The main policy change has not been the abandonment of MCPs but, rather, the proliferation of "civic integration" policies, typically in the form of obligatory language and country-knowledge requirements.

These requirements have been imposed at different stages of the immigration process – initial entry, renewed residency, and naturalization – and have been implemented through a range of tests, courses, and contracts. Sara Goodman has developed a statistical index of such civic integration policies across Europe (CIVIX), and it shows a dramatic change from 1997, when such policies were largely absent, to 2009, when such policies were much more prevalent (see Appendix 2). According to the CIVIX scale, the average EU-15 country score was only 0.56 out of a possible 7.0 in 1997 but had risen to 2.3 by 2009.

So we see an interesting trend: a modest strengthening of MCPs and a more dramatic increase in civic integration requirements. The persistence of MCPs alongside new civic integration policies implies that the two can somehow coexist. But what precisely is the relationship between MCPs and the shift to civic integration?

Civic integration emphasizes the importance of immigrants' integrating more fully into mainstream society and advances a number of core principles, including the following (adapted from Joppke 2007):

- The key role of employment in integration
- Respect for basic liberal-democratic values, such as liberty, democracy, human rights, equalities (such as gender equality), and the rule of law
- Basic knowledge of the host society's language, history, and institutions
- The necessity of antidiscrimination laws and policies.

There is no inherent incompatibility between civic integration and MCPs, as defined here. Certainly, the experience of countries outside of Europe, such as Canada and Australia, confirm that view. Both countries have adopted MCPs, and both have long had robust integrationist strategies for immigrants.

The Canadian model is best described as "multicultural integration." The multiculturalism component of the incorporation regime is quite broad, reflecting most of the elements in the Multiculturalism Policy Index: the recognition of multicultural diversity as a core feature of Canadian life in the constitution, in legislation, and in the curricula used in schools; the requirement in the mandates of broadcasters that they reflect cultural diversity in their programming; exemptions from official dress codes; the acceptance of dual citizenship; grants to ethnic groups; and affirmative action ("employment equity" in Canada) for disadvantaged immigrant groups.

Canadian policy has also long placed a heavy emphasis on integration, including the sorts of policies that are now commonly found in European civic integration programs. This integrationist ethos was reflected in the multiculturalism program itself, whose original goals (as promulgated in 1971) included not only support for cultural diversity, but also assistance for minorities to overcome barriers to wider engagement, promotion of intercultural exchange, and support for immigrants to acquire one of Canada's official languages "in order to become full participants in Canadian society." The integrationist impulse is powerfully reinforced by the immigration program itself and the settlement services offered to newcomers. The federal and provincial governments provide adjustment assistance and extensive language training programs both at the basic level and at more advanced levels for immigrants having trouble acquiring occupation-specific language skills.[27] In addition, Canada has a longstanding tradition of encouraging newcomers to learn about the history, traditions, and political institutions of the country. Applicants for citizenship must pass a written test of their ability to speak English or French and their

---

27 Federal expenditures on these programs have grown dramatically over time, tripling in the past decade to an estimated $1 billion in 2010/2011.

knowledge of Canadian history, geography, political institutions, and traditions. There are also citizenship oaths and ceremonies.[28]

The Canadian model also privileges the protection of liberal-democratic principles and antidiscrimination mechanisms. The Charter of Rights and Freedoms represents a muscular form of liberalism that is enshrined in the constitution and trumps ordinary legislation, including the Multiculturalism Act. The charter, together with federal and provincial human-rights commissions, has protected newcomers from discrimination at the hands of majorities. For example, its guarantee of freedom of religion has helped members of minority religions in several landmark cases concerning religious dress. At the same time, the individual rights and equality rights embedded in the charter counter the danger that multiculturalism might run amok. The charter circumscribes the range of cultural traditions that can be deemed legitimate, helping to ensure that accommodation of differences does not slide into a justification for discrimination or a denial of basic equalities, such as gender equality (Eliadis 2007).

The Canadian regime thus combines multiculturalism and civic integration. But two elements are critical to this combination. First, the instruments of integration are primarily voluntary. Language training and integration programs are provided by governments free of charge, and there is no linkage between participation in them and continued residency or access to social benefits. The only formal leverage is the written citizenship test required for naturalization. Second, the national identity that newcomers are invited to join celebrates diversity. The adoption of bilingualism and multiculturalism in the 1960s and 1970s represented a state-led redefinition of national identity, the culmination of an effort to de-emphasize the historic conception of the country as a British society and to build an identity more reflective of Canada's cultural complexity. The adoption of a new flag, one without ethnic symbols, was a reflection of this wider transition.

---

28 Knowledge of either English or French as a requirement for naturalization dates back to the *Naturalization Act of 1914*.

The Australian case also reveals the compatibility of MCPs and civic integration: Australia has always emphasized learning English as the national language and respecting liberal values as core parts of its multiculturalism. James Jupp, who played a pivotal role in defining Australia's multiculturalism policy, has argued that multiculturalism in Australia "is essentially a liberal ideology which operates within liberal institutions with the universal approval of liberal attitudes. It accepts that all humans should be treated as equals and that different cultures can co-exist if they accept liberal values" (Jupp 1996: 40). Thus, the two countries that were the earliest adopters and remain the most ardent supporters of MCPs have always had strong integration policies, focusing on learning the national language and shared liberal values.

## 1. A Shift from "Rights" toward "Duties"

The data suggest that there is no inherent incompatibility between multiculturalism and civic integration, and this combination has indeed been central to two of the most enduring cases of MCPs. Yet it should be equally clear that not all forms of civic integration are compatible with multiculturalism. The reality is that civic integration policies are themselves very diverse in content and form and, in some cases, the shift to civic integration is a rejection of multiculturalist principles and policies.

Two potential sources of conflict can be identified. One issue concerns the level of coercion involved, or put another way, the relationship between rights and duties. Some countries have developed voluntary approaches that emphasize immigrants' right to integrate and provide supportive programs for them to do so. But other countries have made integration a duty, establishing mandatory programs and denying immigrants access to social rights or residency renewals if they fail to pass certain thresholds of integration.[29] This more illiberal

---

29  Intermediate levels of compulsion are also emerging. In Sweden, for example, immigrants receiving social benefits can have their benefits reduced or eliminated if

version of civic integration cannot be combined with a strong multi-cultural strategy, particularly if it is only or primarily immigrants whose rights are subject to tests of fulfilling duties. It is perhaps revealing that countries that are adopting the most coercive forms of civic integration have never embraced the multicultural strategy, such as Denmark, or have dismantled previous multiculturalism programs as part of the restructuring process, such as the Netherlands. By contrast, those countries that have shifted most significantly in a pro-multicultural direction in recent years, such as Sweden, Finland, Spain, and Portugal, have resisted more coercive forms of civic integration.

We are witnessing a more general shift in the "rights versus duties" continuum in social policy (Borevi 2010). The traditional view underlying the postwar welfare state – articulated most influentially by T. H. Marshall – was that citizens need to have unconditional rights before they are able to fulfill their civic duties. Today, however, in several areas of social policy across the Western democracies (e.g., activation programs and employment policies), there has been a shift toward the idea that citizens have to fulfill certain duties before they can claim certain rights (e.g., "workfare"). If indeed such policies are imposed on all citizens, then they are not inherently anti-immigrant or anti-diversity (although some of us are likely to view them as an erosion of basic liberal or social-democratic values). But the shift from rights to duties raises a danger that those groups deemed "unworthy" of being treated as rights-bearing individuals – in particular, non-white, non-Christian immigrants – will be targeted. Insofar as perceptions of the unworthiness of immigrants underpin coercive integration policies, then a coercive integration strategy negates a multicultural affirmation of diversity.

they do not participate in integration programs, but participation is not linked to either residency or the acquisition of citizenship.

A second issue concerns the definition of the national culture that immigrants are integrated into (coercively or voluntarily) and how open it is to the visible maintenance and expression of difference. In Germany and France, for example, an immigrant may be refused naturalization if he or she is deemed to have an excessive attachment to his or her home country or religion. In these cases, national identity is implicitly presented as having a zero-sum relationship with immigrants' prior identities. Immigrants are not invited to add a new identity to their old ones. Rather, they must relinquish the old. This implicit assumption that prior identities should be relinquished, or at least subordinated and hidden for public purposes, is reflected in a number of ways. Examples include the prohibition of dual citizenship and the stringency of naturalization tests. While most countries require that citizenship applicants pass a language test, some countries set the bar much higher than others, requiring immigrants to acquire close to native-born proficiency in language and cultural knowledge. Such policies are arguably aiming at full assimilation, while preventing incompletely integrated immigrants from gaining citizenship. By contrast, other countries set the bar much lower, requiring only a good-faith effort on the part of the immigrant, and far less than native-born proficiency, on the assumption that immigrants with varying levels of mixed and dual identities can nonetheless become good citizens.

Citizenship tests in Denmark and Canada illustrate this difference.[30] Both countries use citizenship tests to promote a national identity and a national language. But the Canadian citizenship test, both implicitly and explicitly, assumes that many immigrants will want to be multicultural citizens who combine a strong ethnic identity with a strong Canadian national identity, whereas the assimilationist Danish test seeks to exclude such would-be multicultural

---

30  See Adamo 2008. For a broader attempt to measure the ethnic exclusiveness of naturalization policies, see Koning 2011.

forms of citizenship. In this sense, citizenship tests are not inherently incompatible with multiculturalist commitments. On the contrary, citizenship tests are simply one more domain in which countries exhibit their commitment (or lack of commitment) to multiculturalism.

Whether a program is coercive or voluntary is a separate issue from whether the national identity is closed versus open. France may not have mandatory civic integration classes, but it has an assimilationist conception of national identity. Conversely, one could imagine a country that has coercive integration classes but also an open conception of national identity. (Some British proposals to add new tests for residency permits would make the integration process more coercive while retaining a relatively open conception of national identity.) This question of identity concerns the content of civic integration classes or citizenship tests rather than whether they are voluntary or mandatory.

While the openness of national identities is difficult to measure, it is arguably more important than the level of coercion when assessing the (in)compatibility of civic integration policies with MCPs. Highly coercive integration policies are illiberal; as such, they should be offensive to any liberal-minded person, even one who does not particularly embrace multiculturalism. By contrast, assimilationist and exclusionary conceptions of national identity are offensive to multiculturalists, and this is independent of whether the means used to promote that national identity are coercive or voluntary. If we think of Canada as endorsing a "liberal multiculturalism," then coercive integration policies would violate the "liberal" part of the story, and assimilationist conceptions of national identity would violate the "multiculturalism" part of the story. The idea that immigrants have to renounce earlier identities, and/or that they have to achieve the same level of proficiency as the native born in the local language and culture before being welcomed to participate in society, is directly at odds with any meaningful form of multicultural citizenship.

In short, while the shift to civic integration is an important development, it is misleading to equate this with a retreat from multiculturalism. Civic integration policies differ along many dimensions, including in their relationship to multiculturalism. Some countries (e.g., Denmark, Germany, and Austria) have adopted an antimulticultural form of civic integration – one that is coercive and assimilationist. But since these are countries that never embraced multiculturalism in the first place, their new policies can hardly be considered a retreat from multiculturalism. By contrast, other countries with long-standing MCPs (e.g., Sweden) have adopted forms of civic integration policies that are more voluntary and pluralistic. And this model of multicultural integration seems to be the one to which other countries (e.g., Finland) are moving. We lose sight of these profound differences – and important policy options – if we assume prematurely that civic integration entails a retreat from multiculturalism.

### 3. Convergence or Divergence?

And this, in turn, raises questions about the claim that there is a "convergence" on civic integration in Europe. This claim has been popularized by Christian Joppke, who argues not only that there has been a wholesale retreat from multiculturalism in Europe, but that "in response to the integration crisis, distinct national models of dealing with immigrants are giving way to convergent policies of civic integration and anti-discrimination" (Joppke 2004). The evidence discussed here suggests a very different picture. The data show no evidence for convergence either on MCPs or on civic integration policies. On the contrary, European countries display greater divergence today than 15 or 30 years ago in both policy domains. As measured by our MCP Index, the divergence in multiculturalism scores – the standard deviation – has increased from 1980 to 2010.[31] This result is confirmed by Koopmans' index of Indicators of Citizenship Rights for Immigrants, which also shows a growing standard deviation from 1980 to 2008

---

31 For the 16 European countries, the standard deviations increased from 1.03 in 1980 to 1.76 in 2000 to 2.00 in 2010.

along the multiculturalism dimension.[32] And, according to Goodman's Civic Integration Index, the divergence in civic integration scores has increased from 1997 to 2009 (Goodman 2010; Mouritsen 2011 also disputes the convergence hypothesis).

Amid this growing divergence, we can see certain patterns emerging. At one end, we have countries that adopt what Goodman describes as "prohibitive" citizenship strategies (ibid.) based on coercive and assimilative civic integration policies. Not surprisingly, the countries that she categorizes in this way (e.g., Germany, Austria, Denmark) are also countries that score very low on our MCP Index. At the other end, we have countries that adopt what Goodman describes as "enabling" citizenship strategies based on voluntary and open civic integration. Not surprisingly, these are also countries that have increased their MCP score since 2000 (e.g., Sweden, Finland). (Outside of Europe, Canada and Australia also fit this enabling category and also score high on MCPs.) In between, we have a range of countries with intermediary forms and levels of both civic integration and MCPs.

In short, all of the talk about the retreat from multiculturalism and the convergence on civic integration obscures the fact that a form of multicultural integration remains a live option for Western democracies, both in the New World and in Europe. I stress this option not simply for the sake of analytical completeness, but because I think it is an option that warrants serious consideration on both normative and empirical grounds.

From a normative point of view, the combination of enabling civic integration and multicultural accommodation is the option most in line with fundamental liberal values of freedom and fairness. There are valid justifications for the state to promote civic integration, including promoting a common language and national identity. But these policies risk being oppressive and unfair to minorities if they are not supplemented by MCPs. (Conversely, there are valid justifica-

---

32 The standard deviation on Koopmans' multiculturalism dimension in 1980 was 0.19; by 2008, it had risen to 0.30 (Koopmans, Michalowski, and Waibel 2011, Table 5).

tions for minorities to claim multicultural accommodations, but these policies may become unreasonable and destabilizing if they are not supplemented by civic integration policies.) The combination of civic integration and multiculturalism is mutually, normatively reinforcing: Each helps to both justify and constrain the other.[33]

Of course, many critics of multiculturalism accept that it is normatively desirable in principle, but argue that it has failed in practice. As Koopmans puts it, while there are "legitimate normative reasons" for multiculturalism, "we cannot simply assume that what is normatively justifiable will also be practically efficient" (Koopmans 2010: 5). And, indeed, he argues that it has been counterproductive. But, as discussed earlier, it is far from clear that multiculturalism has "failed" in practice. On the contrary, on many of the crucial indicators, it appears that countries with the combination of enabling civic integration and MCPs are doing comparatively well, as measured by levels of political participation, prejudice and far-right xenophobia, and trust and social cohesion.

## Conclusion: The Future of Multicultural Citizenship

This chapter challenges four powerful myths about multiculturalism:
- First, it disputes the 3S account of multiculturalism as the uncritical celebration of diversity and, instead, offers an account of multiculturalism as the pursuit of new relations of democratic citizenship, inspired and constrained by human-rights ideals.
- Second, it challenges the idea that multiculturalism has been in "wholesale retreat" (Joppke 2004: 244) and, instead, offers evidence that MCPs have persisted, even strengthened, over the past ten years.
- Third, it rejects the idea that multiculturalism has failed and, instead, offers evidence that MCPs have had positive effects.

---

33  For a fuller defense of the idea that liberal-democratic principles support robust national integration policies supplemented and constrained by robust MCPs, see Kymlicka 2001.

- Fourth, it disputes the idea that the spread of civic integration pol icies has displaced multiculturalism or rendered it obsolete. The report instead offers evidence that MCPs are fully consistent with certain forms of civic integration policies and that, indeed, the combination of multiculturalism with an enabling form of civic integration is both normatively desirable and empirically effective in at least some cases.

In light of these arguments, the ideal of multiculturalism-as-citizenization should remain a salient option in the toolkit of democracies, worthy of serious consideration by policymakers.[34] However, it must be acknowledged that there are major obstacles to the multiculturalist project: Not all attempts to adopt new models of multicultural citizenship have taken root or succeeded in achieving their intended effects of promoting citizenization.

The crucial question, therefore, is why multicultural citizenship works at some times and in some places and not others. We do not yet have a systematic account of the preconditions for successful experiments in multicultural citizenship, so a certain degree of caution is required when making judgments and recommendations in this area. The theory and practice of multiculturalism suggests that MCPs can contribute to citizenization, but the historical record suggests that certain conditions must be in place for it to have its intended effects.[35]

---

34 To say that multicultural citizenship remains a salient option is not to say that we must or should advocate for the word *multiculturalism*. As is noted earlier, the "*m* word" is now virtually taboo in some countries, and it may not be worth the effort to fight that semantic battle. What matters in the end is whether the underlying principles and policies of multiculturalism-as-citizenization are taken seriously and, in my view, those principles and policies can be enacted without using the "*m* word." They could instead be adopted under the heading of "diversity policies" or "intercultural dialogue" or "community cohesion" or even "civic integration." On the other hand, perpetuating the demonizing of multiculturalism may simply play into the hands of xenophobes. To state that multiculturalism is against human rights, for example, is not just bad history and bad social science; it also risks licensing and legitimating anti-diversity views. It may not be possible to defend multicultural citizenship without countering some of the myths that surround the term "multiculturalism."

35 For a more detailed analysis of these conditions, see Kymlicka 2004 and 2007.

The first is "desecuritization." Where states feel insecure in geopolitical terms (fearful of neighboring enemies), they are unlikely to treat their own minorities fairly. More specifically, states are unlikely to accord powers and resources to minorities that they view as potential collaborators with neighboring enemies. In the past, this has been an issue in the West, particularly in relation to national minorities. For example, prior to World War II, Italy, Denmark, and Belgium all feared that their German-speaking minorities were more loyal to Germany than to their own country and would support attempts by Germany to invade and annex areas of ethnic German concentration. These countries worried that Germany might invade in the name of liberating their coethnic Germans, and that the German minority would collaborate with such an invasion.

Today, as a result of the European Union (EU) and North Atlantic Treaty Organization (NATO), this is a non-issue throughout the established Western democracies with respect to national minorities (or indigenous peoples). It is difficult to think of a single Western democracy where the state fears that a national minority would collaborate with a neighboring enemy and potential aggressor.[36] Unfortunately, it remains an issue with respect to certain immigrant groups, particularly Arab/Muslim groups after 9/11. Where minorities are perceived as security threats, ethnic relations become "securitized." Relations between states and minorities are seen not as a matter of normal democratic debate and negotiation, but as a matter of state security for which the state has to limit the democratic process to protect itself. Under conditions of securitization, minority political mobilization may be banned, and even if minority demands can be voiced, they will be rejected by the larger society and the state. After all, how can groups that are disloyal have legitimate claims against the state? So, the securitization of ethnic relations erodes both the democratic space to voice minority demands and the likelihood that those demands will

---

36 Cyprus and Israel still exhibit this dynamic of viewing their historic Turkish and Arab minorities, respectively, as potential collaborators with external enemies and, coincidentally, have not been able to agree on minority autonomy.

be accepted, and this erodes any potential for multicultural citizenship.

A second precondition is human-rights protection. This concerns security – not of the state, but of individuals who would be subject to self-governing minority institutions. States are unlikely to accept minority autonomy if they fear it will lead to islands of local tyranny within a broader democratic state. In the past, this too has been grounds for opposition to according greater rights to both national minorities and indigenous peoples, who were seen as carriers of illiberal political cultures. While this fear has essentially disappeared in relation to historic minorities – no one fears that the Scots or Catalans will attempt to restrict fundamental human rights in the name of cultural authenticity, religious orthodoxy, or racial purity – it remains a pervasive fear in relation to some recent immigrant groups; here again, Muslims are often singled out. Indeed, as many commentators have observed, much of the backlash against multiculturalism is fundamentally driven by anxieties about Muslims, in particular, and their perceived unwillingness to integrate into liberal-democratic norms.

These two factors are applicable to all forms of multiculturalism – whether for indigenous peoples, national minorities, or immigrant groups. But there are also factors that are specific to the case of immigrant multiculturalism:[37]

*Control over borders.* Multiculturalism is fundamentally about the treatment of immigrants after they have settled, rather than about who is admitted in the first place. However, multiculturalism for settled immigrants is more controversial in circumstances where citizens fear that they lack control over their borders and, hence, lack control over who is admitted. Where countries are faced with large numbers (or unexpected surges) of "unwanted" immigrants – either unauthorized immigrants or asylum-seekers – it often generates a backlash against multiculturalism. It is perhaps not surprising, therefore, that multiculturalism has had an easier time in countries such as Australia and Canada, where immigration is overwhelmingly the re-

37 For a more detailed discussion of these factors, see Kymlicka 2004.

sult of state selection, with few unauthorized entrants. Having a sense of control over one's borders, and hence the capacity to determine who enters and in what number, has several consequences. First, it reduces fear of being swamped by unwanted migrants, therefore lowering the temperature of debates and making citizens feel secure that they are in control of their own destiny. Second, in most Western countries, there is a strong moralistic objection to rewarding migrants who enter the country illegally or under false pretense (i.e., economic migrants making false claims about escaping persecution). Such migrants are seen as flouting the rule of law, both in the way they first enter the country and often in their subsequent activities (e.g., working illegally). Most citizens have a strong moral objection to rewarding such illegal or dishonest behavior. Moreover, such migrants are often seen as "jumping the queue," taking the place of equally needy or equally deserving would-be migrants who seek entry through legal channels. There is also a prudential objection to providing MCPs for unauthorized immigrants, since this may encourage more illegal migration.

*Homogeneity or heterogeneity of immigrants.* Multiculturalism arguably works best when it is genuinely multicultural – that is, when immigrants come from many different source countries rather than coming overwhelmingly from a single source country. In Canada, for example, immigrants are drawn from all corners of the world, and no single immigrant-origin group forms more than 15 percent of the total immigrant stock. In the United States, by contrast, because of the income disparity with its far less wealthy neighbor, 29 percent of immigrants come from Mexico; similarly, North Africans dominate the immigrant stock in Spain and France. This has many consequences for the integration process. In a situation where immigrants are divided into many different groups originating in distant countries, there is no feasible prospect for any particular immigrant group to challenge the hegemony of the national language and institutions. These groups may form an alliance among themselves to fight for better treatment and accommodation, but such an alliance can only be developed within the language and institutions of the host society and, hence, is integrative. In situations where there is a single dominant immigrant group originating in a neighboring country, the dynamics may be very different. The Arabs in Spain or Mexicans in the United States do not need allies among other immigrant groups. One could imagine claims for Arabic or Spanish to be declared a second official language, at least in regions where they are concentrated, and these immigrants could seek support from their neighboring home country for such claims – in effect, establishing a kind of transnational extension of their original homeland into their new neighboring country of residence. This scenario may sound fanciful, but native-born citizens may nonetheless see it as a risk, one that has to be firmly prevented by restricting immigration and opposing multiculturalism.[38]

*Economic contribution.* Multiculturalism – at least in the citizenizing form described earlier – is seen as part of a package of mutual rights and responsibilities in which the state makes good-faith efforts to accommodate immigrants, and immigrants make good-faith efforts to integrate, so as to coproduce new relations of democratic citizenship. Support for multiculturalism therefore depends on the perception that immigrants are holding up their end of the bargain and making a good-faith effort to contribute to society. The most visible manifestation of this, in most countries, is their economic contribution, and so a threat to multiculturalism arises whenever immigrants are perceived as avoiding work and, instead, living off the welfare state. In many cases, of course, immigrants have contributed more to the welfare state than they have taken out – this has historically been the pattern in the United States and Canada. And even when they are disproportionately unemployed or living on assistance, the explanation is often a lack of opportunities and not a lack of good-faith effort. Nonetheless, native-born citizens have both a moral and prudential objection to the idea of extending multiculturalism without tangible evidence of a reciprocal effort on the part of immigrants. And so, it is vital to the success of multiculturalism that the state provide visible

---

38 For an example of this sort of fear, invoking the facts about the contiguity and numerical dominance of Hispanic immigrants in the United States, see Huntington 2004.

means for immigrants to manifest this good-faith effort, including through economic contributions. In some northern European countries, it appears that governments show more concern about facilitating immigrants' access to the welfare state than about facilitating their access to the labor market. This has been called a form of "generous betrayal." But sustainable multiculturalism requires the opportunity for reciprocal contributions.

There are doubtless many other factors that shape the potential for multicultural citizenship, including old-fashioned racial prejudice. For many people, the latter is the key factor. But, of course, prejudice is found in all countries – indeed, its existence is part of the justification for adopting multiculturalism – so it cannot explain the variation across countries (or over time) in support for multiculturalism. And if we try to understand why this latent prejudice and xenophobia sometimes coalesce into powerful political movements against multiculturalism, the answer lies in perceptions of threats to geopolitical security, human rights, border control, and economic reciprocity. Where such perceptions are lacking, as they are in relation to most immigrant groups in North America, then support for multiculturalism can remain quite strong.

If this analysis is correct, it has important implications for the future of multiculturalism in the West. On the one hand, despite all the talk about the retreat from multiculturalism, it suggests that multiculturalism, in general, has a bright future. There are powerful forces at work in modern Western societies driving toward public recognition and accommodation of ethnocultural diversity. Public values and constitutional norms of tolerance, equality, and individual freedom – underpinned by the human-rights revolution – all push in the direction of multiculturalism, particularly when viewed against the backdrop of a history of ethnic and racial hierarchies. These factors explain the ongoing trend toward the recognition of the rights of substate national groups and indigenous peoples. Older ideas of undifferentiated citizenship and neutral public spheres have collapsed in the face of these trends, and no one today seriously proposes that minority rights and differentiated citizenship for historic minorities should be abandoned or reversed. That minority rights, liberal democracy, and human rights can comfortably coexist is now a fixed point in both domestic constitutions and international law. There is no credible alternative to multiculturalism in these contexts.

The situation with respect to immigrant groups is more complex. The same factors that push for multiculturalism in relation to historic minorities have also generated a willingness to contemplate multiculturalism for immigrant groups – and, indeed, such policies seem to have worked well under "low-risk" conditions. However, MCPs for immigrants have run into difficulties where the situation is perceived as high-risk. Where immigrants are seen as predominantly unauthorized, as potential carriers of illiberal practices or movements, and/or as net burdens on the welfare state, then multiculturalism poses perceived risks to both prudential self-interest and moral principles, and this perception can override the forces that support multiculturalism.

On the other hand, one could argue that these very same factors also make the rejection of immigrant multiculturalism a high-risk move. It is precisely when immigrants are perceived as illegitimate, illiberal, and burdensome that multiculturalism may be most needed. Without proactive policies to promote mutual understanding and respect, and to make immigrants feel comfortable within mainstream institutions, these factors could quickly create a racialized underclass standing in permanent opposition to the larger society. Indeed, in the long term, the only viable response to the presence of large numbers of immigrants is some form of liberal multiculturalism, regardless of how or from where these immigrants arrived. But we need to accept that the path to immigrant multiculturalism in many countries will not be smooth or linear. Moreover, we need to better focus on how to manage the risks involved. In the past, defenders of immigrant multiculturalism have typically focused on the perceived benefits of cultural diversity and intercultural understanding, and on condemning racism and xenophobia. Those arguments are sound, but they need to be supplemented with a fuller acknowledgement of the prudential and moral risks involved, and with some account of how those risks will be managed. A fuller exploration of how civic integration policies can work together with multiculturalism may be a crucial step in this process.

# Appendices

## Appendix 1: Immigrant Multiculturalism Policy Scores, 1980–2010

| | Total Score (out of a possible 8) | | |
|---|---|---|---|
| | 1980 | 2000 | 2010 |
| Canada | 5 | 7.5 | 7.5 |
| Australia | 4 | 8 | 8 |
| Austria | 0 | 1 | 1.5 |
| Belgium | 1 | 3 | 5.5 |
| Denmark | 0 | 0.5 | 0 |
| Finland | 0 | 1.5 | 6 |
| France | 1 | 2 | 2 |
| Germany | 0 | 2 | 2.5 |
| Greece | 0.5 | 0.5 | 2.5 |
| Ireland | 1 | 1.5 | 3 |
| Italy | 0 | 1.5 | 1 |
| Japan | 0 | 0 | 0 |
| Netherlands | 2.5 | 5.5 | 2 |
| New Zealand | 2.5 | 5 | 5.5 |
| Norway | 0 | 0 | 2.5 |
| Portugal | 1 | 2 | 3.5 |
| Spain | 0 | 1 | 3.5 |
| Sweden | 3 | 5 | 7 |
| Switzerland | 0 | 1 | 1 |
| United Kingdom | 2.5 | 5.5 | 5.5 |
| United States | 3 | 3 | 3 |
| European average | 0.7 | 2.1 | 3.1 |
| Overall average | 1.29 | 2.71 | 3.48 |

Note: Countries could receive a total score of 8, one for each of the following eight policies:
(a) constitutional, legislative, or parliamentary affirmation of multiculturalism at the central and/or regional and municipal levels and the existence of a government ministry, secretariat, or advisory board to implement this policy in consultation with ethnic communities; (b) the adoption of multiculturalism in school curriculum; (c) the inclusion of ethnic representation/sensitivity in the mandate of public media or media licensing; (d) exemptions from dress codes; (e) allowing of dual citizenship; (f) the funding of ethnic group organizations or activities; (g) the funding of bilingual education or mother-tongue instruction; and (h) affirmative action for disadvantaged immigrant groups.

Source: Multiculturalism Policy Index

## Appendix 2: Civic Integration Index (CIVIX) Scores, 1997–2009

|  | 1997 | 2009 | Change |
|---|---|---|---|
| Sweden | 0.0 | 0.0 | 0.0 |
| Belgium | 0.5 | 0.5 | 0.0 |
| Ireland | 0.5 | 0.5 | 0.0 |
| Italy | 0.5 | 0.5 | 0.0 |
| Finland | 0.5 | 1.0 | 0.5 |
| Greece | 1.0 | 1.0 | 0.0 |
| Luxembourg | 0.5 | 1.0 | 0.5 |
| Portugal | 0.5 | 1.0 | 0.5 |
| Spain | 1.0 | 1.0 | 0.0 |
| France | 0.5 | 3.5 | 3.0 |
| Austria | 0.5 | 4.5 | 4.0 |
| Netherlands | 0.5 | 4.5 | 4.0 |
| United Kingdom | 0.5 | 4.5 | 4.0 |
| Denmark | 0.5 | 5.0 | 4.5 |
| Germany | 1.5 | 6.0 | 4.5 |

Source: Gooodman 2010

## Works Cited

Adamo, Silvia. Northern Exposure: The New Danish Model of Citizenship Test. *International Journal on Multicultural Societies* (10) 1: 10–28, 2008.

Adams, Michael. *Unlikely Utopia: The Surprising Triumph of Canadian Pluralism*. Toronto: Viking, 2007.

Alibhai-Brown, Yasmin. *After Multiculturalism*. London: Foreign Policy Centre, 2000.

Alibhai-Brown, Yasmin. Beyond Multiculturalism. *Canadian Diversity/ Diversité Canadienne* (3) 2: 51–54, 2004.

Ang, Ien, and John Stratton. Multiculturalism in Crisis: The New Politics of Race and National Identity in Australia. In *On Not Speaking Chinese: Living Between Asia and the West*, edited by Ien Ang. London: Routledge, 2001: 95–111.

Back, Les, Michael Keith, Azra Khan, Kalbir Shukra, and John Solomos. New Labour's White Heart: Politics, Multiculturalism and the Return of Assimilation. *Political Quarterly* (73) 4: 445–454, 2002.

Banting, Keith, and Will Kymlicka (eds.). *Multiculturalism and the Welfare State: Recognition and Redistribution in Contemporary Democracies*. Oxford: Oxford University Press, 2006.

Berry, John W., Rudolf Kalin, and Donald M. Taylor. *Multiculturalism and Ethnic Attitudes in Canada*. Ottawa: Supply and Services Canada, 1977.

Berry, John W., Jean S. Phinney, David L. Sam and Paul Vedder. *Immigrant Youth in Cultural Transition*. Mahwah, NJ: Lawrence Erlbaum, 2006.

Bird, Karen. Running Visible Minority Candidates in Canada: The Effects of Voter and Candidate Ethnicity and Gender on Voter Choice. Paper presented at the Conference on Diversity and Democratic Politics: Canada in Comparative Perspective, Queen's University, Kingston, ON, Canada, May 7–8, 2009.

Bissoondath, Neil. *Selling Illusions: The Cult of Multiculturalism in Canada*. Toronto: Penguin, 1994.

Black, Jerome, and Lynda Erickson. Ethno-racial Origins of Candidates and Electoral Performance. *Party Politics* (12) 4: 541–561, 2006.

Bloemraad, Irene. *Becoming a Citizen: Incorporating Immigrants and Refugees in the United States and Canada*. Berkeley: University of California Press, 2006.

Bloemraad, Irene. The Debate Over Multiculturalism: Philosophy, Politics, and Policy. Migration Policy Institute, September 2011. www.migrationinformation.org/Feature/display.cfm?ID=854.

Borevi, Karin. Dimensions of Citizenship: European Integration Policies from a Scandinavian Perspective. In *Diversity, Inclusion and Citizenship in Scandinavia*, edited by Bo Bengtsson, Per Strömblad, and Ann-Helén Bay. Newcastle upon Tyne: Cambridge Scholars Publishing, 2010: 19–46.

Brubaker, Rogers. The Return of Assimilation. *Ethnic and Racial Studies* (24) 4: 531–48, 2001.

Crepaz, Markus. "If You Are My Brother, I May Give You a Dime!" Public Opinion on Multiculturalism, Trust and the Welfare State. In *Multiculturalism and the Welfare State: Recognition and Redistribution in Contemporary Democracies*, edited by Keith Banting and Will Kymlicka. Oxford: Oxford University Press, 2006: 92–117.

Cuperus, René, Karl Duffek and Johannes Kandel (eds.). *The Challenge of Diversity: European Social Democracy Facing Migration, Integration and Multiculturalism.* Innsbruck: Studien Verlag, 2003.

Duyvendak, W. G. J., and P. W. A. Scholten. The Invention of the Dutch Multicultural Model and its Effects on Integration Discourses in the Netherlands. *Perspectives on Europe* (40) 2: 39–45, 2011.

Eliadis, Pearl. Diversity and Equality: The Vital Connection. In *Belonging: Diversity, Recognition and Shared Citizenship in Canada*, edited by Keith G. Banting, Thomas J. Courchene and F. Leslie Seidle. Montreal: Institute for Research in Public Policy, 2007: 547–560.

Entzinger, Han. The Rise and Fall of Multiculturalism in the Netherlands. In *Toward Assimilation and Citizenship: Immigrants in Liberal Nation-States*, edited by Christian Joppke and Ewa Morawska. London: Palgrave, 2003: 59–86.

Ersanilli, Evelyn, and Ruud Koopmans. Do Immigrant Integration Policies Matter? A Three-Country Comparison among Turkish Immigrants. *West European Politics* (34) 2: 208–234, 2011.

Esses, Victoria, Ulrich Wagner, Carina Wolf, Matthias Preiser, and Christopher Wilbur. Perceptions of National Identity and Attitudes toward Immigrants and Immigration in Canada and Germany. *International Journal of Intercultural Relations* (30) 6: 653–669, 2006.

Focus Canada. *Canadian Identity: Bilingualism, Multiculturalism and the Charter of Rights.* Toronto: Environics, 2002.

Focus Canada. *Canadians' Attitudes toward Muslims.* Toronto: Environics, 2006.

Goodhart, David. Has Multiculturalism had its Day? *Literary Review of Canada* (16) 3: 3–4, 2008.

Goodman, Sara. Integration Requirements for Integration's Sake? Identifying, Categorizing and Comparing Civic Integration Policies. *Journal of Ethnic and Migration Studies* (36) 5: 753–772, 2010.

Hansen, Randall. Diversity, Integration and the Turn from Multiculturalism in the United Kingdom. In *Belonging: Diversity, Recognition and Shared Citizenship in Canada*, edited by Keith G. Banting, Thomas J. Courchene, and F. Leslie Seidle. Montreal: Institute for Research in Public Policy, 2007: 351–386.

Harell, Allison. Minority-Majority Relations in Canada: The Rights Regime and the Adoption of Multicultural Values. Paper presented at the Canadian Political Science Association Annual Meeting, May 27–29, 2009. Ottawa, ON, Canada.

Heath, Anthony. Crossnational Patterns and Processes of Ethnic Disadvantage. In *Unequal Chances: Ethnic Minorities in Western Labour Markets*, edited by Anthony Heath and Sin Yi Cheung. Oxford: Oxford University Press, 2007: 639–695.

Hewitt, Roger. *White Backlash and the Politics of Multiculturalism*. Cambridge: Cambridge University Press, 2005.

Hollinger, David A. *Post-ethnic America: Beyond Multiculturalism*, revised edition. New York: Basic Books, 2006.

Howe, Paul. The Political Engagement of New Canadians: A Comparative Perspective. In *Belonging? Diversity, Recognition and Shared Citizenship in Canada*, edited by Keith G. Banting, Thomas J. Courchene and F. Leslie Seidle. Montreal: Institute for Research on Public Policy, 2007: 611–646.

Huntington, Samuel P. The Hispanic Challenge. *Foreign Policy*, March 1, 2004. www.foreignpolicy.com/articles/2004/03/01/the_hispanic_challenge.

Johnston, Richard, Keith Banting, Will Kymlicka, and Stuart Soroka. National Identity and Support for the Welfare State. *Canadian Journal of Political Science* (43) 2: 349–377, 2010.

Joppke, Christian. The Retreat of Multiculturalism in the Liberal State: Theory and Policy. *British Journal of Sociology* (55) 2: 237–257, 2004.

Joppke, Christian. Beyond National Models: Civic Integration Policies for Immigrants in Western Europe. *Western European Politics* (30) 1: 1–22, 2007.

Joppke, Christian, and Ewa Morawska (eds.). *Toward Assimilation and Citizenship. Immigrants in Liberal Nation-States*. London: Palgrave, 2003.

Jupp, James. The New Multicultural Agenda. *Crossings* (1) 1: 38–41, 1996.

Jupp, James. *From White Australia to Woomera: The Story of Australian Immigration*, 2nd edition. Cambridge: Cambridge University Press, 2007.

Kazemipur, Abdolmohammad. *Social Capital and Diversity: Some Lessons from Canada*. Bern: Peter Lang, 2009.

Kesler, Christel, and Irene Bloemraad. Does Immigration Erode Social Capital? The Conditional Effects of Immigration-Generated Diversity on Trust, Membership, and Participation across 19 Countries, 1981–2000. *Canadian Journal of Political Science* (43) 2: 319–347, 2010.

King, Desmond. *The Liberty of Strangers: Making the American Nation*. Oxford: Oxford University Press, 2004.

Koning, E. A. Ethnic and civic dealings with newcomers: naturalization policies and practices in 26 immigration countries. *Ethnic and Racial Studies* (34) 11: 1974–1994, 2011.

Koopmans, Ruud. Trade-Offs Between Equality and Difference: The Crisis of Dutch Multiculturalism in Cross-National Perspective. Danish Institute for International Affairs, Brief, Copenhagen, December 2006.

Koopmans, Ruud. Trade-Offs Between Equality and Difference: Immigrant Integration, Multiculturalism and the Welfare State in Cross-National Perspective. *Journal of Ethnic and Migration Studies* (http://www.informaworld.com/smpp/title~db=all~content=t7134 33350~tab=issueslist~branches=36 - v3636) 1: 1–26, 2010.

Koopmans, Ruud, Ines Michalowski, and Stine Waibal. Citizenship Rights for Immigrants: National Opportunity Structures and Cross-National Convergence in Western Europe, 1980–2008. Paper presented at the 18th annual International Conference of European Studies, Barcelona, June 20–22, 2011.

Kymlicka, Will. *Politics in the Vernacular*. Oxford: Oxford University Press, 2001.

Kymlicka, Will. Marketing Canadian Pluralism in the International Arena. *International Journal* (59) 4: 829–852, 2004.

Kymlicka, Will. *Multicultural Odysseys: Navigating the New International Politics of Diversity*. Oxford: Oxford University Press, 2007.

Laczko, Leslie. National and Continental Attachments and Attitudes towards Immigrants: North America and Europe Compared. Paper presented at the Annual Meeting of the Canadian Sociology Association, Saskatoon, June 3–5, 2007.

Marc, Alexandre. *Delivering Services in Multicultural Societies*. Washington, DC: World Bank, 2009.

McGhee, Derek. *The End of Multiculturalism? Terrorism, Integration and Human Rights*. Milton Keynes: Open University Press, 2008.

Mouritsen, Per. On the Liberal Plateau: Civic Integration Policies in North Western Europe. Paper presented at the conference on Multiculturalism and Nordic Welfare States, Aalborg University, Denmark, March 21–23, 2011.

Multiculturalism Policy Index. www.queensu.ca/mcp.

OECD – Organization for Economic Cooperation and Development. *Where Immigrant Students Succeed: A Comparative Review of Performance and Engagement in PISA 2003*. Paris: OECD, Program for International Student Assessment, 2006. www.oecd.org/dataoecd/2/38/36664934.pdf.

Putnam, Robert. E Pluribus Unum: Diversity and Community in the Twenty-first Century. *Scandinavian Political Studies* (30) 2: 137–174, 2007.

Reitz, Jeffrey. Assessing Multiculturalism as a Behavioural Theory. In *Multiculturalism and Social Cohesion: Potentials and Challenges of Diversity*, edited by Raymond Breton, Karen Dion, and Kenneth Dion. New York: Springer, 2009: 1–47.

Schönwälder, Karen. Germany: Integration Policy and Pluralism in a Self-Conscious Country of Immigration. In *The Multiculturalism*

*Backlash: European Discourses, Policies and Practices*, edited by Steven Vertovec and Susanne Wessendorf. London: Routledge, 2010: 152–169.

Sides, John, and Jack Citrin. European Opinion about Immigration: The Role of Identities, Interests and Information. *British Journal of Political Science* 37: 477–505, 2007.

Smith, Anthony. *The Ethnic Revival in the Modern World*. Cambridge: Cambridge University Press, 1981.

Sniderman, Paul, and Louk Hagendoorn. *When Ways of Life Collide: Multiculturalism and Its Discontents in the Netherlands*. Princeton, NJ: Princeton University Press, 2007.

Tully, James. The Challenge of Reimagining Citizenship and Belonging in Multicultural and Multinational Societies. In *The Demands of Citizenship*, edited by Catriona McKinnon and Iain Hampsher-Monk. London: Continuum, 2000: 212–234.

Uberoi, Varun. Do Policies of Multiculturalism Change National Identities? *Political Quarterly* (79) 3: 404–417, 2008.

Vertovec, Steven. Towards post-multiculturalism? Changing communities, conditions and contexts of diversity. *International Social Science Journal* 61: 83–95, 2010.

Vertovec, Steven, and Susan Wessendorf (eds.). *The Multiculturalism Backlash: European Discourses, Policies and Practices*. London: Routledge, 2010.

Weldon, Steven. The Institutional Context of Tolerance for Ethnic Minorities: A Comparative Multilevel Analysis of Western Europe. *American Journal of Political Science* (50) 2: 331–349, 2006.

Wong, Lloyd, Joseph Garcea, and Anna Kirova. An Analysis of the "Anti- and Post-Multiculturalism" Discourses: The Fragmentation Position. Prairie Centre for Excellence in Research on Immigration and Integration. Edmonton, 2005.

# The Relationship Between Immigration and Nativism in Europe and North America

*Cas Mudde*

## Introduction

Migration is as old as mankind itself, yet it has increased dramatically in scope and consequences in recent decades. Millions of people migrate or have migrated as transportation has become affordable, opportunity has expanded, and countries have become increasingly connected. While the vast majority of migrants stay fairly close to their homeland, a growing group sets out for farther shores, most notably Western Europe and North America.

This chapter focuses primarily on the effects of migration on political extremism in three industrialized regions: North America, Western Europe, and Central and Eastern Europe. Although all three regions are internally diverse, they share some key features that are relevant: In North America, both Canada and the United States have long traditions as countries of immigration; Western Europe has seen mass immigration since the end of World War II (although some countries, France and the United Kingdom among them, experienced it much earlier than others, such as Ireland and Spain); and Central and Eastern Europe have only been confronted in recent decades with generally low levels of immigration and higher levels of emigration.

The focus here is on the political extremism of the host population, or the native born, not of the immigrants. While extremism among some immigrant groups, ranging from Turkish nationalist groups to Arab jihadists, has increased, this is only addressed indirectly, in the ways in which it has influenced the immigration debate in the host country. The chapter examines on the various nativist reactions to immigration. Nativism, a combination of nationalism and xenophobia, is "an ideology which holds that states should be inhabited exclusively by members of the native group (the nation) and that non-native elements (persons and ideas) are fundamentally threatening to the homogeneous nation-state" (Mudde 2007).

The chapter's first section defines and introduces the main nativist actors by region, as well as highlights ways in which nativists mobilize in the different regions and their respective strengths and weaknesses. The second section examines the importance of migration to the identity and political relevance of the nativist actors, and analyzes how these actors frame migration and how central it is to their discourse and electoral success. The third section shifts the focus onto how nativist actors have affected migration policies in their country. The fourth section touches briefly on the effects that the recent economic crisis has had on immigration and nativism in the three regions. The final section summarizes the chapter's main findings and addresses state responses to anti-immigrant extremism.

## The Main Nativist Actors

The extremists discussed in this study go by many different, if often related, names. Academics and journalists use terms such as "xenophobes," "nativists," "racists," "right-wing populists," the "radical right," "radical right-wing populists," the "extreme right," "(neo-)fascists," and "neo-Nazis." While the intrinsic details of the definitional debates are not discussed here, it is important to provide at least some broad clarifications of the main terms used. As mentioned previously, the overarching category examined is nativism (for a full discussion, see Mudde 2007, chapter 1).

There are two fundamental distinctions that are relevant here: right-left and radical-extreme. However, these relative terms don't help much in a broad interregional comparison. At the same time, the socioeconomic distinction between a pro-state left and a pro-market right seems at best secondary to the main concern of this chapter. Therefore, for the purposes of this analysis, the distinction between left and right is in line with that of Italian philosopher Norberto Bobbio (1994), who differentiates on the grounds of the attitude toward (in)equality. In this interpretation, the left considers the key inequalities between people to be artificial and wants to overcome them by active state involvement, whereas the right believes the main inequalities between people to be natural and outside the purview of the state.

The distinction between *extreme* and *radical* is not merely of academic importance but can have significant legal consequences. For example, in Germany, extremist organizations can be banned, whereas radical groups cannot (Backes 2003). To keep things simple, this analysis defines extremism as antidemocratic, in the sense that the key aspects of democracy – majority rule and one person, one vote – are rejected. Radicalism, on the other hand, accepts the basic tenets of democracy but challenges some key aspects of liberal democracy, most notably minority protections. Hence, there is a fundamental difference between radical and extreme forces, which have significant consequences for the way (liberal) democracy can deal with them.

The main groups dealt with here are the radical right. This is not to argue that nativism is exclusive to the radical right, or even to the right per se (as some left-wing parties have at times voiced nativist arguments as well, particularly at the local level),[39] but only that the radical right has nativism as a core ideological feature. Radical-right groups accept both inequalities and basic democracy but espouse an ideology that challenges minority protections. The most important representatives of the radical right, at least throughout Europe, are political parties; in Europe, parties dominate politics. These parties share an ideology that includes core features, such as nativism, authoritarianism, and populism (Mudde 2007). In addition, non-party organizations, both of the radical and extreme right, are examined. The most important groups, at least in terms of physical threats to im-

---

39 Among the first local politicians to take an anti-immigrant position in France were communist mayors in the Paris area (e.g., Baldwin-Edwards 1992).

migrants, are violent extreme-right groups, such as neo-Nazi organizations and skinhead gangs.

## Western Europe

Since the early 1980s, there has been a third wave of postwar radical-right parties with much more success in electoral terms than the previous two waves (von Beyme 1988). That stated, the development and success of radical-right parties in Western Europe has been quite uneven.

The *pater familias* of the contemporary radical right is the French National Front (FN), which was founded in 1972 as a collection of radical and extreme-right groups. Under the charismatic leadership of Jean-Marie Le Pen, the party gained its electoral breakthrough in the mid-1980s even though its parliamentary representation would be mostly minimal because of the French electoral system, FN has become the leading example for most contemporary radical-right parties in Europe (Rydgren 2003). Many parties have adopted FN propaganda and slogans, and some have even copied its name and logo (e.g., the Belgian National Front).

While most contemporary radical-right parties are relatively new, having been founded since the 1980s, some have much longer institutional legacies, although often not as radical-right parties. The most influential of these, in terms of gaining electoral success and political power, are the Austrian Freedom Party (FPÖ) and the Swiss People's Party (SVP). The former developed from a small national(ist)-liberal party into one of the biggest radical-right parties after Jörg Haider took over the leadership in 1986. The latter originated as a farmers' party and changed into a mainstream conservative party in the 1970s; Zurich-based leader Christoph Blocher had transformed it into a full-fledged radical-right party by the early 2000s.

Radical-right parties have been electorally successful (winning over 15 percent of the vote in two or more elections since 1980) in only a few Western European countries (notably Austria and Switzerland).

In about one-third of the countries (e.g., Belgium, Denmark, France, Italy), they have had moderate electoral success, receiving between 5 percent and 15 percent of the national vote. However, in most Western European countries, radical-right parties have never had serious electoral support and have polled below 5 percent (see Table 1).

**Table 1: Support for Radical-Right Parties in Parliamentary Elections in Western Europe, 1980–2011**

| Country | Party | Highest Ever (%) | Most Recent (%) |
|---------|-------|------------------|-----------------|
| Austria | Alliance for the Future of Austria | 10.7 (2008) | 10.7 (2008) |
|  | Austria Freedom Party (FPÖ) | 26.9 (1999) | 17.5 (2008) |
| Belgium | National Front (Belgian) (FNb) | 2.3 (1995) | 0.5 (2010) |
|  | Flemish Interest (VB) | 12 (2007) | 7.8 (2010) |
| Britain | British National Party (BNP) | 1.9 (2010) | 1.9 (2010) |
| Denmark | Danish People's Party (DFP) | 13.8 (2007) | 12.3 (2011) |
| France | National Front (FN) | 14.9 (1997) | 4.3 (2007) |
| Germany | The Republicans (REP) | 2.1 (1990) | 0.4 (2009) |
| Greece | Popular Orthodox Rally (LAOS) | 5.6 (2009) | 5.6 (2009) |
| Italy | Northern League (LN) | 10.1 (1996) | 8.3 (2009) |
| Netherlands | Centre Democrats (CD) | 2.5 (1994) | – |
|  | Party for Freedom (PVV) | 15.5 (2010) | 15.5 (2010) |
| Portugal | National Renovator Party (PNR) | 0.3 (2011) | 0.3 (2011) |
| Spain | New Force (FN) | 0.5 (1982) | – |
| Sweden | Sweden Democrats (SD) | 5.7 (2010) | 5.7 (2010) |
| Switzerland | Swiss People's Party (SVP) | 28.9 (2007) | 26.6 (2011) |

Source: Álvarez-Rivera n.d.

In addition, many of the (once) successful radical-right parties passed their peak in the late 1990s. In fact, the prototype FN itself seemed to be close to a meltdown until Marine Le Pen took over the party leadership from her father in January 2011. Le Pen has been able to bring FN back into the center of the political debate in France, and the recent 2012 parliamentary and presidential elections determined the party can survive its founder-leader. Even Belgium's Flemish Interest

(VB) seems destined for a decline, having lost fairly substantially in all elections since 2006. Moreover, past years have been defined by internal struggles, which have led to the exit (sometimes forced) of many prominent members.

The only three real powerhouses are: the Austrian FPÖ, which has rebounded from internal strife and electoral defeat; the Danish People's Party (DFP), which has provided essential support for the minority government for ten years; and the Swiss SVP, which, despite a recent split and conflicts between its party leader and other governmental party elites, is still operating as part of the Swiss government and remains the most popular party in the country in terms of public support. In addition, the Party for Freedom (PVV), founded in 2005, has fast become the third-largest party in the Dutch parliament and the support party of the current right-wing government. Although the party is not traditionally organized (it lacks party members), it seems quite stable and could survive for some time to come.

There are a few Western European parties that could be counted as radical-right but, at least for the purposes of this study, are borderline cases. Most notably, the Norwegian Progress Party (FRP) has been ideologically eclectic and chaotic, at times supporting a strong anti-immigrant agenda. It is one of the largest parties in Norway, but has had its image damaged by the gruesome terrorist attack in July 2011; the shooter was a former member of the party. Another party sometimes considered radical-right is the Finnish True Finns (PS) party, which became a major player in Finnish politics after gaining a surprising 19.1 percent of the vote in the 2011 elections. Like FRP in Norway, PS has been responsible for putting immigration on the national political agenda, but its nativism is more episodic than structural and doesn't define the core ideology of the party (Arter 2010).

In addition to these political parties, there are various extreme and radical-right non-party organizations in Western Europe, many of which are sectarian and cater to a few hundred people (at best) in their country. Some of the most notable organizations have developed only recently, focusing their agendas almost exclusively on Muslim immigrants. Examples include the English Defence League (EDL) and Stop the Islamification of Europe (SIOE). SIOE seems mainly to exist as an online organization and its "success" a consequence of its tight connection to politicians from radical-right parties (including DFP and VB) as well as to prominent conservatives in the United States. Moreover, like various other "counter-Jihadist" groups in Western Europe, SIOE has chosen to adopt a less prominent profile (even dismantling its website) in light of the fallout from the recent Norway terrorist attack; the terrorist quoted SIOE and other counter-Jihadist groups regularly and approvingly in his 1,500-page manifesto.

EDL is probably the most active and prominent nativist non-party organization in Western Europe today, organizing demonstrations throughout the United Kingdom (predominantly within England), at times mobilizing thousands of mostly young white men. Its loose "membership" is more diverse than traditional radical-right parties (e.g., BNP), but it seems that much of its core is quite similar. However, unlike the traditional radical right in Britain, EDL has reached out to non-Muslim minorities (particularly Jews and Sikhs as well as gays and lesbians) and to like-minded people and organizations abroad. So far, their success has been limited; minorities are only sparsely represented within the organization and its activities. EDL activities abroad (e.g., in Canada and the Netherlands) attract few people.

### Central and Eastern Europe

Although the parties and party systems of Central and Eastern Europe are not yet as institutionalized as in the western part of the continent, political parties are also the main actors in the former communist part of Europe. While received wisdom holds that Central and Eastern Europe are a hotbed for nationalist extremists, radical-right parties are hardly more successful there than in "Old Europe" (Mudde 2005b) (see Table 2).

## Table 2: Radical-Right Parties in Eastern Europe with the Largest Share of Support in Parliamentary Elections, 1990–2012

| Country | Party | Highest Ever (%) | | Most Recent (%) | |
|---|---|---|---|---|---|
| Bulgaria | National Union Attack (NSA) | 9.4 | (2009) | 9.4 | (2009) |
| Croatia | Croatian Party of Rights (HSP) | 5.0 | (1995) | 3.0 | (2011) |
| Czech Republic | Assembly of the Republic – Republican Party of Czechoslovakia (SPR-RSČ); Sovereignty – Jana Bobošíková Bloc | 8.0 (1996) 3.7 | (2010) | – 3.7 | (2010) |
| Hungary | Hungarian Justice and Life Party (MIÉP) Movement for a Better Hungary (Jobbik) | 5.5 16.7 | (1998) (2010) | 0.0 16.7 | (2010) (2010) |
| Latvia | Popular Movement for Latvia-Zigerista Party (TKL-ZP) National Alliance (NA) | 15 13.9 | (1995) (2011) | – 13.9 | (2011) |
| Poland | League of Polish Families (LPR) | 8.0 | (2005) | – | |
| Romania | Greater Romania Party (PRM) | 19.5 | (2000) | 3.2 | (2008) |
| Russia | Liberal Democratic Party of Russia (LDPR) | 22.9 | (1993) | 11.7 | (2011) |
| Serbia | Serbian Radical Party (SRS) | 29.5 | (2008) | 29.5 | (2008) |
| Slovakia | Slovak National Party (SNS) | 11.7 | (2006) | 4.6 | (2012) |

Source: Álvarez-Rivera n.d.; Wikipedia

Only in four countries have radical-right parties ever gained over 15 percent of the vote; however, in two of them, the respective parties have since lost most of their support (the Liberal Democratic Party of Russia, or LDPR, and Greater Romania Party, or PRM), while in the third, the party has recently split (the Serbian Radical Party, or SRS). The newest star on the radical-right front is the Hungarian Movement for a Better Hungary (Jobbik), which started with a bang but still has to prove its longevity. The Latvian National Alliance (NA) is a coalition of the national-conservative For Fatherland and Freedom/LNNK party, one of the oldest parties in the country but with decreasing support, and the radical-right All for Latvia!, which started as a youth movement in 2000. While it has been able to jump from 7.7 percent support in 2010 to 13.9 percent in 2011 and joined the government, NA remains an untested quantity.

In only four countries was the most recent score also the highest support score for parliamentary elections since 1990; in two other countries, the parties no longer have independent parliamentary representation (Croatia and Poland). In other words, as in the western part of the continent, radical-right parties are without significant electoral support in a majority of Central and Eastern European countries and without governmental participation as of September 2011.

Central and Eastern Europe do seem to have a stronger non-party radical right, which includes old mainstream nationalist organizations, such as Slovak Motherland (Matica Slovenská) in Slovakia, revisionist organizations such as the Marshal Antonescu League in Romania, or orthodox-religious organizations such as Radio Maria in Poland (Mudde 2005a). However, in most cases, their political relevance has been closely related to the electoral strength of the domestic radical-right party or to their relationships with idiosyncratic postcommunist parties, such as the Movement for a Democratic Slovakia (HZDS) or the Socialist Democratic Party of Romania (PDSR ), both of which have lost most of their power since the 1990s. The only exception is Radio Maria, which remains closely allied with the national-conservative Law and Justice (PiS), the second-biggest party in Poland.

Finally, several Central and Eastern European countries have significant neo-Nazi groups and extreme-right skinhead gangs, most notably Russia and Serbia (ADL 1995). Unlike in much of the West, these groups were until recently seldom confronted with strong state or antiracist resistance. In countries such as the Czech Republic and Slovakia, both state and local security agencies now take the extreme right seriously, while antiracist initiatives have successfully generated media and public attention. In Russia, which had seen a massive growth of these movements, the state has reacted late, but particularly vigilantly; it has passed draconian new laws, which have been criticized by domestic and foreign human-rights organizations, to ban organizations and imprison activists.

The United States and Canada have very different political systems, and it is therefore unsurprising that the structure of their nativist movements also differs significantly. They do share two main features, though: (1) there are no noteworthy nativist political parties; (2) nativists confront strong pro-immigration forces in the political and public debates.


## Canada

Canada has no nativist political parties. The Nationalist Party of Canada is a tiny white-supremacist organization that is not registered to contest elections, although some members have run in local elections (with very marginal returns). Some people consider Canada Action a nativist party because of its push to halve the level of immigration to Canada. However, this would bring it down to US levels, which are among the highest in the world; therefore, this is hardly a nativist position. Similarly, while immigration and multiculturalism have become more openly debated in recent years, few important voices have really criticized the fundamentals of Canada's official policies, which are extremely liberal from a global perspective.

In recent years, there has been a toughening of the discourse on immigration in elections in Quebec, under pressure from the Democratic Action of Quebec (ADQ), but the effects seem marginal in terms of policy and short-lived and regional in terms of discourse (Kymlicka 2010: 16). Moreover, ADQ's call for "reasonable accommodation" might be radical within the pro-multicultural context of Canada, but it is far removed from the policies supported by nativist parties in Europe.

Some groups try to lobby mainstream parties and the public to support a drastic decrease in migration. Arguably the most prominent is Immigration Watch Canada, and even its party members do not want to do away with immigration entirely. Instead, the group wants to bring immigration levels back to 50,000 a year; according to the organization, this would constitute "about 20 percent of the current annual 260,000 intake" (IWC n.d.). In addition, there are some small neo-Nazi and white-supremacist groups, often Canadian branches of US-based groups.[40]

## United States

Although the United States boasted some of the first nativist parties in the world, notably the Know-Nothing Party or American Party in the mid-19th century (e.g., Higham 1955), they have been nonexistent or irrelevant throughout the 20th century. The only recent example of a notable nativist party was the Reform Party under Patrick J. Buchanan in 2000. Since then, the Reform Party has supported non-nativist politicians for the US presidency. Today, only minor parties with at best regional appeal promote an openly nativist agenda. Probably the most significant is the long-standing American Constitution Party, which recently created some waves in the Colorado gubernatorial elections. Its surprise candidate was former Republican Congressman Tom Tancredo, one of the most prominent nativist US politicians of the past decades, who came in second with a staggering 36 percent of the vote, more than three times as much as the Republican candidate.[41]

The United States does count a broad variety of nativist non-party organizations, however, most of which are politically marginal at the federal level. This includes virtually all white-supremacist groups, including the various incarnations of the formerly powerful Ku Klux Klan, and neo-Nazi and skinhead gangs. It should be noted, though, that while these groups have no relevance in the political arena, their

40  One of the few significant groups still active is the National Alliance in Ontario, now that the Heritage Front (1997–2005) and the Aryan Guard (2006–2009) have been dissolved.
41  An outspoken anti-immigration politician, Tom Tancredo also sought the Republican presidential nomination in 2008 on an immigration-control platform.

local presence does at times adversely influence the life of immigrants in the area.

The most prominent organization of anti-immigration politicians is arguably the House Immigration Reform Caucus (IRC), founded by Tom Tancredo, which touts itself as "an organization dedicated towards identifying legislative solutions to address the issue of illegal immigration" (IRC 2011a). Although the caucus was created, among other reasons, "to create a much-needed forum in Congress to address both the positive and negative consequences of immigration," it almost exclusively focuses on the negative aspects, and all the supported legislation is aimed at restricting illegal immigration (Building Democracy Initiative 2007).

Since 2007, Representative Brian Bilbray (R-CA) has run the caucus, which has seen its membership fall significantly in his tenure, from 112 members in the summer of 2008 to 91 in the summer of 2011 (virtually all Republicans).[42] Despite its clear anti-immigration stance, IRC is careful in its wording and does not use an openly nativist discourse. In May 2011, newly elected Representative Lou Barletta (R-PA), who gained notoriety as mayor of Hazleton, Pennsylvania, for his fight against illegal immigration, announced the formation of a new Congressional Immigration Reform Caucus, to be chaired by himself (Antle 2011).

The most important anti-immigration actors in the United States are single-issue groups that are able to connect to mainstream media and politicians. This includes the various organizations linked to John Tanton, a retired Michigan ophthalmologist who has been instrumental in creating a host of anti-immigration organizations (SPLC 2009). Among the most active and influential Tanton organizations are the grassroots group NumbersUSA and the lobby group Federation for American Immigration Reform (FAIR). In certain regions, notably in the South, more openly racist groups, such as the Council of Conser-

---

42  In September 2011, only 65 members were listed on the website. However, the website doesn't seem to be updated often, perhaps a reflection of the inactivity of the caucus. At the time of publication, the latest news update on the site was dated February 17, 2011 (IRC 2011b).

vative Citizens, and various neo-Confederate groups, such as the Heritage Preservation Association, also are active in the immigration arena and have connections to some mainstream politicians (SPLC 2000).

## Immigration and the Radical Right

The rise of radical-right parties is considered to be closely linked to the phenomenon of mass migration, particularly in Western Europe. Indeed, the German political scientist Klaus von Beyme (1988) defined the "third wave" of "right-wing extremism" as a response to mass immigration and the consequent development of multicultural societies in Western Europe. But while there clearly is a relationship, it is not as straightforward as is often assumed. Moreover, immigration plays much less of a role in elections in North America and, particularly, in Central and Eastern Europe.

### Western Europe

Much of the literature on the Western European radical right considers the phenomenon to be first and foremost a majority response to the perceived threat of mass immigration. In fact, some authors go even a step further and consider radical-right parties by and large as single-issue parties, referring to them as "anti-immigrant parties" (e.g., Gibson 2002). However, the single-issue thesis is inaccurate on at least two counts: First, radical-right parties have a broader ideology and stress multiple issues and, second, people vote for radical-right parties on the basis of different issues (Mudde 1999).

Radical-right parties share a core ideology of nativism, authoritarianism, and populism (Mudde 2007). The three core ideological features are closely linked to three major political issues: immigration, crime, and corruption. Hence, radical-right parties are clearly not single-issue parties. Despite this, immigration features prominently in both the internally and externally oriented literature of these parties (Mudde 2000). In line with their nativism, migration and migrants are seen as multifaceted threats. At least four frames (cultural, religious, security, and economic) are used in the propaganda of Western European nativist movements.

The predominant frame is *cultural*, in which migration is seen as a threat to the cultural homogeneity of the home nation. Depending on how strictly the nativist ideology is interpreted, migrants are considered to be either unable or unwilling to assimilate in the host culture. And, as the nation is flooded by a "tsunami" of migrants,"[43] the core of its culture is threatened. Some parties even go so far as to speak of a "bloodless genocide" (*BBC News,* April 23, 2009).

At least since the 9/11 terrorist attacks, a *religious* frame has accompanied the cultural one. Increasingly the immigrant is seen as a Muslim, not a Turk or Moroccan. While Muslims have been migrating to Western Europe since the 1960s, their numbers and visibility have increased significantly since the 1980s, in part as a consequence of family reunification and growth in the number of asylum-seekers. Today, by conservative estimates, approximately 13 million Muslims live within the European Union (an estimated 2.5 percent of the EU population). The vast majority of Muslims live in Western Europe, most notably in France (3.5 million), Germany (3.4 million), and the United Kingdom (1.6 million). Countries with the largest Muslim populations per capita include the Netherlands (6 percent) and France (5 percent) (EUMC 2006). In many Western European countries, the Muslim population is relatively young and growing much faster than the non-Muslim population; for example, in both Austria and Switzerland, the Muslim population quadrupled between 1980 and 2000 (Dolezal, Helbling and Hutter 2010).

With the realization that the "guest workers" were not all going to return, and with legal economic immigration severely limited since the mid-1970s as a consequence of the oil crisis, the integration of already present "immigrants" became an important part of the "immi-

---

43  Dutch PVV leader Geert Wilders often refers to a "tsunami of Islamization."

gration debate." In fact, since the early 1990s, when most West European countries further tightened immigration and political-asylum laws, the immigration debate has become predominantly an integration debate (Messina 2007; Schain 2008). This debate has become more prominent and more focused on religion, in general, and Islam, in particular, since 9/11. In various countries, intellectuals and politicians have started to debate the question of the compatibility of Islam with democracy, leading to calls for a growing range of restrictions. While many debates start at the local level, mostly in large, multicultural cities, they often end with legal proposals at the national level. For example, in Belgium, the so-called burqa ban, which outlaws the public wearing of face veils, was first debated and implemented in the city of Antwerp. Today, it is national law, just as in France, while the Dutch government was preparing a burqa ban of its own as this book went to print (Corder 2012).

While much of Islamophobia is in fact cultural xenophobia, the religious angle adds important aspects to the debate. Most importantly, nativists consider Islam a fundamentalist religion; Dutch PVV leader Geert Wilders, for example, has called Islam "an intolerant and fascist ideology" (Hendricks 2008). Nativist politicians, such as VB leader Filip Dewinter, flat out deny the possibility of a moderate Islam (*Metro*, June 15, 2005). Others, Wilders included, officially distinguish between Muslims and Islam, claiming their problem is with the latter and not the former, but even their propaganda paints the average Muslim immigrant as an at least potential Islamic extremist. They argue that Muslims threaten key aspects of Western democracies, such as the separation of state and church, the equal position of women, and growing support for gay rights (although many radical-right parties are too homophobic to take up this point).

The third most important theme is *security*, in which immigration and (often low-level) crime are linked. Some parties argue, in line with ethnopluralist ideology, that immigrants become criminals because they have been uprooted from their natural environment. Radical-right magazines are full of short news articles about criminal offenses, such as murder and rape, committed by "aliens." They argue that immigrants are much more likely to commit criminal acts than the host population, but that the real level of crime is being kept from the public by politically correct politicians. Moreover, they decry the allegedly soft way in which the state deals with these criminals and want them to be either expelled or punished more severely. As in the case of the religious frame, the security frame is used not just by the radical right. Particularly after 9/11, the immigration debate in Europe and North America has become "securitized," with immigration policy increasingly made in light of national security.

In recent years, the security frame has come to include the link between migration and terrorism. With the migrant increasingly defined in religious terms, and with Islamist attacks – such as 9/11 in New York and Washington, 11-M in Madrid and 7/7 in London – on the public radar, nativists create a dark picture in which Muslim immigrants are considered the "fifth column" of the Muslim empire. The ultimate goal, they warn, is "Eurabia," a Euro-Arab axis that is connected by Islam and will be fiercely anti-American and anti-Zionist (Ya'or 2005).

Oddly enough, the "Eurabia" thesis is still more popular in the United States than in Europe. It is widely disseminated within mainstream conservative circles in the United States and popularized in the books of authors such as American writer and expatriate Bruce Bawer and *The Weekly Standard*'s senior editor, Christopher Caldwell, with telling titles that include *While Europe Slept: How Radical Islam is Destroying the West from Within* and *Surrender: Appeasing Islam, Sacrificing Freedom*, published by highly respectable publishing houses (Random House and Doubleday, respectively). They are even reviewed positively in liberal publications, such as the *New York Times* (Pollard 2009). *While Europe Slept* was even nominated for the 2006 National Book Critics Circle award, which did raise some critique (Cohen 2007).

Until recently, the "Eurabia" thesis was limited to the margins of the radical right in Europe. Only in the Netherlands and the United Kingdom was the thesis expressed by mainstream actors, such as Melanie Phillips, columnist for the popular British tabloid *Daily Mail*;

Ayaan Hirsi Ali, former Dutch parliamentarian (now with the conservative think tank American Enterprise Institute in Washington, DC); and Afshin Ellian, columnist for the broadsheet *NRC Handelsblad*. The relatively obscure "Eurabia conspiracy" became world news with the publication of excerpts of the 1,500-page manifesto *"2083 – A European Declaration of Independence"* of Anders Behring Breivik, the Norwegian right-wing extremist who killed 77 people (mostly teenagers) in July 2011.

The fourth frame employed in nativist discourse is *economic*. Here, immigrants are depicted as a financial burden to the host society, taking jobs away from the natives and/or draining social benefits. Slogans popular among radical-right parties note the number of unemployed natives, juxtaposed with the larger number of immigrants. This is often combined with a welfare-chauvinist agenda in which welfare programs are supported, but only for the natives. The argument is that if immigrants are sent back to their countries of origin, there will be enough money to provide decent services to natives.

The fifth and final frame is *political*, in which immigrants are seen as mere tools of sinister political forces. With varying degrees of conspiracy theories – some more anti-Semitic, others more anticapitalist – mass immigration is presented as a willing plot of (inter)national politicians, business leaders, and trade-union leaders to strengthen their own position at the expense of the average citizen. Moreover, in line with their populism, the elite (seen as a homogenous, corrupt entity) are accused of covering up the real costs of immigration and of muffling the people through antidiscrimination laws and political correctness.

Many studies have looked into the relationship between the number of immigrants and the number of votes for radical-right parties in Western Europe. So far, the results have been highly contradictory, which is in part the result of the use of different datasets, indicators and units of analysis. For example, some authors have found a clear, positive correlation between the number of foreign-born citizens and the electoral success of a radical-right party in a country (e.g., Golder 2003), while others have not (e.g., Messina 2007; Kitschelt and Mc-

Gann 1995). Similarly, some studies show a significant positive correlation with the number of new immigrants or asylum-seekers (e.g., Lubbers 2001) at the national level, but others find a negative (cor)relation or none at all (e.g., Kitschelt and McGann 1995).

Still, immigration and immigrants do play an important role in the electoral success of radical-right parties. But the relationship is not as simple as is often assumed: that the more immigrants in a country, the higher the electoral success of a radical-right party. Immigration is not inherently a political issue; in fact, while mass immigration started in most Western European countries in the 1960s and 1970s, it only became a salient political issue in the 1980s and 1990s. To become a salient political issue, immigration has to be (made) visible to a significant section of the population. Once this has happened, different narratives will emerge, and there will be a political struggle over the right narrative.

In many countries, notably the Netherlands and the United Kingdom, the hegemonic narrative was for a long time a positive one, which saw multiculturalism as an enrichment of national culture (Messina 2007). Only since the late 1980s has this started to change, with more leading political and societal actors subscribing to various interpretations of the multiculturalism-as-a-problem/threat narrative.

### Central and Eastern Europe

In Central and Eastern Europe, immigration levels are relatively low. According to a recent Eurostat report (Vasileva 2011), virtually all Central and Eastern European countries had fewer non-European Union (EU) immigrants per 1,000 inhabitants than the EU average in 2010.[44]

---

44 The only two exceptions are Estonia and Latvia, with 15.1 percent and 17.0 percent citizens of non-EU countries, respectively, but here it refers to Russian speakers who "immigrated" one or two generations ago within the then-existing Soviet Union.

In addition, in most Central and Eastern European countries, the main immigrant community is from a neighboring state, often with significant cultural similarities to (parts of) the native population: Russians in Latvia, Belarusians in Lithuania, Romanians in Hungary, Moldovans in Romania, and Bosnians in Slovenia (ibid.).

Moreover, while immigration into Central and Eastern Europe is low by comparison to other EU states, emigration from Central and Eastern Europe, particularly into western EU countries, has been rather high since 2004, when most of the countries joined the European Union. For example, in 2010, more than 2 million Romanian and more than 1.5 million Polish migrants lived in other EU countries. In fact, Poles are the largest foreign population in countries such as Ireland and Norway, while in Italy and Spain it is Romanians (ibid.).

Consequently, few political actors, radical-right or otherwise, have made immigration an important issue in their propaganda. Although the number of immigrants has been rising slowly but steadily in recent years, and immigrants have become more visible in many of the larger cities in the region, including Budapest and Prague, radical-right parties tend to focus on indigenous minorities (notably the Roma) rather than on immigrants. And while anti-immigrant attitudes are at least as widespread in the East as in the West of the continent (Mudde 2005a), so far, few Central and Eastern European voters have considered immigration a key concern.

One of the few exceptions is Slovenia, where the radical right responded to the influx of Bosnian and Serbian refugees from the Yugoslav civil war in the early 1990s (Kuzmanic 1999). However, even here, the impact was relatively modest and only short-lived despite continuously high levels of former Yugoslav immigrants. In later years, the Slovenian National Party (SNS) moderated its ideology and shifted its primary focus to Croatians and Roma (Trplan 2005). The most recent exception is Russia, where the single-issue party Russian Movement against Illegal Immigration (DPNI) was founded in 2002. While electorally irrelevant, its emergence does signify the rising salience of the immigration issue in Russia. Most interesting is the striking similarity between its anti-immigration positions and those of the radical right in Western Europe. The group links migrants to societal problems and even shares the Islamophobia. For example, DPNI states that "migrants from the Caucasus states and from Central and South-Eastern Asia are the first part of the foreign expansion" (Mudde 2007: 71). The party was banned in 2011 for pursuing "extremist goals and objectives," under draconian new anti-extremism legislation. DPNI has since appealed the ruling, which has not yet been enforced (Washington 2011).

## North America

North America has a much longer history of mass immigration. Unlike the European countries, Canada and the United States are officially immigration countries. This means that they not only accept relatively large groups of immigrants annually, but they also (try to) regulate the influx of immigrants. Consequently, the annual number of new (legal) immigrants is fairly constant, which makes it less explosive as a political issue. For various reasons, neither Canada nor the United States has a relevant radical-right party, such as exist in many European countries. Still, with more than 11.5 million unauthorized immigrants in the United States (DHS 2012), particularly from Latin America, illegal immigration will at times explode onto local and national public agendas in the United States, not in the least through the advocacy of anti-immigration organizations and politicians.

In the United States the positions on immigration do not so much distinguish the two major parties as divide them. Both parties have significant anti- *and* pro-immigration voices. Consequently, it is not surprising that immigration became a hot-button issue in the Republican primaries. At one of the first major debates of the Republican presidential hopefuls, organized by CNN and the Tea Party Express, Texas Governor Rick Perry was attacked by almost all other candidates for his alleged pro-immigration position. Candidates and audience alike loudly criticized Perry's defense of legislation permitting the children of unauthorized immigrants to attend universities at in-state tuition rates. Attacks on candidates as being soft on immigration are bolstered by powerful anti-immigration organizations, such as FAIR, or nativist lobbies, such as Team America PAC, that of former Republican Tancredo (2011). At the same time, many people inside and outside of the GOP argue that the party has to moderate its position on immigration to court the growing Latino vote (Hunt 2011).

The discourse on immigration in the United States is quite similar to that in Western Europe. In fact, there is contact among nativists from both regions. For example, British National Party (BNP) leader Nick Griffin spoke at the annual meeting of American Renaissance in Virginia in 2006, while former presidential candidate and political commentator Pat Buchanan met with VB leader Filip Dewinter and Frank Vanhecke in Washington, DC, in 2007 (ADL 2009). Self-proclaimed hater of Islam Geert Wilders is probably the most well-connected European nativist in the United States, regularly gracing the opinion pages of *The Wall Street Journal* as well as prime time on Fox News, being very close to "counterjihadists," such as Pamela Geller and Robert Spencer, and even being invited to Congress by Representative Jon Kyl (R-AZ) for a screening of Wilders' anti-Islam film "Fitna" (which Congressman Keith Ellison (D-MN) opposed and compared to showing the racist film "Birth of a Nation" at the White House) (O'Connor 2009). As in Western Europe, cultural, religious, security, economic, and political themes are prevalent. There are some subtle differences, however.

First of all, in many cases, the cultural theme is more racial in the United States. This is in part a linguistic matter; except for in the United Kingdom and United States, the term "race" is no longer widely used in European languages. Whereas Americans might be taught that all races are equal, Europeans are taught that there is only one race, the human race. Consequently, much of the racial nativism in the United States is very similar to the cultural nativism in Europe. Moreover, most of the recent nativist debates are about ethnic outsiders, notably Hispanics and Muslims, rather than the traditional racial outsider, African-Americans.

Second, with regard to security, Islam plays a less dominant role among US nativists. Oddly enough, it seems to be most present among neoconservatives and paleoconservatives, who see the threat predominantly as a European issue. As mentioned previously, a good example is *While Europe Slept*. Neoconservatives see the "Muslim threat" also in the Middle East (endangering the existence of the Jewish state of Israel). While Islam was initially seen almost exclusively as an issue in foreign policy, it is slowly but steadily emerging on the domestic agenda. Now, these conservatives are increasingly rallying against perceived Muslim terrorist threats within the United States (see Ali et al. 2011).

Most paleoconservatives are not sympathetic to Israel, or America's activities within the Middle East, and still see the main danger within the United States as the "Mexican threat." The most prominent and prolific writer on "alien invasions" of the United States is Pat Buchanan, whose nativist books can be found in all major bookstores. In *State of Emergency*, he argues that Mexico is slowly but steadily taking back the American Southwest (Buchanan 2006). This is the key threat according to American nativists. They refer to it as the "Aztlan Plot" for *"la reconquista,"* to recapture lands lost by Mexico in the Texas War of Independence and the Mexican-American War. While these ideas are far removed from those of mainstream political actors in the United States, most notably the two main political parties, they were expressed in Lou Dobbs' program on CNN (until November 2009) and by various right-wing talk-radio hosts. Moreover, Buchanan himself was until recently a well-known pundit on the national cable-TV network MSNBC.

## Effects of Political Extremism

While public attitudes and, particularly, political violence are important aspects of politics, the true test of power is in whether or not nativist actors have influenced policies. It is worth distinguishing between two different types of influence: direct and indirect.

Direct influence means that nativist groups directly influence immigration policy, either by implementing it themselves or by (directly) making other actors implement it. Indirect influence works more slowly and unclearly; nativist actors influence non-nativist actors, who would then implement anti-immigrant policies – obviously, establishing "influence" here is problematic.

### Direct Effects

Overall, there are very few documented cases of nativist actors directly affecting immigration policy in all three regions. The reason is simple: Only in a few cases have nativist actors been part of government (see Table 3). Moreover, most of these cases were in Eastern Europe, where immigration has so far not been a major issue, not even for nativist parties. Where nativist parties have been represented in the parliament but not in the government, their law initiatives have mostly been boycotted by the governmental (and even most other oppositional) parties. In other words, nativist parties have had relatively few direct effects on politics, even on immigration politics.

In Western Europe, only five nativist parties have made it into government so far: the Northern League (LN) in Italy (1994, 2000–2005, 2008–2011), the FPÖ and the Alliance for the Future of Austria (BZÖ) in Austria (2000–2006), the SVP in Switzerland (2000–2008, 2008–), and the Popular Orthodox Rally in Greece (2011–2012). The few academic studies of radical-right parties in office all agree on one thing: They have been mainly successful in introducing more restrictive immigration policies (e.g., Zaslove 2004; Minkenberg 2001).

**Table 3: Nativist Parties in European National Governments since 1980**

| Country | Party | Period(s) | Coalition Partners (party ideology) |
|---------|-------|-----------|-------------------------------------|
| Austria | FPÖ | 2000–2002 | ÖVP (Christian democratic) |
|         |     | 2002–2005 | ÖVP |
|         | BZÖ | 2005–2007 | ÖVP |
| Croatia | HDZ | 1990–2000[1] | |
| Estonia | ERSP | 1992–1995 | Isamaa (conservative) |
| Greece | LAOS | 2011–2012 | PASOK (social-democratic) and ND (conservative) |
| Italy | LN | 1994 | FI (neoliberal-populist) and AN (conservative) |
|       |    | 2001–2005 | FI and AN and MDC (Christian-democratic) |
|       |    | 2008–2011 | PdL (right-wing) |
| Latvia | NA | 2011– | ZRP (center-right) and Unity (conservative) |
| Poland | LPR | 2006–2008 | PiS (conservative) and Samoobrona (social-populist) |
| Romania | PUNR | 1994–1996 | PDSR (diffuse) and PSM (social-populist) |
|         | PRM | 1995 | |
| Serbia | SRS | 1998–2000 | SPS (social-populist) and JUL (communist) |
| Slovakia | SNS | 1994–1998 | HZDS (diffuse) and ZRS (communist) |
|          |     | 2006–2010 | Smer (social-populist) and HZDS |
| Switzerland | SVP | 2000–2008 | SPS (social-democratic) and FDP (liberal) and |
|             |     | 2008– | CVP (Christian-democratic) |

Notes: HDZ changed into a conservative party after 2000. The SVP only became a full-fledged radical-right party in/around 2000.

Source: Mudde 2007

Austria and Switzerland tightened their asylum laws at the initiative of the radical right in 2003 and 2006, respectively. Interestingly, the Austrian radical-right government did not introduce stricter general immigration laws; previous mainstream governments had already done so (Gächter 2008). The most notable examples in the Italian case are the Bossi-Fini Law, which came into force in August 2002 and was named after the LN and AN leaders who proposed the bill. The bill aimed to curb immigration, except for highly skilled workers, although it also included a limited amnesty for some unauthorized immigrants (Colombo and Sciortino 2003). A more recent law, adopted in August 2009, goes much further by, among other things, making illegal presence a criminal offense (Lewis 2009).

Although most countries will allow nongovernmental parties to submit proposals for legislation, in very few cases does this lead to actual laws. This is even more apparent with proposals from the radical right, which tend to be shunned by the other parties in the parliament (e.g., the VB in Belgium). There are three important exceptions, however: DFP in Denmark, PVV in the Netherlands, and SVP in Switzerland. Although DFP has never been an official part of the Danish government, it was the major support party of the right-wing minority governments between 2001 and 2011. As a consequence, the party played a crucial role in drafting the immigration law of 2002 for the government, which, among other things, limited grounds for political asylum and stipulated financial requirements for marrying a foreigner (*CNN*, May 31, 2002). This law is described as "one of Europe's strictest immigration laws" by the United Nations High Commissioner for Refugees (UNHCR 2009). In 2011, the party was instrumental in tightening border controls, despite the fact that Denmark is in the "borderless" Schengen zone, to fight organized crime and illegal immigration (Eriksen 2011). A similar role is currently played by PVV, which has been supporting the Dutch right-wing government since 2010. The Swiss situation is even more complex; while the nativist SVP is part of the broad four-party coalition government, as a consequence of the particular Swiss constitution, it fights many of its political battles through Switzerland's strong system of direct democracy, which includes referendums initiated by the public. A recent example of this, which gained much attention and condemnation around the world, was the referendum that banned the construction of minarets, which was passed by 57 percent of the voters and in 22 of the 26 Swiss cantons in 2009 (*BBC News*, November 29, 2009).

While Central and Eastern Europe have seen more radical-right government participation, only a small minority of post-communist Central and Eastern European governments have included the radical right. Furthermore, this has not had an effect on immigration policies. As previously noted, immigration is simply a non-issue in the region, even for the radical right, which, instead, focuses primarily on indigenous minorities, such as Hungarians, Russians, and "Gypsies" or Roma. In fact, most pressure to implement tougher border regimes came from the European Union, which was worried that Central and Eastern European states did not exert sufficient control of their borders, which were soon to become and now are EU borders (e.g., Lavenex 1999).

The situation in North America is more complex. Canada has no nativist party with parliamentary, let alone governmental, representation. But while the United States does not currently have any successful nativist parties, unlike in the 19th century (the Know Nothing Party), there are some powerful nativist voices within the main parties, most notably the Republican Party. None has made it into prominent positions within Republican administrations, however. Hence, nativist actors have had, at best, only indirect effects.

The situation is different at the local and regional levels, where nativist groups have advanced their agenda through assistance and collaboration on immigration legislation. For instance, various US communities have tried to limit or decrease illegal immigration by pushing through a broad variety of legislation. Much of this legislation seeks to punish businesses that use or cater to unauthorized immigrants or to exclude unauthorized immigrants from local community services (ranging from schools to hospitals). While in many cases these changes were pushed through by mainstream actors, groups such as FAIR have provided technical assistance to several state legislators in passing bills that curtail immigrant rights (e.g., requiring proof of citizenship to get a driver's license, mandating employer verification, restricting immigrant access to public benefits). Similarly, groups such as FAIR and California's Save Our State (SOS) have been instrumental in pushing for versions of the so-called Illegal Immigration Relief Act, which aims to exclude unauthorized immigrants from housing, in a number of communities. Moreover, there are other prominent state actors who can foster anti-immigrant sentiment in an area (Massa and Abundis 2007). A key example here is Maricopa County Sheriff Joe Arpaio from Arizona, the subject of a US Department of Justice civil-rights lawsuit in 2012 alleging his police force discriminates against Latinos while enforcing federal immigration law (James 2009).

One US state with polarizing debates about such measures is California, which, despite its progressive image and Democratic legislative majorities, has seen significant nativist campaigns and anti-immigration legislative successes (particularly through referendums) (e.g., HoSang 2010). The most notable of these was the 1994 Proposition 187, listed on the ballots as the "Save Our State Initiative," which called for strict and punitive measures against unauthorized immigrants. The initiative was cosponsored by the nativist California Coalition for Immigration Reform (CCIR) and passed by an overwhelming 59 percent of the vote, though it was later ruled unconstitutional by a federal court and never implemented (Building Democracy Initiative 2007: 2).

Probably the biggest subnational success of the nativist lobby has been Arizona's 2010 immigration law, SB 1070, which observers called at that time "the nation's toughest bill on illegal immigration" (Archibold 2010). Among the main authors of SB 1070 was immigration-control activist Kris Kobach, who is Kansas Secretary of State and counsels the Foundation for American Immigration Reform (FAIR) (*New York Times*, January 11, 2012). Criticized nationwide by prominent leaders, such as President Barack Obama and Cardinal Roger M. Mahony of Los Angeles, but widely popular among the public (Alfano 2010), the law has become a blueprint for similar legislative proposals enacted in a number of states, including Alabama, Georgia, and South Carolina. While the laws are publicly popular, they have also generated protest from both the left and the right, with lawmakers even reconsidering the measures' effects both on business and the states' image (*Fox News Latino*, December 8, 2011). And key aspects of the laws have been blocked by the courts.

However, while there are many examples of successful anti-immigration measures at the subnational level, with or without pressure from nativist actors, there are also countless examples of successful pro-immigration mobilization, particularly at the local level (e.g., Hanley et al. 2008). For example, since the 1980s, a growing group of cities has banned city employees and police officers from asking people about their immigration status. Although the number of cities involved is not impressive (ca. 30), it does include practically all *major* cities in the United States (e.g., Chicago, Dallas, Los Angeles, Miami, New York, San Francisco, and Washington, DC) (Ridgley 2008).

### Indirect Effects

Obviously, governments don't make policies in total isolation. They are influenced by public opinion, the media, lobby groups, international organizations, and other competing political parties. Both opponents and supporters of the radical right have argued that mainstream parties have implemented anti-immigration legislation under pressure from radical-right electoral success. In a few cases, the respective governments have acknowledged this. In some of these cases, governments have been criticized for offering what sounded like a convenient excuse rather than a credible explanation. For example, former British Prime Minister Tony Blair, former German Chancellor Gerhard Schröder, and former Spanish Prime Minister José María Aznar all called for stricter immigration laws to prevent the rise of the radical right despite the fact that their countries have marginal radical-right parties (Hooper, Tremlett, and Henley 2002).

While there are many national and regional differences, one can detect some general shifts in the debate on immigration in Western Europe. First and foremost, there *is* a debate on immigration. Up until the 1980s, the established parties in most Western European countries were engaged in a "conspiracy of silence" (Messina 2007: 86) or an explicit or implicit agreement to keep immigration outside of the public debate. Mainly due to public pressure, often expressed loudly by the tabloid media, the mainstream parties reluctantly started to address immigration as a political issue, while nativist parties further heightened the salience of the issue.

Second, the consensus in the debate has shifted in most countries from a (implicit or explicit) pro-immigration to an *anti-immigration* standpoint. Nowadays, virtually all but a few radical-left and green parties consider immigration a fundamental challenge to their society, at best, and a threat, at worst (Zaslove 2004; Minkenberg 2001). Hence, whereas mainstream parties in the Netherlands or the United Kingdom tended to sing the praises of the many enrichments of multiculturalism in the 1970s and 1980s, they now ponder the ways in which "Dutchness" and "Britishness" can be protected against outside influences (also Kymlicka 2010: 11–13). Overall, right-wing parties have co-opted radical-right positions more often and more radically than left-wing parties; the best examples include the British Conservative Party, the Dutch People's Party for Freedom and Democracy, and the French Union for a Popular Movement. That stated, there are many examples of social-democratic, and even communist, parties that have adopted anti-immigration positions, from the Dutch Labor Party to the French Communist Party (Alonso and Claro da Fonseca, forthcoming). In fact, in many cases, immigration laws were tightened by governments that included social-democratic parties, sometimes under (perceived) electoral pressure from radical right-right parties (e.g., Austria and Germany in the early 1990s), sometimes without (e.g., the United Kingdom in the 1990s) (e.g., Messina 2007).

Third, the debate has shifted from immigration to *integration*, as in most countries no significant party calls for more immigration. As Western European countries do not typically present themselves as immigration countries, and mainstream politicians do not want to encourage immigration, they still have few integration policies in place despite several decades of immigration. Hence, from Belgium to Norway and from Spain to Denmark, the public is debating what the rights and duties of the host population and immigrants are, with an increasing emphasis on the duties of the immigrants. It is important to stress that, in many countries, the vast majority of the "immigrants" being debated about are, in fact, not immigrants as most people think of the word. Many such "immigrants" are European citizens, born and raised in (Western) Europe, who have only "ethnic" connections to their parents' countries of origin.

Fourth, the immigration debate has shifted from the cultural to the *religious*. For example, traditionally, the typical Dutch or German immigrant was seen as "a Turk"; but, after 9/11, she or he had become "a Muslim." This has had significant influence on the debate, most notably on the anti-immigrant position. Initially, immigration could only be opposed on the basis of economic and cultural grounds. In most countries, cultural opposition was outside of the realm of the respectable, as it linked to (ethnic) nationalism. The struggle against Islamist terrorism has shaped the post-9/11 debate about immigration, linking it to religion and security, and widening the scope for anti-immigration positions. Nowadays, parties will oppose immigration on the basis of mainstream liberal-democratic arguments rather than marginal nationalist positions (Mudde 2010). A good example was the infamous Dutch politician Pim Fortuyn, who framed his attacks on Muslim immigrants in terms of his defense for gay rights, equality of men and women, and the separation of state and church (Akkerman 2005). Right-wing Italian Prime Minister Silvio Berlusconi while in office as well as left-wing Scandinavian feminists made similar arguments (Akkerman and Hagelund 2007).

The relationship between the strength of radical-right parties and the adoption of anti-immigrant positions by mainstream parties is not always clear. For example, while countries such as Denmark and France exemplify the received wisdom that strong radical-right parties have pushed mainstream parties "to the right," other countries do not. The best counter-example is Belgium, where most mainstream parties are among the most pro-immigrant in Europe precisely *because of* the strong VB. And then there are many mainstream parties, from the British Labour Party to the German Christian Social Union, that have adopted relatively strong anti-immigration positions despite the lack of a successful radical-right party in their country. For example, in the past two years, British Prime Minister David Cameron, then President Nicolas Sarkozy of France, and German Chancellor Angela Merkel have all, in one way or another, declared that multiculturalism has failed (*The Daily Mail*, February 11, 2011). Of these, only France has a somewhat successful radical-right party.

A similar point can be made about immigration *policies* in Western Europe. As far as cross-national comparative studies of immigration laws are available, they show that European immigration policies are increasingly converging, not least because of cooperation within the European Union (Messina 2007; Givens and Luedtke 2004). Recent developments indicate that this will only increase in the future. From the European Commission:[45] "During the last decade, the need for a common, comprehensive immigration policy has been increasingly recognised and encouraged by the European Commission and the EU's Member States. The Commission is therefore now proposing concrete principles and measures – accompanied by a new strategy on immigration governance – on which to base the further development of the common immigration policy over the coming years" (EC 2008).

Still, at this moment, the level of convergence remains rather limited. And while there are some important changes that might facilitate further convergence, such as the Stockholm Programme 2010–2015 (which is the European Council framework for policies to be developed in the area of Justice and Home Affairs) and the introduction of Qualified Majority Voting under the Lisbon Treaty, progress is glacial, and the European Commission might be an unreliable barometer of such progress (Faist and Ette 2007). Most importantly, given their marginal role in both the European Parliament and European Council, radical-right parties will most likely not play an important role in these initiatives.

A significant success supported by the immigration-restrictionist movement in the United States was in 2007, when a major bipartisan immigration-reform package proposed by Senators Edward Kennedy (D-MA) and John McCain (R-AZ), and backed by President George W. Bush, was defeated. While various factors played a role, not least the

---

45 An overview of EU-wide immigration initiatives can be found on the EU website: http://ec.europa.eu/justice_home/fsj/immigration/fsj_immigration_intro_en.htm.

internal divisions within major progressive forces, such as the trade unions, defeat of the bill was assisted from the anti-immigration mobilization efforts undertaken by restrictionist groups, such as Numbers USA; reportedly, the phone system of the US Congress collapsed under the weight of more than 400,000 calls opposing the legislation (SPLC 2009). Moreover, in recent years, representatives of nativist and anti-immigration organizations have become mainstream in the media – appearing most notably on CNN's *Lou Dobbs Tonight* (now on Fox Business) and repeatedly testifying as experts to Congress. FAIR, for instance, claims it has testified to Congress "more than any other organization in America" (SPLC 2009).

While the "nativist lobby" has access to the mainstream media and policymakers, its influence should not be exaggerated. Even the defeat of the "amnesty" bill in 2007 was a defensive victory. With regard to implementing new legislation, nativists and anti-immigration advocates more broadly have been much less successful, at least at the federal level. While they have been able to profit from the post-9/11 securitization of the immigration debate, most notably with the construction of the border fence, they have also faced a powerful pro-immigration lobby that includes big business, immigrant groups, and libertarians (Tichenor 2002). This is in sharp contrast to the situation in Western Europe, where pro-immigration forces have been almost invisible in the debate.

## The Economic Crisis, Immigration, and Nativism

The association between crisis and extremism has a lengthy history. In 1919, the famous German scholar Max Weber (1987) argued that charismatic leaders benefit from crisis situations. But it was particularly the rise of Adolf Hitler and his National Socialist German Workers' Party (NSDAP) amid Germany's depression, in the aftermath of the Wall Street Crash of 1929, that has linked economic crisis and the rise of political extremism. In fact, most contemporary studies of the radical right link its emergence to some form of crisis, though not always (exclusively) economic, connected to some type of modernization process (e.g., Kitschelt and McGann 1995; Betz 1994).

Despite the strength of this received wisdom, the empirical evidence is thin. For example, while the Great Depression led to the rise of German extremist parties, it did not in many other European countries (e.g., the Netherlands and United Kingdom) or in the United States. Similarly, neither the oil crisis of the 1970s nor the democratic transition in Central and Eastern Europe in the 1990s, which involved massive economic hardship for large portions of the people, led to the clear rise of extremist politics.

The recent economic crisis seems to follow this pattern so far. If one looks at the national elections in European countries that have been conducted since the global recession began in mid-2008, there is no clear trend toward the rise of "extremist" (i.e., radical-right) parties. While some radical-right parties have gained traction in recent elections, most notably the Hungarian Jobbik in 2010 and the Latvian National Alliance in 2011, others have lost (slightly), such as the DFP in Denmark or the VB in Belgium. And even though various radical-right parties have done well in national and local elections, such as the Austrian FPÖ and the French FN, they are nowhere near their peaks in the 1990s.

The lack of a clear trend toward radical-right electoral success can also be seen in the results of the elections for the European Parliament in June 2009. Against the striking victory of Jobbik in Hungary (gaining 14.8 percent in its first European election) stands the complete implosion of the League of Polish Families (LPR) in Poland (which had gained 15.2 percent in 2004 but didn't even contest in 2009). Similarly, while much attention in Western Europe went to the gains of the British National Party (+1.4 percent) and the Dutch PVV (+17 percent), few noted the clear losses of the Belgian VB (–3.4 percent) and French FN (–3.5 percent). Moreover, in most European countries, radical-right parties did not contest the European elections, or they didn't make it into the European Parliament (e.g., ones from the Czech Republic, Germany, Finland, Ireland, Latvia, Luxembourg, Spain, and Sweden).

## Table 4: Performance of Nativist Parties in the European Election in 2009 and Comparison with 2004 Election

| Country | Party | European Election 2009 (%) | Difference 2004–2009 (%) |
|---|---|---|---|
| Austria | Alliance for the Future of Austria | 4.6 | +4.6 |
| | Austria Freedom Party (FPÖ) | 12.7 | +6.4 |
| Belgium | National Front (Belgian) (FNb) | 1.3 | −1.5 |
| | Flemish Interest (VB) | 9.9 | −3.4 |
| Britain | British National Party (BNP) | 6.2 | +1.4 |
| Bulgaria* | National Union Attack (NSA) | 9.4 | −2.8 |
| Denmark | Danish People's Party (DFP) | 13.9 | +7.1 |
| France | National Front (FN) | 6.3 | −3.5 |
| Greece | Popular Orthodox Rally (LAOS) | 7.2 | +3.1 |
| Hungary | Movement for a Better Hungary (Jobbik) | 14.8 | +14.8 |
| Italy | Northern League (LN) | 10.2 | +5.2 |
| Netherlands | Party for Freedom (PVV) | 17.0 | +17.0 |
| Poland | League of Polish Families (LPR) | --- | −15.9 |
| Romania* | Greater Romania Party (PRM) | 8.7 | +4.5 |
| Slovakia | Slovak National Party (SNS) | 5.6 | +3.6 |

* For Bulgarian and Romania, the difference is between the 2009 and 2007 European elections, as they only joined the European Union in 2007.

Source: All data are from the Norwegian Social Science Data Services (NSD).

Although it is too early to discern clear trends, data from the Organization for Economic Cooperation and Development (OECD) show that immigration to Europe and North America has actually decreased since the beginning of the economic crisis (e.g., Chrisafis 2009). Some anecdotal evidence even indicates that return migration from the United States has increased in recent years (Papademetriou and Terrazas 2009). At the same time, Eurobarometer surveys show that immigration has become a less salient issue for Europeans. Whereas 15 percent of Europeans considered immigration to be one of the two most important issues facing their country in September 2007, this had dropped to 9 percent by August 2008. This has stabilized since; in October/November 2009, 9 percent was again the EU average, though with some striking national variations. Most importantly, in the United Kingdom, the figure was 29 percent, which served as a reflection and a reason for the sharply increased salience of immigration in the campaign preceding the May 2010 parliamentary elections.

The situation in the United Kingdom seems to be exceptional, however. In most European countries, the debate is fully focused on the dire economic situation and the worrying increase in unemployment, but immigration plays a small role. In the United States, the political debate in 2010 was dominated by health care and the country's financial system and rising debt load. Although President Obama promised to propose comprehensive immigration reform, the ongoing economic crisis, and fear of a "double dip" recession have so far kept him primarily focused on economic issues. At the same time, the entrance of Texas Governor Rick Perry into the Republican primaries in late 2011 momentarily moved immigration back to the forefront of the political agenda, as other Republican candidates used his seemingly "pro-immigration" past against him.

## Conclusion

As has been demonstrated, many of the assumptions about the relationship between immigration and nativism are based upon feeble empirical evidence. In many cases, academic research is inconclusive, not in the least because of a lack of reliable cross-national data. Hence, it is absolutely vital that more cross-national data projects are created and supported over longer periods of time. Recent developments, such as the creation and activities of EUMC/FRA and the European Social Survey (ESS), are important steps forward. Nevertheless, it is critical that policymakers base their assumptions about policy and law on what is known. Policy-relevant findings from the literature include:

- *The most extreme reactions to immigration and migrants are fomented by the radical or extreme right, not the left, but their popularity is highly circumscribed across North America, Western Europe, and Central and Eastern Europe.* The most significant extremist reaction to immigration comes from radical-right parties in Western Europe. However, radical-right parties are successful only in a minority of European countries and not at all in North America. In the United States, the most important nativist actors are non-party organizations that are at times well-connected to mainstream media and politicians. In addition, extreme-right violence against immigrants is a significant problem in some countries, including Germany and Russia. Research shows that this violence is not directly related to radical-right parties; as far as the perpetrators are active within political organizations, it is in small neo-Nazi groups and skinhead gangs.

- *Migration patterns do not drive radical-right voting, although immigration as a political issue has contributed to their electoral success.* There is no straightforward relationship between immigration patterns and radical-right voting. Immigration has to be *translated* into a political issue, which involves many different steps. And while immigration is certainly not the only issue of the radical right, it clearly plays an important role in their propaganda and electoral success.

- *There is no clear relationship – either way – between rising numbers of immigrants and extremist incidents.* Logically, with the growth of the immigrant population, anti-immigrant crimes have increased, too. However, no clear relationship exists between the electoral strength of a radical-right party in a country and the level of anti-immigrant violence. As EUMC/FRA started to collect reliable cross-national data several years ago, future research might find more conclusive evidence on the exact relationship between the two factors.

- *Both the process of globalization and the (related) public attitudes toward immigrants influence the support for radical-right parties in a much more complex manner than is often assumed.* Mass attitudes toward immigration and immigrants have always been relatively negative in the sense that, at the very least, a large minority in every country will hold nativist attitudes. While radical-right groups have clearly profited from this, they tap into only a minority of the nativist population. While globalization is also influencing the support for radical-right parties, the relationship is highly complex and seriously underdeveloped theoretically. Clearly, with globalization affecting most highly industrialized countries in roughly similar ways, and with the electoral successes of radical-right parties diverging significantly, there is no linear relationship between globalization and radical-right electoral success.

- *The radical right frames the immigration debate consistently across countries on the basis of two main themes: a cultural threat (recently amalgamated as a cultural-religious threat) and a security threat (recently amalgamated as a criminal-terrorist threat). Secondary themes include economic competition and an anti-elite/anti-politics narrative.* Although individual parties will emphasize specific points more than others in their discourse, all share a roughly similar set of themes. The key theme is cultural, in which immigrants are considered a threat to the cultural homogeneity of the nation because of an inability or unwillingness to assimilate. In recent years, particularly in Western Europe, the cultural has been accompanied by a religious theme, in which (radical) Islam is seen as a threat to liberal-democratic values. Parties in all countries also share a strong security theme, in which immigration is linked to crime and, increasingly, terrorism. Two secondary themes are the economic, in which immigration is seen as a threat to the wealth or welfare of the nation, and the political, in which a corrupt elite is accused of using immigration for financial and political gains. Of all these themes, the security, religious, and economic frames have been adopted most by mainstream actors, though often in watered-down versions.

- *States have tightened immigration policies, but the radical right is only one causal factor; furthermore, counterforces, particularly state-sponsored anti-discrimination laws, have blunted the rise of more extremist parties*. European countries have tightened their immigration policies in recent decades. However, the electoral pressure of radical-right parties has been only one of many important factors. In many cases, the most significant policies were implemented well before the radical right became successful. Moreover, European integration complicates the distinction between domestic and international factors. There is increasing pressure to develop an EU-wide migration policy; while this is yet to be implemented, national policies have already started to converge significantly.

But not everything has gone the radical right's way. In various countries, antiracist and pro-immigrant groups have sprung up in direct reaction to radical-right success, pushing through an alternative, pro-immigration discourse. These initiatives have often been subsidized and expanded by local and national governments. Finally, many states have used anti-discrimination legislation to hinder the development of the radical right, including the banning of political parties.

– *There is a complex relationship between immigration and extremism in which some parties have profited, especially in Western Europe, though many countries do not have a relevant party – and not at all in Central and Eastern Europe.*

In conclusion, the relationship between immigration and extremism is unclear and complex. Increased levels of immigration have given rise to nativist reactions in Europe and North America, but not yet in Central and Eastern Europe. While immigration has helped some radical-right parties obtain moderate electoral success, most European and North American countries do not have a politically influential nativist movement. And while nativist sentiments and organizations have played a role in the tightening of immigration laws, particularly those regarding asylum, they have lost the big battle, as both Western Europe and North America are increasingly multiethnic societies.

# Works Cited

Akkerman, Tjitske. Anti-Immigration Parties and the Defense of Liberal Values: The Exceptional Case of the List Pim Fortuyn. *Journal of Political Ideologies* (10) 3: 337–354, 2005.

Akkerman, Tjitske, and Anniken Hagelund. 'Women and Children First!' Anti-Immigration Parties and Gender in Norway and the Netherlands. *Patterns of Prejudice* (41) 2: 197–214, 2007.

Alfano, Sean. Arizona Immigration Law SB 1070 Has Support of 55% of Americans, New Poll Shows. *Daily News* July 28, 2010. http://articles.nydailynews.com/2010-07-28/news/27071095_1_immigration-law-immigration-status-arrests-of-illegal-immigrants.

Ali, Wajahat, Eli Clifton, Matthew Duss, Lee Fang, Scott Keyes, and Faiz Shakir. *Fear, Inc. The Roots of the Islamophobia Network in America*. Washington, DC: Center for American Progress, 2011. www.americanprogress.org/issues/2011/08/islamophobia.html.

Alonso, Sonia, and Saro Claro da Fonseca. Immigration, Left and Right. *Party Politics*, forthcoming.

Álvarez-Rivera, Manuel. "Election Resources on the Internet: Western Europe," n.d. (accessed March 4, 2012). http://electionresources.org/western.europe.html.

Anti-Defamation League (ADL). *The Skinhead International: A Worldwide Survey of Neo-Nazi Skinheads*. New York: ADL, 1995.

Anti-Defamation League (ADL). *Patrick Buchanan: Unrepentant Bigot*. New York: ADL, 2009. www.adl.org/special_reports/Patrick_Buchanan2/extremists.asp.

Antle, W. James III. Barletta Forming Immigration Reform Caucus, Cracking Down on Sanctuary Cities. *The American Spectator*, May 4, 2011. http://spectator.org/blog/2011/05/04/barletta-forming-immigration-r.

Archibold, Randal C. Arizona Enacts Stringent Law on Immigration. *New York Times* April 23, 2010. www.nytimes.com/2010/04/24/us/politics/24immig.html.

Arter, David. The Breakthrough of Another West European Populist Radical Right Party? The Case of the True Finns. *Government & Opposition* (45) 4: 484–504, 2010.

Backes, Uwe. Extremismus und politisch motivierte Gewalt. In *Demokratien des 21. Jahrhunderts im Vergleich: Historische Zugänge, Gegenwartsprobleme, Reformperspektiven*, edited by Eckhard Jesse and Roland Sturm. Opladen, Germany: Leske & Budrich, 2003: 341–367.

Baldwin-Edwards, Martin. Recent Changes in European Immigration Policies, *Journal of European Social Policy* (2) 1: 53–56, 1992.

Barta, Patrick, and Paul Hannon. Economic Crisis Curbs Migration of Workers. *Wall Street Journal* July 1, 2009. http://online.wsj.com/article/SB124636924020073241.html.

Bawer, Bruce. *While Europe Slept: How Radical Islam is Destroying the West from Within*. New York: Anchor, 2006.

Bawer, Bruce. *Surrender: Appeasing Islam, Sacrificing Freedom*. New York: Doubleday, 2009.

*BBC News*. BNP Leader Defends Policy on Race. April 23, 2009. http://news.bbc.co.uk/2/hi/uk/politics/8011878.stm.

*BBC News*. Swiss Voters Back Ban on Minarets. November 29, 2009. http://news.bbc.co.uk/2/hi/8385069.stm.

Betz, Hans-Georg. *Radical Right-Wing Populism in Western Europe*. Basingstoke, UK: Macmillan, 1994.

Bobbio, Norberto. Rechts und Links. Zum Sinn einer politischen Unterscheidung. *Blätter für deutsche und internationale Politik* (39) 5: 543–549, 1994.

Buchanan, Patrick J. *State of Emergency: The Third World Invasion and Conquest of America*. New York: Thomas Dunne, 2006.

Building Democracy Intiative. *Nativism in the House: A Report on the House Immigration Reform Caucus*. Chicago: Center for New Community, 2007.

*CNN*. Denmark Passes Tough Migrant Laws. May 31, 2002. http://archives.cnn.com/2002/WORLD/europe/05/31/denmark.immigration.

Cohen, Patricia. In Books, A Clash of Europe and Islam. *The New York Times* February 8, 2007. www.nytimes.com/2007/02/08/books/08circ.html.

Colombo, Asher, and Giuseppe Sciortino. The Bossi-Fini Law: Explicit Fanticism, Implicit Moderation, and Poisoned Fruits. In *Italian Politics: The Second Berlusconi Government*, edited by Jean Blondel and Paolo Segatti. New York: Berghahn, 2003: 162–180.

Corder, Mike. Dutch Burqa Ban Legislation Planned. *Huffington Post* January 27, 2012. www.huffingtonpost.com/2012/01/27/dutch-burqa-ban-_n_1236625.html.

DHS Office of Immigration Statistics. Estimates of the Unauthorized Immigrant Population Residing in the United States: January 2011. *Population Estimates* March 2012. www.dhs.gov/xlibrary/assets/statistics/publications/ois_ill_pe_2011.pdf.

Dolezal, Martin, Marc Helbling, and Swen Hutter. Debating Islam in Austria, Germany and Switzerland: Ethnic Citizenship, Church-State Relations and Right-Wing Populism. *West European Politics* (33) 2: 171–190, 2010.

Eriksen, Lars. Denmark's populist border controls reintroduced but many remain skeptical. *The Guardian* May 12, 2011. www.guardian.co.uk/world/2011/may/12/denmark-border-controls-reintroduced-populist.

EC – European Commission. A Common Immigration Policy for Europe. Press release, June 17, 2008. http://europa.eu/rapid/press ReleasesAction.do?reference=MEMO/08/402.

European Monitoring Centre on Racism and Xenophobia (EUMC). *Muslims in the European Union: Discrimination and Islamophobia.* Vienna: European Monitoring Centre on Racism and Xenophobia, 2006.

Faist, Thomas, and Andreas Ette (eds.). *The Europeanization of National Politics and Politics of Immigration: Between Autonomy and the European Union.* New York: Palgrave, 2007.

*Fox News Latino.* Alabama Immigration Law May Get Second Look After Big Business Backlash. December 8, 2011. http://latino.fox news.com/latino/politics/2011/12/08/alabama-immigration-law-may-get-second-look-after-big-business-backlash/.

Gächter, August. Migrationspolitik in Österreich seit 1945. Working Paper No. 12, Migration und soziale Mobilität, 2008.

Gibson, Rachel. *The Growth of Anti-Immigrant Parties in Western Europe*. Ceredigian, UK: Edwin Mellen, 2002.

Givens, Terri, and Adam Luedtke. The Politics of European Union Immigration Policy: Institutions, Salience, and Harmonization. *The Policy Studies Journal* (32) 1: 145–165, 2004.

Golder, Matt. Explaining Variations in the Success of Extreme Right Parties in Western Europe, *Comparative Political Studies* (36) 4: 432–466, 2003.

Hanley, Lisa M., Blair A. Ruble and Allison M. Garland (eds.). *Immigration and Integration in Urban Communities: Renegotiating the City*. Baltimore, MD: Johns Hopkins University Press, 2008.

Hendriks, Dolf. "Ondertekenaars oproep zijn onnozel." *Algemeen Dagblad* January 2, 2008.

Higham, John. *Strangers in the Land: Patterns of American Nativism, 1860–1925*. New Brunswick, NJ: Rutgers University Press, 1955.

Hooper, John, Giles Tremlett, and Jon Henley. Immigration the key as left faces loss of power. *The Guardian* May 16, 2002. www.guardian.co.uk/world/2002/may/16/thefarright.politics1.

HoSang, Dan. *Racial Propositions: Genteel Apartheid in Postwar California*. Berkeley: University of California Press, 2010.

Hunt, Albert R. Republican Anti-Immigrant Stance Bodes 2012 Risk. *Bloomberg Businessweek* January 16, 2011. www.businessweek.com/news/2011-01-16/republican-anti-immigration-stance-bodes-2012-risk-albert-hunt.html.

Immigration Reform Caucus (IRC). 2011a. www.house.gov/bilbray/irc.

Immigration Reform Caucus (IRC). 2011b. Membership. http://bilbray.house.gov/.

Immigration Watch Canada (IWC). Who are we? Why have we organized? n.d. www.immigrationwatchcanada.org.

James, Randy. Sheriff Joe Arpaio. *Time* October 13, 2009. www.time.com/time/nation/article/0,8599,1929920,00.html.

Kitschelt, Herbert, and Anthony McGann. *The Radical Right in Western Europe. A Comparative Analysis*. Ann Arbor: University of Michigan Press, 1995.

Kuzmanic, Tonci A. *Hate-Speech in Slovenia: Slovenian Racism, Sexism and Chauvinism*. Ljubljana: Open Society Institute-Slovenia, 1999.

Kymlicka, Will. *The Current State of Multiculturalism in Canada and Research Themes on Canadian Multiculturalism 2008–10*. Ottawa: Minister of Public Works and Government Services Canada, 2010.

Lavenex, Sandra. *Safe Third Countries: Extending EU Asylum and Immigration Policies to Central and Eastern Europe*. Budapest: Central European University Press, 1999.

Lewis, Aidan. Italian Migration Policy Draws Fire. *BBC News* March 7, 2009. http://news.bbc.co.uk/2/hi/europe/7880215.stm.

Lubbers, Marcel. Exclusionistic Electorates: Extreme Right-Wing Voting in Western Europe. PhD dissertation. Nijmegen: Radboud University, 2001.

Massa, Justin, and Cecelia Abundis. The New Battleground: Anti-Immigrant Ordinances Attack Housing Rights. *Building Democracy Monthly*. February 2007.

Messina, Anthony W. *The Logics and Politics of Post-WWII Migration to Western Europe*. Cambridge: Cambridge University Press, 2007.

*Metro*. Multicultureel betekent multicrimineel. June 15, 2005.

Minkenberg, Michael. The Radical Right in Public Office: Agenda-Setting and Policy Effects. *West European Politics* (24) 4: 1–21, 2001.

Mudde, Cas. The Single-Issue Party Thesis: Extreme Right Parties and the Immigration Issue. *West European Politics* (22) 3: 182–197, 1999. http://works.bepress.com/cgi/viewcontent.cgi?article=1021&context=cas_mudde.

Mudde, Cas. *The Ideology of the Extreme Right*. Manchester: Manchester University Press, 2000.

Mudde, Cas (ed.). *Racist Extremism in Central and Eastern Europe*. London: Routledge, 2005a.

Mudde, Cas. Racist Extremism in Central and Eastern Europe. *East European Politics and Societies* (19) 2: 161–184, 2005b.

Mudde, Cas. *Populist Radical Right Parties in Europe*. Cambridge: Cambridge University Press, 2007.

Mudde, Cas. The Intolerance of the Tolerant. *Open Democracy.* October 20, 2010. www.opendemocracy.net/cas-mudde/intolerance-of-tolerant.

Norwegian Social Science Data Services (NSD). European Election Database. www.nsd.uib.no/european_election_database.

O'Connor, Anahad. Mr. Wilders Goes to Washington. *New York Times* February 26, 2009. http://thelede.blogs.nytimes.com/2009/02/26/mr-wilders-goes-to-washington/.

Papademetriou, Demetrios G., and Aaron Terrazas. *Immigrants and the Current Economic Crisis: Research Evidence, Policy Challenges, and Implications.* Washington, DC: Migration Policy Institute, 2009. www.migrationpolicy.org/pubs/lmi_recessionJan09.pdf.

Pollard, Stephen. The Appeasers. *The New York Times* July 24, 2009. www.nytimes.com/2009/07/26/books/review/Pollard-t.html.

Ridgley, Jennifer. Cities of Refuge: Immigration Enforcement, Police, and the Insurgent Genealogies of Citizenship in U.S. Sanctuary Cities. *Urban Geography* (29) 1: 53–77, 2008.

Rydgren, Jens. Meso-level Reasons for Racism and Xenophobia: Some Converging and Diverging Effects of Radical Right Populism in France and Sweden. *European Journal of Social Theory* (6) 1: 45–68, 2003.

Schain, Martin. *The Politics of Immigration in France. Britain and the United States: A Comparative Study.* New York: Palgrave, 2008.

Southern Poverty Law Center (SPLC). Neo-Conferederates, *Intelligence Report* 99. Montgomery, Ala.: SPLC, 2000.

Southern Poverty Law Center (SPLC). *The Nativist Lobby: Three Faces of Intolerance.* Montgomery, Ala.: SPLC, 2009.

Tancredo, Tom. Rick Perry not a real conservative. *Politico* August 11, 2011. www.politico.com/news/stories/0811/61076.html.

*The Daily Mail.* Nicolas Sarkozy joins David Cameron and Angela Merkel view that multiculturalism has failed. February 11, 2011. www.dailymail.co.uk/news/article-1355961/Nicolas-Sarkozy-joins-David-Cameron-Angela-Merkel-view-multiculturalism-failed.html.

*The New York Times.* Romney's Hard Line. Editorial. January 11, 2012. www.nytimes.com/2012/01/12/opinion/romneys-hard-line-on-immigration.html?_r=1.

Tichenor, Dan. *Dividing Lines: The Politics of Immigration Control in America.* Princeton, NJ: Princeton University Press, 2002.

Trplan, Tomaz. Slovenia. In *Racist Extremism in Central and Eastern Europe,* edited by Cas Mudde. London: Routledge, 2005: 243–266.

United Nations High Commissioner for Refugees (UNHCR). Freedom in the World 2009 – Denmark. 2009. www.unhcr.org/refworld/country,,,,DNK,4562d8b62,4a6452bfc,0.html.

US Department of Homeland Security, Office of Immigration Statistics (DHS). *Estimates of the Unauthorized Immigrant Population Residing in the United States: January 2009.* Washington, DC: DHS Office of Immigration Statistics, 2010. www.dhs.gov/xlibrary/assets/statistics/publications/ois_ill_pe_2009.pdf.

Vasileva, Katya. 6.5% of the EU population are foreigners and 9.4% are born abroad. Eurostat, (34) Statistics in Focus: 4. Luxembourg: Eurostat, 2011. http://epp.eurostat.ec.europa.eu/cache/ITY_OFFPUB/KS-SF-11-034/EN/KS-SF-11-034-EN.PDF.

von Beyme, Klaus. Right-Wing Extremism in Post-War Europe. *West European Politics* (11) 2: 1–18, 1988.

Washington, Tom. Ultra-nationalist group banned by Kremlin. *The Moscow News* February 18, 2011. http://themoscownews.com/society/20110218/188431564.html.

Weber, Max. *Politik als Beruf.* 8th edition. Berlin: Duncker & Humblot, 1987.

Ya'or, Bat. *Eurabia: The Euro-Arab Axis.* Madison, NJ: Fairleigh Dickinson University Press, 2005.

Zaslove, Andrej. Closing the Door? The Ideology and Impact of Radical Right Populism on Immigration Policy in Austria and Italy. *Journal of Political Ideologies* (9) 1: 99–118, 2004.

# The Role of the State in Cultural Integration: Trends, Challenges, and Ways Ahead

*Christian Joppke*

## Introduction

A widely held view is that states handle the cultural integration of immigrants within sharply distinct national models, "multicultural" in Britain, "assimilationist" in France, or "segregationist" in Germany, to quote some usual suspects. This view exaggerates the differences that undoubtedly exist while downplaying essential commonalities. Indeed, European countries' approaches to cultural integration converge in important respects. One shared feature is the existence of constitutional rights clauses that greatly restrict the scope of liberal state intervention in sensitive identity issues, which are simply for the individual and not the state to decide. A second commonality, for over a decade now, is "civic integration" policies that seek to bind newcomers to majority institutions and culture by requiring them to learn the host-society language and acknowledge basic host-society norms and values (see Joppke 2007). The variations from state to state in Europe today are largely within this overall "liberal" framework. The main challenge – which is found everywhere – is to find a mode of civic integration that is restrained enough to respect the moral autonomy of immigrants and aggressive enough to further the incontrovertible goal of a more cohesive and integrated host society.

## Policy Trends

"Civic integration" originated in the Netherlands in the late 1990s as a remedy for disproportionate immigrant unemployment, school dropout rates, and residential segregation, which plagued especially the Turkish and Moroccan immigrant populations. As this malaise occurred in the shadow of a multiculturalism policy (dubbed "ethnic minorities" policy) that had subsidized institutional separation (by allowing separate schools, media, cultural organizations, etc.), the new démarche was to integrate immigrants rigorously into host-society institutions, above all the labor market. The goal was to make them learn Dutch, not as a matter of "national identity," but to facilitate better access to employment. Due to growing populism and domestic turmoil surrounding Muslims and Islam over the past ten years, an initially neoliberal policy of making immigrants "self-sufficient" (and thus no longer dependent on welfare) morphed into a culture-focused policy of making them adapt to, or at least be cognizant of, "Dutch norms and values." This went along with an increasingly punitive and restrictive approach, making permanent residence permits contingent upon passing a civic integration exam, eventually even handing out temporary visas for (mostly Turkish and Moroccan) family migrants only after they could demonstrate basic civic knowledge and Dutch language competence *before* their arrival (so-called "integration from abroad"). At first a measure of immigrant integration, civic integration quickly was extended to nationality law through a formal (and difficult) citizenship test. Variants of the Dutch model of civic integration have subsequently been adopted in several European countries, including Germany, France, Britain, Austria, and Denmark.

Variations exist in how cultural integration is managed in Europe, but all policies lie largely within the dominant model of civic integration. The biggest differences can be seen mostly with respect to the harshness of the policy. Unlike their Dutch inspiration, the French *contrats d'acceuil et d'intégration* are not punitive but service-oriented, the civics part lasting but a day. At most, some newcomers are obliged to take (state-paid) French language lessons – interestingly, this is a

125

small minority (on average 20 percent) among a largely francophone immigrant pool. The German *Integrationskurse* (integration courses) focus on language acquisition, which is a more significant problem in Germany, as most immigrants do not speak German upon arrival. In cases of non-attendance of courses or failing the exam, one may lose social benefits, but not one's residence permit. German citizenship tests initially focused heavily on culture, and even morality (piloted by the *Länder* of Hesse and Baden-Württemberg, respectively), but were replaced by a federal test in 2008 that focuses on civic-political knowledge and is easy to pass. In Britain, civic integration originated in the context of nationality law, and it was only subsequently extended to the regulation of entry and residence. Given the status of English as the global lingua franca, language acquisition is generally less of a problem in Britain, and one passes the requirement by moving just one step higher on the official European scale that measures language competence. On the other hand, civic integration in Britain has an applied-culture inflection, expecting immigrants to understand British mores and day-to-day life, such as knowing how to pay bills, behave in pubs, and stand in line patiently.

The general thrust of civic integration is to narrow the cultural distance between immigrants and the host society, and to make immigrants understand societal norms, principles, and institutions. However, tested *knowledge* of these norms is one thing; their proved *adoption* in one's own behavior is quite another. British Prime Minister David Cameron's recent plea for a "muscular liberalism" to replace the old "state multiculturalism" clearly aims at more than passive knowledge, asking instead for the actual adoption of liberal norms – this is the whole point of the "muscles" (Cameron 2011).

While the goal of policy must be to bring about behavioral and moral change, policy alone does not necessarily have the tools or the powers to effect this change – especially when it purports to be *liberal* policy. This self-limitation becomes apparent if one looks at outliers that have come under fire precisely for wanting to go further. A notorious example is the "Muslim test" introduced in 2005 in Baden-Württemberg, which seeks to sniff out, by way of morally inquisitional trick questions, whether applicants for citizenship *really* accept the principles of the German Basic Law (which they are formally required to accept by signing a loyalty declaration), or whether they are only pretending to do so in order to obtain a German passport. Exactly to set a counterpoint to this heavily criticized *Gesinnungstest* (attitude test), the German federal citizenship test introduced in 2008 abstains from morality questions and largely limits itself to civic-political knowledge.

A second outlier comes from France, where a female Muslim was denied French citizenship in 2008 for wearing a burqa. Her clothing was found "incompatible with the essential values of the French community, especially equality of the sexes" (Conseil d'Etat 2008). Before this Conseil d'Etat decision (which was immediately adopted as routine administrative practice), the "assimilation" formally required for naturalization under French law had been defined in a thinly linguistic sense, as basic French language competence. In a context of heightened tensions between natives and Muslims post-2001, the meaning of assimilation has obviously thickened. The whole French anti-burqa campaign, which culminated in the controversial 2010 law prohibiting the covering of one's face in public places, is Europe's most extreme case of "muscular liberalism" to date, which in France, of course, has a long tradition in terms of "Republicanism." But the assertion of Republican identity in the political arena should not obscure the overall inclusive leanings of the French state, which recently helped into existence the confederation of Muslims in France (CFCM), supports the building of mosques in indirect yet "compensatory" ways and subsidizes the education of French imams at the Institut Catholique in Paris.

Overall, the illiberal exceptions to inclusive civic integration have become known exactly for that – as exceptions. In most instances, civic integration is self-limited to instilling and testing cognitive knowledge, while abstaining from intervening in the inner sphere of morality. Even the Dutch model – arguably the harshest civic integration variant in Europe – shares this self-limitation: Although it strongly insists on respect for "Dutch norms and values," it does not demand adoption of these same values. For example, when Muslim immigrants are confronted with sexual libertinism in the notorious Dutch information video that many newcomers watch, the gist is not that Muslims are being asked to undress at chilly Dutch beaches, but that they are aware that this is common practice in this "liberal" country (this is well observed by Hansen 2010).

## Challenges

The amount of freedom that liberal states have when designing cultural integration policies depends on what type of cultural difference stands to be integrated. If one scratches the surface a bit, there are only two critical issues: language and religion. They are critical in different ways, first because of their inherent features, and secondly because of their different sociological presence on both sides of the Atlantic. Language is the main cultural integration issue in the United States, in terms of the perception of Spanish as a challenge to the dominant English. Religion is the critical issue in Europe, in terms of Islam as a challenge to dominant Christianity (or, rather, the secularism that has grown out of European Christendom).[46]

If this diagnosis is correct, the United States has much less of a cultural integration problem than Europe. This is because language is not exclusive: Acquiring another language (something required of every schoolchild) does not necessitate giving up one's language of birth.[47] On the contrary, adopting a second language is capacity-enhancing; it does not deprive individuals of anything, least of all their "identity." At the same time, states must operate in a specific (by definition "majority") language; functional necessity and resource scarcity tilt toward an *assimilationist* state response with respect to language.[48] However, this is exactly reciprocated by the behavior of

---

46  I follow here the transatlantic comparison made in Zolberg and Long 1998.
47  This is sharply observed by Zolberg and Long 1998.
48  In the United States, this assimilationist tilt is mellowed by the Spanish- (and other minority-)language and bilingualism provisions that flow out of the 1965 Voting Rights Act and 1968 Bilingual Education Act, respectively.

second- and later-generation immigrants, Hispanics included, who show very high rates of English-language acquisition (noted by, among others, Alba 1999). More than 80 percent of the second generation speaks only English or speaks English very well across all immigrant groups in the United States (Jiménez 2011). In order to succeed and partake in the "American Dream" there is simply no alternative. At the same time, there are institutional incentives for market actors and vote-catching politicians to counterbalance the assimilationist state tilt with a modicum of pluralism by, say, advertising or campaigning in Spanish, which has long been common practice in the United States. No further state policy is required to regulate this process; a functionally differentiated society does all the necessary work.

The situation, meanwhile, is more difficult with respect to religion. Religion is exclusive: One cannot adhere to more than one religion at any one time. In addition, at least in the monotheist variant, religion comes with a moral script that bears no compromise, at least on paper (actual practice may, of course, be full of compromise and eclecticism). Just because religion is so tightly connected, if not historically co-original with morality and ethical views of the "good" life, its practice is strongly protected in terms of individual rights to liberty in liberal-state constitutions. Accordingly, with respect to religion, there is no alternative to a pluralist, *de facto multicultural* state response. However, this is never a response in terms of "policy" because constitutional law *requires* that individuals' right to believe and exercise their religion freely be respected (whereas the notion of "policy" conveys the possibility of other "policies," that is, *choice*).

It is surprising, then, that Islam is considered Europe's main cultural integration problem. American observers, in particular, attribute this to an inherent Christian bias of European societies, from which the United States is said to be luckily free. However, this critique obscures the elasticity of liberal institutions and the strong protection of religious freedoms also in Europe.

Instead, "Islam" is a protest ideology of the socioeconomically marginalized Muslim populations of Europe. Posed as a counterfactual, without the high unemployment and school dropout rates, low income levels, and residential segregation that mark (or mar) the lives of European Muslims, particularly the young, there would be much less of a problem of religious intolerance in Europe, perhaps as little as there is one in North America. In fact, the happier demography of American Muslims, who are generally better educated and earn more than average Americans, helps explain why Islam has generally *not* become a critical domestic issue in America. To say that the European Islam problem is one of deficient cultural integration, and that it can be countered by culture-focused integration policies (whatever they might be), is to ignore the socioeconomic underpinnings of the problem.

In addition, Islam can figure as a domestic protest idiom only because, on an international plane, the global Islamic movement sees itself as the opponent to Western hegemony and "imperialism." Note that Buddhism, Sikhism, Hinduism, etc. are not visible as domestic protest idioms even though marginalized immigrants of those faiths certainly exist in Europe. This is in part because there is nothing akin to "Israel" or "Iraq" that would allow these religions to align into opposition to the "West." By implication, an alternative foreign policy that takes the winds out of global Islamism would be more effective than even the best cultural integration policy. This has long been the demand of British Muslims, whose radicalization took a quantum leap after the Blair government's support of the American invasion of Iraq, which was perceived, however wrongly, as a war against Islam. However, to have foreign policy dictated by a small minority, and one in which some adherents see their main loyalty and affinities outside the British national community at that, is also a tall and questionable order – not to mention that even the most Islam-friendly foreign policy is unlikely to make Israel cease to be a source of disaffection among Muslims.

To these socioeconomic and geopolitical factors must be added a creedal predisposition of most variants of Islam that currently circulate in the West and elsewhere to function as an oppositional identity. Islamic doctrinaires, even those considered reform-minded, such as Yusuf al-Qaradawi or Tariq Ramadan, conceive of European Muslims as a people apart, a quasi-nation that can be integrated only by an extreme program of multicultural recognition – exactly the (most-often imagined) position from which European leaders, from British Prime Minister David Cameron to German Chancellor Angela Merkel, have noisily retreated. The dominant variants of Islam stipulate a tight package of religious rules to cover all aspects of life, including those commonly considered secular or political, which prevents their practitioners from blending more easily into their surroundings. Ramadan, dubbed by *Time* magazine one of the 100 most important figures of the 21st century, insists that an uncompromising, unreconstructed Islam can (and must) be practiced in Western societies and that, in this respect, Muslims may feel "at home" in the West (Ramadan 2002).

The basis for this optimism is "political liberalism" (Rawls 1993), which Islamic reformists have readily embraced (for an academic defense, see March 2007). It argues that consensus or the ties that bind in a liberal society can only be procedural, in terms of an agreement on rules for peaceful coexistence; there can never be agreement on "comprehensive doctrines," ethical views of the good life that forever divide individuals and groups in a pluralistic society. If there could be agreement, we would live in an age of nationalism. Short of nationalism, or beyond it, all one can hope for is an "overlapping consensus," the reaching of a common platform of political rules *from within* one's "comprehensive doctrine."

In an intriguing ethnography of on-the-ground accommodation of Islam in the French *banlieues*, the American anthropologist John Bowen has identified applied political liberalism as "social pragmatism." It allows flesh-and-blood Muslims to acknowledge even a strictly secularist host society by always staying within their religion. Tariq Ramadan provides an example: "A civil marriage already is a Muslim marriage, I think, because it is a contract, and that is what a Muslim marriage is" (Bowen 2010: 168). Surely, this is an example from family law, intrinsically closer to one's ethical or even religious views than polity and politics. But it exposes the weak spot of political liberalism, which is to invite only a pragmatic or instrumental attitude to host-society rules and institutions. In turn, these rules and institutions are likely to be skirted whenever they conflict with one's religious precepts. Political liberalism, as some concede, "cannot require as part of a minimal doctrine of citizenship any robust or emotional attachment to one's community of citizenship" (March 2007: 249). This being the case, if a choice has to be made, the outcome is preordained: "If for being a good Frenchman you have to be a bad Muslim, then I say no," says Tariq Ramadan (quoted in Fourest 2004: 224). The astonishing thing here is not to put religion above worldly attachments – all monotheisms do; no, astonishing is the language of peoplehood that juxtaposes "Frenchman" and "Muslim," which gives a flavor for the particular difficulties of Islam integration.

Against this backdrop, one understands why the British prime minister now rejects the idea of a "passively tolerant society" that is the distillation of the dismissed multiculturalism of old, and that he wants to move on to "muscular liberalism" (Cameron 2011). This essentially means that liberal host-society values and institutions are to be intrinsically and unconditionally accepted for what they are, whatever one's religion prescribes, and not just for their usefulness for pursuing some other project. Muscular liberalism, which wishes to "thicken" liberalism from anodyne procedures into an identity, expresses uneasiness about the laissez-faire approach that had reigned in the past regarding the cultural integration and identity of immigrants. The problem is that implementing this muscular liberalism would entail moral intrusiveness and curtailment of individual liberties that would destroy precisely the liberal values it means to achieve.


## Ways Ahead

If the legal and political space in which policymakers can maneuver is limited, states must be strategic in their efforts to further cultural integration in the future. This report makes six recommendations, ranging from the general level of guiding principles to the more concrete level of policy. The guiding principles are: (1) to be liberal in the right way; (2) to not repress robust political debate; and (3) to recognize the limits of policy. The policy goals are: (1) to protect majority culture; (2) to fight discrimination more effectively; and (3) to select the "right" immigrants.

## Guiding Principles

### 1. Be Liberal – in the Right Way

There are two faces of liberalism: One is an ethic for the right way of life, and another prescribes procedural rules that enable many ways of life to coexist. As states scramble to find cohesion and an identity that can keep diverse societies together, there is a temptation to thicken liberalism into a way of life. This is ultimately destructive of liberalism, as it arrogates to the state an ethical project (much like the former Communist states or today's Islamic states) that should not be its project. Procedural liberalism, which eschews the dress codes, thought control, and pedagogy that go along with the ethical variant, is risky because it gives space for its enemies. But this is a risk that a free society has to shoulder. There, consensus on values is a chimera and, at best, a matter for a self-regulating civil society – but never the business of the state.

### 2. Don't Repress Robust Debate

On the opposite side, proper liberalism cuts both ways, as its free-thought and -speech protections require allowing the rascals, whoever they are, to speak out. Much of the accommodation of Islam in Europe proceeded quietly and unnoticed in the nonpublic settings of court-rooms and state bureaucracy. This guaranteed liberal outcomes, but it also invited political backlash. Particularly the cultural implications of immigration, which touch on the identity of the host society, cannot bypass the court of public opinion. The current turmoil surrounding visible Islam (the burqa and the minarets) signals that this stage has finally arrived. Precisely in the countries where political etiquette had silenced debate, as in the once "liberal" Netherlands and Denmark, the politicization of Islam is all the more vicious and virulent today. In Germany, a best-selling book (Sarrazin 2010) that dared to call "integration above all a task of immigrants" (who could sanely deny this?), and that found the difficulties of Muslim integration not unconnected to "Islam" (thus questioning the reigning firewall between political extremism and religion), led to the ostracizing of its author. Heavily criticized for his theories on intelligence and heredity and his claims that Germany is becoming dumber in part because Muslim immigrants have higher birthrates than ethic Germans, the author was forced to resign from his post at Germany's central bank and narrowly avoided expulsion from the Social Democratic Party.

The stifling of debate only feeds extremism. On the opposite end, direct democracy is not the most suitable venue to process identity-related minority issues, either. The true shock of the Swiss minaret referendum was not its outcome – in other European countries, even larger majorities would have voted against visible representations of Islam – but the fact that it was allowed to take place at all. It is a mistake to leave such matters for mass publics to decide, especially when they are known to be hostile to immigrants and Muslims in *all* Western countries. Representative democracy, whereby "public views" are passed "through the medium of a chosen body of citizens" (Madison 1787), is much better-suited for dealing with delicate minority issues. In fact, political leadership is asked for here. Unfortunately, this is exactly the resource in short supply in our populist "audience democracy" (see Manin 1997), where public opinion and not the best or just solution is the benchmark of political success. There is no golden rule to navigate in this vexed terrain, but the opposite extremes of extreme democracy and no democracy are to be equally avoided.


## 3. Recognize the Limits of Policy

If one wishes to understand the futility of furthering "identity" through state policy, a good way to start is with an interesting exchange before the Canadian Supreme Court between two American academics (*Lavoie v. Canada*, 2002 SCC 23, [2002] 1 S.C.R. 769). Tying more benefits to formal citizenship in order to increase its value, which is how Yale law professor Peter Schuck defended the disputed practice of the Canadian federal government to limit public-sector jobs to citizens only, could in reality only feed an instrumental (and thus "wrong") attitude to Canadian citizenship. Conversely, the flattening of the citizen-alien distinction, which Toronto political scientist Joseph Carens recommended for the sake of a noninstrumental ("right") attitude to citizenship, was equally futile because it could only further devalue Canadian citizenship. One can learn from this exchange that, whatever the state chose to do (it eventually sided with the Yale lawyer), it could only do it wrong.

One could carry this further. Like sleep, love, or happiness, "identity" belongs to a class of "states that are essentially byproducts" (Elster 1983, chapter 2). By wanting it, you will not get it. This is a powerful argument, which points to the futility of furthering "identity" through state policy, apart from the ethical problem of controlling thought and belief in a liberal society. In a brilliant reflection on the "return of assimilation," Rogers Brubaker similarly concluded that assimilation could only be of an "intransitive" kind, something "accomplished by" and not "done to" people, which naturally minimizes the role of policy (Brubaker 2003: 51 f.).

From an American point of view, the European search for the right "integration policy" must be puzzling because the United States has accomplished much more with much less (if any) policy engagement, leaving "integration" entirely to society, especially a famously flexible labor market and absorptive mass culture. The best defense of multiculturalism policy against its critics is to point to its miniscule share within the total state budget, even compared to *other* measures on integration (which is in a proportion of 1:50 in Canada!), so that everything bad on the integration front can hardly be the fault of multiculturalism policy alone (see Banting 2011). Along this line, labor market structures or the education system are vastly more important for helping or hindering "integration" than any, by nature paltry, "integration policy."

## Policy Recommendations

### 1. Protect Majority Culture

When multiculturalism was in better standing than now, the culture deemed in need of protection was only that of minorities. In a way, the view of radical feminists and Marxists that the "Dominant" are culturally invisible, hyping their particulars as the (falsely) universal, carried the day – no need to have mercy with them and to respect majority thinking. Of course, the nation-state is the most potent instrument of reproducing majority culture – what more could the majority want? If Jürgen Habermas once snapped at multiculturalism as misguided "species protection," how infinitely more risible are majority-protective measures like the 1994 Toubon Law (also known as the "Allgood" law), which mandated keeping the French language free of English words, such as "hairdresser," "weekend," or "computer"?

However, the snubbing of majority culture, through an alliance of market forces, radical intellectuals, and a minority-focused legal system, is wind in the sails of the right-wing populism that has become epidemic in Europe. A case in point is the curious repression of the fact that, historically speaking, European societies are Christian societies, with Christianity (and the secularism that could only have arisen from this source) being the single most important maker of European culture and civilization since the early Middle Ages. The high point of repression of this obvious fact was perhaps the denial of a reference to God and Christianity in the preamble of the drafted (but never realized) EU Constitution, which was, of course, no minority conspiracy but pushed for by that torch-bearer of European secularism, France.

In an important counterpoint to this trend, the European Court of Human Rights, in its *Lautsi v. Italy* decision of March 2011 (ECHR 2011), allowed the Italian state to display Christian crosses in public schools, overruling its own lower-chamber decision of November 2009. The ECHR's Grand Chamber reached the exact opposite verdict as the German Constitutional Court had in its notorious 1995 crucifix decision, in which to "learn under the Christian Cross" was deemed a violation of a school child's negative religious right (not to be bothered by the religion of others if the child's atheist parents so wished). As the European court argued instead, the Christian cross on the school wall was above all a cultural, not religious, sign that symbolized the Christian formation of Italian society. Moreover, as a passive symbol, the cross did not amount to active indoctrination of a creed, which would not be permissible by a secular state. Finally, and perhaps most importantly, the cross on the school wall was legitimized in reference to pluralism, as the Italian schools *also* allowed students to wear Islamic headscarves, offered optional instruction on Islam, and was considerate of the Muslim religious calendar. A Maltese judge on the ECHR had called the lower chamber's 2009 prohibition of the cross "historical Alzheimer's" and "cultural vandalism." Indeed, it seems unreasonable, even politically dangerous, to allow a militant atheist from Finland to wipe out a century-old tradition in Italy for the sake of her sacrosanct (negative) "religious freedom." A better path to take is gentle pluralism, in which the minority accommodation that is constitutionally required does not occur at the cost of the "majority," whatever that is in a pluralistic society. This pluralist path, of course, is not far from the nonsecularist, more inclusive state-church arrangements that one already finds in most European states, from Norway to England and Germany to Spain.

## 2. Fight Discrimination More Effectively

If multiculturalism is pushed into retreat today, it would be a cardinal mistake to throw out with it anti-discrimination law and policy, as well. The need to fight ethnic and racial discrimination more effectively has even been recognized by France, long averse to all things *communautarist*. Indeed, the fight against discrimination, which became a matter of European Community law in 2000, has shifted to high gear in the very moment that multiculturalism has been called into question. This suggests that, notoriously fused and confused, the multiculturalism and anti-discrimination agendas have to be strictly kept apart. Multiculturalism seeks to perpetuate difference, while anti-discrimination seeks to abolish difference (see Joppke 2010). The purpose of anti-discrimination is the deracialization of society, as Ronald Dworkin called it with respect to US affirmative action (Dworkin 1985, Chapter 14). It aims at a situation where skin color (much like any other ascriptive marker) is not "seen" when seeing a person – much like small children literally cannot "see" black until they learn that skin color carries social significance. To get there, it is imperative that people of *all* ascriptive endowments, black and white, Muslim and Christian, are found in *every* social station, top to bottom, in complete randomness.

Short of this, when race or religion signals social status, which must be a result of injustice or unearned privilege, it is legitimate and demonstrably effective to preferentially recruit minority individuals into coveted social positions, a policy long known as "affirmative action" in the United States and increasingly known as "positive discrimination" in Europe. The legal basis for this is the recognition of "indirect discrimination," which proceeds by comparing the demographic share of minority individuals against their actual (under)representation in key societal sectors, such as employment, education, or public office. Of course, this opens up a group-recognizing, de facto multiculturalist wedge within a notionally individualistic and universalistic policy because, without a preconceived idea of who is a "minority," one could not observe the existence of "indirect discrimination." This is why anti-discrimination and multiculturalism agendas and social forces closely overlap in the real world – even appear to be one – although they are apart, even opposite from one another philosophically (one being universalistic, the other particularistic). The bottom line is that to favor anti-discrimination is not necessarily to support multiculturalism.

### 3. Select the "Right" Immigrants

Finally, immigrant integration should not be separated from immigrant selection. Canadian officials, who are aware that they manage immigration better than most other countries, tend to argue that the "integration" of immigrants starts with their "selection."[49] Similarly, Canadian academics are often surprised when Europeans perceive "civic integration" and "multiculturalism" as antithetical, the first replacing the second (see, e.g., Banting 2011). Instead, they point to Canada's happy equilibrium of "multicultural integration," which is as "muscular" as it is accommodating (ibid.). Indeed, Canada is blessed with a virtuous circle of integration and selection. But it is premised on rigorously and robustly high-skill-oriented immigrant selection, through its fabled points system, which also happens to let in no more than a trickle of Muslim immigrants. Even Will Kymlicka, reflecting on multiculturalism's "retreat" in Europe, concedes that, in the hypothetical case of an overwhelmingly low-skilled Muslim intake in Canada, there might be a European-style questioning of its multiculturalism (Kymlicka 2005). Conversely, two University of California, Berkeley political scientists speculate that, if the "'visible minorities' in the Netherlands would be well-educated, English-speaking and economically skilled migrants from Hong Kong and India," as they happen to be in Canada, "a good bet is that ... we would not be talking about the rise and fall of multiculturalism in the Netherlands" (Citrin and Wright 2011).

The European conundrum of ever-more-repressive "integration" policies, epitomized by "integration from abroad" – which is no integration policy, but a badly concealed control policy – cannot be decoupled from the fact that most of its legal immigrants (some 80 percent in France or the Netherlands) are not "selected" but, rather, are unchosen and low-skilled "as of right" immigrants in the context of family formation and asylum. Moreover, the large majority are Muslim immigrants, often from North Africa and the Middle East, where Islam is heavily politicized, thus further heating up the *querelles islamiques* within Europe.

---

49  As did Brian Grant (Citizenship and Immigration Canada) at a Forum of Federations conference on "Federalism and Immigrant Integration" in Brussels in November 29, 2010.

As ethnic selectivity has become anathema in liberal societies (see Joppke 2005), the only way forward is rigorously skill-based immigrant selection, on the assumption that poverty and exclusion above all fuel the politicization of cultural (more precisely, religious) difference. At the same time, the demarche, given out by then French President Nicolas Sarkozy, to move *from* "suffered" *to* "chosen" immigration is highly misleading because a modicum of "suffered" immigration has to be accepted for legal-constitutional reasons. There are also ethical problems of creaming off the best and fending off the rest. But, from a realist point of view, there is no alternative to an unsentimental selection policy that "selects" and does not just "accept." The right selection policy, the details of which are obviously outside the scope of this chapter, is vastly more effective than the best "cultural integration" policy could ever be, precisely because it obviates the need for the latter.

## Works Cited

Alba, Richard. Immigration and the American Realities of Assimilation and Multiculturalism. *Sociological Forum* (14) 1: 3–25, 1999.

Banting, Keith. Transatlantic Convergence? The Archaeology of Immigrant Integration in Canada and Europe. Paper presented at "The Political Incorporation of Immigrants in North America and Europe" conference, University of California, Berkeley, March 4–5, 2011.

Bowen, John. *Can Islam be French?* Princeton, NJ: Princeton University Press, 2010.

Brubaker, Rogers. The Return of Assimilation? In *Toward Assimilation and Citizenship*, edited by Christian Joppke and Ewa Morawska. Basingstoke: Palgrave Macmillan, 2003: 39–58.

Cameron, David. Speech to the Munich Security Conference. February 5, 2011. www.number10.gov.uk/news/pms-speech-at-munich-security-conference/.

Citrin, Jack, and Matthew Wright. Are We All Now Multiculturalists, Assimilationists, Neither, or Both? Paper presented at "The Political Incorporation of Immigrants in North America and Europe" conference, University of California, Berkeley, March 4–5, 2011. http://hdl.handle.net/1811/51339.

Conseil d'Etat. Decision on Mme Faiza M., req. no. 286798. June 27, 2008.

Dworkin, Ronald. *A Matter of Principle*. Cambridge, Mass.: Harvard University Press, 1985.

Elster, Jon. *Sour Grapes*. New York: Cambridge University Press, 1983.

European Court of Human Rights (ECHR) (Grand Chamber). *Lautsi and Others v. Italy*. Judgment of March 18, 2011. www.echr.coe.int/echr/resources/hudoc/lautsi_and_others_v__italy.pdf.

Fourest, Caroline. *Frère Tariq*. Paris: Grasset, 2004.

Hansen, Randall. Citizenship Tests: An Unapologetic Defense. In *How Liberal are Citizenship Tests?* edited by Rainer Bauböck and Christian Joppke. Working Papers RSCAS 2010/41, Robert Schuman Centre for Advanced Studies, European University Institute, Florence, 2010: 25–27. http://eudo-citizenship.eu/docs/RSCAS_2010_41.pdf.

Jiménez, Tomás. *Immigrants in the United States: How Well Are They Integrating into Society?* Washington, DC: Migration Policy Institute, 2011. www.migrationpolicy.org/pubs/integration-Jimenez.pdf.

Joppke, Christian. *Selecting by Origins*. Cambridge, Mass.: Harvard University Press, 2005.

Joppke, Christian. Beyond National Models: Civic Integration Policies for Immigrants in Western Europe. *West European Politics* (30) 1: 1–22, 2007.

Joppke, Christian. Minority Rights for Immigrants? *Israel Law Review* (43) 1: 49–66, 2010.

Kymlicka, Will. Testing the Bounds of Liberal Multiculturalism? Paper presented at Canadian Council of Muslim Women's conference "Muslim Women's Equality Rights in the Justice System: Gender, Religion and Pluralism," Toronto, Ontario, April 9, 2005.

Madison, James. The Federalist No. 10. In *The Federalist Papers*. Washington, DC: Library of Congress, 1787. http://thomas.loc.gov/home/histdox/fed_10.html.

Manin, Bernard. *The Principles of Representative Government*. New York: Cambridge University Press, 1997.

March, Andrew. Islamic Foundations for a Social Contract in Non-Muslim Liberal Society. *American Political Science Review* (101) 2: 235–252, 2007.

Ramadan, Tariq. *To Be a European Muslim*. Leicester: Islamic Foundation, 2002.

Rawls, John. *Political Liberalism*. New York: Columbia University Press, 1993.

Sarrazin, Thilo. *Deutschland schafft sich ab: Wie wir unser Land aufs Spiel setzen*. Munich: DVA, 2010.

Zolberg, Ari, and Long Litt Woon. Why Islam is Like Spanish. *Politics and Society* (27) 1: 5–38, 1998.

# Section III:
# Country Perspectives

# Understanding "Canadian Exceptionalism" in Immigration and Pluralism Policy

*Irene Bloemraad*

## Introduction

In many transatlantic countries, we find evidence of significant anti-immigrant sentiment and opposition to multicultural policies directed at immigrants and settled minority groups. Whether among the general public, as measured in opinion polls and votes for far-right parties, or articulated by elected leaders and other elites, such views are found across the political spectrum in Europe and the United States.[50]

Against this backdrop, Canada is a striking outlier. Compared to the citizens of other developed immigrant-receiving countries, Canadians are by far the most open to and optimistic about immigration. In one comparative poll, only 27 percent of those surveyed in Canada agreed that immigration represented more of a problem than an opportunity. In the country that came closest to Canadian opinion, France, the perception of immigration as a problem was significantly higher, at 42 percent. The most widespread objections came from the United Kingdom, where 65 percent of people surveyed saw immigration as more of a problem than an opportunity (GMFUS 2010).

As striking, Canadian public opinion has been supportive of immigration for a long time, and support has been *increasing* over recent

---

50  For more on the relationship between immigration and support for far-right parties in Canada, the United States, and Europe, see Mudde 2012.

decades, a time of economic uncertainty and concerns over foreign terrorists. Asked whether they favor decreasing, increasing, or keeping immigration levels the same, a stable plurality of Canadian respondents, about 45 percent, have favored the status quo between 1975 and 2005.[51] Significantly, the number who wanted to reduce immigration, 43 percent in 1975, declined over this period, while the number favoring more immigration went up. By 2005, roughly equal fifths of respondents held these two positions (ibid.). Another series of polls, asking slightly different questions, indicate that, since 2005, the number of Canadians who feel that there are too many immigrants entering Canada has continued to decline. A significant majority of Canadians surveyed, about two-thirds, said that the number of immigrants coming to Canada was "about right" in 2010 (Survey data from EKOS Research, as reported in Reitz 2011: 9).

These attitudes have no correlation to the underlying proportion of immigrants in the general population, or even the public perception of that proportion. Increasing support for immigration has occurred as Canada has admitted more and more new immigrants. Among transatlantic countries surveyed in 2010, Canada had by far the highest percentage of foreign-born residents, about 20 percent of the population; by comparison, immigrants were only 11 percent of the population in the United Kingdom (GMFUS 2010: 19–20). Canadian optimism about immigration thus exists in a context of high mass migration, with the foreign born making up a far greater proportion of the population in Canada than in countries such as the United States, France, Germany, and Italy.[52]

Canadian exceptionalism is also evident when we consider the competition among Canadian jurisdictions for more immigrants. Not

---

51  Survey data are from the same question asked by Gallup polls in Canada from 1975 to 2005. For an analysis of these data, see Wilkes, Guppy and Farris 2008: 312–314.
52  In the analysis of Canadian public opinion by Wilkes, Guppy, and Farris (2008), they find no statistical relationship between anti-immigrant attitudes and the number of new permanent residents over the 1975–2000 period.

only is the federal government bullish about migration – and has been for quite a while – but every Canadian province and two territories have struck agreements with the federal government so that they can select migrants directly into their jurisdictions through the provincial nominee program.[53] In 2010, 36,428 new permanent immigrants gained entry through provincial nomination, representing 13 percent of all new permanent residents in Canada (CIC 2011: 6).

In comparison, subnational jurisdictions in other federal states – in the United States and in Germany, for example – exhibit significant differences in their reactions to immigration, as evident in subnational legislatures' efforts to discourage or encourage migrants' settlement. In Canada, such regional variation is modest.[54] Asked in a 2010 poll whether they agreed or disagreed with the statement that immigration is "a key positive feature of Canada as a country," 67.2 percent of respondents – the highest level of support – agreed that immigration is positive in the province of British Columbia; this percentage only dropped to 63.3 percent in the Prairies, the provinces with the lowest level of support.[55]

Why is Canada such an outlier?

## Immigration Policy, Economic Growth, and Geography

One frequently cited answer to the question of Canadian exceptionalism is the Canadian points system, which actively selects immigrants based on their potential to join the labor force and contribute to Canada's economy. In the first decade of the 21st century, the majority of new permanent immigrants arriving in Canada, 59 percent, were

---

53  For more information on federal-provincial agreements to bring in new immigrants and to fund settlement services, see Seidle 2010.
54  We find wider regional variation in attitudes toward cultural diversity and multiculturalism policy, as discussed below.
55  Nanos 2010: 11. See also Reitz (2011: 11), who reports regional data for a question with slightly different wording, but comes to a similar conclusion.

economic-class migrants. Such migrants[56] apply for permanent residence papers and are selected by Canadian governments based on their education, language skills, occupational training, work experience, and age, while an additional, smaller group is chosen based on ability to invest in business and job creation in Canada. A further 26 percent of new permanent migrants over the 2001–2010 period entered through family sponsorship, and 11 percent were refugees.[57]

The points system has its critics, and the current government has been keen to modify it – in particular, to reduce the number of immigrants selected for their skills but unable to find highly skilled work. Nonetheless, the economic thrust of Canadian immigration policy presumably alleviates worries about immigration being a drain on the welfare state, a central concern in various European countries. Indeed, Canadians express very high levels of support for the idea that migration is good for the Canadian economy. Seventy percent consider immigration a key tool for Canada to strengthen its economy, while only 32 percent believe that immigrants take jobs away from native-born workers.[58] Over the 1993–2010 period, the proportion of Canadian residents agreeing with the statement that immigration has an overall positive impact on the economy rose from 56 percent to 80 percent (Environics Institute 2011). Even among those who are unemployed, an overwhelming majority – 68 percent – agree with the notion that immigration is beneficial to the economy (Reitz 2011: 13).

There is, of course, some variation in people's attitudes toward immigration. The most determinative factor explaining such variation is an individual's level of education. Whereas 69 percent of those who

56 CIC refers to economic class migrants as distinct from those in family reunification and refugee and humanitarian categories. Economic class migrants include the Federal Skilled Worker Class, the Quebec Skilled Worker Class, the Provincial Nominee Class, the Canadian Experience Class, the Live-in Caregiver Class, the Business Immigration Classes (Investor, Entrepreneur, and Self-Employed Persons), and their immediate family members.

57 Author's calculations from annual figures reported in CIC 2011. The remaining percentage included other pathways to legal permanent residence, including those who move from temporary work or study visas to permanent status.

58 Survey data on the economy comes from Nanos 2010, and on jobs from GMFUS 2010.

have completed university support current rates of immigration, this drops to 43 percent among individuals with a high school degree or less (ibid.: 11). A positive correlation between education and attitudes toward immigration is found in other countries, but it arguably carries extra significance in Canada, given its selection process that favors high-skilled migrants. The possibility that these migrants will compete with highly educated Canadians does not undermine such Canadians' pro-migration attitudes. In countries with less emphasis on high-skilled migration, one can imagine that the educated native-born population faces fewer competitive pressures.[59]

The economic orientation of Canada's immigration system probably also communicates a sense of control over immigration policy absent in places such as the United States, where just under a third of foreign-born residents do not have legal papers and where many perceive the federal government as incapable of dealing effectively with immigration. In a 2010 comparative survey, 48 percent of people in Canada said that the national government was doing a very good or good job on immigration, the highest among all countries surveyed – and double the 24 percent in the United States who said the same.[60]

Canadians are not inoculated against fears of migration, however. Analysis of changes in Canadian attitudes from 1975 to 2000 shows that the proportion of those favoring more restrictive migration has increased somewhat in economically difficult times, regardless of the respondents' own economic situation, though this relationship might be less apparent in the past decade.[61] A survey experiment, in which respondents were asked whether a fictive immigrant should be able to

---

59 Reitz (2011: 12) also finds greater support for immigration among the young, those employed full time, and men, but few statistical differences by income (once controlling for education) or between those living in urban or rural settings.

60 While an approval rating of 48 percent seems modest, it is close to the 54 percent of Canadians who expressed general approval of government. In comparison, 39 percent of Americans approved of the job their government was doing in general, but only 24 percent with the steps taken to manage immigration. See GMFUS 2010: 16.

61 See Wilkes, Guppy, and Farris 2008 on the 1975–2000 period, and Reitz 2011 on more recent trends.

move to and gain citizenship in Canada, found that Canadian respondents were more likely to agree when a person was described as high-skilled rather than low-skilled.[62] Canadians also express some ambivalence about refugee admissions. Environics polls show a significant decline in the proportion of those agreeing with the statement "many people claiming to be refugees are not real refugees," from a high point of 79 percent in 1987 to 59 percent in 2010, but a majority of respondents still agree that many claimants are not "real" refugees (Environics Institute 2011: 30).

Fears over uninvited migrants, especially false asylum-seekers, are readily apparent in periodic public outcries – spurred, for example, by media coverage of ships smuggling foreigners off the Canadian coast. In the summer of 2010, approximately 500 Tamils were found aboard the MV *Sun Sea;* once discovered, the group made claims to refugee status. According to a survey taken at the time, 48 percent of Canadians felt that the boat's passengers should be deported back to Sri Lanka (see Fong 2010). Two months later, in October 2010, the minority Conservative government introduced a bill to target human smuggling; a revised version became law in June 2012 after the Conservatives became a majority in Parliament.[63] Opposition groups, including refugee advocates, denounced the legislation, in part because the bill would allow the government to put certain refugee claimants in mandatory detention for up to 12 months. Those opposing the law claim the government is pandering to anti-refugee sentiment, such as that expressed following the MV *Sun Sea* incident.

Despite fears of "false" asylum-seekers, it is relatively hard for unauthorized migrants to get to Canada. Incidents such as the MV *Sun Sea* controversy occur on an occasional basis, and the number of migrants involved is modest, at most a few hundred people. Indeed, Ca-

---

62  Harrell, Soroka, and Iyengar 2011. The difference between respondents given the profile of a low-skilled construction worker or landscaper or a high-skilled computer programmer or engineer was significant but not dramatic, a 10 percentage point drop in average approval (p. 16).

63  The proposed legislation, Bill C-49, did not become law, but a similar bill, C-31, became law on June 28, 2012.

nadian support for immigration probably owes much to geography: illegal migration laps gently onto Canadian shores; it does not come in large waves. There are no authoritative tallies of the unauthorized population in Canada, although media reports regularly cite between 200,000 and 400,000 individuals, which would constitute 3 to 6 percent of the foreign-born population. These figures are highly speculative but, if roughly accurate, would place the number of migrants without required papers far below figures in the United States, estimated at 11.5 million individuals in 2011 (DHS 2012).

Thus, illegal migration is not a particularly salient public or political issue in Canada. As in other countries, more Canadians are concerned about illegal immigration than legal migration, but, at 50 percent of respondents, their proportion is still quite a bit lower than in the United States, where 61 percent of those surveyed express worry, or in Europe, at 67 percent in 2009 (GMFUS 2009: 10). The contrast with Europe is especially noteworthy given that, in some European countries, the proportion of people without required papers might be comparable to Canada, yet concern about the issue is much greater in Europe.[64]

If irregular migration were to become a salient issue, Canadians' support for immigration might decline. Asked explicitly to consider whether public services, such as state-sponsored health care and public schooling, should be provided to all migrants, legal or not, Canadian respondents tended to express more exclusionary attitudes than populations in a number of European countries.[65] In 2005, when media coverage of unauthorized migrants in Toronto and Montreal put

---

64  For estimates of irregular migrant numbers in European countries, see Clandestino Project 2009. Taking 200,000 and 400,000 as the estimated upper and lower bounds of the number of irregular migrants in Canada yields higher values, as a percentage of a country's total population, for the irregular migrant population in Canada than the estimates for Austria, Denmark, France, Germany, Italy, the Netherlands, and Sweden; similar to Belgium, Ireland, and the United Kingdom; and lower than Greece.

65  Fifty percent of Canadian respondents would provide state-sponsored health care to all migrants, both legal and unauthorized, and only 33 percent would provide access to public schools to all migrants.

the issue in the news for a brief period, one survey sponsored by the federal government found that, nationally, 21 percent of respondents strongly opposed giving legal status to "undocumented skilled workers," 14 percent opposed it "somewhat," 35 percent supported it "somewhat," and only 25 percent strongly supported legalization.[66] Given that the wording of the survey probably privileged attitudes favoring legalization, it seems that Canadians are not particularly open to clandestine migration.

In this context, the current Canadian government's turn to greater use of temporary work visas for migrant laborers carries the danger of increasing anti-immigrant sentiment in the country. Temporary migration goes against the expressed desire of Canadian residents, who favor permanent migration: Compared to eight other countries, respondents in Canada were much more likely, at 80 percent, to favor permanent over temporary migration.[67] Furthermore, if substantial numbers of temporary residents remain in Canada after their visas expire and thus become unauthorized, resentment might rise. As will be argued further in this report, trust in and support for Canadian immigration policy rests in no small measure on a strong preference for permanent over temporary migration.

But are economic selection, geography, and a relatively small population of unauthorized migrants enough to explain Canadian exceptionalism? The British Isles are geographically apart from the continent and share no border with a less-developed country, but public opinion there is decidedly against further migration. In the United States, most migrants work, including the unauthorized, and despite a modest welfare state, Americans are divided about the economic benefits of migration. Indeed, the native born in any country can easily resent rich, highly educated migrants. In Canada, this

---

66 The question states that these unauthorized workers "possess skills that are needed in the Canadian marketplace" and focuses on "skilled workers" rather than all unauthorized residents. See CIC 2005.

67 This was in contrast to the 67 percent of American respondents and 62 percent of Europeans favoring permanent visas over other alternatives; GMFUS 2010: 23.

can be seen in periodic flare-ups in the Vancouver area, where some residents blame well-off Chinese immigrants for making it difficult for ordinary Canadians to enter the exorbitantly priced housing market.

Such flare-ups are quite brief, however; they play out in media commentaries and public debates but almost never result in violence. Riots over immigration and minority issues have occurred in France, the United Kingdom, and Australia over the past decade, but not in Canada. In fact, no riots or incidents of street violence have broken out over diversity issues since the liberalization of immigration laws in the 1960s ushered in massive non-European migration.[68] It is remarkable how peacefully Canada's major cities have transitioned from being predominantly Christian and white to highly multicultural and multireligious.[69]

This quiet transition can be understood only if one recognizes that the Canadian model rests on more than economic selection and favorable geography.

## Immigration, Multiculturalism, and Integration Policy as Nation-Building

A key aspect of the "Canadian model" lies in the view that immigration helps with nation-building. Bolstered by the federal government, this view goes beyond political and intellectual elites to be embraced

68  In the early 20th century, white residents of British Columbia engaged in violent acts against Chinese and Japanese residents and, in 1933, the Christie Pits riots put Torontonians' anti-Semitism on display.
69  Arguably, a partial exception to this claim is the bombing of Air India Flight 182, which resulted in the deaths of over 320 people, the vast majority of whom were Indo-Canadians. But this was about political conflict in India, not Canada, as the bombing was perpetuated by Sikh separatists, some of whom were allegedly operating in Canada. There have been other, more recent cases of planned terrorist plots attempted by Canadians of immigrant backgrounds but, strikingly, these have not generated sustained backlash in the general population against minorities, nor have they provoked anti-immigrant violence.

by a significant proportion of ordinary Canadians. Indeed, one recent paper found that, in Canada, those who expressed more patriotism were also more likely to support immigration and multiculturalism. In the United States, this correlation went in the opposite direction: Those expressing greater patriotism were more likely to express anti-immigrant attitudes (Johnston, Citrin, and Wright, forthcoming).

The Canadian immigration-as-nation-building paradigm is rooted in a particular set of policies and institutions: It is about permanent settlement and integration into a diverse citizenry, where legal systems, public policy, and political structures encourage engagement and membership.

In this way, what at first seems a paradox – high support for immigration in a country with very high levels of new and existing migration – becomes an explanation. Immigrants to Canada generally feel welcomed. Given the predominantly permanent nature of Canadian immigration, government policy promotes integration (often in partnership with community organizations) because it is presumed that both sides are together for the long haul. At the same time, integration does not mean assimilation, given the policy and ideology of multiculturalism articulated by the government. Finally, the overwhelming majority of immigrants acquire citizenship, making it hard for anti-immigrant politicians to gain a foothold. Immigrant votes have consequences for electoral outcomes.

## Permanent Immigration and Settlement

The immigration-as-nation-building paradigm rests on specific features of Canadian policy. As noted earlier, there is very high support for permanent rather than temporary immigration in Canada, with 80 percent of residents preferring the former. One can well imagine that the native-born population has little incentive to see temporary foreigners as future members of the society, or for migrants to feel a sense of inclusion and investment in that society when migration is supposed to be temporary. Historically, Canada has had modest and limited temporary migration programs. Thus, unlike the Bracero program in the United States – arguably a catalyst of today's substantial unauthorized population – or guest-worker programs on the European continent, the vast majority of Canadian migration has been explicitly about permanent settlement (for more on the Bracero program, see Meyers 2005).

Indeed, various temporary labor programs in Canada, such as the live-in-caregiver program, offer visa holders a relatively clear and short pathway to permanent residence. Under the "Canadian Experience Class," introduced in 2008, workers with two years of skilled work experience – which includes work in a skilled trade or technical occupation – can apply for permanent residence based on their experience and demonstrated language skills. Similarly, foreign students who graduate from a Canadian postsecondary institution and who work for a year can also adjust their status to that of a permanent resident. Most analogous programs in other countries, from Japan to the United States, keep migrants temporary. In Canada, 32,827 people transitioned from foreign temporary worker status to permanent residence in 2010, and another 8,667 people moved from temporary student status to permanent residence. This means that 15 percent of total permanent admissions – numbering 280,681 – were individuals already in Canada with a temporary work or study visa (author's calculation from CIC 2011). The proportion of people transitioning from temporary to permanent residence has been increasing over the past decade. In 2001, only 8 percent of permanent residents had previously held temporary work or study visas (ibid.).

Looking to the future, the recent ballooning of temporary visas heralds a new and alarming trend that could upset the pro-immigrant consensus in Canada. The absolute number of temporary residence visas has skyrocketed. In 2001, 186,798 people held temporary work permits in Canada; by 2010, this number stood at 432,682 (CIC 2011: 53). The number of foreign students also increased, though more modestly, from 185,948 in 2001 to 278,146 in 2010 (ibid.). Given the historical reliance on permanent migration as a cornerstone of nation-building, the rapid increase in temporary work visas may be a problem for maintaining public support for migration.

The problem is compounded, in the eyes of some commentators, by the sense that the shift to more temporary visas constitutes a hidden change in immigration policy that has occurred with little public consultation or debate in Parliament. The move to greater use of temporary visas may also lead to problematic outcomes for the migrants involved, especially if they move into the underground economy after their visas expire (Reitz 2010).

## Canadian Multiculturalism

Multiculturalism has played a critical role in reorganizing the symbolic order of membership in Canada. The Bilingualism and Biculturalism Commission of the 1960s, which helped shape what eventually became the multiculturalism policy, still talked about the two "founding races" of Canada: the English (British) and the French. Given the stickiness of national ideologies, it is extraordinary that, within a generation, Canadians have shed these views and that many now support the idea of a diverse citizenry. Indeed, more residents of Canada say that multiculturalism is a key part of Canadian identity than hockey: In 2010, 56 percent of respondents agreed that multiculturalism was "very important" to Canadian identity, compared to just 47 percent for hockey (Environics Institute 2011: 17). This shift has arguably gone further in English-speaking Canada than in Quebec, but even there, Quebecers' embrace of Michaëlle Jean – a Francophone former governor-general who migrated from Haiti to Quebec at a young age – shows that traditional notions of the French-Canadian nation have widened substantially.

Support for multiculturalism and immigration go hand in hand. In 2010, of those who said that multiculturalism was "very important" to Canadian national identity (56 percent of all respondents), 68 percent supported existing levels of immigration. In comparison, only

42 percent of the small group who thought multiculturalism was "unimportant" (12 percent) supported existing immigration.[70]

Why and how has this transformation of national identity – one that includes immigrants – occurred? In part, it is due to the fortuitous timing of multiculturalism's birth. In the 1960s and 1970s, Canadians were searching for a sense of national cohesion that was not British and not American, and one that could in some way accommodate the growing separatist movement in Quebec. Multiculturalism served to distinguish Canada from the perceived American melting pot and from images of a homogenous, Protestant Britishness. It also acknowledged (though insufficiently) Quebecois nationalism, which rests on the cultural specificity of Francophones.[71]

While it is often argued in Europe that traditional immigration countries, such as the United States and Canada, are more able to incorporate an "immigrant" story into their national identities, this greatly underestimates the Britishness of Canadian society until the late 20th century.[72] Government recognition and celebration of diversity, within an overarching Canadian nation, has provided a doorway through which new Canadians can enter into the national community. On the ground, initiatives such as multicultural curricula in

---

70  Reitz 2011: 15. Between these two positions, among those who felt that multiculturalism was "somewhat important" to Canadian identity, 50 percent supported current immigration levels.

71  In fact, many Francophone Quebecers interpreted multiculturalism as undermining their claims to special status within Canada. Thus, rather than being acknowledged as a national minority, they fear that multiculturalism renders them just a small tile, similar in importance to Somali Canadians or Vietnamese Canadians, in the larger mosaic. The Quebec government has consequently articulated its own diversity policy, called "interculturalism," which places more emphasis on French language integration and is seen as distinct from multiculturalism. The actual differences in the two policies are not, however, large.

72  The view of North America as "naturally" more able to incorporate diversity due to its immigrant past also might underestimate the way national histories can be re-imagined even in Europe. For example, in the Dutch case, the migration of persecuted religious minorities dates back centuries and was likely critical to the Netherlands' emergence as a world power during the Golden Age. In Portugal, the spirit and courage of Portuguese explorers is celebrated and could easily be interpreted to celebrate the courage of modern-day migrants.

schools incorporate a history of migration and the contributions of long-standing minorities into the national narrative.

Of course, multiculturalism is not a panacea. While there may be no widespread or strong backlash against public recognition and celebration of diversity, there have been controversies about the use of Sharia during arbitration in the Ontario judicial system, the right of Sikhs to wear turbans in the Royal Canadian Mounted Police and the accommodation of religious minorities in Quebec. Asked whether ethnic groups "should try as much as possible to blend into Canadian society and not form a separate community," 76 percent of Canadian respondents agreed with this sentiment in a 2010 poll. The proportion was the highest in Quebec, where an overwhelming 88 percent agreed that ethnic groups should blend in (Environics Institute 2011: 31).

Canadians' expressed desire that immigrants integrate into the receiving society, rather than maintain separate communities, has been a constant in public opinion polls since the 1970s (Reitz 2011: 16). Such a view should not necessarily be read as opposition to multiculturalism or diversity in the Canadian context. Indeed, the original government pronouncement on multiculturalism, articulated by then-Prime Minister Pierre Elliott Trudeau in a 1971 speech to federal Parliament, promoted multiculturalism precisely because cultural recognition and accommodation were presumed to help facilitate peaceful integration and two-way adjustment by immigrants and the native-born majority. According to an analysis of public opinion conducted by Jeffrey Reitz, a favorable attitude toward multiculturalism "bolsters support for immigration by fostering a more open or flexible standard for assessing immigrant integration, leading people to believe more often that immigrants are meeting that standard" (Reitz 2011: 17). In an important sense, the Canadian story is based on "multicultural integration" rather than an ethnic or civic assimilation strategy or a program of cultural separatism.

It is in Quebec that we see the greatest skepticism toward diversity and multiculturalism policies and a greater preference that immigrants assimilate into the dominant Francophone culture. For example, asked in 2010 whether headscarves worn by Muslim women

158

should be banned in public places, including schools, a majority of Canadians outside Quebec, 52 percent, said this was a bad idea; in Quebec, however, 64 percent of respondents considered it a good idea (Environics Institute 2011: 33). Concern over immigrant integration is distinct from attitudes toward migration more generally; as noted above, Quebecers are similar to other Canadians in their support for current Canadian immigration policy.[73]

Quebecers' distinct views on multiculturalism and accommodation lie partially in a centuries-old concern about Francophones' place in overwhelmingly English North America. Pride in French-Canadian history has also, traditionally, rested on the Catholic faith, although today Quebecers are among the least practicing of any of Canada's faith communities. These two elements – historical Catholicism, but contemporary secularism – make Francophone Quebecers arguably more sensitive about religious accommodations for Orthodox Jews, Sikhs, and practicing Muslims. In addition, it is likely that the greater links between Quebec and French intellectuals might color Francophone Canadians' approach to diversity, especially around issues of Islam, in a way distinct from Anglophones. This is especially apparent in debates around the veil, which some Francophone elites interpret (as do some feminists in France) as an issue of women's subjugation, while among Anglophone Canadians, it is seen more as a debate about freedom of religion.

Among advocates for immigrants and minorities, concerns over multiculturalism take a different form. Some scholars and community groups have suggested that public multiculturalism has provided national and provincial governments with a smoke screen to appear tolerant and inclusive without taking aggressive action on issues of racial discrimination. They point to evidence of unequal economic outcomes for "visible minorities" compared to those of European origins. Statistical analyses of Canadian census data over the past three

---

73 According to an analysis by Reitz (2011: 11), support for immigration policy among Francophones is higher, at 64 percent, compared to Anglophones, at 57 percent, based on a 2010 Focus Canada survey.

decades show that visible minorities tend to earn less than Canadians who are not visible minorities, even after controlling for education, age, and similar determinants of economic outcomes, and even among those born in Canada.[74] Audit studies of job-hunting, in which identical résumés are submitted for the same job, but where researchers vary the ethnic origins of candidates' names and place of birth, find that job applicants with "Anglo" names have an advantage despite identical credentials (Oreopoulos and Dechief 2011).

Inequality in incomes or job prospects based on race or national origin sets off alarm bells, not only for the wasted human capital, but also because economic inequality might undermine minorities' sense of belonging and their subsequent integration into Canadian society – and it might undermine the majority's belief in the economic benefits of migration. Indeed, there is evidence that second-generation visible-minority Canadians perceive higher levels of discrimination than their immigrant parents, perhaps because they expect, but do not receive, equal treatment and opportunities. Thus, whereas 35.5 percent of visible-minority immigrants who had lived in Canada more than ten years perceived discrimination against people of color, the proportion rose to 42.2 percent among those in the second generation (Reitz and Banerjee 2007). Increases in perceived discrimination were especially noteworthy among those with parents with South Asian, African or Afro-Caribbean origins. These perceptions are disquieting, especially when we consider that Canadians are divided as to whether a problem actually exists. In one opinion poll from 2010, 52 percent of respondents disagreed with the statement that "it is more difficult for non-whites to be successful in Canadian society than it is for other groups" (Environics Institute 2011: 32).

---

74  Pendakur and Pendakur 2011. Income inequality varies somewhat by gender, location in Canada, and ethnic background, with some evidence of larger gaps for those with origins in South Asia and the Caribbean, and smaller gaps for those from East Asia. It also appears that inequality is greater in the private sector and much smaller in the public sector, and that it is greater in smaller compared to larger businesses.

Discrimination and inequality of outcomes thus remain serious issues in Canada. On one hand, Canada has established a broad anti-discrimination infrastructure – it ranks, alongside the United States, as the country with the most developed anti-discrimination policies, according to the Migrant Integration Policy Index (MIPEX) survey of 31 countries.[75] A recent survey experiment also suggests that Canadians do not make ethnically based distinctions in their preferences for one group of migrants over another as potential future citizens.[76] But it is also clear that Canadian governments and the general population can do more to ensure that origins and ethnoracial backgrounds do not impede economic integration, given strong evidence of unequal outcomes.

## Institutionalized Inclusion: The Charter and Integration Policies

Permanent migration and ideologies around diversity probably would not matter as much if these notions of inclusive citizenship were not institutionalized. To this end, we find a relatively robust legal structure. The enshrinement of a Charter of Rights and Freedoms in 1982 – which outlawed discrimination, affirmed equality guarantees, protected equity hiring, and even instructed justices to keep the multicultural heritage of Canada in mind when rendering decisions – is one of the top three things that Canadians name as foundation stones of Canadian identity. According to a poll conducted in 2010, 85 percent of respondents rate the health care system as "very important" to Canadian identity, 78 percent say the same thing about the Charter of Rights and Freedoms, and 73 percent name the Canadian flag (Environics Institute 2011: 17). Institutions that facilitate immigrants' in-

---

75  For more on the Migrant Integration Policy Index, see www.mipex.eu/anti-discrimination.

76  Harrell, Soroka, and Iyengar 2011. This was especially true of Anglophone respondents; Francophone respondents were slightly less likely to favor immigration and citizenship for an immigrant from a Middle Eastern country.

clusion, such as the charter, are thus both a source of national pride and a resource that minorities can use to combat unequal treatment.

Other universal public policies, notably health care, also matter. The importance of the health care system to Canadian identity and integration might seem strange to outsiders, but it has to be understood in terms of Canada's relationship to the United States. Since a part of Canadian nation-building is about making distinctions from Americans, Canadians celebrate their universal health care system as compared to the US system, which leaves millions of Americans uninsured. Once more, this is a point around which a majority of native-born Canadians and new Canadians can rally, and thus serves as a source of inclusion.

There are also targeted policies and programs that help explain Canadian exceptionalism. In the 1970s, when Canadian governments began to elaborate an ideology and policy of multiculturalism, they also expanded immigrant settlement and integration policies, including programs to facilitate immigrants' transition into the labor market and to help newcomers learn one of Canada's two official languages. The messages of cultural recognition and the value of diversity are thus accompanied by messages of integration. According to one estimate, projected spending for Citizenship and Immigration Canada's integration programs, including transfers to provincial counterparts, stood at slightly over $1 billion in the 2010/2011 fiscal year (Seidle 2010: 4). Remarkably, the amount has been increasing despite the recent global recession.

Importantly, public funding for integration initiatives gets channeled to community-based organizations. Public-private partnerships are behind the success of Canadian settlement policy. By contracting with community-based organizations, governments send a message that they want to partner with immigrant communities, and that they trust them with public funds. They also allow different migrant communities to offer language training, employment services, and other programs in culturally appropriate ways suited to community needs. Such public-private partnerships help frame integration programs as about helping immigrants find jobs or assisting with social inclusion, rather than as a project by which the majority society "teaches" newcomers proper values, an approach which is predicated on the idea that immigrants come with problematic beliefs.

The lesson from Canada, therefore, is that public and private sectors can work together toward economic and social integration. Such partnerships generate feelings of attachment and membership among immigrants in Canada (see, e.g., Bloemraad 2006). Comparative survey data about the relative importance of ethnicity and the national community in forming identity show that immigrants in Canada are more likely to report that their ethnicity is important to their identity than in the United States – but this does not come at the expense of a sense of national belonging. Indeed, they are also more likely to report attachment to the nation than immigrants in the United States (Wright and Bloemraad 2012). Ethnic and Canadian attachments are complementary, not opposing.

It is important to note that settlement funding and diversity policies provide resources that build the *political* capacity of immigrant communities. This is because such policies fund community organizations and foster community leaders who can speak up and mobilize community members around immigrant issues. In this way, immigrants become engaged in public debates and can attempt to shape future policies.

What evidence do we have that this matters? If we look at citizenship acquisition, we find that an astounding 85 percent of foreign-born individuals who had lived in Canada at least three years (the minimum residency requirement for citizenship) reported Canadian citizenship in the 2006 Census.[77] They became citizens despite the fact that, as a matter of costs and benefits, the advantages of Canadian citizenship are modest: You do not need it for most jobs, to access public health insurance, or to sponsor relatives entering the country. In addition, despite concern in some Canadian corners that certain immigrants acquire citizenship as a passport of convenience, a 2010

---

77 Author's calculation of 2006 Canadian Census data, www12.statcan.ca/census-recensement/2006/rt-td/immcit-eng.cfm.

poll found that almost four out of five immigrants (78 percent) reported stronger attachment to Canada than their country of birth, and another 7 percent felt attached to both equally.[78]

High immigration and high levels of citizenship have created feedback loops that make it difficult for anti-immigrant politicians to gain a foothold in Canadian politics.[79] There is no Canadian Geert Wilders or Pat Buchanan. The early Reform Party, the closest to anti-foreigner populism in contemporary Canadian politics, is now part of the governing Conservative Party, one that actively sought immigrants' support in the 2011 federal election.[80]

Indeed, the remarkable transformation of the Canadian political right is a striking case in point. At its founding in 1987, the Reform Party was antagonistic to multiculturalism and suspicious of immigration. These concerns stemmed from fears of rapid ethnic and cultural change; opponents of the party branded it as racist. In its 1988 "Blue Book," which outlined the nascent party's platform on a myriad political, economic, and social issues, the party proclaimed that "immigration should not be based on race or creed, as it was in the past; nor should it be explicitly designed to radically or suddenly alter the ethnic makeup of Canada, as it increasingly seems to be" (Reform Party 1988: 23). The 1991 Blue Book moderated this stance, dropping language over the "ethnic makeup" of Canada, but it committed the party to opposing "the current concept of multiculturalism and hyphenated Canadianism" and to abolishing the program and ministry dedicated to multiculturalism (Reform Party 1991: 35).

---

78  Environics Institute 2011: 16. Only 13 percent report greater attachment to their country of birth, and 3 percent of respondents said "neither" or "don't know." Percentages do not necessarily add up to 100 percent due to rounding.

79  The Canadian electoral system, where districts with a single representative win by getting a plurality of the votes, also impedes the success of anti-immigrant parties.

80  As Reitz (2011: 4) comments: "In the party leaders' debate preceding the May 2011 election, a voter posed a question on immigration and multiculturalism. Each of the four prime ministerial candidates attempted to adopt the most pro-immigration position, defending policies that aimed to facilitate immigration and promote the interests of immigrants in Canada."

Twenty years later, key activists from the old Reform Party – including the current prime minister, Stephen Harper – form the majority Conservative government in power. To win the 2011 federal elections, the party actively, and successfully, sought out new Canadians, including those termed "visible minorities" in Canada. The Conservative government, apparently in a bid to keep wooing immigrant-origin voters, is staying the course, with significant numbers of new immigrants admitted annually, and it has not made any moves to eliminate multiculturalism policy or rescind the 1988 Multiculturalism Act.

These actions by right-wing politicians in Canada are all the more remarkable given that one recent analysis of Canadians' attitudes toward immigration and multiculturalism show significantly less enthusiasm for either policy among people with strong partisan ties to the Conservative Party (Reitz 2011: 20). Thus, Canada is unlike many other countries where political elites seem to be setting the tone for stronger anti-immigrant and anti-minority discourse.

In fact, all of the federal Canadian political parties count at least one foreign-born member of parliament (MP) among their ranks. Based on unofficial election results, 11 percent of MPs in the House of Commons are foreign born. The proportion of foreign-born MPs in each party ranges from 100 percent (the lone Green Party MP was born in the United States) to 9 percent for the Conservative Party. Even the separatist Bloc Québécois (BQ) has a foreign-born MP (Maria Mourani, born in the Côte d'Ivoire of Lebanese parents), which means a quarter of the BQ's representation is "immigrant." Since so many immigrants have citizenship, and so many feel part of Canadian society, they vote and shape politics. This means that those on the right (and left) must moderate anti-immigrant or anti-minority rhetoric in order to win office.

## Conclusions

In Canada, citizens' support for immigration is widespread among almost all segments of the population and, remarkably, support has been increasing over the past decade despite significant inflows of new migrants, the global recession, and fears over foreign terrorists. Unlike the situation in many other countries, the demographic transformations and diversity brought into Canadian society by immigration have spurred no violence and very little political backlash. The populist and anti-multiculturalist Reform Party, established in the late 1980s, is today incorporated into the majority ruling party, a party that is actively reaching out to visible-minority Canadians and retaining the Canadian policy of mass migration. Among immigrants, identification with Canada is very high and echoes the majority's support for such things as universal health care, the Charter of Rights and Freedoms, and the Canadian flag.

The success of the Canadian model is due in part to the economic orientation of immigration policy; the vast majority of Canadians view immigrants as beneficial to Canada's economic future. The relatively small group of unauthorized migrants, in no small part thanks to Canada's isolated geography, certainly helps cement the pro-immigrant consensus.

As this report has argued, however, economic selection and geography are not sufficient to explain Canadian exceptionalism. The Canadian view of immigration as nation-building is key. Canada has reinvented its national identity away from that of a British colony or a shadow of the United States to one as a society that embraces immigration, diversity, and tolerance. This national project is supported through government policies and ideologies of multiculturalism, anti-discrimination law, and settlement programs that promote integration through public-private partnerships. The focus on permanent, rather than temporary, migration has also been critical since it gives both immigrants and the receiving society a stake in promoting favorable long-term outcomes. Supportive institutions and policies are thus an important part of the story.

We must also recognize the engagement of immigrants and their children in forging a place in Canadian society. Immigrants have revitalized urban spaces, they are working in myriad industries and businesses, and they become citizens at incredibly high rates. The second generation is even more likely to go to university than the children of native-born Canadians and is making inroads in all areas of life, from membership in the House of Commons to winning the top Canadian literary prizes. Canada might have followed the turn – witnessed in other nations – against diversity and immigration if it were not for the fact that most immigrants acquire citizenship and participate in electoral politics, and that the second generation receives automatic Canadian citizenship at birth.

Canada is no utopia, however, and some storm clouds might be gathering on the horizon. To the extent that the Canadian model rests on a firm belief that immigration is good for the economy, reports of inequality between people of different national origins or racial backgrounds is a cause for significant concern. Not only might this undermine majority Canadians' faith in the system if certain immigrant groups are doing badly, but it could generate resentment among the Canadian born of minority background.

The recent move to increased temporary migration also raises significant concerns. Canadians overwhelmingly favor permanent migration. Temporary visas also open up the possibility of a ballooning population of unauthorized migrants if people stay in the country past the expiration date on their visas. There is little evidence that Canadians are particularly sympathetic to unauthorized migrants, and a rapid increase in this population could have a big effect on public opinion.

Finally, Canadian support for diversity and multiculturalism goes hand in hand with the assumption that newcomers will integrate and blend into Canadian society. As in other countries, new migration prompts a certain disquiet. In particular, concerns over religious accommodation – primarily, but not exclusively, centered on Muslim migrants – erupt in periodic media controversy. If a group of political entrepreneurs were to stoke such fears, it is possible that attitudes against immigrants might become more negative. Immigration is both an economic and cultural issue.

At present, however, such concerns appear unlikely. Since immigration and multiculturalism have become part of Canadian nationbuilding and identity, a radical turn against migrants and diversity would necessitate a dramatic change in Canadian nationalism. In addition, unless established immigrant Canadians completely turn their backs on would-be migrants, the significant share of immigrants in the voting population will likely mitigate radical anti-immigrant politics. Time will tell whether Canada continues to be an exception in the area of immigration or whether other transatlantic societies will also modify their national identities in the face of growing immigrant and second-generation populations.

## Works Cited

Bloemraad, Irene. *Becoming a Citizen: Political Incorporation among Immigrants and Refugees in the United States and Canada.* Berkeley: University of California Press, 2006.

CIC – Citizenship and Immigration Canada. *Freeze Frame: Public Environment Overview on Undocumented Workers.* Ottawa: CIC, 2005.

CIC – Citizenship and Immigration Canada. *Facts and Figures: Immigration Overview, Permanent and Temporary Residents, 2010.* Ottawa: CIC, 2011. www.cic.gc.ca/english/pdf/research-stats/facts2010.pdf.

Clandestino Project. *Clandestino Project Final Report.* Athens: Hellenic Foundation for European and Foreign Policy, 2009. http://clandestino.eliamep.gr/wp-content/uploads/2010/03/clandestino-final-report_-november-20091.pdf.

DHS Office of Immigration Statistics. Estimates of the Unauthorized Immigrant Population Residing in the United States: January 2011. *Population Estimates* March 2012. www.dhs.gov/xlibrary/assets/statistics/publications/ois_ill_pe_2011.pdf.

Environics Institute. *Focus Canada 2010.* Toronto: Environics Institute, 2011. www.environicsinstitute.org/uploads/institute-projects/pdf-focuscanada2010.pdf.

Fong, Petti. 3 Months on the MV Sun Sea: Tamil Migrants Describe Their Journey. *Toronto Star* August 21, 2010. www.thestar.com/news/canada/article/850885--3-months-on-the-mv-sun-sea-tamil-migrants-describe-their-journey.

GMFUS – German Marshall Fund of the United States. *Transatlantic Trends: Immigration, Key Findings 2009.* Washington, DC: GMFUS, 2009. http://trends.gmfus.org/files/archived/immigration/doc/TTI_2009_English_Key.pdf.

GMFUS – German Marshall Fund of the United States. *Transatlantic Trends: Immigration, Key Findings 2010.* Washington, DC: GMFUS, 2010. http://trends.gmfus.org/files/archived/immigration/doc/TTI2010_key.pdf.

Harrell, Allison, Stuart Soroka and Shanto Iyengar. Attitudes toward Immigration and Immigrants: The Impact of Economic and Cultural Cues in the US and Canada. Paper presented at the American Political Science Association meetings, Seattle, Wash. August 31–September 3, 2011.

Hoefer, Michael, Nancy Rytina and Bryan Baker. *Estimates of the Unauthorized Immigrant Population Residing in the United States: January 2011.* Washington, DC: Department of Homeland Security, Office of Immigration Statistics, 2012. www.dhs.gov/xlibrary/assets/statistics/publications/ois_ill_pe_2011.pdf.

Johnston, Richard, Jack Citrin and Matthew Wright. National Identity in Canada and the United States: Where do Immigration and Multiculturalism Fit In? *Canadian Journal of Political Science.* Forthcoming.

Meyers, Deborah Waller. *Temporary Worker Programs: A Patchwork Policy Response.* Washington, DC: Migration Policy Institute, 2005. www.migrationpolicy.org/ITFIAF/TFI_12_Meyers.pdf.

Mudde, Cas. *The Relationship Between Immigration and Nativism in Europe and North America.* Washington, DC: Migration Policy Institute, 2012. www.migrationpolicy.org/pubs/Immigration-Nativism.pdf.

Nanos, Nik. Canadians Strongly Support Immigration, But Don't Want Current Levels Increased. *Policy Options* (31) 7: 10–14, 2010. www.irpp.org/po/archive/jul10/nanos.pdf.

Oreopoulos, Philip, and Diane Dechief. Why Do Some Employers Prefer to Interview Matthew, but Not Samir? New Evidence from Toronto, Montreal, and Vancouver. Metropolis British Columbia Working Paper Series No. 11–13. Vancouver: Metropolis British

Columbia, 2011. http://mbc.metropolis.net/assets/uploads/files/wp/2011/WP11-13.pdf.

Pendakur, Krishna, and Ravi Pendakur. Color by Numbers: Minority Earnings in Canada 1995–2005. *Journal of International Migration and Integration* 12: 305–329, 2011.

Reform Party. Platform and Statement of Principles of the Reform Party of Canada. 1988. http://contentdm.ucalgary.ca/cdm4/document.php?CISOROOT=/reform&CISOPTR=197&REC=9.

Reform Party. Reform Party of Canada: Principles and Policies. 1991. http://contentdm.ucalgary.ca/cdm4/document.php?CISOROOT=/reform&CISOPTR=2212&REC=6.

Reitz, Jeffrey G. Selecting Immigrants for the Short Term: Is It Smart in the Long Run? *Policy Options* (31) 7: 12–16, 2010. www.utoronto.ca/ethnicstudies/Reitz2010IRPP.pdf.

Reitz, Jeffrey G. *Pro-immigration Canada: Social and Economic Roots of Popular Views.* Montreal: Institute for Research on Public Policy, 2011. www.irpp.org/pubs/IRPPstudy/IRPP_Study_no20.pdf.

Reitz, Jeffrey G., and Rupa Banerjee. Racial Inequality, Social Cohesion, and Policy Issues in Canada. In *Belonging? Diversity, Recognition and Shared Citizenship in Canada*, edited by Keith Banting, Thomas J. Courchene, and F. Leslie Seidle. Montreal: Institute for Research on Public Policy, 2007: 489–545.

Seidle, F. Leslie. *The Canada-Ontario Immigration Agreement: Assessment and Options for Renewal.* Toronto: Mowat Center for Policy Innovation, 2010. www.mowatcentre.ca/research-topic-mowat.php?mowatResearchID=12.

Wilkes, Rima, Neil Guppy, and Lily Farris. "No Thanks, We're Full": Individual Characteristics, National Context, and Changing Attitudes Toward Immigration. *International Migration Review* (42) 2: 302–329, 2008.

Wright, Matthew, and Irene Bloemraad. Is There a Trade-off between Multiculturalism and Socio-Political Integration? Policy Regimes and Immigrant Incorporation in Comparative Perspective. *Perspectives on Politics* (10) 1: 77–95, 2012.

# French National Identity and Integration: Who Belongs to the National Community?

*Patrick Simon*

## Introduction

How French national identity is both defined and expressed has been the subject of a long and controversial public debate in France since the mid-1980s. In May 2007, the government created the Ministry of Immigration, Integration, National Identity and Co-Development, which, among other things, was tasked with "promoting national identity." Two years later, in November 2009, a "Great Debate on National Identity" was launched by the government with the objective of codifying "what it means to be French." The highly controversial initiative fostered a series of 350 public meetings during its first three months, and a dedicated website received 58,000 submissions as replies to the question chosen by the government: "For you, what does it mean to be French?" (Besson 2010). Perceived more as a political ploy than as a real attempt to foster social cohesion around a unified collective identity (see Davies 2009; Crumley 2009), the "great debate" has indeed revealed the shadow of doubt constantly cast on the loyalty of immigrants and their descendants.

Concerns that the split allegiances of "foreigners" might weaken social cohesion in France are not new; similar claims have been voiced since the early Third Republic (1870–1940) (Schor 1985; Gastaut 2000; Noiriel 2007). In autumn 2010, the radical right of the conservative party issued a parliamentary amendment to ban dual citizenship for French citizens. While the amendment was turned down, the debate resumed again in spring 2011 when high-level officials from the national soccer team criticized promising young players of dual nationality for electing to play with their second-nationality national team instead of the French one. In these recent debates, dual nationality was criticized for its alleged threat to national cohesion and the unfair advantage it brings to those who have choice of loyalty. Dual nationals were urged to make a choice between their citizenships and select one country in which to exercise their political rights. Beyond the practical consequences of dual nationality, the critics focused on the lack of commitment to French national identity among second-generation North Africans and sub-Saharan Africans. Ethnic minorities were accused of fostering the "balkanization" of French society with their "communitarianism"[81] and prompting the decline of social cohesion.

This debate needs to be set against its historical background: the formation of the French nation-state. The incorporation of common norms and values is tied to the sharing of memory, history, sentiments, and attitudes that define a national body. This combination of political and cultural dimensions, outlined in Ernest Renan's *Discours sur la Nation* (1882), was central to the French model of integration from the outset and characterizes most national models in Europe (Brubaker 1992; Thiesse 1999). Seen against this background, the identity of immigrants and their descendants is subject to a range of expectations, questions, and, all too often, suspicions (Weil 2008).

Whereas countries that have adopted multiculturalism treat multiple national or ethnic identities as positive marks of a diverse heritage (e.g., Canada, the United States, Australia, the United Kingdom), assimilationist countries, with France in the lead, tend to insist on exclusive choices and consider the retention of an ethnic identity to be a sign of incomplete assimilation (Bloemraad 2007). Any public claim to an identity combining references to both France and a minority culture or a foreign country – what some might call a "hyphenated

---

81  A French term that is not equivalent to "communitarian" in English. It refers to a propensity to favor in-group networks, interests, and values, and is defined by opposition to participation in society.

identity" – is perceived negatively (Simon 2005). This fear reveals a conception of identity as a sort of finite stock: Any sense of belonging to another country must necessarily weaken an individual's sense of being French. This conception of belonging is challenged by the findings of the *Trajectories and Origins: a Survey on Population Diversity in France (TeO)* survey outlined in this chapter, which polled individuals who claim multiple identities – a claim that theoretically applies as much to the general population as to immigrants and their descendants. To what extent ethnic minorities and "natives" differ in their definition of identity lies at the core of this chapter.

As previously noted, the public debate frames the belonging of immigrants and their descendants in France in terms of a "conflict of loyalty." This chapter puts this discourse in the light of survey respondents' own experiences. Feelings of belonging and constructions of ethnicity will be understood not only as preferences toward a minority identity, but also as a consequence of the repeated experiences of discrimination and stigmatization (see the notion of "reactive identity" developed by Portes and Rumbaut 2001). An analysis of the dialectical relationship between the mainstream society and minority groups continues in the final section. A discussion of French national feeling is framed by responses to the *TeO* survey's open-ended question about origins. What terms (national, geographic, cultural, religious, etc.) do the respondents use to define their origins? Should the results obtained be interpreted as the emergence of a "hybrid" minority identity that does not signify a lack of integration but, rather, the emergence of a "symbolic ethnicity"?[82] Such an ethnicity is not necessarily a reproduction from one generation to the next (from immigrants to their children born in France) but involves the invention of a

---

82  This term was coined by Herbert J. Gans in 1979 to refute the idea that an "ethnic revival" was occurring in the United States. He argued that the increasing use of visible ethnic symbols did not herald a reversal of the processes of integration, but was rather the product of an increasingly upwardly mobile second and third generation choosing easy and intermittent ways of expressing their ethnic identity *precisely because* they were so well-integrated. Rather than defining them, their ethnicity had become a choice or a "symbolic ethnicity." See Gans 1979.

new identity. This creative process is also marked by the patterns of stigmatization and exclusion experienced in French society.

## Methodology

Data on ethnicity are not collected in the French census or in social science surveys. The census asks questions on citizenship and place of birth, which makes it possible to describe the situation of immigrants or foreigners. A few surveys collect data on the second generation (the Labor Force Survey and Housing Survey, for example), but there is an overall lack of data on this population group (Simon 2010). Data on religion, gathered mainly in polls and opinion surveys, are even scarcer.

This chapter analyzes a unique data set from the largest survey ever conducted in France on ethnic minorities,[83] one that asks questions about dual nationality, feelings of national belonging ("being French"), and "feeling at home" in France. *TeO* was conducted in metropolitan France between September 2008 and February 2009 using a sample of 22,000 people. Respondents were divided into five subsamples representing:

- Immigrants (see Appendix: Glossary) (8,500)
- Descendants of immigrants (8,200)
- French migrants from overseas departments (DOMs)[84] (650)

83 The survey is the largest ever conducted of immigrants and the second generation; although other surveys have included immigrants in recent years, none has used such a large sample or covered so many areas of social life. See Beauchemin, Hamel, and Simon 2010.

84 The French Overseas Departments (*départements d'outre-mer*, or DOMs) consist of four non-European territories with a status of "département": French Guiana, Guadeloupe, Martinique, and Réunion. Since May 2011, Mayotte has been made the fifth DOM. The DOMs send representatives to the French Parliament, and DOM inhabitants are full French citizens and, consequently, have the right to vote in elections, including those of the European Parliament. As of January 2011, 2.9 percent of the population of the French Republic lived in the French Overseas Departments; INSEE 2011. There are also French overseas territories with a different status (French Polynesia, New Caledonia, Saint Barthélemy, Saint Martin, Saint Pierre and Miquelon, and Wallis and Futuna).

- The descendants of DOM migrants born in mainland France (750)
- Persons born in mainland France without an immigrant background, from two generations (3,600).

The census records citizenship in three categories that are mutually exclusive: French citizen at birth, French citizen by acquisition (including second generations born in France), and foreigners. Since data on multiple nationalities simply do not exist in official records, the *TeO* survey is the main source of information on dual nationality.

This chapter analyzes the identity patterns of immigrants and their descendants, focusing on how these relate to French national identity. We rely here on self-declaration by respondents.

## French Citizenship Acquisition

According to the *TeO* survey, 41 percent of immigrants aged 18–60 living in metropolitan France are French citizens. Official data on citizenship acquisition state that 143,275 foreigners acquired French nationality in 2010 (Croguennec 2011). Some 94,600 were naturalized by decree, and 22,000 obtained nationality by request following marriage to a French national (ibid.: 8). These are in addition to the 800,000 new citizens who have acquired nationality since the early 2000s.

The acquisition of French citizenship is directly linked to immigrants' age at arrival and length of residence in France; those who arrived younger and who have stayed longer are more likely to be French citizens.[85] Indeed, 64 percent of immigrants who arrived be-

---

85  Immigrants who arrive as children are more likely to acquire French citizenship for two reasons: the effect of the naturalization of their parent(s), and the relative similarity of their position to that of descendants of immigrants born in France, which often leads them to identify themselves as French in the same way. Length of residence is also a determining factor in the decision to be naturalized, since living in a country in a more permanent way transforms people's original purpose at the time of migration. The possibility of returning to the home country grows more distant as attachment to the country of residence increases and the obstacles related to foreign nationality become harder to tolerate.

fore the age of 10 acquired French citizenship, as did 53 percent of those who came between the ages of 10 and 16, and 32 percent of those who arrived after age 16. The assimilation criteria required for naturalization tend to favor the "established" profile, that is, older, married people who are employed and, above all, who have mastered both oral and written French. As a result, in 2008, the average number of years of residence in France for new citizens was 19 years for naturalization and 9.5 years for acquisition of citizenship by marriage.[86]

Children born in France of foreign parents come under a deferred *jus soli* nationality law: They are considered foreigners at birth[87] and automatically become French when they reach 18, or earlier by request. Consequently, the vast majority of descendants of immigrants are French, with less than 3 percent, on average, reporting only a foreign nationality. There is, however, variation across nationalities: The rate increases to 5 percent for descendants of Turkish immigrants and 8 percent for descendants of Portuguese immigrants.

More than 80 percent of Southeast Asian immigrants are French citizens, which may be explained by their lack of intention to return to their country of origin when they came as refugees. Spanish and Italian immigrants also show high rates of French citizenship acquisition, largely explained by the fact that they came as children with their parents.[88] When considering only immigrants who arrived as adults, North Africans and sub-Saharan Africans more frequently acquire French citizenship than southern European immigrants. The harmonization of status for European nationals living in another European Union country has made the acquisition of French nationality less attractive, and it is likely that EU-27 citizens refrain from opting for French citizenship for this reason.

---

86  A minimum of five years' residence is required before applying, and the procedure takes 18 months on average (or a total of 545 days, according to 2008 figures from Ministère de l'intérieur, de l'outre-mer, des collectivités territoriales et de l'immigration 2010: 48).

87  Unless one of their parents was born in France (a case of double *jus soli*, i.e., two generations born in France) or is a French citizen, in which case they are French at birth.

88  Seventy percent of Italian and Spanish immigrants in the survey (aged 18- to 60-years-old) entered France before the age of 16.

## Dual Nationality, Dual Loyalty?

French law permits dual nationality and does not require foreigners who obtain French nationality to give up their original one. It is therefore legally possible for a naturalized immigrant to be a citizen of both France and another nation. The same holds true for descendants of foreigners born in France: When they come of age, they can choose to keep their former nationality or not. One should, however, emphasize that the legal framework is not known by most immigrants and members of the second generation – not to mention the mainstream population.

Dual nationality is not widespread in the mainstream population (see glossary in Appendix), including among those born in foreign countries. Only 4 percent of repatriates and 16 percent of French nationals born abroad reported having dual nationality. Dual nationality is more common among immigrants (21 percent). Nearly half of the immigrants who acquired French nationality have also kept their foreign nationality. Binationals are very rare among Southeast Asians (less than 10 percent), whereas more than two-thirds of North African immigrants, 55 percent of Turkish immigrants, and 43 percent of Portuguese immigrants combine French nationality with that of their countries of origin. Excluding Spanish and Italian immigrants, most immigrants from the EU-27 countries do not apply to naturalize after they have moved to France.

Increasing numbers of naturalized immigrants have been choosing to keep their former nationalities in recent years. The proportion of binationals recorded in the *TeO* survey in 2008 was far higher than in the 1992 *Geographic Mobility and Social Insertion Survey* (MGIS) (Tribalat, Simon, and Riandey 1996: 145–171). For Algerian immigrants, the number of binationals rose from 7 percent in 1992 to 67 percent in 2008; for Portuguese immigrants, from 18 percent to 43 percent. While there have been no notable changes to the law since 1992, immigrant practice with regard to dual nationality has changed considerably. The dramatic growth of binationals has to be understood as a new framing of multiple belongings. For ethnic minorities, having multiple nationalities is seen as compatible with a full commitment to their Frenchness and, indeed, even as an enhancement to their Frenchness. They clearly do not see any contradiction in terms of loyalty.

Descendants of immigrants reveal an attachment to their parents' nationality of origin. While 95 percent are French, nearly one-third of descendants with two immigrant parents report dual nationality. This drops to 13 percent for descendants of mixed parentage. Descendants of Turkish immigrants are the most attached to their parents' nationality, but one-third of descendants of Algerians, Moroccans, and Tunisians are also binational. This is especially significant in the case of Algerians, who, because of their dual *jus soli*,[89] hold French citizenship at birth. However, very few descendants of Southeast Asian immigrants have dual nationality, and it is also quite rare among individuals whose parents originally came from Italy or Spain.

**Table 1: Type of Citizenship, by Population Group\***

|  | French Only | Dual Nationality | Foreign Only | Total |
|---|---|---|---|---|
| Immigrants | 10 | 18 | 72 | 100 |
| Generation 1.5 | 35 | 24 | 41 | 100 |
| 2nd Generation | 62 | 33 | 5 | 100 |
| Generation 2.5 | 87 | 13 | 0 | 100 |
| Mainstream Population | 99 | 1 | 0 | 100 |
| **Total** | **88** | **5** | **7** | **100** |

Note: Population ages 18–50.

\* The groups are defined as (1) immigrants: born abroad with a foreign nationality, arrived in France after 15 years of age; (2) Generation 1.5: born abroad with a foreign nationality, arrived in France before 16 years of age; (3) 2nd generation: born in France from two immigrant parents; (4) Generation 2.5: born in France from mixed parentage; and (5) mainstream: French, born of French parents.

Source: Beauchemin, Hamel, and Simon 2010

89 Defined as being born in France to at least one parent born in France, Article 23 of the French Nationality Law, and Article 19–3 of the Civil Code.

## Nationality and the Sense of Belonging

In addition to collecting data on citizenship, the *TeO* survey asks respondents about something harder to measure: their "national belonging," defined as feelings of attachment to France or their country of origin (or the one of their parents for the second generation). The questions were formulated the same way for all reference territories: "I feel French, Algerian, Guadeloupian, etc." For the descendants of immigrants, the question was duplicated for each parent and referred to the country of origin of the immigrant mother and father. That these questions are separate allows the *TeO* survey to avoid the errors of many immigrant-focused surveys, which confront one identity with another or at least place them in competition. Instead, the identification-focused questions first address France alone and then describe various combinations with a country of origin (of self or parent). A lack of attachment to France does not necessarily mean a preference for another country; it may just as well express a lack of interest in any national feeling. Each answer was broken down in four modalities: "strongly agree," "agree," "disagree," and "strongly disagree." We pick the more assertive feelings ("strongly agree") for references in Tables 2 and 3.

As expected, immigrants differ from other respondents in terms of national feeling: Only 35 percent said they "strongly feel French," as opposed to 81 percent of the mainstream population, and 77 percent of descendants of immigrants (a proportion close to that of the DOM-born and their descendants, 75 percent in both cases; see Tables 2 and 3). Age upon arrival affects national feeling, as does having at least one French parent: Generation 1.5 reports a strong feeling of Frenchness twice as often as immigrants who came as adults, and descendants with a mixed parentage come close to the mainstream population. There is thus a linear rise in French national feeling with each successive immigrant generation, which confirms the incorporation of a national ethos as generations go by.

### Table 2: Feelings of Belonging among Immigrants

| | I feel at home in France | I feel French | | I feel [ethnic label] |
| --- | --- | --- | --- | --- |
| | | All | French Citizens | |
| Metropolitan France | 75 | 81 | 85 | – |
| Mainstream Population | 78 | 88 | 88 | – |
| Immigrants | 51 | 25 | 47 | 62 |
| Generation 1.5 | 66 | 50 | 59 | 46 |
| DOMs | 54 | 75 | 75 | 77 |
| Algeria | 60 | 42 | 56 | 44 |
| Morocco and Tunisia | 63 | 41 | 53 | 55 |
| Sub-Saharan Africa | 42 | 33 | 51 | 60 |
| Southeast Asia | 61 | 40 | 46 | 59 |
| Turkey | 50 | 21 | 37 | 40 |
| Portugal | 69 | 43 | 79 | 54 |
| Spain and Italy | 61 | 36 | 72 | 57 |
| EU-27 | 56 | 22 | 52 | 56 |
| Others | 54 | 31 | 49 | 48 |

Note: Population aged 18–50.

Source: Beauchemin, Hamel, and Simon 2010

This national ethos does, however, vary by origin. As there is a significant impact with the acquisition of French nationality, the percentages are given for all immigrants and only for those who are French citizens. Among the French citizens, a relative distance can be observed among immigrants from Turkey (37 percent of strong feeling of Frenchness), Sub-Saharan Africa, North Africa, and other EU-27 countries (a bit more than 50 percent). The mainstream population is more eager to "strongly agree" (88 percent), as is the case for descendants of parents from Spain, Italy, and other EU-27 countries (86 percent) or from the DOMs (81 percent). Descendants of immigrants report rankings similar to immigrants, with those from outside Europe having lower figures than those with a European background.

If three-quarters of naturalized immigrants "feel French," nationality is not everything. The adoption of a French national feeling among non-naturalized immigrants is quite noteworthy here: More than half of non-naturalized immigrants feel French, and two-thirds of those from North Africa. If a result deserves comment, it is not the lack of adoption of national identity by immigrants and their descendants but, rather, the strength of that adoption.

However, is feeling French the same as "feeling at home in France?" An individual may very well not share a national feeling and yet feel very close to the country where he resides.[90] This is verified in Table 2, which shows that some immigrants may feel at home in France although they do not "feel French." Even though there is a fairly high correlation between the two variables, building one's life in France and feeling attached to the country do not necessarily entail a sense of national belonging. This distinction is revealed by the fact that 61 percent of respondents who do not feel French say that they feel "at home in France."[91] The proportion of immigrants who feel at home in the country is systematically higher than of those who feel French, with particularly high discrepancies among immigrants from Turkey (30 points), from EU-27 countries (35), and from Morocco, Tunisia, Southeast Asia, Spain, and Italy (from 20 to 24 points). Conversely, there are very few people who define themselves as French but do not feel at home where they live. The DOM born represent an exception: 10 percent state that they "feel French" but do not feel at home in metropolitan France. "Feeling at home" encompasses symbolic, affective, and material dimensions of personal investment in one's place of residence (see Duyvendak 2011). Whatever their legal citizenship, most immigrants and members of the second generation consider themselves "locals."

90  Closeness refers to a concrete attachment to a style of life and social codes that do not necessarily transmute into a "national identity." As Evelyne Ribert points out, questions about closeness to the French nation may have more than one meaning and be vague to say the least, especially in quantitative surveys. See Ribert 2006.
91  Fifty-five percent for foreigners, and 70 percent for French citizens.

## Table 3: Feelings of Belonging among Second Generation

|  | I feel at home in France | I feel French | I feel [ethnic label] |
|---|---|---|---|
| Metropolitan France | 75 | 81 | – |
| Mainstream Population | 78 | 88 | – |
| 2nd generation | 69 | 63 | 41 |
| Generation 2.5 | 83 | 85 | 15 |
| DOMs | 68 | 75 | 44 |
| Algeria | 69 | 68 | 32 |
| Morocco and Tunisia | 67 | 64 | 38 |
| Sub-Saharan Africa | 56 | 58 | 34 |
| Southeast Asia | 71 | 66 | 24 |
| Turkey | 64 | 42 | 44 |
| Portugal | 81 | 75 | 37 |
| Spain and Italy | 85 | 85 | 21 |
| EU-27 | 85 | 86 | 9 |
| Others | 75 | 73 | 30 |

Note: Population aged 18–50.

Source: Beauchemin, Hamel, and Simon 2010

### National Identities: A Zero-Sum Game?

The other side of belonging is allegiance to one's country of origin. Public debate systematically portrays multiple allegiances as conflictual, but many immigrants and their descendants see them as complementary. Dual nationality enables them to legally reconcile their simultaneous real commitments, just as declaring one's attachment to the country where one lives *and* the country one comes from (and may often visit) is a type of syncretism that is likely to become more common as globalization intensifies and supranational institutions increase in number. However, the opportunity to combine allegiances and national or ethnic identities is a privilege attached to the condition of migrants. By contrast, the mainstream population has no option when it comes to hyphenating their national identity. This lack of resources may explain the highly sensitive nature of the national-identity issue and the criticisms against dual nationality: Apparently, choices must be made between competing references. The criticism of multiple allegiances – whether such allegiances are legally expressed in dual nationality or symbolic and affective – is based on the assumption that commitment to one country weakens commitment to another. Are the "rules" of this zero-sum game supported by evidence, or must they be abandoned in the face of a new paradigm?

The first observation is that national feeling is relatively strong toward both references: here and there. The second observation is that variation in the intensity of French national feeling is only moderately correlated with that of allegiance to one's country of origin. The relationship between the two is connected rather than competitive. Although a lower intensity of French national feeling is observed among the descendants of immigrants than within the mainstream population, it is not explained by an increased national allegiance to their parents' country of origin. Except for the descendants of Turkish immigrants, where the two allegiances are equally strong (76 percent and 81 percent), the discrepancies in other groups are strongly in favor of France: Among second-generation Algerians, for example, 68 percent said they "feel French," and only 34 percent said they "feel Algerian;" for those of African background, the figures are 58 percent and 34 percent, and for those of Asian background, 66 percent and 24 percent.

A closer look at the different combinations of allegiance results in a typology with four positions: feeling exclusively French, feeling exclusively ethnic/foreign, feeling both, and feeling neither. The fourth combination corresponds to a lack of national feeling of any sort. Figure 1 illustrates the distribution of the four immigration-related groups across the four combinations of allegiance. For immigrants who arrived in France as children and for the descendants of immigrants, a dual allegiance is the most common situation (58 percent and 66 percent, respectively). A stronger allegiance to the country of origin is found mostly among immigrants who arrived as adults (40 percent), while feeling exclusively French is found in significant numbers among descendants of mixed parentage (58 percent). Feeling neither allegiance is rare across all groups (less than 5 percent).

**Figure 1: Feeling French and/or Foreign by Migration Background**

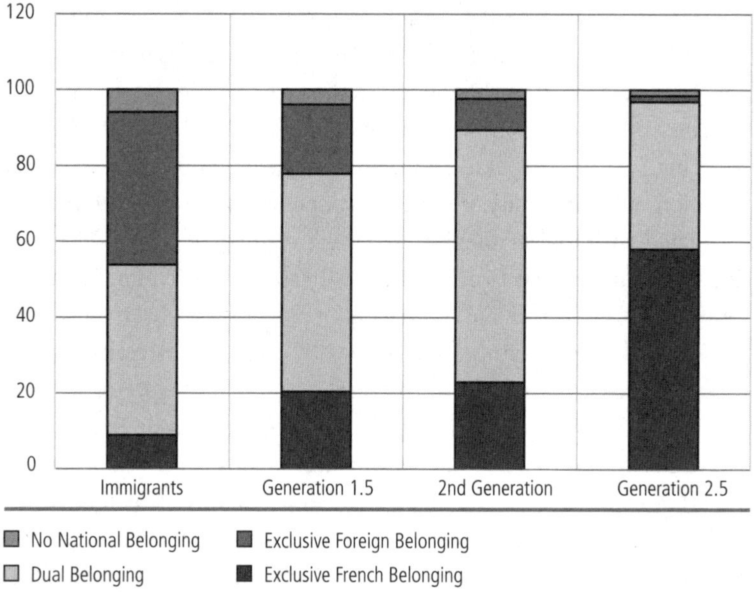

No National Belonging
Dual Belonging
Exclusive Foreign Belonging
Exclusive French Belonging

Source: Beauchemin, Hamel, and Simon 2010

What can be observed is the emergence of a dual allegiance combining identification with France with loyalty to the country of origin (whether of oneself or one's parents). This is becoming the dominant pattern for the second generation. But the opposite seems to be true for the descendants of mixed parentage (Generation 2.5), marking a shift over time from one symbolic and material territory to another. The declining significance of ethnic belonging for Generation 2.5 may reflect the slow pace of the integration process. Whether this decline has to be expected for the third generation depends on the differential.

## Defining One's Origin

The *TeO* survey assessed national identity by asking respondents an open question about their family "origins" that could be very broadly interpreted. The wording was: "When you think about your family history, what would you say your origin(s) is/are? You may give more than one answer." No examples were given. This question referred to the respondent's parents and grandparents ("family history"), while allowing the respondent to make her own personal statement ("your origin[s]"). The reference to family history was intended to guide respondents toward influences that went beyond their own direct experience.[92] Would the responses to the *TeO* survey mention parents' characteristics, or would the idea of origin evoke generations further back or other dimensions of personal identity?

The first fact to be noted about the responses is their wide variety: Even eliminating different spellings of the same proper names, there were 4,630 different responses. Although the question allowed more than one answer, nearly 89 percent of respondents defined their origin in one term, and only 10 percent chose two.

Immigrants and descendants of immigrants, especially those of mixed parentage, were slightly more likely to cite a second reference. The dominant pattern of a single origin contradicts the idea of a plurality inherited from the historic intermixing of populations and regional histories. If assimilation means the erosion of particular regional and ethnic identities, the process seems to be on track in light of this result alone. French assimilationists' political model is *actively* unfavorable to the expression of multiple identities or "hyphenation." This context encourages respondents to make a selection among their origins: Beyond the reality of plural ancestries, answers reflect exclusive choices.

---

92  It is known that responses to this sort of question are basically subjective and only imperfectly reflect the family genealogy. See Mary Waters (1990) for a detailed analysis of the ancestry question in the 1980 US census and its meanings as supplemented by qualitative interviews.

**Table 4: Terms Cited in Response to an Open-Ended Question about Origins (in percent)**

| Cite at least | Immig-rants | 2nd Gene-ration | Genera-tion 2.5 | Main-stream Population | Metro-politan France |
|---|---|---|---|---|---|
| France | 17 | 41 | 66 | 58 | 53 |
| Single quotation | 8 | 23 | 47 | 51 | 45 |
| France + other country | 8 | 15 | 17 | 4 | 6 |
| Other combina-tion | 1 | 3 | 2 | 3 | 2 |
| Country (other than France) | 61 | 45 | 16 | 4 | 13 |
| Region | 2 | 2 | 5 | 17 | 14 |
| Large geogra-phical entity/ continent | 5 | 3 | 4 | 3 | 3 |
| Ethnocultural | 7 | 5 | 5 | 2 | 3 |
| Social and personality | 2 | 2 | 3 | 11 | 9 |
| Cosmopolitan and other wide identities | 3 | 3 | 3 | 4 | 4 |
| No response/ Don't know | 6 | 4 | 4 | 7 | 6 |

Note: Population aged 18–50.

Source: Beauchemin, Hamel, and Simon 2010

The terms mentioned by respondents confirm national identity as the main means of expressing origin: 66 percent cited one or more country names to define their origins; of these, 53 percent cited France. The other terms in the reclassified responses refer to areas similar to countries (regions, continents), explicit ethnocultural references (ethnic groups, such as Berber, Creole, or Kurd; color [black]; or religion), social references (middle-class, modest origins, working-class, rural), family (large family, single-parent family), or personality (honest, sincere). The last group included "multicultural," "cosmopolitan," and "human," together with general remarks and opinions on the question.

It is mainly among the mainstream population that the terms used cover dimensions other than country name. Regional identity is an important form of identification among the mainstream population, and 17 percent used it in lieu of, rather than in addition to, the country.[93] Other responses from the mainstream population concern social background or personality (11 percent). Allowing for the nonspecific nature of the question, the fact that 84 percent of respondents with no migration background in two generations interpreted their origins in national or regional terms shows that this topic is strongly influenced by national debates and internalized by the respondents. This open question could also be used to identify those respondents in the mainstream population who had immigrant origins more than two generations back. Only 4 percent of the majority population cited a country other than France, which shows how the memory of immigrant origins in the third generation and later is eroded by the internalization of French national identity.

The responses of immigrants and their descendants are less varied: Four-fifths of them refer to a country. Few mention social background or personality but, rather, ethnocultural references or geographical regions (Maghreb, Europe, Africa, Asia, etc.). Most cited a combination of France and one or more of the family's countries of origin. Only 8 percent of immigrants named France alone as their origin, out of 17 percent who mentioned France in one way or another. Of descendants of two immigrant parents, 23 percent declared solely French origin, which expresses quite clearly the strength of an assimilation process that tends to dissolve minority identities. Since the question concerns "origins" and not current nationality, one might expect few sole mentions of France where the family roots are in other countries. Paradoxically, the descendants of mixed parentage did not

---

93 Brittany (18 percent of regional citations), well ahead of Alsace (7 percent), is a notable reference, claimed by 3 percent of the mainstream population.

declare plural origins any more than other population groups. The choice of a solely French origin mirrors the *preferences* observed by Mary Waters in her analysis of the answers to the "ancestry question" in the 1980 US census and meets the conclusion of Anthony Perez and Charles Hirschman that "census questions about race and ethnicity measure identity, which is theoretically distinct from ancestry."[94] Consequently, those who combined France and another country in their responses – the hyphenated French – are relatively few, or only 15 percent of descendants of immigrants, with little variation if the parents are of mixed origin.

## "Being" French or "Looking" French?

National feeling is constructed not only by the patterns of attachment and belonging that develop during an individual's life, but also in relation to the perception that others have of one's identity. This interaction is revealed particularly clearly in the dimension of national feeling – a feeling that can be denied by a restrictive definition of national identity based on, say, skin color or sociocultural norms.

We have thus far analyzed indicators of national belonging from the point of view of individuals, but the survey also recorded data about third-party perceptions of "Frenchness." By asking the respondents to consider how they are perceived in their daily lives, this question captures the image of belonging. It is not unusual for there to be dissonance between one's own representation of oneself ("I feel French") and others' perceptions ("but people do not see me as French"). This dissonance is undeniably a source of tension and generates feelings of rejection. While the French population is ethnically and religiously diverse, this diversity is not yet fully incorporated in the representation of "Frenchness." Therefore, visible minorities are

94  In her 1990 study, Mary Waters analyzes the influences on ancestry choices, showing that, for Americans who have multiple ancestries, choice of a single ethnicity is influenced by different factors, including the popularity of ethnicities in public opinion (Waters 1990). See also Perez and Hirschman 2009.

perceived as not belonging to the French mainstream and are frequently singled out as "others." The term "othering" refers to this process of labeling members of the community on the basis of their visibility, primarily skin color, but also language, accent, self-presentation, or surname, which contribute to signaling otherness and thus lead to questions about origins. Two indicators of "othering" have been computed in the survey to measure the extent of the phenomenon (see Table 5). They are completed with two indicators of experiences of racism and discrimination.

Table 5: Indicators of Rejection and Othering, by Group

| | Experience of Racism | Experience of Discrimination | Rejection of Frenchness* | Questions about Origins |
|---|---|---|---|---|
| Immigrants | 30 | 27 | 45 | 32 |
| 2nd Generation | 43 | 31 | 36 | 27 |
| Generation 2.5 | 31 | 17 | 11 | 20 |
| Mainstream Population | 18 | 11 | 4 | 6 |

Note: Population aged 18–50.

* This indicator is calculated only for French citizens.

Source: Beauchemin, Hamel, and Simon 2010

The first indicator is based on the frequency of questions about one's origins. To be frequently asked about where one comes from is not in itself pejorative and does not necessarily imply a value judgment; but, when it recurs, it reinforces a feeling of cultural difference. The second indicator reflects the conviction of not being seen as French ("rejection of Frenchness"). Nearly half of immigrants with French nationality consider that they are not perceived as French. This is also true for one-quarter of descendants of immigrant parents. Second generations with mixed parentage are somehow protected from othering: 11 percent feel rejected from Frenchness compared to 36 percent of descendants of two immigrant parents. The feeling of having one's Frenchness denied clearly follows a "line of visibility" affecting primarily immigrants from sub-Saharan Africa and their descendants, then immigrants and descendants from North Africa, Turkey, and Southeast Asia. The pattern is completely different for immigrants from Europe, who feel accepted in the national community. This acceptance is even more marked among their French-born descendants. Clearly, "Frenchness" is not attributed on the basis of nationality or cultural codes, such as the language spoken, but rather on a restricted vision of who "looks French."

These indicators are correlated with experiences of discrimination more than those of racism. Being perceived as an outsider reinforces the stereotypes and prejudices that foster discrimination.

**Table 6: Indicators of Rejection and "Othering" by Ethnoracial Groups**

|  | Experience of Racism | Experience of Discrimination | Rejection of Frenchness* | Questions about Origins |
|---|---|---|---|---|
| Europeans/ Whites | 23 | 12 | 10 | 18 |
| Africans and DOMs/Blacks | 49 | 39 | 41 | 42 |
| Maghrebians/ Arab | 42 | 34 | 43 | 28 |
| Asians | 33 | 22 | 44 | 38 |
| Turks | 29 | 26 | 43 | 25 |
| Others | 33 | 26 | 24 | 39 |

Note: Population aged 18–50.

* This indicator is calculated only for French citizens.

Source: Beauchemin, Hamel, and Simon 2010

The line of visibility that divides assimilated migrants and second generations and those who remain out the French community is materialized in the classification used in Table 6. In this table, all generations are conflated in a proxy of ethnoracial classification. If only 10 percent of the white (European) group immigrants and their descendants feel the denial of their Frenchness, all other minorities experience the same level of rejection four times more. Blacks and Arabs report significantly more discrimination and racism, meaning that their sense of belonging matches the way they are perceived. Conversely, immigrants and descendants from North Africa, Southeast Asia, and sub-Saharan Africa report a substantial mismatch between their feeling French and the perception of their otherness. The dissonance is even slightly greater for descendants than for immigrants of a given origin. "Othering" is sharper for the second generation: The descendants of postcolonial migrations, who are also the most "visible" in French society, crystallize the tensions surrounding the definition of national identity.

## Conclusions: Compatibility and Coexistence of National and Minority Identities

Multiculturalism is overwhelmingly rejected by French political elites as a model relying on the recognition and valorization of ethnic communities and their cultural differences. It is strongly associated with foreign experiences, especially the British and US models, and perceived as the opposite of the French model of integration. It is seen to conflict with Republican values and national cohesion, and defined only in negative terms: as what the French society is *not* and should not become. It is closely associated with what is referred to as "communitarianism" (*communautarisme*): a form of cultural separatism seen as the inevitable outcome of group recognition and the promotion of cultural differences.

Yet, France is multicultural in the sense that its population is increasingly diverse: Not only do immigrants and the second generation comprise 20 percent of the population in metropolitan France, but these groups reach higher proportions locally – such as 43 percent in the Paris metropolitan area and 75 percent in the *département* of Seine Saint Denis. Diversity has fostered the expression of multiple cultural identities. But despite this "hyper diversity," the French national identity remains more or less unchanged. In 2012, it is still expected that cultural identities will remain settled in the private sphere of life without the need for public or political recognition. The recent debate on national identity and the 2012 presidential campaign have clearly shown that the definitions of "Frenchness" that have been most heatedly promoted do not, unfortunately, offer an inclusive perspective for ethnic minorities but, instead, stigmatize those who allegedly are not "French enough" and who are threatening the national cohesion with their "broken Frenchness."

The findings of the *TeO* survey challenge the idea that plural identities undermine national cohesion. They show that the importance of ethnicity in one's identity does not exclude the development of a French national feeling. Most descendants of immigrants – and many immigrants – share this feeling, even when they do not possess French citizenship (47 percent of immigrant foreign nationals say they feel French). Not only can an ethnic affiliation be maintained alongside a strong French allegiance, but this allegiance does not exclude having a strong national feeling toward one's own or one's parents' country of origin. A pattern of plural allegiances, not necessarily ranked, emerged from the findings of the *TeO* survey, debunking the common belief that trust and civic participation are negatively correlated with higher ethnic retention.

The strength of national identification is confirmed by the responses to an open-ended question on defining one's origins. Given all the possible responses, those respondents whose families have roots outside metropolitan France define themselves mainly in terms of ethnic-national origin, usually citing both France and the country of origin. We might note that these two references are not the same in nature: The country of origin is both a matter of subjective identity and objective fact, whereas for immigrants and descendants of immigrants, to cite France is the expression of an allegiance. To have been born in France shifts the center of gravity of origin but does not eliminate a continued reference to one's parents' country: Three-quarters of descendants of immigrants state it among their origins.

Our results show the formation of what one may call a minority identity that does not contradict, but in fact complements, French national feeling. This identity does not reflect reluctance to incorporate elements from majority society into individual references, as might be predicted by a theory of integration based on a fear of "communitarianism." It is striking to note that over 90 percent of those who mention their ethnicity as a feature of their identity also feel "at home in France." However, the process of adopting plural identities and allegiances – normal practice among most immigrants and their descendants – is impeded by external perceptions. Other members of society can assign people an identity that may contradict or undermine their own self-definition. Immigrants' sense of belonging is hindered less by a withdrawal into their community (not supported by our data) than by the fact that this belonging is not sufficiently recognized. The rejection of Frenchness mainly concerns immigrants but also affects those descendants whose origins are highly visible in the public space. Those from overseas France (DOM) experience a similar paradox despite their long-standing membership in the national community. The concept of "visible minorities," used in connection with discrimination, takes an eloquent shape along this dividing line. Here, we see the attitudes of French society toward its own diversity.

## Policy Implications:
## The Need to Update the National Identity Discourse

Considering the findings of the *TeO* survey, it is hard to support the mainstream discourse and widespread beliefs about the lack of allegiance to the French national identity of immigrants and their descendants. The problem lies in the restrictive definition of this national identity: It ends up excluding visible minorities and Muslims from the national community. The French model of integration pretends to be colorblind and to ensure cohesion through a process of soft assimilation, that is, civic integration and cultural convergence to the mainstream. The counterpart to this soft assimilation is the full equality of rights and opportunities. One can call this give-and-take game a "soft assimilation contract." This contract has, in fact, not been enforced by the receiving society since full admission into the mainstream and the effective equality that should ensue from this invisibilization are not achieved for non-European ethnic minorities. The role of national identity as a framework for equality needs to be profoundly reconsidered:

- The compromise on a "soft assimilation contract" should be revised with respect to the accuracy of the cultural convergence condition. Not only is value of a convergence toward a mainstream culture (itself impossible to define) in question, but the resources for this convergence are hard to identify. More coercive requirements, such as linguistic and civic tests that a significant share of native citizens would not be able to fulfill, are strengthening the boundary between "us" and "them." *Rather than insisting on what immigrants and their descendants should achieve to be part of the national community, an update of the French conception of integration is necessary to make it more efficient.*

- The debate over national identity is divisive rather than inclusive. It does not help incorporate outsiders into the national community; rather, it increases their exclusion by defining national identity negatively, that is, by stating what it should *not* be. *Maintaining an open national identity that is more flexible and adaptive to the new realities of French diversity is the key objective for cohesion policies. Even if multiculturalism as a policy is not an objective in the French context, ethnic and cultural diversity should be acknowledged in a symbolic and practical dimension.*

- The real threat against national cohesion is the persistence of ethnic and racial discrimination, which targets Muslims more than ever. This discrimination is challenging the French model of integration and the Republic's promises of equality. Beyond the loss of opportunities in the labor market and social life, experiences of discrimination are associated with a higher feeling of rejection from Frenchness and a sense of isolation. Ethnic and racial discrimination discredits the value and significance of common values and norms. Instead, it leads to the emergence of a double standard in citizenship. *Positive action against discrimination should be implemented in a more effective way. For a decade now, anti-dis-*

194

*crimination policies have lacked coherence and failed to improve equality. The inability of these policies to change the nature and the extent of discrimination reinforces the feeling among ethnic minorities that they do not deserve the same attention from public authorities.*

– Relations between police forces and minority youths have fueled tensions, sparking sporadic riots – the 2005 riots being an extreme example. Being stopped for identity checks is a common experience for young people from ethnic minorities, as proved by the study done by the Open Society Foundations (OSF 2009). The conviction of being substandard citizens under constant suspicion and harassment by the police is now shared by a large number of these young members of ethnic minorities. Ethnic and racial tensions are partly produced by these relations. *To stop the dreadful dynamic of confrontations and violence, a high-level national symposium with representatives of police forces, nongovernmental organizations (NGOs) from youth in suburbs, key political actors, and academics should be organized to build a shared diagnosis of the situation and revise the practices of stop-and-search.*

## Appendix: Glossary of Terms

*Immigrants:* Persons born abroad with a foreign nationality at birth. This definition excludes French citizens born abroad (children of expatriates, former colonizers).

*Descendants of immigrants:* Persons born in metropolitan France with at least one immigrant parent.

*DOM native born:* Persons born in one of the French overseas departments.

*Descendants of DOM native born:* Persons born in metropolitan France with at least one parent born in a DOM.

*Mainstream population:* Persons who are not immigrants or descendants of one or more immigrant(s) or who are not DOM native born or descendants of one or more DOM native born. Most of the mainstream population is born in metropolitan France with two parents born in metropolitan France, but the group also includes French citizens born abroad (repatriates from the former French colonies or children of expatriates).

*Foreigners:* Persons without French citizenship.

## Works Cited

Beauchemin, Cris, Christelle Hamel, and Patrick Simon (eds.). *Trajectories and Origins: Survey on Population Diversity in France, Initial Findings.* Documents de Travail n° 168. Paris: Institut national d'études démographiques (INED), 2010. www.ined.fr/fichier/t_telechargement/45084/telechargement_fichier_fr_dt168.13 janvier11.pdf .

Besson, Eric. Conclusion of the first phase of the Great Debate on National Identity, November 2, 2009–February 2, 2010. Written remarks by the Minister of Immigration, Integration, National Identity and Co-Development, February 5, 2010. www.immigration.gouv.fr/IMG/pdf/DiscGDINat050210.pdf.

Bloemraad, Irene. Unity in Diversity? Bridging Models of Multiculturalism and Immigrant Integration. *DuBois Review: Social Science Research on Race* (4) 2: 317–336, 2007.

Brubaker, Rogers. *Citizenship and Nationhood in France and Germany.* Cambridge, Mass.: Harvard University Press, 1992.

Croguennec, Yannick. Les acquisitions de la nationalité française en 2010. Infos migrations 25. Paris: Ministère de l'intérieur, de l'outre-mer, des collectivités territoriales et de l'immigration, 2011. www.immigration.gouv.fr/spip.php?page=actus&id_rubrique=254&id_article=2587.

Crumley, Bruce. Berets and Baguette? France Rethinks its Identity. *Time* November 4, 2009. www.time.com/time/world/article/0,8599,1934193,00.html.

Davies, Lizzy. France is Torn Asunder by Great Debate over its National Identity. *The Guardian* November 7, 2009. www.guardian.co.uk/world/2009/nov/08/france-national-identity-debate-race.

Duyvendak, Jan Willem. *The Politics of Home: Belonging and Nostalgia in Europe and the United States*. New York: Palgrave MacMillan, 2011.

Gans, Herbert J. Symbolic Ethnicity: The Future of Ethnic Groups and Culture in America. *Ethnic and Racial Studies* (2) 1: 1–20, 1979.

Gastaut, Yvan. *L'immigration et l'opinion en France sous la Ve République*. Paris: Seuil, 2000.

INSEE – Institut national de la statistique et des études économiques. Estimation de population par région, sexe et grande classe d'âge – Années 1990 à 2010. 2011. www.insee.fr/fr/ppp/bases-de-donnees/donnees-detaillees/estim-pop/estim-pop-reg-sca-1990-2010.xls.

Ministère de l'intérieur, de l'outre-mer, des collectivités territoriales et de l'immigration. *Tableau de bord de l'intégration*. Paris: Département des statistiques, des études et de la documentation, 2010. www.immigration.gouv.fr/IMG/pdf/indicateurs_integration_122010.pdf.

Noiriel, Gérard. *Immigration, antisémitisme et racisme en France (XIXe–XXe siècle): Discours publics, humiliations privées*. Paris: Fayard, 2007.

OSF – Open Society Foundations. *Profiling Minorities: A Study of Stop-And-Search Practices in Paris*. 2009. www.soros.org/initiatives/justice/articles_publications/publications/search_20090630.

Perez, Anthony D., and Charles Hirschman. The Changing Racial and Ethnic Composition of the US Population: Emerging American Identities. *Population and Development Review* (35) 1: 1–51, 2009.

Portes, Alejandro, and Rubén Rumbaut. *Legacies: The Story of the Immigrant Second Generation*. Berkeley: University of California Press, 2001.

Ribert, Evelyne. *Liberté, égalité, carte d'identité: les jeunes issus de l'immigration et l'appartenance nationale*. Paris: La Découverte, 2006.

Schor, Ralph. *L'opinion française et les étrangers en France: 1919–1939*. Paris: Publication de la Sorbonne, 1985.

Simon, Patrick. La République face à la diversité: comment décoloniser les imaginaires? In *La fracture coloniale*, edited by Nicolas Bancel, Pascal Blanchard, and Sandrine Lemaire. Paris. La Découverte, 2005: 237–246.

Simon, Patrick. Statistics, French Social Science and Ethnic and Racial Relations. *Revue Française de Sociologie* 51: 159–174, 2010.

Thiesse, Anne-Marie. *La création des identités nationales. Europe XIIIe–XXe siècle*. Paris: Seuil, 1999.

Tribalat, Michéle, Patrick Simon, and Benoît Riandey. *De l'immigration à l'assimilation. Enquête sur les populations d'origine étrangère en France*. Paris: La Découverte, 1996.

Waters, Mary. *Ethnic Options: Choosing Identities in America*. Berkeley and Los Angeles: University of California Press, 1990.

Weil, Patrick. *Liberté, Égalité, Discriminations: "L'identité nationale" au regard de l'histoire*. Paris: Grasset, 2008.

# Contested Ground:
# Immigration in the United States

*Michael Jones-Correa*

## Introduction

The United States is in the midst of a sustained period of immigration that began in the 1960s. This has coincided with the nation's transition from a manufacturing to a service economy, a rise in wage inequality (Tienda and Mitchell 2006; Levy 1998; Danziger and Gottschalk 1993), and the overall aging of the population as the baby-boomer generation approaches retirement (Myers 2007). Between 1960 and 2000, immigration (and immigrant fertility) not only added over 47 million people to the US population, but also brought about unprecedented ethnic and racial diversity, dramatically altering the demography of the country. The diversification of the migrant streams to the United States and the fact that a significant percentage of these flows are unauthorized have both contributed to the tenor of the immigration debate.

This chapter outlines trends in recent immigration to the United States; the anxieties triggered by this immigration, complicated by the current economic downturn and demographic change; the policy response at the national and state levels; and the unexamined implications of the second generation – the children of immigrants – and their role in American society. As the chapter looks at the reasons for the current unease around US immigration, it points out that the fixation on state and federal enforcement as the primary response overlooks a central fact: However much immigrants are debated or deported, the demographic future of the country will be shaped by their children.

## A Nation of Immigrants

The United States has a long history of immigration and is often described as a nation of immigrants. In 2010, nearly 40 million of the approximately 309 million residents of the United States were foreign born (US Census Bureau, American Community Survey). The United States currently grants legal permanent residence to more than 1 million immigrants every year – more than any other country in the world (DHS Office of Immigration Statistics 2012a). During the 1990s alone, over 14 million immigrants arrived to the United States (Meissner et al. 2006); another 13 million arrived between 2000 and 2010 (US Census Bureau 2010, Table 2.1). However, the United States has sometimes been ambivalent about immigration, and this ambivalence is often more pronounced as immigration flows peak, as is the case today.

Alongside this increase, there have been three other key changes in immigration patterns over the past four decades: a shift in the country of origin of immigrants to the United States, an increasing proportion of illegal immigration, and the geographic dispersal of immigrant settlement beyond traditional destinations. As illustrated in Figure 1, in 1970, soon after the passage of the landmark 1965 immi-

**Figure 1: Immigration to the United States, by Region of Origin, 1970 and 2010**

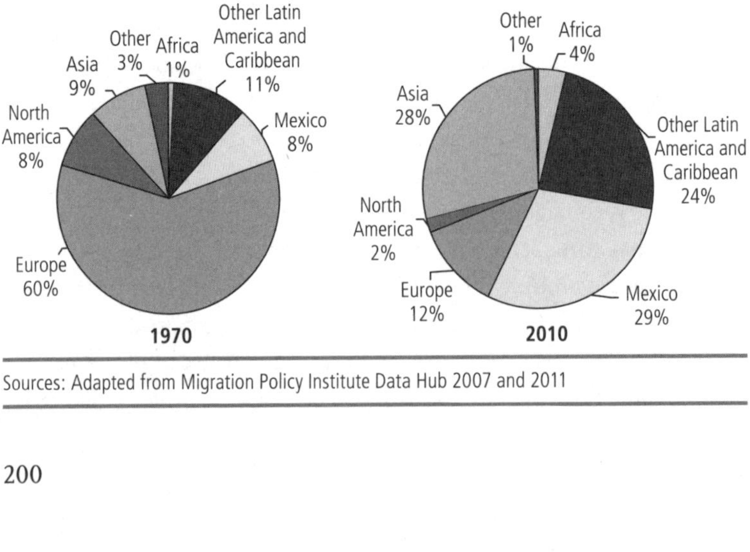

Sources: Adapted from Migration Policy Institute Data Hub 2007 and 2011

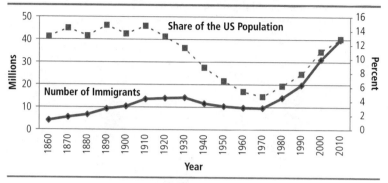

**Figure 2: Foreign-Born Population in the United States, 1860–2010**

Source: Migration Policy Institute Data Hub 2010

gration act that would trigger dramatic changes in the composition of immigration to the United States, most of the immigration flows to the United States were still from Europe. Forty years later, arrivals from Europe make up about one in ten immigrants. Most now arrive from Latin America and Asia. More than half of all immigrants come from Latin America, 29 percent from Mexico alone. Arrivals from Asia make up 28 percent of recent immigrants.

More immigrants are coming to the United States from more places than ever before but, in percentage terms, the United States is only now approximating the scale of immigration last reached a hundred years ago. Immigrants today make up about 13 percent of the US population, but this is still below the peak reached during the last great wave of immigration (see Figure 2). Of the 39 million foreign-born residents in the United States, 17 million are naturalized citizens. That leaves 22 million who are not citizens, about half of whom are thought to lack the authorization to live or work in the United States (Martin and Midgley 2010).

Immigration has long been concentrated in certain states, such as California, Texas, New York, and Florida. But the recent flows are increasingly dispersed, with immigrants gathering in metropolitan areas and smaller localities across the country – including places that

## Figure 3: States with the Largest and Fastest-Growing Immigrant Populations, 1990–2009

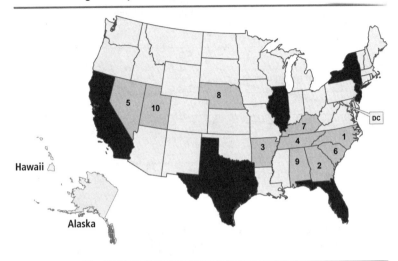

■ States with 1.7 million or more immigrants (2010)
☐ States (ranked) with 280 percent or higher growth (1990 to 2010)

Source: Migration Policy Institute Data Hub 2011

had experienced little in the way of immigration over the last century (Singer, Hardwick, and Brettell 2008; Odem and Lacy 2009).

The map above (Figure 3) illustrates how the states with the fastest-growing immigrant populations between 1990 and 2009 were those with little recent immigration experience.

The seven states experiencing the most rapid change over this period were North Carolina, Georgia, Arkansas, Nevada, Tennessee, South Carolina, and Nebraska. None of these had attracted significant numbers of immigrants before 1990. In each of them, the immigrant population increased by at least 200 percent between 1990 and 2000. Immigration to these new receiving areas is overwhelmingly Latin American in origin and, in many Southern and Midwestern states, a significant portion of this migrant flow is unauthorized or "illegal." Arriving in smaller towns and cities to work in agriculture, construc-

202

tion, meat processing, furniture manufacturing, and other industries, Latino migrants have dramatically altered local populations and, in the South, introduced a new dynamic into historical black/white racial relations. In short, as early as 2000 and certainly by 2010, recent immigration to the United States had reshaped the demographics of almost every state, introducing new ethnic diversity, particularly from Latin America, and eliciting strong local reactions, which in turn sharpened the national debate on immigration.

## Anxieties about Immigration

Together, these four factors – the scale of immigration, its increasing ethnic diversity, the fact that a substantial portion of it is unauthorized, and its dispersal across the country over a short period of time – have triggered unease about immigrants and their role in American society. This unease has complicated attempts in Congress to pass comprehensive reform of the immigration system. The last successful effort to tackle major reform of the immigration system was in 1986 (major efforts in 2006 and 2007 foundered in Congress); then, as now, there was considerable disagreement about how to respond to the influx of immigrants, many of them entering the country illegally. On the one hand, there is a sizeable business lobby that benefits from these labor flows, both skilled and unskilled, and would like to see them continue. This lobby is bolstered by immigrant advocates who would like unauthorized immigrants to have some kind of pathway to legalization, and by Hispanic voters who increasingly interpret anti-immigrant rhetoric as aimed not only at those without papers, but at all Hispanics. On the other hand are restrictionists, who argue that America's porous borders impact native-born employment and contribute to the erosion of American society and culture.

It would be a mistake to interpret the debate around immigration as solely about economics (Papademetriou and Terrazas 2009). While immigration anxieties have been aggravated by the recession that began in 2008 and the lagging recovery, the correlation between anti-immigrant sentiment and the nation's economic performance has weakened overall since the mid-1990s. This is illustrated by Figure 4, which charts public opinion on restricting immigration against unemployment rates in the United States from 1987 to 2010. As the impact of immigration has been felt in localities around the United States, it became clear that immigration anxieties were more than just about economics.

The greatest support for curtailing immigration was seen in the early to mid-1990s. This period also saw the implementation of the North American Free Trade Agreement (NAFTA), which lowered trade barriers with Canada and Mexico but arguably increased pressures on American workers. Also during this time, then-governor Pete Wilson pushed for the passage of Proposition 187 in California,

**Figure 4: Views on Immigration Restriction vs. Unemployment in the United States, 1987–2010**

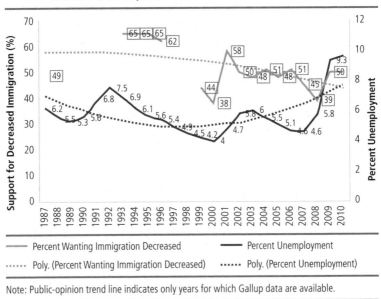

Note: Public-opinion trend line indicates only years for which Gallup data are available.

Source: Gallup 2011; Bureau of Economic Analysis, n.d.

which passed by a wide margin and intended to withhold a wide range of government benefits from unauthorized immigrants in the state.[95] In 1996, Wilson and Pat Buchanan both ran for president on populist, anti-immigrant platforms. Meanwhile, Congress approved the 1996 welfare reform act, which included restrictions on federal benefits to both legal and unauthorized immigrants.

Public opinion favoring restrictions on immigration has trended downward since the mid-1990s, even taking into account an upward spike in restrictionist sentiment following the 9/11 attacks in 2001 and again since the recession started in 2008. However, even when unemployment rates recently soared as high as 9.6 percent, public opinion favoring immigration restrictions did not touch the highs reached in the mid-1990s, when the economy was expanding briskly and the unemployment rate was about half what it was in 2010.

If not just reflecting economic concerns, what explains anti-immigrant sentiment in the United States? Public-opinion data reflect concerns that immigration is *changing* society, largely for the worse. Results from national surveys indicate that while a significant number of respondents believe that immigrants negatively affect the job opportunities of native-born Americans and make the economy worse off in general, most respondents believe, in addition, that immigrants increase crime rates, drive up tax burdens, and encourage the deterioration of social and moral values (Gallup 2011). Significant percentages of the native born believe that recent immigrants are a negative influence on American society. This is compounded by the fact that American society is aging.[96] Today's elderly – who exercise disproportionate influence on the political system – came of age during a lull in immigration to the United States, before the effects of the 1965 immigra-

---

95 The California referendum Proposition 187 passed in November 1994, denying unauthorized immigrants access to public education, medical care, and a variety of other services. Immediately challenged in court, Proposition 187 was never implemented; its provisions were ruled unconstitutional. See Nieves 1999.
96 See Frey 2011. Frey notes that the population that is 45 years and over in the United States grew 18 times as fast as the population under 45 years between 2000 and 2010.

tion reform were felt. The America they recall from their youth was considerably more racially and ethnically homogenous. This generation is the most likely to feel threatened by the recent influx of immigrants (Parker and Barreto 2011; see also Salam 2011).

Their concerns, however, are countered by existing evidence. For instance, one recent study indicates that there is no proof that immigrants crowd out US-born workers in the short or long run and that, over the long run, immigration actually increases income per worker. The study found that immigration to the United States from 1990 to 2007 was associated with a 6.6 to 9.9 percent increase in real income per worker (Peri 2010). Similarly, there is evidence that higher proportions of the foreign born and new immigrants appear to *decrease*, not increase, robbery and homicide rates (Wadsworth 2010; see also Butcher and Piehl 2008). Countering concerns that English will be taken over by Spanish, all the data on language acquisition indicate that immigrants and their children learn English, and that, indeed, within a single generation, the children of immigrants use English as their primary and often only language (Portes and Rumbaut 2001; see also the results from the 2006 *Latino National Survey*, presented in Fraga et al. 2012).

To point to research indicating that immigrants learn English, that immigration is not, as a whole, detrimental to the job prospects of the native born (see also Smith and Edmonston 1997; Borjas 2006; Card 2001, 2007 and 2009; Card and Lewis 2007) or that the presence of immigrants is correlated with a reduction rather than an increase in crime (Ousey and Kubrin 2009; Martinez Jr. 2006; Butcher and Piehl 1998) does not necessarily make anxieties about immigration any less real to the people who have them. The anxieties of the native born may not be objectively borne out but, rather, capture concerns about loss and dislocation, about once-familiar communities undergoing change. These concerns are illustrated by an oft-repeated story: Older residents tell of walking into a neighborhood grocery store only to hear Spanish and no English being spoken, triggering feelings of displacement and anger. It is these anxieties among the native born that, real or not, fuel restrictionist immigration policy.

## Developments in Immigration Policy

### Federal Enforcement

Anxieties triggered by changing communities have been tugging national immigration policy in the United States in a more restrictive direction since the 1970s – though, remarkably enough, the emphasis on family reunification that has been at the center of US immigration policy since 1965 remains in place. However, other aspects of immigration, particularly around illegal migration, have been receiving increased scrutiny. Enforcement along the US-Mexico border has increased, as have removals of unauthorized immigrants residing in the United States, sometimes in partnership with local law-enforcement agencies.

Beginning in the 1980s, in a trend that accelerated dramatically after the September 11, 2001 terrorist attacks, the United States began to bolster the policing of its borders (particularly its border with Mexico) as well as its capacity to arrest and deport unauthorized immigrants already in the country. These efforts accelerated after 2003, when, in response to the 9/11 attacks, the newly constituted Department of Homeland Security (DHS) expanded its immigration-enforcement capabilities (DHS 2005). Detentions and returns at the border peaked in 2000 at 1.7 million, then declined steadily (see Figure 5) to just over 476,000 in 2010, the lowest number of apprehensions at the border since 1972.

As border detentions dropped, attention shifted to immigration enforcement in the interior of the country (DHS 2006). In the years following the passage of the 1986 *Immigration Reform and Control Act* (IRCA), work-site investigations focused principally on fining the employers of unauthorized workers. However, the popular backlash against the 2006 immigration marches, in which millions of Latinos and other immigrants turned out in major cities across the United States to call for comprehensive immigration reform and a path to legalization for the more than 11 million unauthorized residents then living in the United States (Pew Hispanic Center 2006) – and the fail-

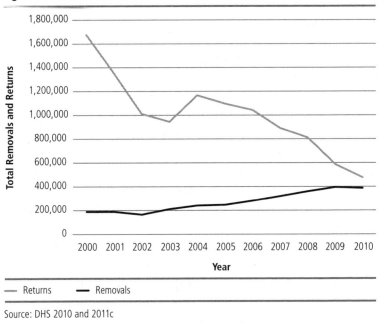

**Figure 5: ICE Removals and Returns of Non-citizens, FY2000–2010**

Source: DHS 2010 and 2011c

ure of reform efforts in Congress in 2006 and 2007 – marked a significant shift in US immigration enforcement policy. Under the new work-site enforcement policy, workplace raids began targeting unauthorized workers, not the employers who had hired them. Following this shift, workplace arrests increased steadily, from 510 arrests in fiscal year (FY) 2002 to 6,287 arrests in FY 2008 (see Figure 6).

Similarly, "fugitive operations teams" set up throughout the United States to track down, detain, and deport unauthorized immigrants who had failed to show up for deportation hearings or had other complications with the law (including criminal records) expanded substantially after 2003, when they were first instituted. Arrests of "fugitive" unauthorized immigrants increased from 1,900 in 2003 to over 34,000 arrests in 2008 (see Figure 7). These fugitive operations arrests, while not as high-profile as the Immigration and Customs Enforcement (ICE) workplace raids, affected many more individuals.

**Figure 6: ICE Work-site Enforcement Arrests by Fiscal Year, 2002–2010**

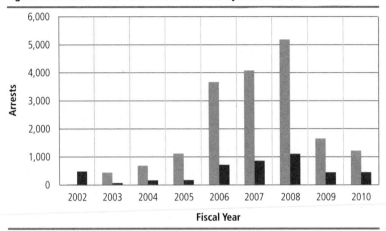

**Fiscal Year**

☐ Administrative Arrests    ■ Criminal Arrests

Sources: 2002–2008 data: US Immigration and Customs Enforcement 2009;
2009 data: Bruno 2011, Table 3

Such policies were pursued most vigorously under the Bush administration. Under the Obama administration, there has been a shift not in law, but in practice, as Obama has tried to keep his promise to supporters, particularly Latino voters, that he would move away from punitive anti-immigrant policies. As a result, immigrant arrests carried out in the course of workplace enforcement (see Figure 6) declined significantly between FY2008 and FY2009, as the new administration indicated that it would redirect ICE resources to the criminal prosecution of employers hiring illegal workers, which it called the "root cause of illegal immigration" (US Immigration and Customs Enforcement 2009).

On the other hand, Obama has tried to placate conservatives who have signaled that immigration enforcement is a precondition to any comprehensive immigration reform, presiding over a record number of removals (US Immigration and Customs Enforcement n.d.). The Obama administration has not shied away from several enforcement initiatives put into effect in the Bush years, in particular, partnerships

209

**Figure 7: Fugitive Operations Team Arrests, 2003–2008**

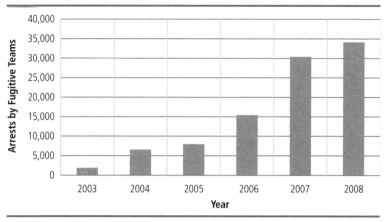

Source: US Immigrant and Customs Enforcement 2011b

between DHS and local law-enforcement agencies meant to better identify and deport unauthorized immigrants (US Immigration and Customs Enforcement 2011a). By the end of the Bush administration, 69 state and local police agencies had entered into agreements with DHS to cooperate on immigration enforcement (ibid.). Over 217,000 persons have been identified for deportation as the result of these agreements (ibid.). Under the Obama administration, these arrangements have morphed into a broader program titled Secure Communities (ABC News 2011; see also Homeland Security Advisory Council 2011). This program, now implemented in 48 states, is designed to target criminal aliens once in custody, aiding local law enforcement in their identification and removal (US Immigration and Customs Enforcement 2012). Over 387,000 non-citizens were deported in 2010 alone – almost double the number in 2000 (see Table 5).

Recent trends indicate a sharp drop in border apprehensions (DHS Office of Immigration Statistics 2011b), the result of a combination of increased policing at the US-Mexico border, a slowing economy in the United States, and growing opportunities in Mexico. As noted, there has been a shift away from work-site enforcement toward the expansion of a variety of programs to apprehend unauthorized immigrants within the United States. There are now almost as many unauthorized migrants arrested and deported through these programs as there are detained at the border (DHS Office of Immigration Statistics 2011a). Meanwhile, the dilemma of the millions residing in the country without documents remains unresolved, and the United States is perhaps further away from a major overhaul of its immigration system than it ever has been.

## State and Local Responses

Even before the failure of federal immigration reform in Congress in 2006 and 2007, the responsibility for immigration policy had been shifting to states and localities.[97] The rapid pace of immigration, dispersed to new places and perceived through the lens of social anxiety, prompted a wide variety of legislation at the state and local levels (Varsanyi 2010a; Olivas 2007). States, localities, and communities in the United States have responded in various ways to the increased presence of immigrants, implementing radically different immigration policies (Varsanyi 2010b; Walker 2010), ranging from relatively benign accommodation to outright hostility, presumably with very different outcomes for immigrant settlement and integration.

The number of bills introduced in state legislatures increased fourfold between 2005 and 2010, and the legislation enacted by the states increased ten times during this six-year period (see Figure 8). A majority of this legislation was designed to discourage illegal immigration. A number of states, most notably Arizona, Georgia, Indiana, Alabama, and South Carolina, have passed sweeping legislation targeting unauthorized immigrants. The *Legal Arizona Workers Act*, passed in 2007, requires all employers in the state to use the federal

---

97  For instance, the 1996 federal welfare reform act gave states the leeway to exclude permanent legal residents from federal programs, and states chose very different paths in addressing issues such as insurance coverage for the children of unauthorized immigrants, with some states choosing universal coverage (Massachusetts) and other states choosing dramatically reduced coverage (Texas).

**Figure 8: Immigration-Related Legislation Introduced and Enacted at the State Level, 2005–2010**

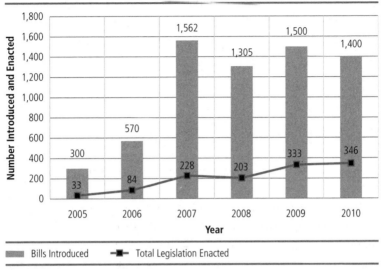

Source: National Conference of State Legislatures, n.d.

E-Verify program to check on the legal status of all employees. A ruling by the US Supreme Court in June 2011 upholding the Arizona employment verification law left the path clear for similar laws in Alabama, Georgia, Mississippi, South Carolina, and Utah to move forward (*Chamber of Commerce of the United States v. Whiting*).

Arizona's disputed SB 1070 law, while still awaiting full resolution of legal challenges, has also been emulated by several other states. It gives local police broad scope to detain suspected unauthorized immigrants and, if unable to show proof of legal residency, to arrest them pending federal confirmation of their legal status (Archibold 2010). Alabama, Georgia, Indiana, and South Carolina have passed similar legislation, in some respects going even further. Alabama's legislation, for instance, in addition to having provisions on the role of local law enforcement and requirements for the use of E-Verify, also bars unauthorized immigrants from attending public colleges in Alabama, asks public schools to determine the citizenship and immigra-

212

tion status of all students and report their findings to state officials, and makes it a felony to transport an unauthorized immigrant (Chishti and Bergeron 2011a; Associated Press 2011). Much of this legislation is now being challenged in the courts (Severson 2011; Chishti and Bergeron 2011b; Berkes 2011).

On the other hand, some states are taking a more positive approach to immigration. Utah's state legislature, while supporting an expanded role by local enforcement and a requirement for all employers to use E-Verify, also issued a "compact" outlining the state's commitment to the inclusion of immigrants[98] and, until recently, states such as Tennessee issued "driving certificates" to non-citizen residents (see Tennessee Department of Safety and Homeland Security, n.d.). Four states – Alaska, Montana, New Mexico, and Oregon – explicitly prohibit the use of state resources for the purpose of immigration enforcement (National Immigration Law Center 2008). Even as other states move to require employers in their states to check on employees' legal status, Illinois restricts employers' use of the federal government's E-Verify system (*Illinois Right to Privacy in the Workplace Act*). In 2011, Maryland approved a measure that would allow some unauthorized immigrants to pay in-state tuition to state colleges and universities, joining ten other states (Davis 2011; Russell 2007), while Illinois has proposed establishing a scholarship fund for the children of immigrants seeking to attend college (Chishti and Bergeron 2011b).

There is a similar differentiation of approaches at the local level, too. At least a dozen municipalities have passed local ordinances restricting unauthorized immigrants' access to housing and employment, though most of these have been successfully challenged in the courts.[99] At the same time, however, other municipalities have been working to foster immigrant integration into American society. For instance, two municipalities – San Francisco, Calif., and New Haven,

---

98   *New York Times* 2010. The Utah Compact has been taken up as a model by other states, see: http://pachurchesadvocacy.org/weblog/?p=8367; Graham 2011.

99   See, for example, *Lozano v. City of Hazleton, 496 F. Supp. 2d 477* (M.D.Pa. 2007), which struck down an ordinance restricting the housing or employment of unauthorized aliens on pre-emption and Fourteenth Amendment grounds.

Conn. – have issued municipal identity cards to allow their residents, regardless of legal status, access to both public and private services, ranging from health care to banking (Junta for Progressive Action, Inc. and Unidad Latina en Acción 2005; Buchanan 2007). Accommodation and adaptation has been taking place in states with new, fast-growing immigrant populations, as well: In 2009, voters in Nashville, Tenn., rejected a proposal under a referendum election to prohibit the city's government from using languages other than English. The initiative failed by a substantial margin (Cowles 2009). Several dozen jurisdictions (such as Asheville, N.C.) in 23 states have enacted laws that seek to keep police and immigration enforcement separate so as to preserve immigrants' access to public life and civic participation (Department of Justice, Office of the Inspector General, Audit Division 2007; Seghetti, Vina, and Ester 2006; National Immigration Law Center 2008). These include some of the largest cities in the United States – such as New York City, Los Angeles, San Francisco, the District of Columbia, Chicago, Baltimore, Boston, Detroit, Minneapolis, St. Louis, Newark, Philadelphia, Austin, and Seattle – all of which have passed legislation limiting the role of local law enforcement in applying federal immigration laws (Loftin 2011) with the support of their police chiefs, who were increasingly concerned that local enforcement of immigration would "undermine [the] trust and cooperation" necessary for effective policing.[100]

## The Real Policy Challenge: The New Americans

Much of the current debate, and many of the policies proposed by states and localities around immigration, has been centered on the issue of illegal immigration. There are, at last estimate, about 11.5 million unauthorized residents in the United States (DHS Office of Im-

---

100  IACP 2007. In 2009, the Police Foundation came out explicitly against local law-enforcement cooperation with federal immigration agencies; see Police Foundation 2009.

migration Statistics 2012b), out of slightly under 40 million immigrants in all; however, more than two out of every three foreign-born residents are *legal* residents. Over the past 20 years, more than 1 million individuals have been granted legal permanent residency every year, including an average of more than 80,000 refugees who are settled across the country (DHS 2011a; Department of State, Bureau of Population, Refugees, and Migration 2011). Every year from 2000 to 2010, an average of 670,000 of these legal permanent residents became naturalized US citizens (DHS 2011a). Policy debates focusing on illegal immigration to the exclusion of other issues have obscured the fact that most immigrants – the large majority of whom have arrived in the United States through legal channels – remain in the country, eventually becoming citizens.

More than this, much contemporary policy ignores the fact that the demographic changes taking place across the United States today are driven as much or more by the *children* of immigrants as by immigrants themselves. As illustrated in Figure 9, in 2000, 18.8 percent of all people under the age of 18 in the United States were either first- or second-generation immigrant children; by 2009, almost one out of every four people under 18, or 17.4 million youths, was an immigrant or the child of immigrants. The shift that has been taking place over time has been the increasing proportion of second-generation immigrants who are born in the United States and are US citizens: In 2009, second-generation children outnumbered first-generation children by more than six to one (Child Trends 2010). Many children of immigrants are at risk of falling behind educationally and economically, to the general detriment of all Americans (Tienda and Haskins 2011; Zhao 1997). The figures for Hispanics, the nation's largest minority group, are illuminating here: By age 26, 82 percent of all Hispanic high school completers have enrolled in college, but only 18 percent have completed a bachelor's degree, compared with 38 percent of their white peers. Hispanics are more likely to attend local two-year community colleges and trade schools than four-year universities (Pew Hispanic Center 2004).

215

**Figure 9: First- and Second-Generation Immigrant Children under Age 18 in the United States in 1990, 2000, and 2009**

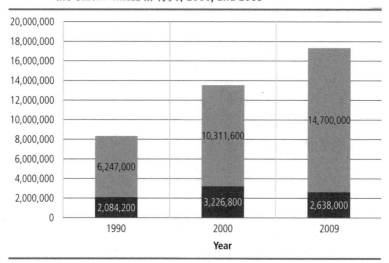

■ First Generation

□ Second Generation (US-born children with at least one foreign-born resident parent)

Source: Child Trends 2010[101]

It might be tempting to believe – as suggested by recent state legislative actions – that the policy challenges posed by immigration in the United States are all about unauthorized immigrants. In fact, the central policy challenge is how to ease the integration of permanent foreign-born residents and their US-born children. Historically, the United States has relied on immigrants to integrate themselves, often with the help of voluntary agencies and locally supported venues,

101 Data for 1990 and 2000: Estimates for non-immigrant children and immigrant children overall: Beavers and D'Amico 2005. Data for first- and second-generation immigrant children: Child Trends calculations of unpublished estimates from the Population Reference Bureau, analysis of US Census 1990, 5-Percent Public Use Microdata Sample (PUMS) Files and Population Reference Bureau, analysis of US Census 2000. Data for 2005–2009: US Census Bureau, "Current Population Survey, Characteristics of the US Foreign-Born by Generation;" Urban Institute, n.d.

such as public schools and libraries. Integration efforts at the national level have been almost nonexistent. The naturalization process in the United States, for instance, is financed by the fees immigrants pay to naturalize and has few resources to spare to support immigrant integration. Only a tiny fraction of the DHS budget – a few million dollars out of a $47 billion budget – is allocated to immigrant integration programs (DHS 2011b). For all the public handwringing about immigration's impact on American culture and society, there is a curious absence of creative public policy framing a constructive response.

## Conclusion

Even as a nation of immigrants, the United States has a long history of ambivalence toward immigration. Almost every wave of immigrants arriving to America – Chinese, Irish, German, Jewish, Italian, Japanese, to name a few – survived a period of sometimes intense, racialized, anti-immigrant sentiment from the native born before eventually, over generations, being accepted as American.[102]

In recent decades, the rapid pace of immigration and the dispersal of immigrants across the United States have exacerbated tensions between residents born in the United States and those born abroad, requiring adjustments from both the communities where immigrants settle and from the immigrants themselves. As immigration reaches every corner of the country, it is now shaping communities that have had little historical experience with immigration and that have little preparation for large and rapid incoming flows, triggering a backlash. However, the fact is that most immigrants and their children are here

---

102 The arrival of each new immigrant nationality has sparked its own reaction. For instance, the American (or Know-Nothing) Party began in the 1840s in response to large numbers of Catholic immigrants from Germany and Ireland, who seemed so jarring to the then-overwhelmingly Protestant population. In 1882, Congress passed the *Chinese Exclusion Act* and, later in the century, the millions of immigrants from Southern and Eastern Europe eventually led to the *Quota Act of 1921*, which restricted immigration based on nation of origin. See King 2000; Shrag 2001; Higham 1994 [1955].

to stay, and their presence will continue to shape the United States over the long run. This requires attention to the promise, and challenges, posed by the process of their integration into American society, workforce, and politics.

Historically, in the end, immigrants *have* integrated into American society, although this can take generations. Every indication is that the course for current immigrants will be no different (Alba and Nee 2003; Fuchs 1991). The United States offers an object lesson: Countries confronting the challenge of immigrant integration are in it for the long haul.

## Works Cited

ABC News. DHS Task Force Criticizes Immigration Fingerprint Program. *ABC News Blogs* September 16, 2011. http://abcnews.go.com/blogs/politics/2011/09/dhs-task-force-criticizes-immigration-fingerprint-program/.

Alba, Richard, and Victor Nee. *Remaking the American Mainstream: Assimilation and Contemporary Immigration.* Cambridge, Mass.: Harvard University Press, 2003.

Archibold, Randal C. US's Toughest Immigration Law is Signed in Arizona. *New York Times* April 23, 2010. www.nytimes.com/2010/04/24/us/politics/24immig.html?ref=us.

Associated Press. Alabama's Illegal Immigration Law Tougher Than Arizona's. June 10, 2011. http://blog.al.com/wire/2011/06/alabamas_illegal_immigration_l.html.

Beavers, Laura, and Jean D'Amico. *Children in Immigrant Families: US and State-Level Findings from the 2000 Census.* Baltimore, Md.: Annie E. Casey Foundation, 2005. www.prb.org/pdf05/ChildrenIn Immigrant.pdf.

Berkes, Howard. Utah Immigration Law Goes into Effect, But Court Quickly Blocks It. *National Public Radio* May 10, 2011. www.npr.org/blogs/thetwo-way/2011/05/10/136177436/utah-immigration-law-goes-into-effect-but-court-hearing-looms.

Borjas, George J. Native Internal Migration and the Labor Market Impact of Immigration. *Journal of Human Resources* (41) 2: 221–258, 2006.

Bruno, Andorra. *Immigration-Related Worksite Enforcement Measures.* Washington, DC: Congressional Research Service, 2011. http://assets.opencrs.com/rpts/R40002_20110301.pdf.

Buchanan, Wyatt. S. F. Supervisors Approve ID Cards for Residents. *San Francisco Chronicle* November 14, 2007. www.sfgate.com/cgi-bin/article.cgi?f=/c/a/2007/11/14/BAB9TBP5H.DTL&tsp=1.

Bureau of Economic Analysis. Employment and Unemployment. News releases, various months. n.d. www.bls.gov/bls/newsrels.htm#OEUS.

Butcher, Kristin F., and Anne Morrison Piehl. Cross-City Evidence on the Relationship Between Immigration and Crime. *Journal of Policy Analysis and Management* (17) 3: 457–493, 1998.

Butcher, Kristin F., and Anne Morrison Piehl. *Crime, Corrections, and California: What Does Immigration Have to Do with It?* San Francisco: Public Policy Institute of California, 2008. www.ppic.org/main/publication.asp?i=776.

Card, David. Immigrant Inflows, Native Outflows, and the Local Labor Market Impacts of Higher Immigration. *Journal of Labor Economics* (19) 1: 22–64, 2001.

Card, David. How Immigration Affects US Cities. Discussion Paper 11/07, Centre for Research and Analysis of Migration Discussion, University College London, 2007. www.econ.ucl.ac.uk/cream/pages/CDP/CDP_11_07.pdf.

Card, David. Immigration and Inequality. *American Economic Review, Papers and Proceedings* (99) 2: 1–21, 2009.

Card, David, and Ethan Lewis. The Diffusion of Mexican Immigrants during the 1990s: Explanations and Impacts. In *Mexican Immigration to the United States*, edited by George J. Borjas. Chicago: University of Chicago Press, 2007: 193–228.

*Chamber of Commerce of the United States v. Whiting* (09-115). www.lawmemo.com/supreme/case/Chamber2/.

Child Trends. Immigrant Children. 2010. www.childtrendsdatabank.org/?q=node/333.

Chishti, Muzaffar, and Claire Bergeron. DHS Announces End to Controversial Post-9/11 Immigrant Registration and Tracking Program. *Migration Information Source* May 17, 2011a. www.migrationinformation.org/USFocus/display.cfm?ID=840.

Chishti, Muzaffar, and Claire Bergeron. Supreme Court Upholds Legal Arizona Workers Act with Limited Implications for Other State Immigration Laws. *Migration Information Source* June 15, 2011b. www.migrationinformation.org/USFocus/print.cfm?ID=843.

Cowles, Isabel. English-Only Measure Defeated in Nashville. *finding-Dulcinea* January 23, 2009. www.findingdulcinea.com/news/Americas/2009/jan/English-Only-Measure-Defeated-in-Nashville.html.

Danziger, Sheldon, and Peter Gottschalk. *Uneven Tides: Rising Inequality in America.* New York: Russell Sage Foundation, 1993.

Davis, Aaron. Md. Voters to Decide Immigrant Tuition Law. *Washington Post* July 7, 2011. www.washingtonpost.com/local/dc-politics/md-voters-to-decide-immigrant-tuition-law/2011/07/07/gIQAfAsr2H_story.html.

DHS – Department of Homeland Security. Fact Sheet: Secure Border Initiative. Washington, DC: DHS, 2005. www.hsdl.org/?view&did=440470.

DHS – Department of Homeland Security. Department of Homeland Security Unveils Comprehensive Immigration Enforcement Strategy for the Nation's Interior. News release, April 20, 2006.

DHS – Department of Homeland Security. Enforcement Integrated Database (EID). DHS, Washington, DC, December 2010.

DHS – Department of Homeland Security. *Yearbook of Immigration Statistics: 2010.* Washington, DC: DHS, 2011a. www.dhs.gov/files/statistics/publications/LPR10.shtm.

DHS – Department of Homeland Security. *FY 2012 Budget in Brief – US Department of Homeland Security.* Washington, DC: DHS, 2011b. www.dhs.gov/xlibrary/assets/budget-bib-fy2012.pdf.

DHS – Department of Homeland Security. ENFORCE Alien Removal Module (EARM). Washington, DC: DHS, 2011c.

DHS Office of Immigration Statistics. *Immigration Enforcement Actions: 2010.* Washington, DC: DHS, 2011a. www.dhs.gov/xlibrary/assets/statistics/publications/enforcement-ar-2010.pdf.

DHS Office of Immigration Statistics. *Apprehensions by the U.S. Border Patrol: 2005–2010*. Washington, DC: DHS, 2011b. www.dhs.gov/xlibrary/assets/statistics/publications/ois-apprehensions-fs-2005-2010.pdf.

DHS Office of Immigration Statistics. *U.S. Legal Permanent Residents: 2011.* Washington, DC: DHS Office of Immigration Statistics, 2012a. www.dhs.gov/xlibrary/assets/statistics/publications/lpr_fr_2011.pdf.

DHS Office of Immigration Statistics. *Estimates of the Unauthorized Immigrant Population Residing in the United States: January 2011.* Washington, DC: DHS Office of Immigration Statistics, 2012b. www.dhs.gov/xlibrary/assets/statistics/publications/ois_ill_pe_2011.pdf.

Department of Justice, Office of the Inspector General, Audit Division. Cooperation of SCAAP Recipients in the Removal of Criminal Aliens from the United States (redacted public version). January 2007. www.justice.gov/oig/reports/OJP/a0707/final.pdf.

Department of State, Bureau of Population, Refugees, and Migration. Worldwide Refugee Admissions Processing System (WRAPS), Fiscal Years 1980 to 2010. 2011. www.dhs.gov/files/statistics/publications/YrBk10RA.shtm.

Fraga, Luis, John Garcia, Rodney Hero, Michael Jones-Correa, Valerie Martinez-Ebers, and Gary Segura. *Latinos in the New Millennium: An Almanac of Opinion, Behavior, and Policy Preferences.* New York: Cambridge University Press, 2012.

Frey, William. The Uneven Aging and "Younging" of America: State and Metropolitan Trends in the 2010 Census. State of Metropolitan America Papers no. 35, Brookings Institution, 2011. www.brookings.edu/papers/2011/0628_census_age_frey.aspx.

Fuchs, Lawrence. *The American Kaleidoscope: Race, Ethnicity and the Civic Culture.* Hanover, NH: Wesleyan University Press, 1991.

Gallup. Immigration. 2011. www.gallup.com/poll/1660/immigration.aspx.

Graham, Troy. Philadelphia Councilman Opens Hearing on Immigration. *Philadelphia Inquirer* June 29, 2011. http://articles.philly.com/2011-06-29/news/29717400_1_immigration-public-hearing-latest-census.

Higham, John. *Strangers in the Land: Patterns of American Nativism, 1860–1925.* New Brunswick, NJ: Rutgers University Press, 1994 [1955].

Homeland Security Advisory Council. Task Force on Secure Communities Findings and Recommendations. Washington, DC: DHS, 2011. www.dhs.gov/xlibrary/assets/lisac-task-force-on-secure-communities-findings-and-recommendations-report.pdf.

IACP – International Association of Chiefs of Police. *Police Chiefs Guide to Immigration Issues*. Alexandria, Va.: IACP, 2007. www.theiacp.org/Portals/0/pdfs/Publications/PoliceChiefsGuidetoImmigration.pdf.

*Illinois Right to Privacy in the Workplace Act*. www.ilga.gov/legislation/95/SB/09500SB1878eng.htm.

Junta for Progressive Action, Inc. and Unidad Latina en Acción. *A City to Model*. New Haven, Conn.: Junta for Progressive Action, Inc. and Unidad Latina en Acción, 2005. www.newhavenindependent.org/archives/2005/10/A_City_to_Model.pdf.

King, Desmond. *Making Americans: Immigration, Race and the Origins of the Diverse Democracy*. Cambridge, Mass.: Harvard University Press, 2000.

Levy, Frank. *New Dollars and Dreams: American Incomes and Economic Change*. New York: Russell Sage Foundation, 1998.

Loftin, Josh. Utah Immigration Law Joins Arizona Measure – In Court. *Huffington Post* May 11, 2011. www.huffingtonpost.com/2011/05/11/utah-immigration-law-_n_860572.html.

Martin, Philip, and Elizabeth Midgley. *Population Bulletin Update: Immigration in America in 2010*. Washington, DC: Population Reference Bureau, 2010. www.prb.org/Publications/PopulationBulletins/2010/immigrationupdate1.aspx.

Martinez Jr., Ramiro. Coming to America: The Impact of the New Immigration on Crime. In *Immigration and Crime: Race, Ethnicity, and Violence*, edited by Ramiro Martinez Jr. and Abel Valenzuela Jr. New York: New York University Press, 2006: 1–21.

Meissner, Doris, Deborah Meyers, Demetrios G. Papademetriou, and Marc Rosenblum (eds.). *Immigration and America's Future*. Washington, DC: Migration Policy Institute, 2006. www.migrationpolicy.org/ITFIAF/finalreport.pdf.

Migration Policy Institute (MPI) Data Hub. Ten Source Countries with the Largest Populations in the United States as Percentages of the Total Foreign-Born Population: 1970. 2007. www.migrationinformation.org/datahub/charts/10.70.shtml.

Migration Policy Institute (MPI) Data Hub. Foreign-Born Population and Foreign Born as Percentage of the Total US Population, 1850–2009. 2010. www.migrationinformation.org/datahub/charts/final.fb.shtml.

Migration Policy Institute (MPI) Data Hub. Ten Source Countries with the Largest Populations in the United States as Percentages of the Total Foreign-Born Population: 2010. 2011. www.migrationinformation.org/datahub/charts/10.2010.shtml.

Myers, Dowell. *Immigrants and Boomers: Forging a New Social Contract for the Future of America*. New York: Russell Sage Foundation, 2007.

National Conference of State Legislatures. Immigrant Policy Project. n.d. www.ncsl.org/default.aspx?tabid=21857.

National Immigration Law Center. Laws, Resolutions and Policies Instituted Across the US Limiting Enforcement of Immigration Laws by State and Local Authorities. 2008. http://v2011.nilc.org/immlawpolicy/LocalLaw/locallaw-limiting-tbl-2008-12-03.pdf.

*New York Times*. The Utah Compact. Editorial. *New York Times* December 4, 2010. www.nytimes.com/2010/12/05/opinion/05sun1.html.

Nieves, Evelyn. California Calls Off Effort to Carry Out Immigrant Measure. *New York Times* July 30, 1999. www.nytimes.com/1999/07/30/us/california-calls-off-effort-to-carry-out-immigrant-measure.html?pagewanted=all&src=pm.

Odem, Mary, and Elaine Lacy. *Latino Immigrants and the Transformation of the US South*. Athens, Ga.: University of Georgia Press, 2009.

Olivas, Michael. Immigration-Related State and Local Ordinances: Preemption, Prejudice, and the Proper Role for Enforcement. *University of Chicago Legal Forum*: 27–56, 2007.

Ousey, Graham C., and Charis E. Kubrin. Exploring the Connection between Immigration and Violent Crime Rates in US Cities, 1980–2000. *Social Forces* (56) 3: 447–473, 2009.

Papademetriou, Demetrios G., and Aaron Terrazas. Immigrants in the United States and the Current Economic Crisis. *Migration Information Source* April 1, 2009. www.migrationinformation.org/Feature/display.cfm?ID=723.

Parker, Christopher, and Matt Barreto. Change We Can't Believe In: Exploring the Sources and Consequences of Tea Party Support. Paper presented at the 2011 APSA Meeting, Seattle, Wash., September 1–4, 2011.

Peri, Giovanni. The Effect of Immigrants on US Employment and Productivity. *Federal Reserve Bank of San Francisco Economic Letter* August 30, 2010. www.frbsf.org/publications/economics/letter/2010/el2010-26.html.

Pew Hispanic Center. Fact Sheet: Hispanic College Enrollment: Less Intensive and Less Heavily Subsidized. January 2004. www.pewhispanic.org/files/factsheets/7.1.pdf.

Pew Hispanic Center. Size and Characteristics of the Unauthorized Migrant Population in the U.S. March 7, 2006. www.pewhispanic.org/2006/03/07/size-and-characteristics-of-the-unauthorized-migrant-population-in-the-us/.

Police Foundation. *The Role of Local Police: Striking the Balance Between Immigration Enforcement and Civil Liberties.* Washington, DC: Police Foundation, 2009. www.policefoundation.org/strikingabalance/strikingabalance.html.

Portes, Alejandro, and Rubén Rumbaut. *Legacies: The Story of the Second Generation.* Berkeley: University of California Press, 2001.

Rumbaut, Rubén, and Alejandro Portes. *Ethnicities: Children of Immigrants in America.* Berkeley: University of California Press, 2001.

Russell, Alene. In-State Tuition for Unauthorized Immigrants: States' Rights and Educational Opportunity. Policy brief, American Association of State Colleges and Universities, August 2007. www.aascu.org/uploadedFiles/AASCU/Content/Root/PolicyAndAdvocacy/PolicyPublications/in-state_tuition07%282%29.pdf.

Salam, Reihan. Don't Call it Racism. Op-ed. *The Daily* August 19, 2011. www.thedaily.com/page/2011/08/19/081911-opinions-column-racism-salam-1-2/.

Seghetti, Lisa M., Stephen R. Vina, and Karma Ester. *Enforcing Immigration Law: The Role of State and Local Law Enforcement*. Washington, DC: Congressional Research Service, 2006. http://trac.syr.edu/immigration/library/P1072.pdf.

Severson, Kim. Parts of Georgia Immigration Law Blocked. *New York Times* June 27, 2011. www.nytimes.com/2011/06/28/us/28georgia.html.

Shrag, Peter. *Not Fit for Our Society: Immigration and Nativism in America*. Berkeley: University of California Press, 2001.

Singer, Audrey, Susan Hardwick, and Carole Brettell. *Twenty-first Century Suburban Gateways: Immigrant Incorporation in Suburban America*. Washington, DC: Brookings Institution, 2008.

Smith, James P., and Barry Edmonston (eds.). The *New Americans: Economic, Demographic, and Fiscal Effects of Immigration*. Washington, DC: National Academy Press, 1997.

Tennessee Department of Safety and Homeland Security. Tennessee Certificate for Driving (Class TD). n.d. http://articles.philly.com/2011-06-29/news/29717400_1_immigration-public-hearing-latest-census.

Tienda, Marta, and Faith Mitchell (eds.). *Multiple Origins, Uncertain Destinies: Hispanics and the American Future*. Washington, DC: National Academies Press, 2006.

Tienda, Marta, and Ron Haskins. Immigrant Children: Introducing the Issue. *The Future of Children* (21) 2: 3–18, 2011. http://futureofchildren.org/futureofchildren/publications/docs/21_01_01.pdf.

Urban Institute. Children of Immigrants Data Tool. n.d. http://datatool.urban.org/charts/datatool/pages.cfm.

US Census Bureau. Current Population Survey, Characteristics of the US Foreign-Born by Generation. n.d. www.census.gov/population/www/socdemo/foreign/.

US Census Bureau. Community Population Survey – March 2010. Detailed Tables. 2010. www.census.gov/population/foreign/data/cps2010.html.

US Census Bureau. American Community Survey (ACS). Selected Social Characteristics in the United States. n.d. http://factfinder2.

census.gov/faces/tableservices/jsf/pages/productview.xhtml?pid=
ACS_10_1YR DP02&prodType=table.

US Immigration and Customs Enforcement (ICE). Removal Statistics. n.d. www.ice.gov/removal-statistics/.

US Immigration and Customs Enforcement (ICE). Fact Sheet: Worksite Enforcement Overview. Washington, DC: DHS, 2009. www.ice.gov/news/library/factsheets/worksite.htm.

US Immigration and Customs Enforcement (ICE). Fact Sheet: Delegation of Immigration Authority Section 287(g) Immigration and Nationality Act. Washington, DC: DHS, 2011a. www.ice.gov/news/library/factsheets/287g.htm.

US Immigration and Customs Enforcement (ICE). Fact Sheet: ICE Fugitive Operations Program. Washington, DC: DHS, 2011b. www.ice.gov/news/library/factsheets/fugops.htm.

US Immigration and Customs Enforcement (ICE). Activated Jurisdictions, as of April 17, 2012. 2012. www.ice.gov/doclib/secure-communities/pdf/sc-activated.pdf.

Varsanyi, Monica. Neoliberalism and Nativism: Local Anti-Immigrant Policy Activism and an Emerging Politics of Scale. *International Journal of Urban and Regional Research* (35) 2: 295–311, 2010a.

Varsanyi, Monica (ed.). *Taking Local Control: Immigration Policy Activism in US Cities and States.* Palo Alto: Stanford University Press, 2010b.

Wadsworth, Tim. Is Immigration Responsible for the Crime Drop? An Assessment of the Influence of Immigration on Changes in Violent Crime between 1990 and 2000. *Social Science Quarterly* (9) 2: 531–553, 2010.

Walker, Kyle. Local Policy Responses to Immigration in the United States. *CURA Reporter* (40) 3/4: 27–34, 2010. www.cura.umn.edu/publications/catalog/reporter-40-3-4-2.

Zhao, Min. Growing Up American: The Challenge Confronting Immigrant Children and Children of Immigrants. *Annual Review of Sociology* (23): 63–95, 1997.

# Identity and (Muslim) Immigration in Germany

*Naika Foroutan*

## Introduction

This chapter explores how international immigration influences national identity in Germany and the reciprocal influence that German national identity has on immigrants. Although one-fifth of Germany's inhabitants are immigrants or the children of immigrants, German politics and public discourse have long ignored the implications of the nation's changing population. Meanwhile, German public opinion includes some of the deepest anti-Muslim sentiments in Europe. Perceptions of Muslims as backward, fanatical, intolerant, and a threat to Germany's national security and national identity are commonplace (Pollack 2011: 6; Heitmeyer 2011: 38). Much of this was evident in the debates over Thilo Sarrazin's controversial depiction of Muslims in his best-selling 2010 book, *Deutschland schafft sich ab* ("Germany Does Away with Itself").

The chapter provides an overview of the demographics, trends, and current debates and linkages concerning national identity and immigration in Germany, and concludes by presenting recommendations for policymakers. These recommendations are focused on how German policymakers should challenge the stereotypes of Muslims that pervade the media and public discourse, and how to tackle structural factors that lead to unequal opportunities and outcomes for immigrants and their descendants.

# Germany as a Recent Country of Immigration

## Demographic Overview

Over recent decades, transnational migration has become a self-evident characteristic of German society. One-fifth of Germany's 82 million inhabitants have a so-called migration background,[103] including one-third of children under the age of 6 (see Figure 1).[104] It is interesting, though, that only 5 percent of all migrants or persons with a migration background live in the eastern German states; however, anti-immigrant sentiments and xenophobia are the highest there.[105]

---

**Figure 1: German Population by Migration Background, 2011**

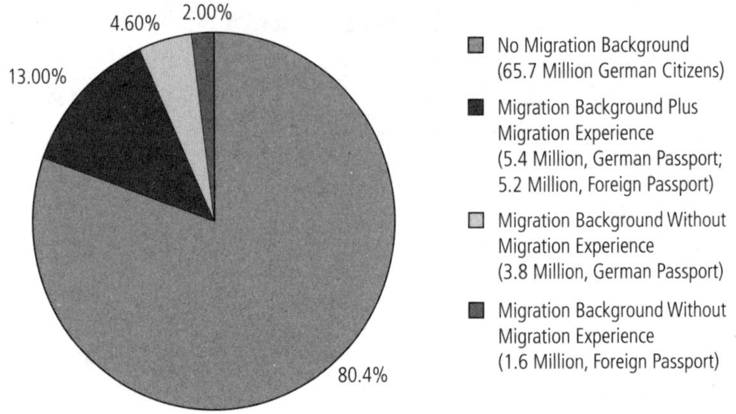

Legend:
- No Migration Background (65.7 Million German Citizens) — 80.4%
- Migration Background Plus Migration Experience (5.4 Million, German Passport; 5.2 Million, Foreign Passport) — 13.00%
- Migration Background Without Migration Experience (3.8 Million, German Passport) — 4.60%
- Migration Background Without Migration Experience (1.6 Million, Foreign Passport) — 2.00%

Source: Statistisches Bundesamt 2011

---

103 This term includes foreigners living in Germany, people who acquired German citizenship, repatriates of "German origin" and their children, children born to foreigners (who acquired citizenship at birth), and children whose father or mother migrated. Generation is an additional factor; the label "migration background" is officially lost after the third generation. See Statistiches Bundesamt 2010: 33.

104 The estimates in this section are taken from Haug, Müssig, and Stichs 2009.

105 Allensbach Archives 2010; Pollack 2011. The archives contain data from the 1950s to the present, allowing a tracking of public views on immigration and integration over a lengthy period of time.

**Figure 2: Share of German Population with Migration Background in Select Large Cities, 2007**

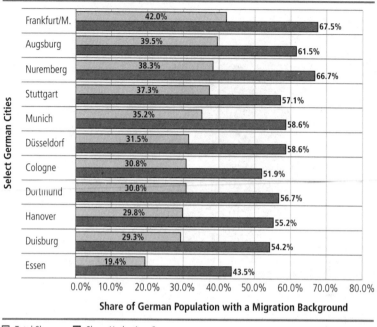

Share of German Population with a Migration Background

☐ Total Share    ■ Share Under Age 6

Source: DGB Bildungswerk Bund 2010b

At the national level, one-third of the estimated 16 million people with a migration background living in Germany did not immigrate, but were born in Germany. In some federal states, those labeled as "Germans with a migration background" make up more than 35 percent of all children under the age of 10.

As seen in Figure 2, in some metropolitan areas, such as Frankfurt, Augsburg, or Nuremberg, over 60 percent of all children who started school in 2011 had a migration background.

Of the 10.6 million people who have immigrated to Germany since 1950, 70.6 percent are from other European countries, including 32.3 percent from European Union (EU) member states; a further

## Figure 3: Muslims in Germany by Region of Origin, 2008 (percent)

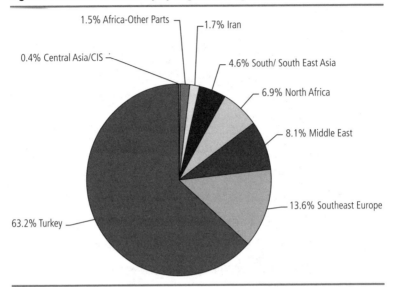

1.5% Africa-Other Parts

1.7% Iran

0.4% Central Asia/CIS

4.6% South/ South East Asia

6.9% North Africa

8.1% Middle East

13.6% Southeast Europe

63.2% Turkey

Source: Haug, Müssig, and Stichs 2009

16.4 percent originate from Asia or Oceania (Brückner 2010). Only one-quarter of German residents with a migration background are Muslim, of which the largest group is of Turkish origin (2.9 million). People of Arab origin, so often overrepresented in negative news coverage concerning migration, number around 400,000 – less than 1 percent of the German population.

According to the Pew Forum on Religion and Public Life, there are about 4.2 million Muslims living in Germany, comprising about 5 percent of the country's population (Pew Forum on Religion and Public Life 2011). In absolute numbers, Germany ranks second in the European Union, after France, in Muslim population size. Germany ranks fifth in size of the Muslim population as a share of total population, after France, Belgium, Austria, and the Netherlands (ibid.).

Where migration is linked to settlement, it leads to changes in the structure of the population. These changes are not only demographic and social, but also reshape the fundamental identities and narratives of a country (Koopmans et al. 2005). However, while Germany has become a country of immigration in recent decades, the emotional public discourse often presents German society as a homogenous one, in which those with a migration background cannot fully belong. A considerable number of Germans experience postmodernity in their day-to-day life, in which anything seems to go – whether by claiming patchwork identities (Keupp 2008), being exposed to mobile and flexible work and life concepts (Beck 1986), or practicing new partnership models beyond the heterosexual nuclear family. And, still, there are large numbers of voters who long for the more homogenous and "clear" Germany that, in their perception, existed before the 1961 recruitment agreement with Turkey began the inflow of Turkish workers to Germany.

To this day, racism and negative conduct toward people perceived to be "strangers" are still pervasive in Germany. A long-term study measuring group-focused enmity, carried out yearly by the University of Bielefeld over a ten-year period, provides empirical evidence that there is an "ideology of inequality" underlying these prejudices (Heitmeyer 2011), continuing the classic social conflict that Norbert Elias called the crisis of the established versus the outsiders (Elias and Scotson 1994). More than one-third of Germans (30.8 percent) think that "people who have always lived here should have more rights than those who have moved here later." Nearly half (47.1 percent) agrees with the sentence: "There are too many foreigners living in Germany." A clear majority (54.1 percent) believes that "someone who is new someplace should be content with less in the beginning" (Heitmeyer 2011).

Despite the fact that plurality has become the norm for most adolescents and many adults living in Germany, a rising insecurity concerning national identity can be observed among those aware that the country has in fact become diverse through immigration.

## Perceptions of Muslims

Since the terrorist attacks of September 11, 2001, and the subsequent proclamation by the United States of a "global war on terror," the image of Muslims as terrorists, archaic warriors, or anachronistic religious believers has trickled into the German national *Diskursraum* (public dialogue).

This was especially evident throughout the 2010–2011 debates led by the Bundesbank's executive board member and former Berlin state finance minister Thilo Sarrazin. His controversial book *Deutschland schafft sich ab* ("Germany Does Away with Itself") (Sarrazin 2010) argues that Muslims are less intelligent because of their cultural ties, prefer to live off the state rather than work, and have too many children (while well-educated native Germans are having too few) (Aslan 2011). The book was the best-selling book in Germany in 2010 and has sold more than 1 million copies (for a critical analysis of Sarrazin's central assumptions, see Foroutan et al. 2010).

Common attributes and associations linked to Muslims in Germany include terms such as *fanatic, backwards, intolerant,* and *undemocratic,* as found in a study by the German Institute for Human Rights (Bielefeldt 2008). According to the study, 21.4 percent of Germans think that "Muslim immigration to Germany should be stopped." When asked whether "Muslim culture fits into our Western world," three-quarters of respondents answered negatively (ibid.: 5–7). Islam and being Muslim are perceived as being in stark contrast to being German. After 9/11, "Muslims" have been largely perceived as a security threat (Cesari 2009), leading to alienation and estrangement.

A recent study conducted by the Social Democratic Party-affiliated Friedrich Ebert Foundation entitled *Intolerance, Prejudice and Discrimination: A European Report* analyzed antidemocratic attitudes in eight European countries (Zick, Küpper, and Hövermann 2011). It concluded that "Europeans are largely united in their rejection of Muslims and Islam. The significantly most widespread anti-Muslim attitudes are found in Germany, Hungary, Italy and Poland, closely followed by France, Great Britain and the Netherlands" (ibid.: 63). Almost *half* of all Germans said that there are too many Muslims living in the country – even though they make up only 5 percent of the population, that they are too demanding and that their religion is intolerant.[106]

A comparative study conducted by the University of Münster in 2010 researching "Perception and Acceptance of Religious Diversity" found that Germans have a worse perception of adherents of non-Christian religions than publics in other European countries, such as Denmark, France, the Netherlands, or Portugal (Pollack 2011: 5). When asked "How is your personal attitude towards the members of the following religious groups?" 62.2 percent of surveyed Germans living in the former East German states and 57.7 percent living in the former West German states answered "negative" or "extremely negative" concerning Islam. By comparison, the "negative" or "extremely negative" sentiment was 35.6 percent in Denmark, 36.7 percent in France, 35.9 percent in the Netherlands, and 33.5 percent in Portugal. Germans also answered significantly more negatively than other nationalities when asked about Hinduism, Buddhism, or Judaism. When the same study referred to positive attributions, nearly one-third of Dutch respondents (32.6 percent) associated Islam with peace and 44.9 percent with solidarity, while in Germany attributions of peace and solidarity with Islam were given by only 6.6 percent (former East German states) and 8.1 percent (former West German states) of the German population. Among Danish respondents, 25.9 percent associated Islam with peace and 37.6 percent with solidarity; among French respondents, it was 13.6 percent and 31.9 percent; and among Portuguese respondents, 19.8 percent and 27.4 percent (ibid.: 6).

These biased attitudes are sometimes expressed violently or aggressively. There have been several attacks on mosques, people perceived to be Muslim have been threatened, Muslim organizations re-

---

106 Ibid.: 61: 46.1 percent respond "There are too many Muslims in Germany," 54.1 percent "Muslims are too demanding," and 52.2 percent "Islam is a religion of intolerance."

233

ceive daily hate mail, and anti-Muslim Internet blogs are increasingly popular.[107]

Moreover, on a social and economic level, people of Muslim background are less likely to be hired; if their name is recognizably non-German, they may not even get a job interview (Kaas and Manger 2010). They have a harder time finding an apartment for the same reasons, and students with a migration background are less likely to receive teacher recommendations for higher-education opportunities (Jürges and Schneider 2006).

## Policies on Migration and Integration

Politicians and policymakers began to address such threats to social cohesion around 2006. They realized that not only Islamic fundamentalism, but also rising anti-Muslim racism had to be monitored and controlled in order to achieve a rapprochement. This was a paradigmatic shift in politics, as well as for the academic community and security agencies. The latter, especially, shifted from only looking at Muslims as a security risk and adjusted many of their programs, particularly concerning prevention of expressions of bias and bigotry (Kury 2008). Then-Interior Minister Wolfgang Schäuble established the Deutsche Islamkonferenz (German Islam Conference) in 2006 in order to create a national framework for dialogue between the German state and Muslims living in Germany (Federal Ministry of the Interior 2006). He opened the conference by stating that "Islam is a part of Germany and Europe. It is part of our past and of our future. Muslims are welcome in Germany" (Schäuble 2006).

Parallel to this significant, symbolic act, German Chancellor Angela Merkel initiated an integration summit to explore new concepts on how to deal with diversity in a changing Germany (Bundesregierung 2006). The Ministry of the Interior for the first time ordered a

---

107 Relating to hate mail: Jung 2010; relating to attacks on Berlin mosques: Petzinger 2010; relating to anti-Muslim networks: Townsend 2012.

234

nationwide representative study on Muslims in Germany (Haug, Müssig and Stichs 2009). This was followed up by many studies covering a wide range of topics relating to Muslim life in Germany (for more information on studies concerning Muslims, see Projekt HEyMAT).

This shift in policy is also linked to the fact that the German economy increasingly demands high-skilled workers from abroad; creating a more welcoming climate for foreign workers is therefore in the economic and national interest. It is only slowly, however, that this realization is trickling down into the general population.

## The Reality of Muslim Integration

Reviewing the structural, cultural, and social integration quantified in academic studies of the past six years makes clear that the integration of "Muslims" in Germany is far better than often assumed (numbers taken from Federal Office for Migration and Refugees 2009; Bundesamt für Verfassungsschutz 2010):

- More than 50 percent of Muslims are members of a German association; a mere 4 percent are only members of an association affiliated with their country/culture of origin.
- Ninety-five percent of all Muslim boys and girls take part in coed sports and swimming classes at school (even as media reports might lead the public to believe that most Muslim parents are keeping their girls separate).
- Eighty percent of Muslim immigrants make a living from income as employees or from being self-employed.
- Thirty-four percent receive the *Abitur* or *Fachabitur* (the diploma qualifying pupils for university admission); 22.3 percent finish intermediate secondary school (*Realschule*); and 28.8 percent finish secondary general school (*Hauptschule*). Collectively, this means that 85.2 percent achieve a school qualification needed to enter Germany's diversified job market.
- Only 1 percent of Muslims in Germany can be considered part of the Islamist milieu.

Similar successes can be seen in economic integration. Businesses owned by the foreign born have become an important component of the German economy over the past 15 years. The Board of Trade noted that self-employment rates among Muslim immigrants in Germany have constantly risen over the past 20 years, proving they are increasing productivity by establishing new jobs with new employees. Considering the Turkish population alone – the largest single Muslim immigrant group – one can observe an increase in self-employment rates of more than 200 percent since 1991 (Institut für Mittelstandsforschung der Universität Mannheim 2005).

## National Identity and Immigration

Social scientists posit that, for the self to be defined, there must be a contradicting "other" established (Tajfel and Turner 1986). In the German context, this "other" has for quite a while – beginning with the Iranian Islamic revolution in 1979 and surely after 9/11 – been the figure of "the Muslim." The idea of "other" has always been one of an antithesis. In the 1960s, wheras Germans defined themselves as hardworking, proper, and punctual, the figure of the immigrant – who, at the time, was a southern European guest worker from Italy, Spain, Greece, or Turkey – was considered unambitious, lazy, and always late (Terkessidis 2004: 98). Now that the idea of being German is more embedded into a larger European identity, being German is associated with tolerance, democracy, and enlightenment, while the opposing figure of the Muslim is described as intolerant, antidemocratic, and unenlightened (Attia 2009: 43). There are several reasons for the current anti-Muslim climate grounded both in historical and contemporary developments.

The process of excluding Muslims and immigrants from the society-building process by positioning them outside the narrative of German identity – and, thus, out of the normalization procedure of plural societies – has to do with the fact that German politics has long denied the evolution of Germany into a country of immigration (Thränhardt 1992). It has thus failed to develop a concept for the transformation not only of the political, but also of the public debate. The negative perception of "foreigners" – in recent debates, synonymous with Muslims (Spielhaus 2011: 54) – goes hand in hand with challenges to Germany's changing national identity. The unanswered questions surrounding national identity between the end of World War II and German reunification in 1990 – as well as the challenge of uniting two very different Germanys – together with the subcutaneous continuity of an ethnic idea of "Germanness" have resulted in the making of an essential stranger: the Muslim. This process of othering is not unique to Germany and is observable within most EU countries (Zick, Küpper, and Hövermann 2011), where Islam seems to be the counterfoil to what European identity is perceived to represent (Göle 2008: 9).

*Germany as a post-National Socialist country.* In the decades after 1945, the idea of being German was associated mainly with World War II brutalization and shame – not only outside, but also inside the country. Even though the idea of guilt and responsibility was not internalized in the first decades after the war and Nazi ideology lived on in German institutions into the 1950s, there was a growing awareness and question about the propriety of formulating a concept of national identity. Thus, talking or thinking about the question of a German identity was to a certain extent locked out of the national consciousness and mainly articulated within the trauma of the Holocaust (Giesen 2004).

*Pervasiveness of a blood-and-soil concept of German identity.* The *jus sanguinis* (citizenship derived through descent) basis of German citizenship law was partially changed into *ius soli* (citizenship derived from birth in the territory) in 2000. Since then, it has formally become easier to be naturalized – but only on the official level. Concerning the emotional sentiments of belonging, things have very much remained the same. The idea that "Germanness" is founded on the idea of blood and soil – based in 19th-century romanticism that reached its peak during National Socialism – remains held on to by a large part of the population. Being German is still linked to specific phenotypes. The general self-perception of a highly homogenous, ethnically based nation and the indefinable *Leitkultur* is established as a border of non-verbal norms to be passed. As a consequence, people who have lived in Germany for 50 years or were born on German soil to migrant parents are still not unconditionally accepted as "normal" members of society, leading to constant feelings of non-belonging.

*German reunification.* In the 1980s, with the reunification of the two Germanys, national identity was reborn: one nation, one Germany. But, in reality, these reunited parts were very different from each other in terms of norms and values (Kramer 1996). Forty years of different socialization processes, of hostility and antagonism could not be reconciled without a connecting unit. There were two different Germanys uniting, thus the need for a "docking station." This search for a national connector may explain the tremendous need to differentiate the "other" in Germany, a country that has long struggled with its identity-building process. In reality, the cohesion and storytelling of these two distinct Germanys could only have started with a social identity theory that upgraded the peer group, thereby creating and downgrading the out-group. This might explain the atmosphere of xenophobia and the rise in German nationalism at the beginning of the 1990s, which ended with the pogroms of Hoyerswerda, Solingen, and Mölln, where migrants were attacked or burned in their houses while Germans stood outside without helping them (Panayi 1994).

*Generational influence.* The generation born between 1925 and 1955 was socialized in a Germany that was homogenous like never before, a Germany deeply influenced by National Socialist ideas. This generation now includes many decision makers and statesmen (in their mid-50s to 80s). Several polls indicate that it is chiefly members of this generation who have bought Thilo Sarrazin's book (Kniebe 2011). Wilhelm Heitmeyer states that it is mainly this age group, irrespective of party preferences, that scores highest in polls on group-focused enmity, especially when it comes to religious and cultural discrimination (Heitmeyer 2011: 13; Zick, Küpper and Hövermann 2011: 90).

*Failure of European identity.* During the 1970s, when the young generation yearned to emancipate itself from its parents' war-ridden past, the idea of being German changed in some parts of society. Participants and supporters of the 1968 European protest movements saw themselves as members of a freedom-loving generation; their dislike for borders opened up room for a new identity beyond exclusive national identities, one of European collective identity (Habermas 1987). The strength of this European identity, however, has wavered amid fracturing emotional solidarity sparked by the recession and particularly the euro crisis that the European Union has confronted since 2007. Faced with shrinking economic growth, rising unemployment, a debt crisis that influences political elections, and other challenges, this generation doesn't seem to have the power to clearly draw new visions for a new Germany as they have done before. Instead, even within this liberal and traditionally open-minded group, anti-Muslim sentiment can be observed, argued mainly through post-liberal motives (such as opposing Muslims because "they" are against women, homosexuals, or Jews).

*Debates on national security issues.* It is no accident that a rise in racism against Muslims has been observed since the September 11, 2001 terrorist attacks. Concerns about Muslim fundamentalism and national security issues have too often fed into nationalist and anti-Muslim discourse. With fears of a "clash of civilizations" already expressed by some going back to the 1990s, German residents of a Muslim migration background were looked upon with mistrust that only grew after 9/11. Shortly after the attacks, then-Interior Minister Otto Schily initiated the computer-assisted profiling of Muslim students, which had the effect of implicitly asking Muslims to publicly distance themselves from the terrorist acts and terrorism itself. This and other acts tested Muslims' loyalty toward Germany and fostered the "Muslimization" of the security debate in Germany. And even though politically motivated violence, particularly from the right, has been much more pronounced than Islamist violence over the past decade, to this day, Interior Minister Hans-Peter Friedrich conceives of Islamic terrorism as the biggest threat to Germany (Federal Ministry of the Interior 2011).

*Economic crisis.* As studies mentioned earlier have shown, anti-Muslim attitudes are linked to a general increase in prejudice and social exclusion taking place in a climate of growing competition, fear of unemployment, and a reduction in social services.[108] Such fears, spurred by global financial crisis, have led to rising nationalist sentiment and right-wing populism and especially to anti-Muslim sentiment in a number of European countries (Zick, Küpper, and Hövermann 2011).

## Recommendations for New Inclusive Narratives

The recent *Transatlantic Trends* study, in which 78 percent of Germans identified Germany as a country of immigration, gives reason for hope (GMFUS 2011: 48). Another opinion poll from the German Council on Migration and Integration shows an increasing pragmatic attitude among non-immigrant Germans who believe that a peaceful coexistence between people with and without migration backgrounds is possible (Sachverständigenrat deutscher Stiftungen für Integration und Migration 2011). Though the reasons for this potential shift in attitudes are not yet clear, they may have to do with an increased realization that the German economy requires more workers than the country produces. Such attitudes, however, are not yet strong enough; they need to become part of a general discourse and a new narrative of collective identity:

*From "Kulturnation" to "Nation of Immigrants" via "Verfassungspatriotismus."* To this day, Germany perceives itself as a *Kulturnation*, with an essential German culture that is inherently linked to language. As *Transatlantic Trends* shows, Germans perceive knowledge of the language as the most important precondition to obtaining citizenship – much more than other European nations (GMFUS 2011: 27). Even talking with an accent somehow singles you out. Instead of such a homogenous and exclusionist concept of national identity, the idea

---

108 Interestingly enough, Thilo Sarrazin was not only known for his anti-Muslim attitudes, but also for prejudice against welfare recipients. It is no coincidence that these attitudes of exclusion go hand in hand (*Süddeutsche Zeitung* 2008).

of a *Verfassungspatriotismus* (patriotism to the constitution) should again be strengthened. This idea was established exactly because there was a need for defining a basis of citizenship through the law and constitution and not through diffuse moments of mythical or ancestral belonging (Sternberger 1990). The constitution *(Verfassung)* offers a set of norms and values that is much more tangible and real than the oft-proclaimed idea of a *Leitkultur* meant to guide immigrants toward German integration. It can serve as a base on which all Germans can rely – be they immigrants or ethnic Germans. Having this shared base makes the idea of perceiving Germany as it really is today seem like less of a threat; a country of immigration no longer has to be viewed as a country without stable ground.

*From hybrid selves to hybrid society.* Hybrid identities and multiple places of belonging are commonplace for (post-)migrants (Foroutan 2010). Theirs is an increasingly hybrid, post-national, self-empowered, and self-confident identity, through which they perceive themselves as active members of German society and for whom integration is no longer a category of achievement. In fact, they do not feel like outsiders having to be integrated somewhere themselves (Liljeberg Research International/INFO GmbH 2009). The challenge is how to transport these hybrid constitutions of heterogeneous narratives from the intrapersonal level to the narrative of a *society.* The pluralist narratives of identity and belonging that already exist for many German citizens – be they ethnic Germans or hyphenated ones (Spielhaus 2011) – can serve as a starting point to build a societal German identity marked by hybridity and plurality (Kraus 2006).

*From national to postnational.* Despite difficulties in strengthening the development of a European identity, this project is still gaining strength as a utopian vision: It presents a glimpse of a collective identity that goes beyond the national level and dangerous exclusionist implications. Instead, it opens the way for thinking beyond this form of collective identification again and trying to create a new "post-national constellation" in a postmodern world (Habermas 1998).

*From "old Germanness" to "New Germany."* Finally, Germany needs a strong multicultural narrative similar to the founding myth of the

United States as a nation of immigrants. This myth, though present from the earliest days of the United States, did not turn into a narrative of social cohesion until the social upheaval of the 1960s (Gabaccia 2002). Certainly, a similar process in Germany would have to take into account the country's specific national history. One element of that narrative could focus on the decades after World War II, when Germany underwent an "economic miracle." During this period, the economic prosperity of swaths of society was secured by foreign "guest workers" working hand in hand with postwar Germans. This can be a bonding narrative: *Auferstanden aus Ruinen* – hand in hand we built this country, and hand in hand we tell our children how we did it. Challenging homogenous concepts of national identity and pointing out Germany's diverse past and present – and making clear that homogeneity was only a fiction of National Socialism – can help strengthen a perception of a "New Germany" as a heterogeneous, pluralistic society.

## Implications for Policymakers

The shift in the national narrative on identity and its new formulation must be strengthened by policymakers and educators working at all levels of society, whether through media, schools and universities, or public discourse.

More concretely, there is a need to tackle stereotypical communication and representation of Muslims in a Germany that is much more pluralistic than public opinion suggests. This leads to the following recommendations for policymakers:

- *Review school books.* Break stereotypical depictions of migrants, Muslims, and people of color and point out their contributions to Germany's past and present (Georg-Eckert-Institut 2011).
- *Diversify collective symbols.* Whether through the national anthem, government agencies, or advertising campaigns, expressions of diversity can help shape a new understanding of what society can look like.

- *Develop media guides for how to represent Muslims.* Stereotypical portraits, specifically of Muslims, in the media reinforce existing imagery. Sensitizing journalists and other media figures to challenge these pictures will be a positive step toward changing public opinion of immigrants and Muslims.
- *Communicate academic findings concerning positive integration achievements.* As described above, there have been many positive developments concerning integration in Germany over the past half century. This success needs to be communicated to the public in order to embed it in the collective memory.
- *Communicate that the skills and potential of people with a migration background are valuable as well as necessary resources for the entire country.* Germany's position as a leading global exporter and political player is dependent on its international image. It needs to communicate its de facto heterogeneity and get rid of its outdated (and fictional) image of homogeneity.

Beyond this, there are several problems that government and security agencies need to address in their day-to-day work:
- *Challenge racism and xenophobia.* Government programs such as *Vielfalt tut gut: Jugend für Vielfalt, Toleranz und Demokratie* ("Diversity is good for us: Youth for Diversity, Tolerance and Democracy")[109] or the more recent *Toleranz fördern – Kompetenz stärken* ("Advance Tolerance – Improve Your Skills")[110] have done a good job of challenging racism on a local level, taking into account specific communal needs and situations. These are positive examples of educational programs that need to be continued and strengthened.
- *Monitor the rise of right-wing populist parties,* such as the National Democratic Party (NPD), or newer groups, such as Pro Deutschland or Die Freiheit and, where applicable, take legal action. Right-wing populist Internet blogs must be exposed and their hate speech analyzed just like that of radical Islamist websites and blogs.

109 www.vielfalt-tut-gut.de.
110 www.toleranz-foerdern-kompetenz-staerken.de/.

- *Enforce equal-employment initiatives and consider the introduction of affirmative action*, with the intent of making people with a migration background more visible in corporations, the media, and public office. This would also help in creating role models for young people. This step should also include long-term support for programs such as the *Allgemeines Gleichbehandlungsgesetz (General Equal Treatment Act)*, which allows people to go to court on the grounds of racially based discrimination. Currently, only between 2 and 3 percent of government and public service employees have a migration background.[111] Similarly, only about 3 percent of journalists in public media (see Neue deutsche Medienmacher n.d.) and 4.5 percent of teachers come from a migrant background, compared to 35 percent of the entire student population (DGB Bildungswerk Bund 2010a).

- *Continue the Deutsche Islamkonferenz.* The *Deutsche Islamkonferenz* (German Islam Conference) has been a major step in a sponsored dialogue between German state institutions and members of Muslim communities. Despite inevitable difficulties, this institution has proven relevant and productive, and should be continued.

---

111 These numbers are taken from a data analysis of public service/government employees in the state of North Rhine-Westphalia. In other states, an even smaller quota is to be expected. See Ministerium für Arbeit, Integration und Soziales des Landes Nordrhein-Westfalen n.d.

# Works Cited

Allensbach Archive. IfD-Umfrage 10061. September 2010.

Aslan, Ali. *New Approaches to Muslim Engagement – A View from Germany*. Washington, DC: German Marshall Fund of the United States, 2011. www.gmfus.org/galleries/ct_publication_attachments/ Aslan_MuslimIntegration_Feb11.pdf.

Attia, Iman. *Die "westliche Kultur" und ihr Anderes. Zur Dekonstruktion von Orientalismus und antimuslimischem Rassismus*. Bielefeld: Transcript, 2009.

Beck, Ulrich. *Risikogesellschaft. Auf dem Weg in eine andere Moderne*. Frankfurt a.M.: Suhrkamp, 1986.

Bielefeldt, Heiner. *Das Islambild in Deutschland – Zum öffentlichen Umgang mit der Angst vor dem Islam*. Berlin: Deutsches Institut für Menschenrechte, 2008. www.institut-fuer-menschenrechte.de/ fileadmin/user_upload/Publikationen/Essay/essay_no_7_das_ islambild_in_deutschland.pdf.

Brückner, Gunter. Pressemitteilung 248. News release, Statistisches Bundesamt, July 14, 2010. www.destatis.de/DE/PresseService/ Presse/Pressemitteilungen/2010/07/PD10_248_122.html.

Bundesamt für Verfassungsschutz (Federal Office for the Protection of the Constitution). *Yearly Report*. Berlin: Bundesamt für Verfassungsschutz, 2010. www.verfassungsschutz.de/de/publikationen/ verfassungsschutzbericht/vsbericht_2010/.

Bundesregierung (Federal Government). *Erster Integrationsgipfel*. Berlin: Bundesregierung, 2006. www.bundesregierung.de/Content/ DE/Artikel/IB/Artikel/2008-11-06-integrationsgipfel.html.

Cesari, Jocelyne. The Securitisation of Islam in Europe. Challenge Research Paper 14, April 2009. Brussels: Centre for European Policy Studies, 2009. www.ceps.eu/node/1648.

Decker, Oliver, Marliese Weißmann, Johannes Kiess and Elmar Brähler. *Die Mitte in der Krise – Rechtsextreme Einstellungen in Deutschland 2010*. Berlin: Friedrich-Ebert-Stiftung, 2010. http://library. fes.de/pdf-files/do/07504.pdf.

DGB Bildungswerk Bund. Zunehmende segregative Erscheinungen. *Forum Migration Newletter* 7/2010a. www.migration-online.de/ data/publikationen_datei_1277900145.pdf.

DGB Bildungswerk Bund. Menschen mit Migrationshintergrund Anteil der Bevölkerung mit Migration Hinterland. *Forum Migration Newletter* 10/2010b. www.migration-online.de/data/publikationen_ datei_1285751517.pdf.

Elias, Norbert, and John L. Scotson. *Etablierte und Außenseiter.* Frankfurt a.M.: Suhrkamp, 1994.

Federal Ministry of the Interior. Deutsche Islam Konferenz am 27. News release, September 19, 2006. www.deutsche-islam-konferenz. de/nn_1864812/SharedDocs/Pressemitteilungen/DE/DIK/060927-pressemitteilung-01-06-bmi.html.

Federal Ministry of the Interior. Verfassungsschutzbericht 2010: Bundesinnenminister Dr. Friedrich stellt Ergebnisse vor. News release, July 1, 2011. www.bmi.bund.de/SharedDocs/Pressemittei lungen/DE/2011/mitMarginalspalte/07/vsb2010.html.

Federal Office for Migration and Refugees. *Muslim Life in Germany.* Berlin: Federal Office for Migration and Refugees, 2009. www. bamf.de/SharedDocs/Anlagen/EN/Publikationen/Forschungsbe richte/fb06-muslimisches-leben.pdf?__blob=publikationFile.

Foroutan, Naika. Neue Deutsche, Postmigranten und Bindungs-Identitäten. Wer gehört zum neuen Deutschland? *Aus Politik und Zeitgeschichte* 46/47: 9–15, 2010.

Foroutan, Naika, Korinna Schäfer, Coskun Canan, and Benjamin Schwarze. *Sarrazins Thesen auf dem Prüfstand – Ein empirischer Gegenentwurf zu Thilo Sarrazins Thesen zu Muslimen in Deutschland.* Berlin: Humboldt-Universität zu Berlin, 2010.

Gabaccia, Donna. *Immigration and American Diversity – A Social and Cultural History.* Malden, Mass.: Blackwell Publishers, 2002.

Georg-Eckert-Institut. *Keine Chance auf Zugehörigkeit? Schulbücher europäischer Länder halten Islam und modernes Europa getrennt.* Braunschweig: Georg-Eckert-Institut, 2011. www.gei.de/fileadmin/ bilder/pdf/Presse_interviews/Islamstudie_2011.pdf.

GMFUS – German Marshall Fund of the United States. *Transatlantic Trends – Topline Data 2010.* Washington, DC: GMFUS, 2011. http:// trends.gmfus.org/files/archived/immigration/doc/TTI2010_ English_Top.pdf.

Giesen, Bernhard. The Trauma of the Perpetrators: The Holocaust as the Traumatic Reference of German National Identity. In *Cultural Trauma and Collective Identity*, edited by Jeffrey Alexander, Ron Eyerman, Bernhard Giesen, Neil Smelser, and Piotr Sztompka. Berkeley: University of California Press, 2004: 112–155.

Göle, Nilüfer. *Anverwandlungen. Der Islam in Europa zwischen Kopftuchverbot und Extremismus.* Berlin: Wagenbach, 2008. French original: *L'Islam et l'Europe.* Paris: Éditions Galaade, 2005.

Habermas, Jürgen. Geschichtsbewußtsein und postnationale Identität. Die Westorientierung der Bundesrepublik. In *Eine Art Schadensabwicklung*, edited by Jürgen Habermas. Frankfurt a.M.: Suhrkamp, 1987: 161–179.

Habermas, Jürgen. *Die postnationale Konstellation. Politische Essays.* Frankfurt a.M.: Suhrkamp, 1998.

Haug, Sonja, Stephanie Müssig, and Anja Stichs. *Muslim Life in Germany.* Nuremberg: Federal Office for Migration and Refugees, 2009. www.euro-islam.info/wp-content/uploads/pdfs/muslim_ life_in_germany_long.pdf.

Heitmeyer, Wilhelm. *Deutsche Zustände* Vol. 9. Frankfurt a.M.: Suhrkamp, 2010.

Heitmeyer, Wilhelm. *Deutsche Zustände* Vol. 10. Berlin: Suhrkamp, 2011.

Institut für Mittelstandsforschung der Universität Mannheim. *Die Bedeutung der ethnischen Ökonomie in Deutschland.* Mannheim: Universität Mannheim, 2005. www.bmwi.de/BMWi/Redaktion/ PDF/C-D/die-bedeutung-der-ethnischen-oekonomie-fuer-deutsch land-kurzfassung,property=pdf,bereich=bmwi,sprache=de,rwb= true.pdf.

Jung, Dorothea. Politically Incorrect – Allianz der Islamhasser. *Blätter für deutsche und internationale Politik* 11: 13–16, 2010.

Jürges, Hendrik, and Kerstin Schneider. *Age at School Entry and Teacher's Recommendations for Secondary School Track Choice in*

*Germany.* University of Mannheim and University of Wuppertal, 2006. www.vwl.uni-freiburg.de/iwipol/faculty_seminar/age_at_school_entry.pdf.

Kaas, Leo, and Christine Manger. Ethnic Discrimination in Germany's Labour Market: A Field Experiment. IZA Discussion Paper 4741, February 2010. Bonn: IZA. http://ftp.iza.org/dp4741.pdf.

Keupp, Heiner. *Identitätskonstruktionen: Das Patchwork der Identitäten in der Spätmoderne.* Reinbek: Rowohlt, 2008.

Kniebe, Tobias. Wer hat Angst vorm fremden Mann? *Süddeutsche Zeitung* January 8, 2011. www.sueddeutsche.de/kultur/thilo-sarrazin-und-seine-leser-wer-hat-angst-vorm-fremden-mann-1.1043753.

Koopmans, Ruud, Paul Statham, Marco Giugni, and Florence Pass. *Contested Citizenship: Immigration and Cultural Diversity in Europe.* Minneapolis, Minn.: University of Minnesota Press, 2005.

Kramer, Jane. *The Politics of Memory: Looking for Germany in the New Germany.* New York: Random House, 1996.

Kraus, Wolfgang. The Narrative Negotiation of Identity and Belonging. *Narrative Inquiry* (16) 1: 103–111, 2006.

Kury, Helmut. Präventionskonzepte. In *Auf der Suche nach neuer Sicherheit,* edited by Hans-Jürgen Lange, Peter H. Ohly, and Jo Reichertz. Wiesbaden: VS Verlag, 2008: 21–47.

Liljeberg Research International/INFO GmbH. Deutsch-Türkische Wertewelten. News release, November 19, 2009. www.infogmbh.de/aktuell/Pressemitteilung-fuer-pressekonferenz4.pdf.

Ministerium für Arbeit, Integration und Soziales des Landes Nordrhein-Westfalen. Mehr Menschen mit Migrationshintergrund in den öffentlichen Dienst. n.d. www.integration.nrw.de/Meldungen/pm2011/Mehr_Menschen_mit_Migrationshintergrund_in_den_oeffentlichen_Dienst/index.php.

Neue deutsche Medienmacher. Willkommen bei den Neuen deutschen Medienmachern! n.d. www.neuemedienmacher.de.

Panayi, Panikos. Racial Violence in the New Germany 1990–93. *Contemporary European History* (3) 3: 265–288, 1994.

Petzinger, Jill. Arson and Integration: Have Berlin Mosques Become a Target? *Spiegel Online International,* December 29, 2010. www.spiegel.de/international/germany/0,1518,736337,00.html.

Pew Forum on Religion and Public Life. *The Future of the Global Muslim Population – Projection for 2010–2030*. Washington, DC: Pew Forum on Religion and Public Life, 2011. www.pewforum.org/The-Future-of-the-Global-Muslim-Population.aspx.

Pollack, Detlef. Wahrnehmung und Akzeptanz religiöser Vielfalt. Study by the Religion and Politics Excellence Cluster, Westfälischen Wilhelms-Universität Münster, 2011. www.uni-muenster.de/imperia/md/content/religion_und_politik/aktuelles/2010/12_2010/studie_wahrnehmung_und_akzeptanz_religioeser_vielfalt.pdf.

Projekt HEyMAT. Links. www.heymat.hu-berlin.de/links.

Sachverständigenrat deutscher Stiftungen für Integration und Migration. Umfrage: Sarrazin-Debatte trübt Zuversicht bei Zuwanderern in Deutschland. SVR sieht "Eigentor." News release, January 10, 2011. www.svr-migration.de/?page_id=2633.

Sarrazin, Thilo. *Deutschland schafft sich ab*. Munich: Deutsche Verlags-Anstalt, 2010.

Schäuble, Wolfgang. Deutsche Islam Konferenz – Perspektiven für eine gemeinsame Zukunft. 2006. www.deutsche-islam-konferenz.de/nn_1866426/SubSites/DIK/DE/PresseService/RedenInterviews/Reden/20060928-regerkl-dik-perspektiven.html.

Spielhaus, Riem. *Wer ist hier Muslim?: Die Entwicklung eines islamischen Bewusstseins in Deutschland zwischen Selbstidentifikation und Fremdzuschreibung*. Würzburg: Ergon-Verlag, 2011.

Statistiches Bundesamt. *Statistical Yearbook 2010 for the Federal Republic of Germany*. Wiesbaden: Statistiches Bundesamt, 2010.

Statistisches Bundesamt. *Bevölkerung und Erwerbstätigkeit: Bevölkerung mit Migrationshintergrund – Ergebnisse des Mikrozensus 2011*. Wiesbaden: Statistisches Bundesamt, 2011.

Statistisches Landesamt Baden-Württemberg. Indikatoren zum Thema: Migrantenanteil, 2011. www.statistikportal.de/Bevoelk Gebiet/Indikatoren/BV-BS_migranten.asp.

Sternberger, Dolf. Verfassungspatriotismus. Rede bei der 25-Jahr-Feier der 'Akademie für Politische Bildung' (1982). In *Verfassungspatriotismus. Schriften Bd. X*, edited by Dolf Sternberger. Frankfurt a.M.: Insel Verlag, 1990: 17–31.

*Süddeutsche Zeitung.* Einfach 'nen dicken Pulli anziehen. July 29, 2008. www.sueddeutsche.de/politik/finanzsenator-sarrazin-einfach-nen-dicken-pulli-anziehen-1.574212.

Tajfel, Henri, and John C. Turner. The Social Identity Theory of Intergroup Behavior. In *Psychology of intergroup relations*, 2nd edition, edited by Steven Worchel and William G. Austin. Chicago: Nelson Hall, 1986: 7–24.

Terkessidis, Mark. *Die Banalität des Rassismus. Migranten zweiter Generation entwickeln eine neue Perspektive.* Bielefeld: Transcript, 2004.

Thränhardt, Dietrich. Germany – an Undeclared Immigration Country. In *Europe – a New Immigration Continent: Policies and Politics since 1945 in Comparative Perspective,* edited by Dietrich Thränhardt. Hamburg: LIT, 1992: 167–194.

Townsend, Mark. Far-right anti-Muslim network on rise globally as Breivik trial opens. *The Guardian* April, 14, 2012. www.guardian.co.uk/world/2012/apr/14/breivik-trial-norway-mass-murderer.

Zick, Andreas, Beate Küpper and Andreas Hövermann. *Intolerance, Prejudice and Discrimination: A European Report.* Berlin: Friedrich-Ebert-Stiftung, 2011. http://library.fes.de/pdf-files/do/07908-20110311.pdf.

# The Netherlands: From National Identity to Plural Identifications

*Monique Kremer*

## Introduction[112]

After Anders Behring Breivik killed 77 people in Norway in July 2011, portraying the victims as "traitors" who embraced multiculturalism and immigration, the focus of many journalists quickly turned to another small country in northwestern Europe: the Netherlands. In a 1,500-page manifesto posted online hours before the horrific attacks, Breivik mentioned Geert Wilders, the leader of the third-biggest political party in the Netherlands, 30 times. This thrust the Netherlands on the international agenda again, several years after the emergence (and later murder) of right-wing populist Pim Fortuyn by an animal-rights activist and the killing of director Theo van Gogh by an Islamic radical.

How did it come to pass that a political leader in the tolerant, peaceful, globally connected Netherlands served as a source of inspiration for an anti-Muslim, nationalist murderer in Norway?

Shortly after Breivik's rampage, a *New York Times* article revealed the widespread anxiety in the Netherlands, quoting a native Dutch resident as saying: "Sometimes I'm afraid of Islam ... They're taking over the neighborhood and they're very strong. I no longer feel at home" (Erlanger 2011). These sentences exemplify Dutch discontent and the feeling of being displaced in one's own country. The inter-

---

112  This chapter draws substantially from the author's work with Pauline Meurs, Dennis Broeders, and Erik Schrijvers for the Dutch Scientific Council for Government Policies (WRR 2007).

viewee went on to say that, despite her disdain for Wilders' style, he "says what many people think."

In the past decade, there has been a backlash against what people perceive as "political correctness." Citizens who no longer feel "at home" in the Netherlands have been voicing their anxieties and demanding acknowledgment of their concerns from politicians. Fortuyn, a controversial Dutch politician who called Islam "a backward culture," was the first to publicly give voice to discontent with the multicultural society. Although other political parties – both right- and left-wing – had discussed the negative consequences of migration, Fortuyn was the first who made the issue politically prominent. The sociological feelings of discontent, in a country that is one of the world's most densely populated and has welcomed significant inflows as guest workers or from former Dutch colonies since the end of World War II,[113] were made political.

It is in this context that national identity became a political and policy issue. Reinforcing national identity has two purported policy goals: first, it aims to provide a sense of stability and comfort to those who feel anxiety – or a sense of loss – about the changes wrought by globalization and immigration; and, second, it is also seen as a way to encourage integration by giving immigrants the necessary information about their new homeland so they are better able to fit in. In 2004, the Dutch government stated that the idea of multicultural society had failed. The focus on national identity in the Dutch context meant a farewell to the ideal of the multicultural society and a welcome to the culturalization of citizenship – whereby newcomers to the Netherlands have to fully adopt Dutch culture in order to become citizens. This is a more exclusionary approach, allowing only one accepted "Dutch national identity" as opposed to multiple means of identification with the Netherlands.

This chapter describes the discontent within Dutch society and subsequent search for an explanation. It also outlines the dominant

---

113  As of 2011, 20.6 percent of the country's 16.65 million residents were immigrants or had at least one foreign-born parent (CBS n.d.).

policy response, in which national identity is one of the key themes. Finally, the chapter tries to provide an alternative set of recommendations based on the idea that national identity as policy can cause counterproductive effects. Instead, the notion of plural identifications, which is a two-way process, offers more fruitful policy options.

## Polarization in the Netherlands

Group distinctions and boundaries – whether drawn along ethnic, religious, linguistic, or other lines – are a reality for all societies. Even though the Organization for Economic Cooperation and Development (OECD) has ranked the Netherlands as one of the more "equal" countries (based on inequality ratios), this does not mean there are no divisions or tensions between different groups (OECD 2011). Before and after World War II, religious distinctions between neutral, Catholic, and Protestant groups were dominant. The organization of politics and daily life was built on religious pillarization. Around the turn of this century, however, new dividing lines became apparent: Now the twin concepts of *allochtoon* (not from the Netherlands; literally, "not from here") and *autochtoon* (from the Netherlands) came to be perceived as the crucial distinction. The concept of *allochtoon* also applies to children born in the Netherlands to foreign-born parents. Comparative European statistics from 2003 show that 61 percent of Dutch people said most societal tensions were between *allochtonen* and *autochtonen*; far fewer reported tensions between the rich and the poor (25 percent), men and women (9 percent), and old and young (18 percent) (WRR 2006). This pattern is also visible in other European countries, particularly in France and Belgium. In the minds of a fair number of people in Europe, and particularly in the Netherlands, "us versus them" group distinctions are based on people born in the country versus (non-Western) migrants and their children.

These new tensions are also visible in voting behavior. In 2002, Fortuyn's party (Lijst Pim Fortuyn) won 17 percent of the vote in Dutch national elections (just days after his assassination) – the first significant victory for an anti-Islam, anti-immigration party. After forming part of a coalition government, the party collapsed within months and was followed by another, less successful party: Rita Verdonk's newly formed Trots op Nederland (TON, or "Proud of the Netherlands") party. In 2010, Wilders' Partij voor de Vrijheid (PVV, Party for Freedom) received 15.5 percent of the vote for the Dutch Parliament, making it the third-biggest party in the Netherlands.

While not identical, the PVV, TON, and Lijst Pim Fortuyn have much in common. They are nationalist, premised on distinguishing natives from "others," such as immigrants and Muslims; anti-establishment; critical of political institutionalism; anti-European Union; fearful of globalization; and focused on national identity. The parties have been able to reframe the issue of migration from a juridical and legal one to a cultural one; they now consider all social problems, such as public safety and social cohesion, to be linked to migration or Muslims.

The people who have voted for these parties can loosely be labeled as "voters from the periphery," although they now comprise a fair share of the population. Voters for Wilders in 2010 were often low- (sometimes middle-) educated, male, and over 55. They live in specific neighborhoods and regions, particularly in the south of Holland (Limburg), in which Wilders has siphoned votes from the Christian Democrats.[114] Many PVV supporters live in stagnating industrial areas where unemployment and the aging of society are an issue. Voters for Wilders (as for Fortuyn in 2002) also live in suburban areas (such as the planned city of Almere), outside the economic, cultural, and governmental heart of the Netherlands (De Voogd 2011).

Although journalists tend to go to neighborhoods with majority Muslim populations to understand "Dutch discontent," there is no straightforward connection between the areas where people voted for Wilders and the number of Muslims residing there (Van Gent and Musterd 2010; De Voogd 2011). Contrary to popular belief, Wilders

114 Other constituencies are located in the west of Brabant, Rijnmond region, and Zeeuws Vlaanderen.

voters are not the ones likely to have run-ins with misbehaving Moroccan youth and who report that their neighborhoods have been "taken over." This is especially important because the Social Democratic politicians tend to respond to populist victories by campaigning in disadvantaged inner-city neighborhoods. But the people who have stayed in the city center are often the ones who are able to cope with, and even enjoy, cultural diversity. It is not necessarily their day-to-day experiences that shape the views and votes of those who are anti-Muslim, anti-establishment, and anti-immigration. Some live in areas with nearby immigrant communities, so they may be afraid that their neighborhood will be the next to lose its identity. But many Wilders voters also base their views on the images they have of the Netherlands. What they see on TV may take on more importance than what they encounter around the corner from their house.

Anti-immigrant attitudes and cultural conservatism are, however, much more widespread than the voting patterns for Wilders and Fortuyn before him reveal. People who feel that the multicultural society has failed and that the Netherlands has been overwhelmed by immigrants may also support another political party that has grown rapidly: the Socialist Party. Also fishing in the social conservative pond, the Socialist Party expresses anti-Europe standpoints, is in favor of immigrant assimilation into the broader society, and stresses the importance of national identity.[115]

In response to the successes of Fortuyn and Wilders, the Labour Party has also adopted the tough language of assimilation and anti-immigration in order to avoid being considered "too soft" on social issues. For example, Wilders put pressure on former Labour Leader Job Cohen, ridiculing the multiculturalist stance Cohen first undertook as mayor of Amsterdam as little more than an effort to "sit and

115  Previous Socialist Party Head Jan Marijnissen said in 2004: "The Muslim community must understand that there is a collective responsibility to combat excesses such as political Islam. Educators, teachers and imams must choose for our Constitution and bring up children in its spirit. If one is not prepared to conform to our values and obey our laws, the pressing advice is: Seek a country where you feel at home." See Duyvendak 2011: 93.

drink tea with the Muslims." The right-wing Volkspartij voor Vrijheid en Democratie (the People's Party for Freedom and Democracy, or VVD) shows anti-immigrant tendencies and an emphasis on national identity, as well, although the party is split into two camps. One camp is connected to employers who prefer cultural openness and are in favor of immigration as a way to win the battle of globalization and overcome the demographic time bomb; the second faction is more nationally conservative. (Wilders and Verdonk both sprang from the VVD.) Recently departed Prime Minister Mark Rutte employed Wilders' rhetoric by saying: "We will make sure that we give this beautiful Netherlands back to the Dutch" (Zandbergen 2011). Only two smaller parties – D66 and the Green Left Party – continue to fiercely oppose adopting the rhetoric of national identity and cultural assimilation.

### No Consensus on Views toward Immigrants

Dutch politics revolve deeply around anti-immigration, anti-Muslim, and pro-national identity feelings and ideas, which are more widespread than electoral support for the PVV shows. Yet, there is no anti-immigration or anti-Muslim consensus: Dutch society is deeply polarized. This is visible from the regular surveys conducted by the Sociaal en Cultureel Planbureau (Social and Cultural Planning Office, or SCP). For instance, when asked whether the Netherlands would be a nicer country to live in if fewer immigrants lived there, a 2011 survey showed 32 percent disagreed and 41 percent agreed (SCP 2011a). In addition, 54 percent agreed that the national identity of the Netherlands is threatened by immigration and open borders, whereas 24 percent disagreed. This shows that while a small majority fears migration because of the perceived loss of national identity, a substantial number disagree. Moreover, when asked whether the presence of different cultures represents a gain for society, 41 percent agreed, while only 27 percent disagreed. Dutch society shows much ambivalence, but over the last decade, much of the public has connected immigration with social problems and loss of national identity.

Still, these attitudes and feelings can shift over time. Studies show that support for the view that there are too many people of different nationality in the Netherlands dropped to 38 percent in 2009 from 51 percent in 2000 and 48 percent in 1994 (SCP 2011b). While multiculturalism topped the list of most cited social problems during the last decade, since the onset of the economic recession, the issue has dropped from the top five concerns most important to the public (ibid.).

It is social cohesion that has dominated public concern in the Netherlands over the last decade and, until recently, a majority – although small – linked this to issues of immigration and Islam.

This brings us to the question of how to interpret and explain this link. Why have cultural issues of assimilation, national identity, and anti-Muslim sentiment become so pronounced?

## The Link between Cultural Insecurity and Politics

Anti-immigrant views and ethnic intolerance are often connected to education levels. People with higher levels of education tend to be more ethnically tolerant and more pro-immigrant, while less-educated people tend to have the opposite views (Sniderman and Hagendoorn 2007). The academic debate focuses on identifying the underlying factors: Why are less-educated people less tolerant?

In the Netherlands, we have seen that anti-immigrant and anti-Muslim attitudes do not fluctuate predictably according to economic cycles. When Fortuyn made his political debut, the economy was doing well, producing relatively high growth rates and low unemployment. The "ethnic competition theory" – that less-educated people fear they will have to compete with low-skilled migrants – does not necessarily hold: Neither income level nor weak employment situations can reliably predict public opinion toward immigration. Voters for Wilders, for example, tend to live in areas where there is little competition for work or housing between immigrants and natives, though it is possible that some *perceive* this to be the case (van Gent and Musterd 2010).

So far, the conflict in the Netherlands seems to be about culture rather than economic scarcity (Sniderman and Hagendoorn 2007). Less-educated people have less cultural capital and are therefore unable to cope smoothly with ethnic and other differences. This cultural insecurity – when people fear their norms and values are being taken over, and that their national identity itself is at stake – leads people to turn to authoritarianism, rigid social order, and intolerance toward others.[116] Therefore, intolerance seems to be primarily rooted in the *cultural* background of the less educated rather than as a result of competition over resources (Houtman and Duyvendak 2009), and, as such, people who are ethnically and/or culturally different are considered a cultural rather than an economic threat.

Looking at the postwar Netherlands, cultural capital has grown rapidly. Thirty percent of the population has benefited from higher education, so one would expect more people to be able to cope with differences and exhibit increased tolerance. Yet a substantial number of people continue to feel culturally insecure and threatened. The dominant explanation is that the Dutch political establishment pushed multicultural policies too far by giving "special treatment" to newcomers. By 1994, 60 percent believed that the onus should be on immigrants and minorities to adapt to Dutch culture, and they perceived that political leaders ignored their wishes in pursuit of the ideal of a multicultural society (Sniderman and Hagendoorn 2007; Koopmans and Muis 2009). This argument, however, is far from the truth. The Netherlands never pushed through fully fledged multicultural policies promoting diverse religious and cultural identities, focusing instead on socioeconomically disadvantaged ethnic minorities (Duyvendak 2011). Moreover, other countries (e.g., the United Kingdom), have always been more supportive of institutionalized diversity.

---

116  The extensive surveys of van der Waal and Houtman (2011) and van der Waal, de Koster, and Achterberg (2011) show that not only are low education levels linked to authoritarianism and a need to stress social order, but also that the intermediate factor was not income or employment insecurity, but issues of (cultural) insecurity. In addition, the existence of cultural capital was essential.

It is more likely that cultural insecurity, which is more dominant among the less educated, is fueled by processes of globalization. According to the sociologist Zygmunt Bauman, globalization divides societies into small global elites with a hybrid culture, while the majority gets more "local" – turning to local traditions because they do not feel connected to the new global culture of the elite (Bauman 1998). Especially for the less educated, globalization fosters feelings of authoritarianism and ethnocentrism, and parallel processes of secularization and individualization can lead to a possible feeling of loss of control (Houtman and Duyvendak 2009). While the more educated feel better able to deal with globalization and are more able to cope with uncertainties, less-educated people become more insecure and try to keep what they have.

Also possibly contributing to feelings of discontent is the fact that the political establishment and the economic elite, particularly in the Netherlands, have always unequivocally favored global openness and European integration. With Dutch economic well-being largely dependent on international trade, globalization and greater European integration are said to benefit the nation. Therefore, the discontent and the success of populist parties are sometimes seen as a revolt against the establishment by low- and middle-educated publics.

Cultural fears may also be fueled by uneven patterns and perceptions of mobility. Even though the Dutch have one of the highest intergenerational mobility rates in Europe (and much higher than in the United States) (OECD 2011) because of universal education, the majority feel that their children will be worse off. For the first time in decades, social stagnation is visible: 17 percent of the public, mostly men, are less well-off than their parents (RMO 2009). In the meantime, only one group that was previously at the lower end of the economic ladder is finally moving up: Labor market participation rates for Turkish and Moroccan Dutch have increased significantly in 15 years and are "just" 10 percent less than for the native Dutch (CBS 2011). While better-educated migrants are more tolerated, they may also be considered more of a cultural threat because they may be able to better articulate their values and make claims to cultural areas of life. In other words, the narrowing of the employment and education gap between natives and foreigners – perceived or real – also could cause anxiety, as natives will not be able to preserve their comparative advantage. Even if they are not in direct competition, the upward mobility of one group may cause fears for another group.

## Politics

Pim Fortuyn was able to present himself as anti-establishment and thus capitalize upon this discontent that the governing elite was pushing an agenda at odds with majority concerns, arguably even making the unease greater by giving it a specific target. His success lay in the fact that he was able to make anti-immigration, anti-Islam, and pro-national identity rhetoric *socially acceptable*. Because Fortuyn openly discussed issues that resonated with the public, he left the established parties with no choice but to take these concerns on board. Those parties had previously managed to avoid them (van der Brug and Mughan 2007). He made the issues of Islam and migration a normal part of political discourse. The subsequent reactions of media and other politicians created dynamic feedback processes that raised his popularity among the electorate – a phenomenon that Jasper Muis and Ruud Koopmans refer to as a "spiral of discursive escalation" (Koopmans and Muis 2009).

The emergence of Fortuyn's right-wing populist party has Dutch dimensions but is not unique to the Netherlands; it clearly fits into a larger shift of politics in European countries. Hanspeter Kriesi et al. describe a new structural conflict in Western European countries that pits those who benefit from processes of globalization (the "winners") against those who experience disadvantages (the "losers") (Kriesi et al. 2006). In this context, the cultural dimension has been gaining importance. Parties of the populist right do not stand out for their economic profile yet. It is on cultural issues where they support a demarcation strategy much more strongly than mainstream parties. Authoritarianism, according to Dick Houtman and Jan Willem

Duyvendak, has become the crucial pole in Dutch politics, defined on the scale of ethnocentrism and social order (Houtman and Duyvendak 2009). Whereas secularization and individualization left a political void in the Netherlands, globalization has opened up a new demarcation line between those who feel they are not in control and do not have a "grip" over their lives, and those who are able to cope with diversity.

So far, the political debate over globalization – which includes an economic component – has been fought in terms of culture and national identity precisely because it raises issues of well-being and the challenges of economic, social, and ethnic diversity at the national and local levels. Today, with the financial and economic crises rattling Europe and the world, globalization increasingly raises material concerns. It remains to be seen if the economic crisis will focus the globalization debate primarily on economic issues. It is too soon to draw conclusions but, as described before, just recently in the Netherlands, the issue of migration and multicultural society has dropped out of the top five most urgent problems identified by the Dutch population.

## Policy Response: National Identity and Cultural Assimilation

In 2000, Paul Scheffer published an essay titled "The Multicultural Drama" that ignited the controversial debate about integration and immigration in the Netherlands (Scheffer 2000). Scheffer argued that the Dutch should develop a greater sense of national consciousness and become less indifferent to their own society. Doing so would also benefit immigrants, he contended, because if "we" became better at defining and propagating "our" language, history, and culture, immigrants would know in which country they had to integrate. Therefore, following Scheffer's line of reasoning, the dominant policy response to cultural discontent has been to reject the ideal of the multicultural society, stress the (cultural) assimilation of one group (immigrants), remind the Dutch of their national identity by developing a national canon for educational purposes, reinforce this identity by building a national historic museum (the latter failed) and, finally, prohibit dual nationality.

The concept of *inburgering* – becoming an integrated citizen – was introduced in 1994 as just one step in the process of full integration. By 2007, a civic integration exam testing knowledge of Dutch society and language skills had become compulsory for non-Western, non-EU immigrants entering the Netherlands (and even for some already settled immigrants). The demands being placed upon immigrants became heavier and also took on more moral and cultural weight: Immigrants now have to become Dutch. In practice, this means that those who do not speak the language and fail the exam on Dutch history and practices are denied admission to the country. For those who are already here, rules have become stricter: Social assistance, for instance, can be reduced if one does not speak Dutch.

Becoming Dutch also means appearing to be less Muslim in public. In pursuit of electoral gains, Wilders proposed a *kopvoddentax* – a headscarf tax – in 2009. This was an unfeasible policy idea as it is too unpractical to be implemented, yet it insults and alienates those who wear a headscarf. This was followed in 2011 by Interior Minister Piet Hein Donner's (a Christian Democrat) proposing a prohibition on burqas in public spaces. In short, in addition to deepening the criteria for becoming Dutch, these rules now apply to a larger number of people. Nowadays, "integration" already starts abroad, as it has become a criterion for admission to the Netherlands, and people who immigrated a long time ago – the proverbial 55-year-old Turkish-origin housewives – have to follow the set integration trajectories.

Since 2004, the ideal of the multicultural society has been officially rejected by the Dutch government. The new minority has to fit into the existing majority. As former Minister Donner recently underlined in a policy paper (Ministerie van Binnenlandse Zaken en Koninkrijksrelaties 2011): "The persistence of integration problems underlines the image that the model of the multicultural society has not offered a solution for the dilemma of the pluriform society ... Again and again it shows that many Dutch people do not experience ethnic and cultural diversity as an enrichment, but as a threat. The Dutch society, in all her diversity, is the society in which those who settle have to learn to live, to which they have to adjust and fit into."

A national canon and museum focused on Dutch history were proposed to promote the country's culture. The museum, put forward by the Socialist Party, was never built because of political, national, and local power struggles and the economic crises. The canon, in contrast, was developed in 2006 and is obligatory for use in the Dutch education system.[117] Nevertheless, the commission that set up the canon rejected the notion of national identity: "If it has been a valid concept, now less than ever: In the international, multicultural world of today, it is a false, yes, dangerous concept." The commission does believe that the canon can contribute to integration (Commissie Ontwikkeling Nederlandse Canon 2006). However, the canon does not give space to divergence, diversity, or power differences. And even though historians agree that national identity is constructed and evolves according to dominant ideas, the national canon just gives one story about what the Netherlands is.

In the current debate over national identity in the Netherlands, a heated discussion has taken place on the issue of dual nationality. In practice, in the 1990s, people did not have to renounce the citizenship of their country of origin when they wanted to become Dutch. In 2004, when the issue was discussed again, then-Integration and Immigration Minister Rita Verdonk considered dual nationality to be a hindrance to integration and sought to ban it. But, today, a little over 1 million people have dual citizenship – including a member of the royal family and members of the government (which provoked a pub-

---

117 The canon is a set of ideas and historical events that are considered to be crucial for understanding Dutch history, decided upon by a commission of eminent historians. Some of the decisions made by the commission have been criticized fiercely: Migration, for instance, makes up just a tiny part of the canon and only with respect to the recent era. Most of the criticism, however, focuses on the fact that the canon is obligatory for us in the classroom. Schools and teachers are not allowed to discuss how they see Dutch history but must instead draw from the canon. History is thus not free from interpretation and power relations. See WRR 2007.

lic outcry in 2007 when the latter was revealed). Dual nationality is regarded as disloyalty. Such strong views about dual nationality are all the more striking because 68 percent of the Turkish-origin and 74 percent of the Moroccan-origin Dutch citizens who have dual nationality report that they feel at home in the Netherlands, compared to 78 and 80 percent (of the same groups) who only have Dutch nationality (Duyvendak 2011). This shows that dual citizenship is not a hindrance to "feeling at home" in the Netherlands.

## From National Identity to Plural Identities

Modern nation-states are built on a feeling of attachment to a community and culture defined as a "nation"; however, there are many variations in the ways "national identity" is shaped.[118] In the Netherlands, the common understanding of "being Dutch" is based on four categories: race/ethnicity, roots, cultural practices, and moral disposition. The Dutch-Iranian scholar Halleh Ghorashi calls this a "thick" notion of identity – premised on things such as shared heritage that cannot be easily acquired – which makes it possible to distinguish between "us" and "them" (Ghorashi 2003a). As a consequence, people from different backgrounds who are born in the Netherlands, or who have lived most of their lives in the country and have Dutch nationality, are not considered one of "us" (Ghorashi 2003b). This rigid, ancestry-based interpretation of national identity allows little space for multiple identities despite the fact that this is already a practice of millions of people today. By rejecting people's pasts, a group will feel excluded and perhaps alienate itself. By focusing on such a rigid and thick concept of national identity and forcing people into a single identity, the Netherlands may not be ready for a future in a globalized world where multiple identities are more common.

---

118 According to Benedict Anderson (1983), the modern nation-state is an "imagined community" that creates a feeling of attachment to the state in the form of love of the nation.

Therefore it is preferable to look to the future rather than the past and adopt a more dynamic, pluralistic approach. Rather than offering a blueprint for *the* national identity of the Netherlands, it is more useful to promote the idea that there can be several routes toward identification with the Netherlands. Three processes can be distinguished: emotional, normative, and functional identification. Such an approach offers greater scientific and policy opportunity to address present and future tensions in society.

## Emotional Identification

Emotional identification is about a sense of belonging and feeling connected, not only with other people and groups, but also with a country. The public debate in the Netherlands primarily revolves around emotional identification – encapsulated in the ideas of "feeling at home" and feeling pride for the country – which is no surprise in a society that increasingly pays more attention to emotions (Duyvendak 2011). Being proud of the Netherlands – as 87 percent of the Dutch said they were in 2006 – does not automatically lead to exclusion of others (WRR 2007). However, the Dutch intellectual and political elite had previously been reluctant to acknowledge people's emotional identification with the nation-state. Until recently, "becoming Dutch" was nothing more than picking up your passport from the government office. Today, however, there is a ritual at the town hall that accompanies the naturalization process, in which new citizens, surrounded by family and friends, are welcomed.

Emotional identification, however, could also be based on a "thin" definition of national identity – a more fluid concept derived from mutual and individual identification rather than shared ancestry or heritage. As Duyvendak notes: "If the ticket into Dutch society can only be obtained by being part of a longer national history, people with different backgrounds are confronted with insurmountable obstacles. Dutch society then only becomes accessible to people with deep roots in Dutch soil" (Duyvendak 2011: 101). He agrees with Ghorashi, who stresses:

265

"American national discourse allows thick cultural differences within its understanding of a thin notion of national identity. It is possible to be considered American – both by oneself as well as by others – within the diversity of physical appearances, languages, and cultural backgrounds. Thus, the notion of American identity is like an umbrella that includes different particularities" (Ghorashi 2003b: 221 f.).

A thin notion of national identity also allows for dual nationality, understanding that dual nationality as an expression of loyalty is a faulty link: Loyalty is not related to passports. The fact that many people of Moroccan or Turkish descent have Moroccan or Turkish passports may stem from practical motives: They need passports to go back to their country of origin or to protect land or other property there. Not wanting to renounce their nationality or disconnect fully from their country of origin does not necessarily indicate disloyalty toward the Netherlands or a sense that their future is not linked to the Dutch future. The flip situation also applies: The 6 percent of the Dutch population that lives abroad may also want to feel connected to the Netherlands, even if durable ties have been established in the country of settlement. Just recently, 4,000 Dutch expatriates signed a petition asking Donner to allow for double nationality. In a globalizing world, it is increasingly common for people to hold two passports, and this applies not only for immigrants to the Netherlands – the "new Dutch" – but also for Dutch émigrés. Emotional identification with the Netherlands has more chance of success if people are not forced to give up their identification with the country where they have their origins.

Moreover, attitudes toward the nation, like other identifications, are rooted in local, ordinary, necessary, and specific practices, which acquire personal and group meanings. National identity and feelings of belonging are created through other types of identifications, via work, living in a local community, etc. (Johnson 1993). Shared experiences are a necessary condition for the development of the nation and the mutual relationships between people (Castells 2003). Therefore, the route to emotional identification is hard to establish on the level of national policy. It is more likely to be established via the two other routes, normative identification and particularly functional identification.

## Normative Identification

Normative identification means that people have the possibility to follow norms that are meaningful to them and articulate these publicly, and that there is enough space to solve conflicts about norms democratically. Normative identification contains two elements: adjustment *to* the norms (the process by which newcomers adapt to existing cultural practices) and adjustment *of* the norms (the process by which cultural practices are changed – implicitly and explicitly – by immigrant or minority groups). In the latter, newcomers are agents of change; in the former, they also have to adapt. Both processes should take place.

The current political debate is primarily concerned with adjustment *to* the norms. But this is a process that often takes place naturally: most immigrants, after they have spent some time in the Netherlands, develop similar norms as the Dutch, although they often retain their religion. There is no need for specific coercive policies for immigrants to adjust to the prevailing norms. This adjustment is only a matter of time. There are some instances, however, in which people clearly need to adapt to the norms, for example, obeying the law. Some categories of immigrants or their children are overrepresented in crime statistics, mainly young Moroccan-Dutch youth. It is a given that the rule of law is the framework in which people need to behave. In this particular case, the state should enforce the law and restore safety in troubled neighborhoods.

Adjustment *of* the norms is a more multilayered issue. The sociologist Robert Merton argues that problems exist when a sizable group of people can no longer ascribe to the norm or are not able to live as such (Merton 1968). Two reactions can take place: withdrawal or rebellion. Withdrawal can mean that people no longer identify with the Netherlands; a guided process of rebellion is to be preferred, whereby Dutch societies should allow discussion and steer responses toward the existing norms. One could argue that a process of guided rebellion took place in the 1960s, when people in the Netherlands demanded democratization of institutions, freedom of sexuality and women's emancipation. For normative identification with the Netherlands, it is important that people see their conventions represented in public arenas. As a result, societal and political attention should also be given to those who want adjustment of the norms. The problem is that not everybody has a voice in the process: The ability to articulate and advocate for specific norms in the political arena – media and parliament – is not evenly distributed. Access to public goods and services and political representation are key issues, as can be seen in the debate on freedom of speech versus freedom of religion.

Within the public and political debate, a tension exists between those who stress freedom of speech and those who stress freedom of religion – both constitutional rights. A rather dominant school of politicians and intellectuals – sometimes labeled "Enlightenment fundamentalists" – argues that newcomers have to adapt fully and should not be allowed to bring in Islam. Their tone and demands have been extremely insulting and provocative toward Muslims. Those who have felt insulted and stressed other constitutional rights, such as freedom of religion, have been less able to defend themselves and advocate for their ideas. Most Muslims are not in favor of political Islam, but those who are have not been able to explain why and how. The political establishment and the media have reacted with fear when occasionally a political movement or party has sought to establish itself. Moreover, Islamic leaders who are not moderate have no space to articulate their ideas. Of course, the lack of advocacy is also related to the lack of representation (there is no cohesive Muslim community in the Netherlands, only segregated ethnic groups). And, according to the Dutch majority, religion is no longer considered a valid source of political discussion, and for Islam, in particular, little religious tolerance exists.

For normative identification, educators, politicians, and the media have a dual role to play in the public debate. On the one hand, there is a need to create greater space for the more extreme viewpoints, insofar as they exist within the boundaries of the law. This will mean that opposition will increase, but this will improve processes of identification in the long term. When people cannot voice their feelings – even if radical – they will not be able to identify with the larger community. At the same time, there is a continuous need to search for subtle nuance in order to generate insights into the great diversity of positions and views. So far, the lack of subtlety has led to the withdrawal of the insulted. "To say what one thinks," the adage of Fortuyn, does not necessarily lead to solving the conflicts that touch upon constitutional questions. Timing and style are also important, argues Alex Brenninkmeijer, the government's national ombudsman: "Though language is necessary to gain influence, sometimes you reach more with soft language or even silence" (Brenninkmeijer 2006). Engaging in a more civil debate is the responsibility of members of the media, educators and, not least, politicians themselves.

## Functional Identification

Functional identification occurs when a person is no longer seen as a member of a particular (ethnic) group, but as an individual with numerous functional relationships, for instance, as a member of an occupational group, a sports club, or a political party. Shared interests with others open the way for processes of identification that cut across ethnicity.[119] So, when cleaning professionals in the Netherlands united to argue for a pay raise, for example, ethnic diversity was not an issue anymore. Functional identifications can lead to reduction of stereotypes, more empathy, and more tolerance – tools necessary for culturally insecure groups to deal with the newly multicultural global society described earlier.

For functional identification to take place, interaction among groups is crucial. Several conditions must be in place, however, for these interactions to yield positive views of the other group rather than provoke further anxiety. Facilitating conditions include: people having the same status when they meet, mutual interdependence and cooperation toward common goals, interactions that are repeated and

---

119 Pettigrew (1998) defines the process as follows: First, people are seen as part of an ethnic group; then, they become decategorized and individualized; and then they are placed back into another category.

intimate (i.e., with "friendship potential"), and, finally, institutional support (i.e., from the authorities) (Pettigrew 1998). If these conditions are not in place, contact between members of different groups may feel threatening rather than productive.

Defined this way, it may be more realistic for positive interactions to occur in the workplace or at school rather than in neighborhoods. In the workplace, ethnic differences are less important than individual differences. People from diverse ethnic backgrounds who work together on a common goal and have shared interests tend to forget about their group differences (Schaafsma 2006). But, in the Netherlands, the chance of meeting different ethnic groups at work is exceptionally low. Only 6 percent of ethnic Dutch people have coworkers from minority ethnic backgrounds (van der Meer and Roosblad 2004; CBS and WODC 2006). Sectoral segregation occurs frequently, and the more highly educated – who are also more likely to be able to cope better with ethnic differences – are much less likely to meet members of different ethnic groups at work than their less-educated counterparts (Schaafsma 2006).

There are two primary reasons for the lack of interaction among different ethnic groups in the Netherlands. First, the labor market participation of immigrants (and descendants of immigrants) is still comparatively low, about 10 percent less than the native Dutch, although this is improving (Karsten et al. 2005). In 2011, 4.2 percent of the native Dutch population was unemployed, compared to 13.1 percent of the non-Western *allochtone* population (CBS n.d.). Second, immigrants, and even their native-born children, are generally less educated. Nearly one-fifth of the *allochtone* population has only completed primary school, compared to 6 percent of the native Dutch population. About 13.7 percent of second-generation immigrants drop out of school without obtaining a diploma, compared to 10 percent for the native born (CBS 2011). Both are related: Low education also means higher likelihood of being unemployed, especially in times of economic crisis. But there are also two softer factors: Many employees with Dutch-Moroccan or Dutch-Turkish backgrounds have social skills deemed insufficient, have no feeling for the cultural codes at work, show inadequate job search methods, and have fewer networks to find jobs (Klaver, Mevissen, and Odé 2005). Employers, in their own right, show resistance. A typical example: Highly educated refugees are unable to find a job once resettled despite their education level (60 percent of male refugees were unemployed in 2000). In trying to reduce risks in the company's performance, some employers avoid hiring employees who look foreign. In 2004, half of employers in the Netherlands stated that they "did not want employees with a headscarf" (Motivaction 2004).

Policy-wise, it is important to continue to increase the education level of immigrants and their children, to develop social skills allowing them to succeed in Dutch society, and to discuss the dominant cultural codes governing workplaces – all of which is far more practical than teaching them about Dutch national identity. Combating labor market discrimination should also be made a policy priority, and (financial) measures could be taken so employers can more flexibly hire people and limit corporate insecurity. One can think of tax reductions for employers who hire members of marginal groups. At the same time, many immigrants and their children have specific soft skills – such as interethnic communication or "bridging" skills – that are underappreciated. The number of ethnic entrepreneurs making a living out of doing business with their country of origin is increasing (Engelen 2010).

*School*
Learning together can be a source of functional identification, making schools another crucial meeting site. Children at mixed schools have a more positive attitude toward other ethnic groups than those at "white" schools (Verkuyten and Thijs 2000). But, in the Netherlands, segregation in education is very strong. In the period between 1985 and 2000, the percentage of basic education schools with 70 percent or more ethnic minorities grew from 15 to 35 percent in the four biggest cities, and the percentage grew more rapidly in average-sized cities (Karsten et al. 2005).

Much of the educational segregation stems from neighborhood segregation: Parents prefer to bring their child to a school close to home. This, however, is just one part of the explanation. In 2002, 33 percent of schools were disproportionately "white," and 22 percent were disproportionately "black" compared to the ethnic composition of the neighborhood (Sardes 2005). One-third of the ethnic segregation can thus be explained by the wishes of parents: Few parents want to bring their children to a "black" school (with 70 percent ethnic minorities). Highly educated parents may not have internalized their ethnic intolerance: If it comes down to their own child, they also maneuver to avoid more ethnically diverse situations. They can thus be termed "situationally tolerant." School administrative boards also play a role with very subtle exclusionary mechanisms. White schools tend to demand that parents register their children soon after they are born, which excludes parents who are less informed, and sometimes demand high "voluntary" fees. Some schools want to remain as "black" as possible, as this entitles them to more subsidies, a practice which is no longer attractive as subsidies are now no longer based on ethnic composition but on parental socioeconomic background.

Crucial in the Dutch context is that parents have the constitutional right to choose their child's school due to freedom of religion (Article 23 of the Constitution). But religious denominations have become less important. While a small number of Muslim parents still prefer Islamic schools for their children, few such schools exist. Why is promoting social cohesion and interethnic interaction less important than the individual rights of parents? It is important to weigh this with the significance of mutual identification – there are more conflicting values in the Dutch constitution (such as freedom of religion and freedom of speech). Schools and local authorities need greater scope to experiment with mixed schools – not in order to impose a new rule on schools but, rather, to support them in carrying out such experiments. Some municipalities, like Rotterdam and Nijmegen, have attempted to reduce ethnic segregation, but always felt hindered by Article 23.

Finally, functional identification stresses careful and precise use of language. Sweeping distinctions such as "immigrant/indigenous" are often counterproductive. The government, academics, and the media need to tailor their language to the relevant context; the fact that someone is a tram driver or a lawyer is generally more relevant than the fact that his or her parents were born in Morocco. In policy papers and research of government-funded institutions, it was common to make distinctions on the basis of *allochtoon/autochtoon*, initiated by the Wetenschappelijke Raad voor het Regeringsbeleid (Dutch Scientific Council for Government Policies, or WRR). Such distinctions may not always be adequate, and it helps to create boundaries that are not changeable.

## Conclusions

National governments cannot promise to take away the feeling of threat and cultural insecurity felt by many, mainly among lower- and middle-educated people; nor can they fully govern processes of globalization. Thus, these concerns will continue to be part of the public's future, particularly in the Netherlands. Moreover, the immigrant population in the Netherlands is likely to become more upwardly mobile, as the education level of the second generation is rising, especially for girls. In contrast to first-generation immigrants (mostly men from rural areas of Turkey and Morocco), this new generation demands a greater voice. In this context, stressing national identity and demanding cultural assimilation do not constitute the most sensible policy response. Such an approach is highly exclusionary, can lead to the withdrawal of an already marginalized part of society, and will not bring comfort to those who feel loss.

Instead, a focus on maintaining and developing processes of identification seems to be a more sensible solution. To feel connected to others and to the Netherlands, three dimensions of identification are important: emotional identification, normative identification, and functional identification. Such an approach not only contributes to social cohesion, but also allows for fruitful policy alternatives in which many actors have a role to play, such as fighting segregation in the labor markets and at schools, allowing for more extreme but also more civilized political points of view in the public debate, and stressing a fluid and open notion of national identity that permits multiple identities.

## Works Cited

Anderson, Benedict. *Imagined Communities: Reflections on the Origin and Spread of Nationalism*. London: Verso, 1983.

Bauman, Zygmunt. *Globalization: The Human Consequences*. Cambridge: Polity Press, 1998.

Brenninkmeijer, Alex. Een afwegingsmodel voor de vrijheid van meningsuiting. *Nederlands juristenblad* 13: 737, 2006.

Castells, Manuel. *The Power of Identity: The Information Age: Economy, Society and Culture*, Volume II. London: Blackwell Publishing, 2003.

CBS – Centraal Bureau voor de Statistiek. Population; sex, age, origin and generation, 1 January. n.d. http://statline.cbs.nl/StatWeb/pub lication/default.aspx?VW=T&DM=SLEN&PA=37325eng&LA=EN.

CBS – Centraal Bureau voor de Statistiek. *Jaarrapport Integratie 2010*. The Hague: CBS, 2011. www.cbs.nl/nl-NL/menu/themas/dossiers/ allochtonen/publicaties/publicaties/archief/2010/2010-b61-pub.htm.

CBS – Centraal Bureau voor de Statistiek and WODC – Wetenschappelijk Onderzoek- en Documentatiecentrum. *Integraatiekaart 2006*. The Hague: WODC, 2006. http://wodc.nl/onderzoeksdatabase/ integratiekaart-monitoring-integratie-2006.aspx.

Commissie Ontwikkeling Nederlandse Canon. *De canon van Nederland*. Delen A en B. The Hague: Ministerie van OCW, 2006. http:// entoen.nu/over.

De Voogd, Josse. *Bakfietsen en rolluiken. De electorale geografie van Nederland*. Utrecht: Wetenschappelijk Bureau Groen Links, 2011. http://wetenschappelijkbureau.groenlinks.nl/node/71331.

Duyvendak, Jan Willem. *The Politics of Home: Belonging and Nostalgia in Europe and the United States*. Basingstoke: Palgrave Macmillan, 2011.

Engelen, Ewald. Etnisch Ondernemerschap 2.0. *Sociale Vraagstukken.* November 25, 2010. www.socialevraagstukken.nl/site/2010/11/25/ etnisch-ondernemerschap-2-0/.

Erlanger, Steven. Amid Rise of Multiculturalism, Dutch Confront Their Questions of Identity. *New York Times* August 13, 2011. http://query.nytimes.com/2011/08/14/world/europe/14dutch.html? pagewanted=all.

Ghorashi, Halleh. Multiple Identities between Continuity and Change: The narratives of Iranian women in Exile. *Focaal: European Journal of Anthropology* 42: 63–75, 2003a. http://hallehghora shi.com/nl/wp-content/uploads/2009/03/paper-focaal-identity.pdf.

Ghorashi, Halleh. *Ways to Survive, Battles to Win: Iranian Women Exiles in the Netherlands and the United States.* New York: Nova Science, 2003b. Quoted in Jan Willem Duyvendak. *The Politics of Home: Belonging and Nostalgia in Europe and the United States.* Basingstoke: Palgrave Macmillan, 2011.

Houtman, Dick, and Jan Willem Duyvendak. Boerka's, boerkini's en belastingcenten: Culturele en politieke polarisatie in een post-Christelijke samenleving. In *Polarisatie. Bedreigend en Verrijkend,* edited by Raad voor Maatschappelijke Ontwikkeling. Amsterdam: SWP, 2009: 102–119.

Johnson, Richard. Towards a Cultural Theory of the Nation: A British-Dutch Dialogue. In *Images of the Nation,* edited by Annemieke Galema, Barbara Henkes, and Henk te Velde. Amsterdam: Editions Rodopi, 1993: 159–218.

Karsten, Sjoerd, Charles Felix, Guuske Ledoux, Wim Meijnen, Jaap Roeleveld, and Erik Van Schooten. Onderwijssegregatie in de grote steden. *Beleid en Maatschappij* (32) 2: 63–75, 2005.

Klaver, J., J.W.M. Mevissen, and A.W.M. Odé. *Etnische Minderheden op de Arbeidsmarkt: Beelden en feiten, belemmeringen en oplossingen.* Amsterdam: Regioplan, 2005. http://docs.szw.nl/pdf/129/2005/ 129_2005_3_7280.pdf.

Koopmans, Ruud, and Jasper Muis. The rise of right-wing populist Pim Fortuyn in the Netherlands: A discursive opportunity approach. *European Journal of Political Research* 48: 642–664, 2009.

275

Kriesi, Hanspeter, Edgar Grande, Romain Lachat, Martin Dolezal, Simon Bornschier, and Timotheos Frey. Globalization and the transformation of the national political space: Six European countries compared. *European Journal of Political Research* 45: 921–956, 2006. http://onlinelibrary.wiley.com/doi/10.1111/j.1475-6765.2006.00644.x/pdf.

Merton, Robert K. *Social Theory and Social Structure.* New York: The Free Press, 1968.

Ministerie van Binnenlandse Zaken en Koninkrijksrelaties. *Integratienota Integratie, binding, burgerschap.* The Hague: Ministerie van Binnenlandse Zaken en Koninkrijksrelaties, 2011. www.rijksoverheid.nl/documenten-en-publicaties/notas/2011/06/16/integratienota.html.

Motivaction. *Trendmeter van het middenbedrijf.* Amsterdam: Motivaction, 2004.

OECD – Organization for Economic Cooperation and Development. *Divided We Stand: Why Inequality Keeps Rising.* Paris: OECD, 2011. www.oecd.org/document/51/0,3746,en_2649_33933_49147827_1_1_1_1,00.html.

Pettigrew, Thomas F. Intergroup contact theory. *Annual Review of Psychology* 49: 65–85, 1998.

RMO – Raad voor maatschappelijke ontwikkeling. *Nieuwe ronde, nieuwe kansen.* The Hague: RMO, 2010.

Sardes. *Spreiden is geen kinderspel.* In *Spreidingsmaatregelen onder de loep,* ed. Onderwijsraad. The Hague: Onderwijsraad, 2005. www.onderwijsachterstanden.nl/php/download.php/zitdos049.pdf.

Schaafsma, Juliette. *Ethnic Diversity at Work: Diversity Attitudes and Experiences in Dutch Organisations.* Amsterdam: Aksant, 2006.

Scheffer, Paul. Het multiculturele drama. *NRC Handelsblad* January 29, 2000. http://retro.nrc.nl/W2/Lab/Multicultureel/scheffer.html.

SCP – Sociaal en Cultureel Planbureau. *Continu onderzoek burgerperspectieven. Kwartaalbericht 2011,* 2. The Hague: SCP, 2011a. www.scp.nl/dsresource?objectid=28531&type=org.

SCP – Sociaal en Cultureel Planbureau. *Stemming onbestemd.* The Hague: SCP, 2011b. www.scp.nl/dsresource?objectid=27870&type =org.

Sniderman, Paul M., and Louk Hagendoorn. *When Ways of Life Collide: Multiculturalism and its Discontents in the Netherlands.* Princeton: Princeton University Press, 2007.

Van der Brug, Wouter, and Anthony Mughan. Charisma, Leader Effects and Support for Rights-Wing Populist Parties. *Party Politics* (13) 1: 29–51, 2007.

Van der Meer, Marc, and Judith Roosblad. Overcoming marginalisation? Gender and ethnic segregation in the Dutch construction, health, IT and printing industries. Working paper 2004–29, Amsterdam Institute for Advanced Labour Studies, June 2004. www. uva-aias.net/uploaded_files/publications/WP29.pdf.

Van der Waal, Jeroen, and Dick Houtman. Tolerance in the Postindustrial City: Assessing the Ethnocentrism of Less Educated Natives in 22 Dutch Cities. *Urban Affairs Review* (47) 5: 642–671, 2011.

Van der Waal, Jeroen, Willem de Koster, and Peter Achterberg. Stedelijke context en steun voor de PVV. *Res Publica* 2: 189–207, 2011.

Van Gent, W. P. C., and Sako Musterd. Isolement en angst: PVV in Haagse buurten bij de geemteraadsverkiezingen van 2010. *Beleid en Maatschappij* (37) 2: 143, 2010.

Verkuyten, Maykel, and Jochem Thijs. *Leren(en) waarderen: discriminatie, zelfbeeld en leerprestaties in 'witte' en 'zwarte' basisscholen.* Amsterdam: Thela Thesis, 2000.

WRR – Wetenschappelijke Raad voor het Regeringsbeleid. *De verzorgingsstaat herwogen.* Amsterdam: Amsterdam University Press, 2006. www.usgvox.nl/pdf/wrr%20rapport%20de%20verzorgings staat%20herwogen.pdf.

WRR – Wetenschappelijke Raad voor het Regeringsbeleid. *Identificatie met Nederland.* Amsterdam: Amsterdam University Press, 2007. www.wrr.nl/fileadmin/nl/publicaties/PDF-Rapporten/Identificatie_ met_Nederland.pdf.

Zandbergen, Karen. SGP een leuke partij met leuke mensen. Trouw, April 3, 2011. www.trouw.nl/tr/nl/5009/Archief/archief/article/detail/1855391/2011/03/04/SGP-een-leuke-partij-met leuke-mensen. dhtml.

# Building a British Model of Integration in an Era of Immigration: Policy Lessons for Government

*Shamit Saggar, Will Somerville*

## Introduction

The United Kingdom has not developed a fully coherent immigration integration program despite experiencing large-scale immigrant flows and settlement over the past half-century.[120] The political debates around immigrant integration that have accompanied these flows have often been fraught and destabilizing, reflecting a deep-seated ambivalence about immigrants and immigration in British society.

This chapter analyzes developments in integration policy over the past 15 years in the United Kingdom, dating from the election of the Labour government in May 1997 until the present day. The analysis focuses on whether or not policy has influenced (or has been perceived to influence) national identity, immigrant integration outcomes and neighborhood cohesion in communities. Part I explores integration policy in the context of the overall immigration picture and public opinion. Part II focuses on key trends in national identity, differences in outcomes between immigrant groups and the national average, and neighborhood cohesion – the three definitional categories we draw out of the literature and extant empirical measures. Part III reviews integration policy developments, tracking immigrant integration meas-

---

120 Note there have been integration programs dating back at least a century – for example, there were resettlement programs for Belgian refugees in the 1910s and Polish refugees in the 1940s that catered to hundreds of thousands of people. See Rutter and Cavanagh, forthcoming.

ures the government has introduced over the 15 years and the policy drivers behind them – the aggregate of which could be considered a British model of integration. Part IV analyzes whether integration policy affects integration outcomes or perceptions of integration. Finally, the chapter draws conclusions about the future direction of policy.

## The Context of Integration

### Snapshot of Immigration in the United Kingdom

Immigration to the United Kingdom has changed over the past 15 years: Migration has grown in volume and has become more temporary in nature, and its composition has become more diverse.

From 1999 to 2009, net migration to the United Kingdom added 2 million people to the total population (Figures calculated from Salt 2010, Table 1.1). This significant net inflow explains the 70 percent increase in the foreign-born population over recent years, from 3.8 million in 1993 to 6.5 million in 2010, amounting to 12 percent of the United Kingdom's population (Rienzo and Vargas-Silva 2011). Furthermore, emigration has risen steeply, dropping only with the advent of economic recession.

Migration has become more temporary in nature. Net annual long-term migration (defined as those coming to stay in the United Kingdom for more than one year, minus those leaving for more than one year) reached 252,000 in 2010. The gross inflow (i.e., ignoring emigration) stands at approximately 600,000. The short-term inflow (migrants coming for more than three months but less than one year) adds another approximately 300,000.

This picture of human movement is vastly different from that seen even a decade ago. This contrasts significantly with earlier waves of immigration to the United Kingdom mainly from the Caribbean, India, Pakistan, and Bangladesh, which in part gave rise to the race-relations model of addressing integration and inter-group relationships that has been in place since the 1960s. Moreover, a major proportion of immigrants are coming for short periods of time: 72 percent of migrants come for less than five years (Vargas-Silva 2011). A majority of long-term migrants now state that they intend to stay for one to two years only.

Poland and India are now the main origin countries of long-term migrants, and London and the South East of England are the main destinations of choice, as they have been since the 19th century. Fully half of all immigrants live in these areas. However, across all UK regions there have been significant percentage increases in the size of the foreign-born populations. This is in part due to the scale of immigration in recent times, and in part because Eastern European immigrants have a higher propensity to locate outside of Greater London and have accounted for a substantial proportion of flows since 2004.

Immigrants have lower employment rates than UK-born people overall, though, critically, the rates vary widely according to gender and nationality. Men have similar employment rates, while immigrant women have much lower employment rates (Rienzo 2011). In 2010, the employment rates of male workers from the A8 countries[121] (90 percent), other European Union (EU) countries (76 percent), India (81 percent), and Australia (86 percent) were higher than that of UK-born men (75 percent); migrants from Pakistan and Bangladesh, however, experienced significantly lower employment rates than the UK-born. In other words, there has been considerable variation of experiences across different migrant groups, a factor that has been poorly transmitted into policy formulation.

The unauthorized resident population has been estimated at 618,000 (Gordon et al. 2009), or around 10 percent of the foreign-born population. This proportion has been judged higher than those in comparable EU countries, such as Germany and France (Vollmer 2011).

---

121 This refers to eight out of the ten countries that joined the European Union in 2004: the Czech Republic, Estonia, Hungary, Latvia, Lithuania, Poland, Slovakia, and Slovenia.

The critical context to public opinion on integration is British hostility to immigration. Around three-quarters of the population are hostile to immigration (both legal and illegal), higher than across Europe and North America (see GMFUS 2010), making the British public an outlier. Moreover, immigration has been a prominent political issue for a decade after a period when it had not been a feature of political or media debate at all. Its salience rose significantly in the early 2000s, and immigration has consistently ranked among the top issues facing Britain in public opinion surveys ever since – a condition not seen for over a generation.[122]

Public opinion on integration is rather different. There are two identifiable trends. First, slightly over half of the British public thinks that the integration of immigrants is "poor" (GMFUS 2011: 20–23). This is lower than general hostility to immigration but still substantial. Importantly, the public is much more positive about the children of immigrants: Two-thirds report positive integration (including for Muslim second-generation immigrants, where opinion is only slightly less favorable) (ibid.). Importantly, disaggregating public opinion on immigrant integration by age, social class, and education does not reveal major differences (as it would with immigration), with the exception of more sympathetic urban dwellers. Broadly speaking, British society has a consensus view on immigrant integration, but what the public understands integration to mean is less clear. The more positive feelings of city residents are probably related to direct experi-

---

122 See Ipsos-MORI Issue Index polls of public opinion in the United Kingdom over the past 15 years. In December 1999, fewer than 5 percent of respondents identified immigration or race relations as one of the most important issues facing the country; in December 2007, this figure was 46 percent. The percentage of people identifying immigration or race relations as one of the most important issues facing the country has declined since 2008 as economic concerns have become dominant (the other most common responses of crime, education, and the National Health Service have followed the same pattern). Nonetheless, immigration (or race relations) has remained almost constantly among the top four issues identified by the British public. For further discussion, see Blinder 2011.

ence and comparative proximity – a finding that underscores the hypothesis that social contact affects how relationships and perceptions are molded.

Second, the general public in the United Kingdom (England, Wales, Northern Ireland, and Scotland) reports that 75 to 80 percent of people in their neighborhoods get along well with one another – a finding that has been stable over time (Ford 2011). The neighborhoods where people do not get along well are often associated with immigration, but analyses controlling for other factors suggest that this effect is principally caused by poverty and social deprivation (Sturgis et al. 2011). The impacts of further immigrant settlement may, however, serve to exacerbate existing stresses and strains on, for instance, certain public services.

The public may take a skeptical line, believing that certain policies (e.g., anti-discrimination or equality policies,[123] which are often assumed to connote integration) have gone too far, and yet also believe that day-to-day relationships work well.

Put differently, immigration and integration are "vortex" issues that may suck in views on a range of other issues, such as trust in politicians, ability to influence decisions affecting local communities, provision of public services, and so on.

## Trends in Britishness, Integration, and Cohesion

*Integration* means different things to different people, with overlapping definitions dating from the 1930s: Integration is a concept both dazzling (Bommes and Kolb 2004: 5) and treacherous (Banton 2001: 151 f.), and policymakers must use and define it with care.

An examination of the (many) empirical measures used to assess identity, integration, and cohesion reveals three categories:[124] national

---

123  Such policies are rarely reported as popular in public opinion surveys.
124  For more detail on empirical measures and how they can be grouped, see Saggar et al. 2012.

identity (Britishness or measures of whether someone feels more or less English, Scottish, Welsh, or Irish); integration outcomes (this refers to the performance of immigrants, usually set against the national average, in various spheres, such as employment and education, and is probably the definition closest to "immigrant integration" as understood by scholars in comparative analysis of immigrant integration); and cohesion, usually at the local or neighborhood level. Cohesion at the local level may be termed neighborhood cohesion or, in the United Kingdom, community cohesion or social cohesion.

There are various trends and patterns to be observed in each of these three broad categories.

### National Identity: The Changing Meaning of "Britishness"

The concept of Britishness has changed in recent decades. There has been a shift in national identity from an ethnocentric view – a focus on British ancestry – to a civic understanding of Britishness as respect for the rule of law and shared (broadly liberal) values.[125] This trend also applies to conceptions of Englishness, Scottishness, Welshness, and Irishness.[126]

The reasons for this shift are open to debate. Studies of British national identity, whether written by historians (e.g., Linda Colley) or sociologists (e.g., Tom Nairn) have posited that the core British national identity is shaped by recurring wars (especially with France), the Protestant religion, and the image of Britain as an empire builder (Colley 1992 and 1999; Nairn 2000). As these nation-building elements have lost relevance – via diminishing religious affiliation, loss

---

125  Tilly, Exley, and Heath (2004) report that the shift is largely generational, suggesting a civic understanding of Britishness is likely to become standard.

126  Whether people see themselves as British or as Scottish, English, and so on is a more complicated question. Citizens with minority heritage are more likely to consider themselves British, for example. Meanwhile, the Scottish National Party's majority in Holyrood and plans for a referendum on independence are factors now affecting trends in Scottish identity.

of empire, globalization, and devolution of power to Scotland, Wales, and Northern Ireland – a civic understanding of Britishness has replaced the ethnocentric view of national identity. Regardless of the exact causes, immigration and immigrant integration are often embroiled in debates on Britishness.

The immediate implications for integration *policy* are limited in that building a sense of national identity is not the subject of tangible initiatives or public policy programs, and is more located in the arena of public debate and political rhetoric. The most obvious concern is that immigrants – by not sharing certain values or ancestral connections – will weaken a sense of British or national identity. This anxiety has been a staple element of critiques of immigration in Britain over several decades. However, the shift to a civic conception of national identity suggests a more capacious identity, one that could include a greater number of immigrants.

That said, it has been argued that the attempt to define national identity (whether UK or other) in universal and civic terms is paradoxical; since these are by definition universal values, or at least values shared by all liberal states, they cannot be used to define and delimit a particular national identity (Joppke 2010). It is not immediately clear how greater civic understanding eclipsed earlier voids left by decolonization and the decline of religion. Certainly, a fairly active role has been taken by liberal-inclined elites who have pursued a civic discourse of what it means to be British and have selectively drawn from an earlier liberal settlement that tackled discrimination and promoted integration (Saggar 1995).

More concerning is that the insertion of immigration into debates about shifting national identity can make immigrants the vessel of opposition to that trend. In particular, the perceived dilution of national identity (in the ethnocentric sense) has become one of the appeals of the far-right British National Party (BNP). Extremist voting for the far right has been on the rise for the past decade. The BNP received almost 1 million votes in the 2009 European parliamentary elections (a 6.2 percent share of the vote) (see House of Commons Library 2009), which fell to about 560,000 votes in the 2010 general election (1.9 percent of the vote), although the BNP did not contest all seats nationwide (see BBC News 2010). BNP supporters are especially motivated by anti-Muslim sentiment and are troubled by cultural insecurity. Pre-existing skepticism and grievances around ethnic diversity are also bound up in their views toward current and past immigration (Goodwin 2011). In short, when immigration and integration trends are pulled into debates over national identity, they can shape policy directly – or indirectly, by changing the climate in which policy is made.

## Immigrant Outcomes

The second major understanding of integration is gained by comparing the differences between immigrants and natives: What are the gaps in educational, social, and labor-market outcomes, and are they closing over time? However, using an immigrant average can be misleading, as immigrant outcomes vary considerably across particular groups.[127] This means that policy interventions that concentrate on average immigrant outcomes are likely to miss the mark of greatest need. Instead, interventions should be targeted with much greater sophistication. For example, first-generation women of Pakistani background living in economically distressed northern mill towns will typically experience employment outcomes that do not remotely compare with second-generation men of Indian descent living in suburban London boroughs. Additionally, where certain groups have experienced notably successful outcomes, it is useful to consider how far the responsible factors can or cannot be transplanted to groups whose progress has been more muted.

---

127   There are many other issues with such comparisons, as well, such as the fact that the national average may be moving. For a description of some the problems, see Saggar et al. 2012.

We will examine two integration indicators – the economic and employment outcomes of immigrants[128] and intermarriage rates – in order to compare outcomes over time. Many of the political anxieties over immigration in recent years have been driven by worries that particular groups have been left behind. Although we do not examine it directly, there are numerous other indicators and dimensions that we could propose. An obvious one is political integration, where the sources of differences in political behavior among immigrants and natives prompt questions about differential socialization, mobilization, and attitude formation (Heath et al. 2011).

The foreign-born population in the United Kingdom has experienced lower employment rates and higher unemployment rates than the native population for the past 15 years. On average, unemployment rates are 2 to 3 percentage points higher, much of it due to unemployment among foreign-born women (Rienzo 2011). At an aggregate level, the 2008–2009 recession impacted the foreign and native born at similar levels, and the pre-existing gap has remained. However, underneath these not particularly alarming outcomes is a wide variation in trajectories among different immigrant groups, masked by the broad average in employment rates.

Similar trends may be observed across a range of other domains, such as health, housing, and political representation. Explaining differences is difficult, but crucial for policymaking. In particular, there is little policy consensus about the root causes of observed patterns of under- or overrepresentation. Separating immigrant- or minority-specific drivers from wider circumstantial causes is central to arriving at such a consensus.

Unemployment rates are due at least in part to the characteristics of immigrants on arrival. For example, immigrants from low-income countries (where educational qualifications might not match the needs of the complex, service-based UK economy) and who do not

---

128 As noted above, one of the key issues in analyzing immigrant integration in the United Kingdom is that scholarship has mainly focused on minorities and their integration trajectories, eschewing a focus on generation (first, second, third) in favor of a focus on race or ethnicity.

speak English exhibit unemployment rates of at least 25 percent. Further evidence can be found by disaggregating the data by age and gender – where the "immigrant penalty" disappears if we take out women (immigrant women, as mentioned earlier, have much higher unemployment, probably due to a mix of cultural mores and childcare responsibilities) or look at youth (immigrant youth largely track UK averages). On the other hand, visible minorities have higher unemployment rates, which have been only exacerbated by the recession.[129] In addition, the negative impact of policy on those from refugee-producing countries cannot be discounted from the high unemployment rate such communities exhibit. Current policies such as the dispersal of asylum-seekers outside London and the South East (entailing relocation away from community networks and from tighter labor markets) and policy prohibiting asylum-seekers from accessing the labor market for 12 months are good examples of regulations likely to exacerbate unemployment.

Intermarriage rates (considered by many US scholars as the gold standard of integration due to the intimacy and social implications) suggest the same headline: Rates of intermarriage vary enormously. For example, one in four Black Caribbean men have married whites, compared to one in 20 Indian men. Higher social class and income are typically viewed as predictors of out-marriage rates. This is challenged in the United Kingdom, as Indian men in Britain have higher educational achievement and labor-market outcomes than Black Caribbean men. In addition, it is worth noting the pace of change: A generation ago, fewer than one in 50 Indians "married out"; the rate was so low among Pakistanis and Bangladeshis that it could not be measured in major national surveys (Saggar 2008).

Behind such intermarriage rates sit changing public attitudes toward ethnic pluralism. Data from the long-running British Social Attitudes surveys highlight significant erosion of earlier opposition and

---

129 Earlier evidence on this has pointed to visible minorities experiencing hypercyclicality over the economic cycle: fragility in their job tenure resulting in a greater chance of losing jobs during an economic downturn. See, e.g., Cabinet Office 2003.

hostility among indigenous white Britons toward visible minorities as workplace colleagues, bosses, neighbors, and in-laws. The pace of change has been greatest among younger generations, particularly when combined with the effects of higher education, white-collar employment, and existing political orientation.

The crux of much of the discussion around integration (where integration is understood to be how different immigrant groups perform over time) lies in choosing the indicators of integration or the measures of progress. Which yardstick should we use for measuring group integration? Should it be marriage, employment, language, or a vast number of even softer measures around social interaction and group reputation? There is no public agreement or policy consensus on which of these are the most important indicators; there is no "gold standard" used consistently.

Confusingly, public opinion may well conflate the performance of national groups with perceived changes in both national identity and local neighborhoods.

## Successful Local Communities

The third definition of immigrant integration assesses the success of the community as a whole rather than that of immigrant groups, and is oriented around relationships and reputations, usually in neighborhoods. This might be called local integration or cohesion.[130] It is connected to the idea that different groups cannot only coexist harmoniously in local communities, but can also thrive regardless of differences between them. In public opinion surveys, people are almost unanimously agreed (across ethnic and social groups) on the ingredients necessary for successful communities: respect, understanding, awareness, trust, safety, friendliness, and stability.

---

130 The Labour government (1997–2010) had a set of policies under the rubric community cohesion that it introduced in 2001–2003 and is roughly approximate to this definition.

In ascertaining whether or not the presence of immigrants (and how they are doing) affects how much a community is deemed cohesive, we rely heavily on a set of opinion polls and academic survey questions with a variant on one particular theme. This is probing opinion on whether groups (not immigrants) do actually coexist harmoniously. The most regularly asked question is: "Do you feel that, on average, people in your neighborhood get on better or worse than they did a year ago?"

Academic analyses of the datasets that are produced by this question show that the most important predictors of unsuccessful communities are not immigration but socioeconomic deprivation and the quality of public services. In other words, the poorer the community, the less people feel it is integrated – irrespective of the presence of immigrants (Letki 2008; Laurence and Heath 2008; Laurence 2011). Lack of economic resources is seen as the factor most responsible for patterns of atomization and community disintegration. This is in stark contrast to the seminal findings of Robert Putnam (2007) in the United States, who found that diversity reduces cohesion and trust. In fact, some scholars, such as Patrick Sturgis (Sturgis, Jackson, and Brunton-Smith 2011), find diversity *increases* cohesion. These findings are common in studies across the United Kingdom, but are also true of studies in Norway (Ivarsflaten and Stromsnes 2010) and elsewhere.

Views on neighborhood or local integration (cohesion) are therefore driven by poverty levels and public service delivery, and not by immigrants themselves. However, this does not mean that a sudden influx of immigration will not cause local issues and negatively affect social cohesion. Immigrants may, for example, affect community stability or be perceived to drain public resources. For example, a rapid influx of newcomers entails lower per-person funding of public services, and for major influxes there is inevitably going to be significant and difficult adjustment. However, in the longer term, there is no evidence that immigrants or the diversity they produce negatively affect neighborhood cohesion.

There are important insights here for the management of immigration. For instance, where opinion regarding immigrants in local communities is particularly sensitive, it is useful to know how far this is connected to the scale or proportion of immigrant settlement. It may be that the crucial destabilizer is not absolute numbers but, rather, the rate of settlement across relatively short time periods. This is borne out in polling evidence that highlights the rate of population change as driving local patterns of hostility toward immigration.[131] This, again, will have ramifications for the adaptability and responsiveness of public services (additional school places, expanded primary health services, etc.). Where responsiveness is poor, there are clear risks to community relations.

## Integration Policies

### The Arc of Integration Policy from the Mid-1990s to the Present Day

It is important to recognize that the United Kingdom's immigration profile today is very different from the picture prior to 1997. In the past decade and a half, immigration has become more temporary and more diverse in its sources. The country's previous experience of large-scale New Commonwealth immigration now appears a dated chapter from a different era. The integration challenges created by the earlier wave gave rise to a specific policy framework that focused on race/ethnicity and skin color to the exclusion of other factors that have either advanced or held back long-term integration. The more recent experience involving large-scale white migration from Eastern European sources has created a substantially different framing context for integration, arguably rendering the earlier race-centered approach anachronistic (at best) and a distorting of priorities (at worst).

The government's approach to integration has changed substantially since the mid-1990s, with the emphasis shifting toward increas-

---

131 See Ipsos-MORI (2005) for public opinion data on the relationship between the rate of population change and attitudes to immigration.

ing the obligations on new, first-generation immigrants to integrate (for example, a language examination and citizenship test were introduced in 2004). Beginning with the 1997–2010 Labour administration, followed by the current Conservative–Liberal Democrat coalition (in power since May 2010), there has been a clear reaction to the doctrine of multiculturalism (defined as state support and funding for minority groups to preserve their culture and blamed for leading to segregation and a concomitant backlash).

However, this reaction is based on a gross mischaracterization: There was never a clear doctrine or programming on multiculturalism in the United Kingdom, so replacing it with obligations on immigrants to adapt to majority values and practices has been seen through piecemeal initiatives. Policy change has not been on the grand scale implied by rhetoric. This may both represent and result in greater repressive liberalism that requires subscription to certain beliefs as a precondition of acceptance and belonging.

Rhetorical U-turns should not be dismissed, however. They signal an appetite among today's leaders to distance themselves from the policies and priorities of the past. In some cases, such rhetoric has pointed to much larger changes in policy direction and even in national reassessments, as seen in the Netherlands since 2002. Again, the caveat remains, namely, that any golden age of multiculturalism may be exaggerated by critics and supporters of recent directional change.

Nevertheless, significant changes can be inferred from new integration programs for refugees; new citizenship classes, testing, and ceremonies; predeparture language testing; and efforts to promote community cohesion. They can also be seen in the introduction of a points-based system to assess immigrants' potential utility for the UK economy and that favors specific labor-market needs. Ongoing work to improve the accessibility of major public services to certain newcomers (such as low-income immigrant women with minority heritage in the health service or ethnic minority children with poor English in schools) has also been critical, but it is not a departure from past practice.

The new approach can be summed up as "liberal coercion" and loosely reflects the instincts of political leaders in various Western democracies. The key element has been an in-built, liberal corrective force that has applied moderate new pressures on immigrants to shift behavior if not necessarily beliefs or attitudes. Notably, the United Kingdom (where far-right parties have had few breakthroughs) has not gone as far as the more conservative approaches witnessed in Austria, the Netherlands, and Denmark (where the far right has entered government and, partly as a consequence, heaped new demands on immigrants and linked mass immigration to a wider social crisis).

Up until around the turn of the century, a "race-relations" model was the standard shorthand description of UK policy. Integration policy was built around anti-discrimination law, inspired by the US civil-rights movement. The most potent legal measures came in the form of anti-discrimination law, initiated in 1965 and subsequently strengthened in 1968, 1976, and 2000. The legal framework was reinforced by institutions led nationally by the Commission for Racial Equality and by local governments. Furthermore, in line with a history of British empiricism influencing policy and practice, significant government-appointed commissions led to changes in institutional practices, particularly in policing methods and educational curricula (Swann 1985; Scarman 1981).

Critically, it is ethnic diversity, and not immigration, that has driven the UK integration agenda. Statistics have traditionally been collected on ethnic minorities (i.e., not on place of birth or on parental place of birth), and minorities have been the targets of social and economic policies.[132] The adoption of such a race-centered approach was critiqued as a poor match to the immigrant integration context of Brit-

---

132 The General Census from 1971 and 1981 did not contain a direct ethnic origin item and, therefore, estimates of the UK ethnic minority population were derived using a complicated methodology based on the birthplace of heads of households (responsible for completion of the Census pro forma). In 1991, a direct ethnic origin item was introduced, and it was updated and repeated in 2001 and 2011. This was complemented by a religious background item introduced in 2001 and repeated in 2011.

ain in the mid-20th century,[133] reflecting instead the racial scar that hung over the United States at that time, and this lack of fit is a much more relevant critique today.

In 2001, three events shook public and government confidence in a race-relations model already facing rhetorical backlash: riots involving minority communities in the northern towns of Bradford, Burnley, and Oldham; the Sangatte refugee crisis; and the September 11 terrorist attacks in the United States. These events fueled the sense that existing immigration and immigrant integration policy was unsuccessful and in need of change. The July 7, 2005 terrorist attacks on London provoked further concerns about white and minority ethnic and religious groups (especially Muslims) leading segregated lives and being mutually suspicious of one another.

Furthermore, throughout this period, there was rising support in a limited number of areas of the United Kingdom for far-right political parties, particularly the BNP (Ford and Goodwin 2010). Against the backdrop of a general renewal of far-right parties across Europe, the BNP's appeal underlined concern about popular attitudes toward diversity and immigration, and the success of Britain's race-relations model more generally.

The focus of immigrant integration policies consequently shifted away from a race-relations model. There are at least six strands of policy to consider when characterizing this shift: refugee integration policy, community cohesion from 2001 to 2010, a strong and broad emphasis on equality, counterterrorism (CT) policy, mainstream policies with some targeting of immigrant groups embedded within them, and citizenship policy.

---

133 A significant proportion of UK immigrants are white, coming from European countries and from former colonies (e.g., Australia, Canada, New Zealand and South Africa). Immigrants from the United States also form a significant inflow. That said, over the past few decades, two factors have contributed substantially to increasing ethnic diversity in the United Kingdom: immigration from the Commonwealth (notably from India, Pakistan, Bangladesh, the Caribbean, and African countries, such as Ghana, Kenya, Nigeria, and Uganda), and new inflows from countries such as Somalia, Afghanistan, China, and Iraq.

**Policy Measures**

*1. Immigrant Integration Policy*

A formal immigrant integration policy has been applied in the United Kingdom to only one subcategory of migrants: recognized refugees. A coherent vision was first set out in 2000 (Home Office 2000) – and expanded in 2005 (Home Office 2005) – with an aim to raise refugees' awareness of and adjustment to British societal norms and values.

In its third term, from 2005 to 2010, the Labour government briefly flirted with a broader strategy of immigrant integration. This involved a mapping of strategies and projects and some funding for local projects in places with significant numbers of new arrivals (called the Migration Impacts Fund, this was short-lived). Overall, the approach can be called a stock-taking rather than goal-driven approach. Whitehall politics, where responsibility for integration (except, illogically, refugee integration) moved in 2007 to the Department of Communities and Local Government from the Home Office, could have proved decisive but ultimately led to stasis. Any decision on the nascent national immigrant integration strategy was delayed by the Commission on Integration and Cohesion. The commission's remit was not the integration of newcomers, but a response to the 7/7 London attacks. It sought to balance the interests of immigrant identities with wider concerns about the long-term failure to integrate some, but not all, settled immigrant communities. Ultimately, however, "no clear rationale for developing an integration agency" was found, or for committing extensive funding and capacity to an integration strategy (DCLG 2008).

The coalition government has been supportive of refugees and has made efforts to improve the asylum system (e.g., with reforms to reduce the number of families in the detention estate). However, there have also been significant cuts to advice services, core support, and training programs directly benefiting refugees (e.g., funding for the Refugee Integration and Employment Service [REIS] has ended). More predictably, the Migration Impacts Fund has been terminated. This must be seen in the context of a major decrease in voluntary-sector funding generally, but it is likely to have disproportionately affected refugees.

## 2. Community Cohesion Policy

Community cohesion policies are closely associated with a response to the 2001 riots in the northern mill towns of Oldham, Burnley, and Bradford. A series of reports, including the main government enquiry, led by Ted Cantle, suggested that a major cause of the riots was the segregation of Asian and white communities, and recommended a new set of community cohesion policies aimed at bringing those (segregated) communities together (Burnley Task Force 2002; Cantle 2001; Oldham Independent Panel Review 2001). Community cohesion policies followed, including initiatives such as summer youth programs, school-twinning projects, and ethnically mixed housing policies – all largely promulgated at a local level.

Unsurprisingly, questions still remain as to whether the promotion of cohesion through programs that increase intergroup interaction is an appropriate way to accommodate social and cultural differences in the United Kingdom. The current coalition government appears skeptical of this approach, and funding in this area has been severely cut (in the context of an overall decrease in funding to the voluntary sector) (Collett 2011).

It is noteworthy that the communities targeted by community cohesion policies (and from whence the anxiety of integration sprang) are not home to many new immigrants; instead, they belong overwhelmingly to the children of immigrants. This confirms that integration is rarely about new immigrants only.

## 3. Equality and Human Rights Policy and Legislation

Major equality measures have reinforced and extended the anti-discrimination framework. There was incremental but (in aggregate) very substantial change in the equalities framework between 1999 and 2010. Following the Macpherson report in 1999, which identified institutional failings in the police and other parts of the public sector that affected ethnic minorities, the *2000 Race Relations* (Amendment) *Act* aimed to eradicate institutionalized racism by obligating certain public authorities, including the police and immigration services, to take action to correct ethnic inequalities and latent biases in recruitment, employment, and service delivery. The *2010 Equality Act* brought together existing duties and a series of changes over the previous decade into a broad and proactive legal framework for a range of minorities and disadvantaged or vulnerable communities.

The *1998 Human Rights Act*, which enshrined the European Convention on Human Rights into UK law, has further reinforced the anti-discrimination framework. The majority of jurisprudence that has reinforced or developed the rights of refugees and migrants comes from the passage of the 1998 Act.

There has also been some institutional infrastructure that has supported the implementation of rights. For example, a single public body – the Equality and Human Rights Commission (EHRC) – was created in 2007 to further equal rights across ethnicity, gender, sexual orientation, faith, and disability. However, EHRC and its predecessor commissions (notably the Commission for Racial Equality) have always had limited purview over immigration issues and have not taken the lead on immigrant integration.

There is no doubt that immigrants – especially vulnerable groups – have been assisted by the equality and human rights legislation passed over the past 15 years. However, there have been consistent official attempts to undercut or circumvent developments in rights *as they apply to immigrants*. On the one side, the *Human Rights Act* has been successfully used to reduce destitution in asylum cases, to ensure appeal rights in asylum and deportation cases, to remove barriers to family reunion, and so on. Similarly, equality legislation has led to some improvements in service planning, while the passage of the *Children's Act* and the dropping of the immigration reservation to the Convention on the Rights of the Child have increased standards of care for immigrant children, especially unaccompanied asylum-seeking children. And yet, on the other side, there has been, in parallel, a sustained effort to remove or stop the accretion of immigrants' rights – for example, the government has passed legislation to reduce appeal rights, to remove access to welfare, to limit access to the labor market, and, most recently, to substantially curb legal aid for immigration cases. The courts have curtailed only some of these developments.

There has been at best a draw between government and immigrant advocates on advancing rights, but at no point was the government *intending* for the advance in rights to increase the integration of immigrants. This is arguably a classic example of the unintended consequences (and subsequent boomerangs) of policy in action. In this case, no one predicted how the passage of human-rights legislation would affect immigrants.[134]


## 4. Tweaking Mainstream Policies

The very limited support for refugees and the short-lived Migration Impacts Fund, together with the fact that community cohesion and equality measures are largely targeted at existing minority populations, may provide the impression that there is no provision or thinking on any aspect of immigrant integration. This is misleading.

Hidden inside most British mainstream government programs and social policies are deliberate correctives that favor integration, especially of disadvantaged populations. When applied to immigrants, the most obvious example is in relation to education policy. Early childhood education programs have outreach components that are

---

134 One can extend this analysis to another landmark legislative achievement of the first Labour term – devolution. At no point did any politician or senior official see the unintended consequence of that policy for immigration and immigrant integration. However, the Scottish government has developed at various points bespoke immigration visas with integration elements attached, and has invested in tailored schemes that are greater in scope than in England. This point should not be belabored, but it is worth highlighting.

dedicated to minorities and favor immigrants. In schools, the Ethnic Minority Achievement Grant (EMAG) released upwards of £250 million for language learning alone in 2009–2010 (it was also used for other purposes).[135] More generally, area-based grants and additional premiums to schools based on their number of low-income pupils will likely disproportionately favor immigrant youth and second-generation immigrants.[136] For adults, there was a major increase in the budget for English language instruction, especially in the early 2000s.[137]

Put differently, while bespoke measures are small – often little more than garlands – the major weight of social welfare programs favors integration. This reflects a long-standing tenet of British social policy that employs the proxies of area and participation to deliver loose targeting of programs. The result is that socially disadvantaged groups – including many immigrants and second-generation communities – are disproportionate beneficiaries of policies that were originally conceived without reference to the objectives of immigrant integration.

The coalition government is broadly in favor of continuing a focus on the disadvantaged within policy areas such as education, but it has moved away from increased tailoring. This suggests that advances in immigrant integration through more tailored policy measures are unlikely, at least in the near future.

---

135  The EMAG program was preceded by programs that date to the 1960s and focused on adapting classrooms for the specific needs of immigrant schoolchildren.

136  Other examples can be found throughout British welfare state policies and programs. The Child Benefit program supported large families almost as generously as smaller ones (in per-capita terms) and thus benefited many immigrant households. The Educational Maintenance Allowance has channeled funds toward continuing full-time education for youth ages 16 to 19. Both programs have been significantly cut back under the coalition administration.

137  English language provision over the past 15 years has changed substantially, and the impact on integration outcomes is difficult to judge. On the demand side, strategic objectives have changed and, along with them, entitlement criteria – with consequent confusion. On the supply side, provision has been incomplete and of inconsistent quality.

Prior to the July 2005 London attacks, government counterterrorism (CT) policy focused surveillance and intelligence on likely threats from foreign sources and also from domestic ones. The "home-grown" dimension of the 2005 London bombings changed that framework irrevocably. The policies pursued since then contain two core elements: First, measures have been adopted to strengthen the resilience of potential targets of violence (e.g., transport infrastructure) and revolving targets (e.g., media outlets) in response to particular controversies. Second, government policy has sought to tackle potential support for violent extremism from within Muslim communities. This strand has acknowledged the dangerous effects of tacit backing within British Muslim communities for confrontation and violence. A recurring feature of terrorism trials since 2005 has been the appetite of public prosecutors to indict (with mixed results) those who have given practical support to specific plots.

One criticism has been that very little is known about the effectiveness of these local programs; another is that hardly any have been subject to cost-benefit assessments or value-for-money studies. A criticism from a completely different perspective has been that CT measures have themselves contributed to a hardening of attitudes and grievances among peaceful Muslims (Choudhary and Fenwick 2011).

Under the current Conservative-Liberal coalition government, the CT strategy has focused on the roots and causes of domestic radicalization, looking at the problem further upstream than had previously been the case. Tackling extremist ideology was placed at the heart of the new policy, a move designed to create a much larger distinction between general measures to support integration and a strong new push against radical Islamist ideas and values. Such a drive is particularly difficult to implement. It has mostly been couched in a toughened official rhetoric on the unintended consequences of Britain's liberal multiculturalism. That said, the balance of CT has now shifted firmly toward bringing integration and security policy aims into alignment, and also in favor of neo-conservative skepticism toward cultural pluralism and cultural relativism.


## 6. Citizenship Policy

Citizenship and naturalization, long a policy backwater, has undergone a "quiet revolution" (Nick Pearce, quoted in Somerville 2007), with policymakers deliberately encouraging a more proactive (and a longer-horizon and far more expensive) regime to those seeking to acquire citizenship or long-term residency rights.

The promotion of citizenship began in earnest under Home Secretary David Blunkett (2001–2004) and his adviser Bernard Crick,[138] and it involved "activating" the naturalization process. This included the introduction of citizenship tests (which came into force in October 2005), language tests (also mandatory for long-term residence), and, in British terms, eye-catching citizenship ceremonies (first piloted in 2004). This was further elaborated by the 2008 Goldsmith Commission on Citizenship, which endorsed an oath of allegiance, tax rebates for volunteering, and a national British public holiday (none of which has been enacted).

The period required before long-term residence rights are acquired has also been extended. The change to citizenship law and practice has been substantial and marks the biggest direct change in immigrant integration policy. The policy driver behind the changes has been rising numbers of immigrants and a consequent rise in awards of settlement.

Overall, it should be noted, these programs are regarded positively by immigrants, particularly the provision of English-language instruction, though increasing restrictions and extending the period

---

138 Bernard Crick, also a political philosopher, had previously led efforts to include citizenship in the national curriculum in schools. In driving change to the citizenship process, he chaired the Advisory Board on Naturalisation and Integration (ABNI), which advised the government on the content of language and citizenship tests.

before people can apply for citizenship are unlikely to be viewed favorably (MacGregor, Bailey, and Dobson 2009). Aside from citizenship education in schools, little attention has been given to the importance of citizenship among native and settled immigrant communities, and the reaction to the Goldsmith Commission suggests this is not likely to change.

Debates over citizenship since 2008 have largely been proxy debates over who is entitled to settle in the United Kingdom. The coalition government looks to be placing even more value on citizenship and settlement, partly by constraining access to them and partly by increasing testing. Reducing the overall number of immigrants is an expected by-product that would aid other government objectives.


## Future Policy Directions

There are, therefore, at least six strands that make up immigrant integration policy or have been conflated or associated with immigrant integration policy. Only changes to settlement and citizenship – typically associated with the democratic state – actually constitute a targeted area of policy directed at immigrants. The others are either tangential or aimed at other targets entirely.

An important dynamic that has not been discussed thus far is the role of the European Union, which has assumed greater power over immigration policymaking on an incremental basis, particularly since the Treaty of Amsterdam (1997). Driven mainly by intergovernmentalism, there has been a significant pooling of sovereignty on asylum and illegal-immigration issues. There have also been significant efforts toward immigrant integration. These include the Common Basic Principles, agreed in 2004, and a range of research, network-building, and dissemination to spread best practices on immigrant integration.

Three observations are relevant to the European dimension. First, the Lisbon Treaty made clear that immigrant integration was subject to the subsidiary principle and is therefore unlikely to see any major policy influence coming from the European Union in the foreseeable future. However, the European Union will continue to have a gentle effect through sharing of best practice and, in particular, through dedicated resource allocation. Looking back at the last decade, it is clear that cofinancing from the European Refugee Fund and, later, the European Integration Fund has been significant. Finally, intergovernmental networks and exposure at a European level have led to at least some policy transfer, for example, in predeparture integration tests. This is not related to the sharing of best practices but, rather, government concerns over immigration and the interplay with integration issues.

Elsewhere, on CT policy, the coalition government has chosen to concentrate on tackling risks to public safety (as before), while publicly challenging extremist doctrines that are said to encourage radicalization (a change of direction). The general outlook of the coalition toward cultural and religious pluralism is far from settled, given the very broad spread of opinion across the two political parties, and is likely to remain so.

The government's policymaking direction became clearer in the spring of 2012, when the Department of Communities and Local Government released its broad integration strategy, *Creating the Conditions for Integration* (DCLG 2012). It is a slim document that contains no program of action or coordination but, rather, a list of government initiatives from a range of departments of varying degrees of relevance. It is also the first statement in nearly three years of a government position on integration and clearly notes that the state's role should be that of facilitator and, as a matter of principle, an actor only of last resort – noting clearly, for example, that the "government will only act exceptionally" (ibid.: 9).

The direction of integration policy – as indicated by the new strategy – is likely to stay on a similar path for the short term. There are, for example, references to encouraging "mainstream liberal values," which echo past approaches. However, while there is no proactive change of direction, there is a coming change in the direction of integration policy. Whether by default or design, reductions in spending will change how resources are allocated. If the prevailing view (that government should not lead integration activity) holds, resources from government look unlikely to radically increase. For instance, grants to schools for additional language support that have been amalgamated will not likely be replaced – a policy change that will reduce educational support for children with poor English, especially in the medium term as more schools become academies. Second, immigration policy changes will begin to be felt; the impacts of some (such as the current effort to curb settlement rights for work visas)[139] will have integration impacts that are difficult to predict.

Conservative traditionalism is another subliminal influence in both the current coalition government's general philosophy and in its initial integration strategic framework. This comprises at least two interlocking elements: The first of these is (and, centuries after the Enlightenment, remains) skepticism toward and about the power of reason. Modern policymaking that aims to alter or transform social relationships is therefore questionable as a Burkean principle. Secondly, there is instinctive opposition to allocating natural, let alone human, rights to citizens and to potential citizens as opposed to "prescriptive rights" – rights established by practice over time. For example, there is strong opposition to the *Human Rights Act* among the majority of Conservative politicians, and this inevitably constrains the operational headroom available for current rights-based strategies to integrate migrants.

The new integration strategy, spearheaded by Secretary of State Eric Pickles, has been contained by this caution and also by a general reluctance to become too closely involved (as a national government) in fostering positive intergroup relations. In that sense, the approach is a minimalist one that represents a modest retrenchment and focusing of effort. It also chimes with a much longer empiricist tradition in Britain that does not start by defining long-term immigrant integra-

---

139  The government has stated its intention of "breaking" the link between immigration and settlement, largely in order meet another policy objective (the government's "cap" on immigration numbers).

tion as a public policy challenge for government, let alone one that necessitates an overarching, fixed model of what integration is and how it should be attained.

## Multiculturalism: Crisis and Continuity

In précis, the various strands of immigrant integration indicate a policy shift away from multiculturalism but not a regression to the acculturation and assimilationist frameworks publicly adopted by some European countries in recent years. Much as French republicanism has been a label, the British race-relations model has also been the poster child for certain proponents or opponents of multiculturalism.

Quantitative comparative indices[140] of integration policy and citizenship laws tend to report the United Kingdom as neither favorable nor unfavorable to immigrant minorities and place it in the middle of the European spectrum, though they also highlight that the United Kingdom has recently implemented less-generous policies than in the past.

There has been a noticeable tendency to criticize the excesses and unintended consequences of British multiculturalism. This tendency, it should be stressed, has been largely couched in political rhetoric, albeit influential in its reach.

Crucially, the central principle has shifted toward a loosely framed public acceptance that migrants themselves must change outlooks and behaviors in order to "fit in." In many other Western democracies, this may not be novel, let alone challenging. In today's Britain, it represents a substantive move away from the past. Thus, "liberal coercion" is reasonable shorthand for the current model – and a heavy hint about the direction of future travel.

---

140 Examples include the Multiculturalism Policy Index, MIPEX and the European Union Democracy Observatory on Citizenship.

## Policy Impact

Does policy have an identifiable impact on immigrant outcomes? This question is relevant in relation to both the small handful of policies that deliberately target immigrants and refugees and, as previously emphasized, the much larger volume of policy measures that affect immigrants' integration indirectly. Evidence tends to be locked into individual program and project evaluations (often on the community scale), and the counterfactual (outcomes in the absence of policy intervention) is problematic.

The limited evidence on specific immigrant integration policies suggests small-scale projects have only marginally impacted immigrant outcomes, which are more affected by mainstream public policy. Given the small investments made in targeted programs, this is unsurprising.

Employment outcomes, for example, are affected more by active labor-market policy interventions and the aggregate demand for particular kinds of labor within the economy. In schools, the impacts of general policies aimed at raising attainment have far overshadowed the impacts of a very limited number of policy interventions aimed at immigrants. Likewise, where a bundle of policy measures have targeted particular schools or school districts (using geography as a proxy for group in effect), the resulting impacts have been crucial in evaluating the drivers of educational integration. A good example of this approach has been the floor target regime used by the previous government to help drive up educational attainment performance. The successful use of this regime in several East London education districts in the past ten years has been linked to significantly improved attainment scores for these students in general, with a turnaround in scores among second-generation Bangladeshi girls in particular (OFSTED 2004; Strand et al. 2010).

Critically, advocacy and much academic investigation centers on the inverse of impact. It assumes that policy is a key variable *but one that negatively affects outcomes by erecting barriers to opportunity.* This is most clear among a subset of immigrants who have limited rights, such as asylum-seekers or illegally resident immigrants. Some relatively new immigrant groups (e.g., Somalis and Sri Lankans), many of whom enter as refugees, have very poor employment outcomes (GLA 2005). The question is how far their skills, knowledge, awareness, and lack of employment-related networks preclude advancement and how far policy (which, for example, bars access to the labor market during the asylum process) is responsible.

Immigrant outcomes are more affected by broad currents of public policy: active labor-market policy interventions, the state of the economy, regional economic drivers, public spending on deprived areas, and education policies. Thus, previous Labour government efforts to raise school standards had a major impact on new immigrant children and second-generation immigrant children (Dustmann, Machin, and Schönberg 2008; Strand et al. 2010; Rutter and Cavanagh, forthcoming). However, that impact was not as high as it could have been, even with "top up" or "add-on" policies, such as EMAG[141]. One cause of this shortfall was that even large and successful mainstream policy levers can result in poor outcomes for particular subgroups, as success is measured and rewarded across an entire cohort. Thus, successful, high-attaining schools can also be the same schools where immigrants and minorities "slip between the cracks."

Nevertheless, tweaks to mainstream policy offer a more cogent and long-term solution to integration challenges. The history of integration initiatives for refugees is one of bespoke, small-scale and well-intentioned projects that are not scaled up and therefore inadequate to the task. For instance, experts learned from integration initiatives with the Vietnamese in the 1980s that it was important to embed employment advice in mainstream job centers (which was lacking). Some of the poor labor-market outcomes among Vietnamese immigrants

---

141 Ibid. There is consensus in the literature that language fluency raises attainment. Some academic observers (e.g., Phillips 2005) credited the EMAG grant and its predecessors with raising attainment directly. EMAG was subsumed into a general "schools grant" in April 2011, and the tailored provision doesn't currently exist.

can be attributed in part to patchy advice. Similar outcomes are now being recorded for more recent refugee populations as, once again, significant public monies are being spent on isolated projects not connected to mainstream job advice and placement services. As advocates correctly point out, few mainstream welfare-to-work programs have the expertise to understand complex needs (or, in some cases, to access certain groups at all); as a result, tailored programming is essential. Where mainstream programs are "tweaked" – as was done for the Trellis project in Birmingham and Solihull[142] – outcomes are typically positive.

## Conclusions and Recommendations for Policy

### Dimensions of Integration

This chapter has sought to draw lines among three sets of policies and debates: national identity, immigrant group outcomes, and local neighborhood integration or local cohesion. All are captured under the rubric of integration in debates in the United Kingdom.

### 1. National Identity

National identity involves confidence in the idea that the values, traits, and allegiance of newcomers do not collide with those of natives. Where these understandings are nested in various ethnocultural factors, this can be hard to achieve; however, shared ideas of national belonging that are contingent on attachment to civic values can make this easier. This first understanding of government measures on integration – which often dominate public debate – is clearly important but only loosely connected to integration policy. The realm is the public square – of debate, commentary, and political rhetoric. Where policy measures

142  Ahson 2008. The Trellis project is one of several that have not been continued.

are involved, they refer mainly to citizenship or to grand projects, such as the national volunteering service that is being undertaken by the coalition government, or to the projection of institutions, such as the massive engagement with the public regularly undertaken by the BBC with an intention to speak to the United Kingdom as a whole.

One key question for policymakers is whether, or how far, immigration policy or immigration itself undermines integration. In 1965, at the height of an earlier chapter of immigration controversy, notable Labour politician Roy Hattersley said in the House of Commons: "Integration without limitation is impossible; equally, limitation without integration is indefensible." The causal link, if there is one, can operate indirectly via polarized, heated national debates on immigration (that create a lack of confidence locally); alternatively, it can be more direct via substantial, unplanned local settlement (that disrupts existing expectations, distribution and consumption patterns, and, critically, extant fairness norms).

## 2. Immigrant Outcomes

There are several concrete factors that drive successful immigrant outcomes. One of these is proximity to, and flexibility in relation to, buoyant local labor markets. In London, the professional service and corporate business sectors have been important in generating demand for highly educated and skilled employees. This signal has been received and reflected in middle-class Indian educational patterns, which have prized such employment opportunities. This has not been seen in the case of many Pakistani immigrants, whose settlement patterns were concentrated in declining heavy industrial areas of northern England.

A further important driver has been a basket of social-capital factors. Some of these have allowed immigrants to gain rapid knowledge of changing opportunity structures in education and in housing markets. Others have been vital in pointing to growth-oriented sectors for entrepreneurial investment.

309

Mainstream social policies (schools, welfare-to-work, labor-market regulation, health, and so on) have been more important in closing outcome gaps for immigrants than smaller-scale initiatives aimed at particular groups.

Immigration policies also have an impact, which is usually assumed to be negative, especially for the outcomes of immigrant groups who have come largely through humanitarian routes.

*3. Successful Communities*

The quality and cohesion of a neighborhood is not *primarily* driven by immigration or immigrant integration outcomes. Nevertheless, new arrivals may add to existing diversity and less-than-optimal delivery of services (such as health and housing), both of which have some predictive value for less-cohesive communities. It is therefore critical that local needs are (and are perceived to be) met efficiently and equitably.

**Recommendations**

Immigration to the United Kingdom is likely to continue at relatively high rates. A substantial, new generation will emerge from current and future influxes (over half of London's school-age pupils are the children of immigrants, for example). The need for a well-considered approach that is responsive to the barriers to integration is clear. Equally clear is the need to nest that approach in the history and context of British practice. Reassuringly, there is strong support for integration policy by the public. This chapter points to three key recommendations.

First, there has been insufficient attention paid to planning for and understanding the changing characteristics and movement of new arrivals. A system that can finance the adjustments to services equitably is important, as is finding new ways to deliver services to mobile populations (some new arrivals, others the children of new arrivals) and mitigate any negative impacts on existing populations and communities. In short, immigrant integration cannot be left to chance and requires that close attention be given to immigrant selection, pressure points in local neighborhoods, and bottlenecks and muddled priorities in local public services facing large numbers of newcomers.

Second, and related, a strategy to improve immigrant integration outcomes in the United Kingdom should focus on improving mainstream social policies. Where necessary, this would involve adapting intelligently and incrementally to identify and address the "negative trends" for underperforming migrant groups. The biggest danger is, on the one hand, having immigrant groups settle into long-term disadvantage in conjunction with a grievance-based identity against the broader society and, on the other, having a broader society that blames immigrant groups for issues of community security and failures in public service delivery. Heading off this danger requires some shared-risk calculus if it is to address the biggest challenges, achieve buy-in politically, and remain sustainable beyond the short term.

Setting priorities lies at the heart of tackling the most persistent integration challenges of "at-risk" populations. Currently, that amounts to targeting the poor educational and employment achievements of second-generation Pakistani, Bangladeshi, and Black Caribbean boys, as compared to those of white working-class boys. Even more fine-grain analysis is needed moving forward – for example, targeting the educational underachievement of Somali and Portuguese students. In the future, policy may target other population groups and subgroups. It is as much a craft as a science to arrive at the optimum blend of incrementally adapted macro policies to meet these specific group needs. For example, it may be more effective to target particular areas with an expectation that certain groups will be beneficiaries as a result.

Ensuring accurate information is a precondition to effective priority-setting and intelligent adaptation, and policymakers should work harder to understand where the disadvantage lies and what drives it.[143] Furthermore, policymakers should work creatively to adjust mainstream policies – for instance, in the commissioning of services (procurement), various levers are open to policymakers, many of them cost-neutral. Similarly, policymakers have much to learn from pilots and initiatives that do work and could be scaled up.

Survey respondents are able to distinguish between the experiences of particular immigrant groups. Therefore, we should be cautious in extrapolating these group-centered trajectories into significant area-centered impacts. In practice, both places and groups are bundled together in polling on where and who is best or most integrated. This fusion has implications for the reputation of immigrant integration. Members of the public sense – but may not effectively articulate – what has worked and what has not, and how existing policies align with the grain of British public attitudes and norms. It is equally important, therefore, to focus on strengthening neighborhoods; this will contribute to and change perceptions on immigrant integration. The better immigrant outcomes are, the more room there will be for immigration policy and change. The two are – to some degree – interwoven.

An evidence-based strategy of intelligent adaptation should be overlaid with a strong and inclusive national narrative that acknowledges that successful integration is about ensuring that *all* groups move toward parity. The development of successful local communities relies on addressing deprivation, diversity management, and the sensitive delivery of public services (especially housing).

Third, a clearer assessment of negative *policy* impacts on the trajectory of immigrant outcomes is necessary. This could lead to better outcomes and greater refinement in the design of policy interventions to meet specific barriers to progress. Where negative policy impacts exist, they should be proportionate to the policy goal being addressed. For example, refusing asylum-seekers access to the labor market is expensive to the public purse and affects integration outcomes nega-

---

143 Examples might include better use of the extended ethnicity codes in the National Pupil Database or the refugee marker in Jobcentre Plus.

tively to a degree that is disproportionate to the policy goal of reducing the incentives of illegal immigration. In contrast, the retargeting of English language support may adversely affect some immigrant-group outcomes but is based on a wider effort to target the need more effectively. There are a range of other examples, from credentialing through to the incentives and disincentives associated with access to welfare and training and support programs.

Together, these recommendations would ensure that large policy levers target needs more effectively while highlighting the rationale to intervene to support integration when it would be damaging and costly to take a laissez faire stance.

## Works Cited

Ahson, Kemal. *Refugees and Employment: The Trellis Perspective.* Life-world, 2008. www.employabilityforum.co.uk/documents/Trellis ImpactReportFINAL2008.pdf.

Banton, Michael. National Integration in France and Britain. *Journal of Ethnic and Migration Studies* (27) 1: 151–168, 2001.

BBC News. Election 2010 National Results. 2010. http://news.bbc.co.uk/2/shared/election2010/results/.

Blinder, Scott. *UK Public Opinion toward Immigration: Overall Attitudes and Level of Concern.* Oxford: Migration Observatory, 2011. www.migrationobservatory.ox.ac.uk/sites/files/migobs/Pubic%20 Opinion-Overall%20Attitudes%20and%20Level%20of%20Con cern.pdf.

Bommes, Michael, and Holger Kolb. *Economic Integration, Work, Entrepreneurship.* State of the Art Report Cluster B4. Osnabrück, Germany: Institute for Migration Research and Intercultural Studies, 2004. www.eukn.org/dsresource?objectid=147405.

Burnley Task Force. *Report of the Burnley Task Force, chaired by Lord Clarke.* Burnley: Burnley Council, 2002.

Cabinet Office. *Ethnic Minorities in the Labour Market.* London: Cabinet Office, 2003.

Cantle, Ted. *Community Cohesion: A Report of the Independent Review Team, Chaired by Ted Cantle.* London: Home Office, 2001.

Choudhary, Tuyful, and Helen Fenwick. The Impact of Counter-Terrorism Measures on Muslim Communities. *International Review of Law, Computers and Technology* (25) 3: 151–181, 2011.

Collett, Elizabeth. *Immigrant Integration in Europe in a Time of Austerity.* Washington, DC: Migration Policy Institute, 2011. www.migrationpolicy.org/pubs/TCM-integration.pdf.

Colley, Linda. *Forging the Nation 1707–1837.* New Haven, Conn.: Yale University Press, 1992.

Colley, Linda. *Britishness in the 21st Century.* Prime Minister's Millennium Lecture, 1999, 10 Downing Street website.

DCLG – Department of Communities and Local Government. *Review of Migrant Integration Policy in the UK.* London: DCLG, 2008. www.northwestrsmp.org.uk/images/stories/documents/pdfs/cohesion/838994.pdf.

DCLG – Department of Communities and Local Government. *Creating the Conditions for Integration.* London: DCLG, 2012. www.communities.gov.uk/documents/communities/pdf/2092103.pdf.

Dustmann, Christian, Stephen Machin, and Uta Schönberg. *Educational Achievement and Ethnicity in Compulsory Schooling.* London: Centre for Research and Analysis of Migration, 2008.

European Union Democracy Observatory on Citizenship. http://eudo-citizenship.eu/publications/comparative-analyses#.UDUIPqDLNIO.

Ford, Robert. *Public Opinion and Immigration: Policy Briefing.* London: All-Party Parliamentary Group on Migration, 2011. http://appgmigration.org.uk/sites/default/files/APPG_migration-Public_opinion-June_2011.pdf.

Ford, Robert, and Matthew Goodwin. Angry White Men: Individual and Contextual Predictors of Support for the British National Party. *Political Studies* (58) 1: 1–26, 2010.

GMFUS – German Marshall Fund of the United States. *Transatlantic Trends: Immigration.* Washington, DC: GMFUS, 2010. http://trends.gmfus.org/files/archived/immigration/doc/TTI2010_English_Key.pdf.

GMFUS – German Marshall Fund of the United States. 2011. *Transatlantic Trends: Immigration*. Washington, DC: GMFUS, 2011. http://trends.gmfus.org.php5-23.dfw1-2.websitetestlink.com/wp-content/uploads/2011/12/TTImmigration_final_web.pdf.

Goodwin, Matthew. *New British Fascism: Rise of the British National Party*. Abingdon: Routledge, 2011.

Gordon, Ian, Kathleen Scanlon, Tony Travers, and Christine Whitehead. *Economic Impact on London and the UK of an Earned Regularisation of Irregular Migrants in the UK*. London: Greater London Authority, 2009. http://legacy.london.gov.uk/mayor/economic_unit/docs/irregular-migrants-report.pdf.

GLA – Greater London Authority. *Country of Birth and Labor Market Outcomes in London*. DMAG Briefing 2005/1. London: GLA, 2005. http://legacy.london.gov.uk/gla/publications/factsandfigures/DMAG-Briefing-2005-1.pdf.

Heath, Anthony, Stephen Fisher, David Sanders, and Maria Sobolewska. Ethnic heterogeneity and the social bases of voting at the 2010 British General Elections. *Journal of Elections, Public Opinion and Parties* (21) 2: 255–277, 2011.

Home Office. *Full and Equal Citizens – A Strategy for the Integration of Refugees into the United Kingdom*. London: Home Office, 2000.

Home Office. *Integration Matters: A National Refugee Strategy*. London: Home Office, 2005.

House of Commons Library. European Parliament Elections 2009. Research paper 09/53. London: House of Commons, 2009. www.parliament.uk/documents/commons/lib/research/rp2009/rp09-053.pdf.

Ipsos-MORI. Issue Index polls. Various years. www.ipsos-mori.com/researchpublications/researcharchive/poll.aspx?oItemID=56&view=wide.

Ivarsflaten, Elisabeth, and Kristin Stromsnes. Inequality, Diversity and Social Trust in Norwegian Communities. Paper presented to the National Norwegian Conference in Political Science Kristiansand, January 6–8, 2010. www.humanities.manchester.ac.uk/socialchange/seminars/documents/Diversityandsocialcapital.pdf.

Joppke, Christian. *Citizenship and Immigration*. Oxford: Polity, 2010.

Laurence, James. The Effect of Ethnic Diversity and Community Disadvantage on Social Cohesion: A Multi-Level Analysis of Social Capital and Interethnic Relations in UK Communities. *European Sociological Review* (27) 1: 70–89, 2011.

Laurence, James, and Anthony Heath. *Predictors of Community Cohesion: Multi-Level Modelling of the 2005 Citizenship Survey*. Report for the Department for Communities and Local Government. London: DCLG, 2008. www.communities.gov.uk/documents/communities/pdf/681539.pdf.

Letki, Natalia. Does Diversity Erode Social Cohesion? Social Capital and Race in British Neighbourhoods. *Political Studies* (56) 1: 99–126, 2008.

MacGregor, Sherilyn, Gavin Bailey, and Andrew Dobson. The New British Citizen: The Political Implications of Citizenship Tests and Ceremonies in the UK. Paper presented at Political Studies Association annual conference, Challenges for Democracy in a Global Era, University of Manchester, April 7–9, 2009. www.psa.ac.uk/2009/pps/MacGregor.pdf.

MIPEX. www.mipex.eu.

Mudde, Cas. *The Relationship between Immigration and Nativism in Europe and North America*. Washington, DC: Migration Policy Institute, 2012. www.migrationpolicy.org/pubs/Immigration-Nativism.pdf.

Multiculturalism Policy Index. www.queensu.ca/mcp/index.html.

Nairn, Tom. *After Britain: New Labour and the Return of Scotland*. London: Granta Books, 2000.

OFSTED – Office for Standards in Education, Children's Services and Skills. *Achievement of Bangladeshi Heritage Pupils*. London: OFSTED, 2004. www.ofsted.gov.uk/resources/achievement-of-bangladeshi-heritage-pupils.

Oldham Independent Panel Review. *One Oldham, One Future, Panel Report, Chaired by David Ritchie*. Oldham: Oldham Metropolitan Borough Council, 2001.

Phillips, Coretta. *Ethnic Inequalities under New Labour: Progress or Retrenchment?* In *A more Equal Society?* edited by John Hills and Kitty Stewart. Bristol: Policy Press, 2005: 189–208.

Putnam, Robert. E Pluribus Unum: Diversity and Community in the Twenty-First Century. The 2006 Johan Skytte Prize Lecture. *Scandinavian Political Studies* (30) 2: 137–174, 2007.

Rienzo, Cinzia. *Outcomes and Characteristic of Migrants in the UK Labour Market.* Oxford: Migration Observatory, 2011. www.migration observatory.ox.ac.uk/briefings/characteristics-and-outcomes-mig rants-uk-labour-market.

Rienzo, Cinzia, and Carlos Vargas-Silva. *Migrants in the UK: An Overview.* Oxford: Migration Observatory, 2011. www.migrationobser vatory.ox.ac.uk/briefings/migrants-uk-overview.

Rutter Jill, and Matt Cavanagh. *Back to Basics: Making Integration Work in the UK.* London: Institute for Public Policy Research, forthcoming.

Saggar, Shamit. Integration and adjustment: Britain's liberal settlement revisited. In *Immigration and Integration: Australia and Britain,* edited by David Lowe. Canberra: Bureau of Immigration, Multi-cultural and Population Research/Sir Robert Menzies Centre for Australian Studies, 1995: 105–131.

Saggar, Shamit. *Pariah Politics: Understanding Western Radical Islamism and What Should Be Done.* Oxford: Oxford University Press, 2008.

Saggar, Shamit, Will Somerville, Robert Ford, and Maria Sobolewska. *The Impacts of Migration on Social Cohesion and Integration.* London: Migration Advisory Committee, 2012.

Salt, John. *International Migration and the United Kingdom.* Report of the United Kingdom SOPEMI Corresponent to the OECD, 2010. www.geog.ucl.ac.uk/research/mobility-identity-and-security/mi gration-research-unit/pdfs/Sop10_final_2112.pdf.

Scarman, Lord. *Brixton Disorders 10–12 April 1981: Report of an Inquiry by the Rt. Hon. the Lord Scarman (The Scarman Report).* London: HMSO, 1981.

Somerville, Will. *Immigration under New Labour.* Bristol: Policy Press, 2007.

Strand, Steve, Augustin de Coulon, Elena Meschi, John Vorhaus, Lara Frumkin, Claire Ivins, Lauren Small, Amrita Sood, Marie-Claude

Gervais, and Hamid Rehman. *Drivers and Challenges of Raising the Achievement of Pupils from Bangladeshi, Somali and Turkish Backgrounds*. London Department of Children, Schools and Families, 2010. www.education.gov.uk/publications/eOrderingDownload/ DCSF-RR226.pdf.

Sturgis, Patrick, Ian Brunton-Smith, Sanna Read, and Nick Allum. Does ethnic difference erode trust? Putnam's hunkering-down thesis reconsidered. *British Journal of Political Science* (41) 1: 57– 82, 2011.

Sturgis, Patrick, Jonathan Jackson, and Ian Brunton-Smith. Ethnic Diversity and the Social Cohesion of Neighbourhoods: the Case of London. Draft paper, European Consortium for Political Research, 2011. www.ecprnet.eu/MyECPR/proposals/reykjavik/uploads/papers/ 470.pdf.

Swann, Lord. *Education for All: The Report of the Committee of Inquiry into the Education of Children from Ethnic Minority Groups*. London: Her Majesty's Stationery Office, 1985.

Tilley, James, Sonia Exley, and Anthony Heath. Dimensions of British Identity. In *British Social Attitudes: the 21st Report*, edited by Alison Park, John Curtice, Katrina Thomson, Catherine Bromley, and Miranda Phillips. London: Sage, 2004: 147–167.

Vargas-Silva, Carlos. *Long-Term International Migration Flows to and from the UK*. Oxford: Migration Observatory, 2011. www.migration observatory.ox.ac.uk/briefings/long-term-international-migration-flows-and-uk.

Vollmer, Bastian. *Irregular Migration in the UK, Definitions, Pathways and Scale*. Oxford: Migration Observatory, 2011. www.migration observatory.ox.ac.uk/briefings/irregular-migration-uk-definitions-pathways-and-scale.

# Exceptional in Europe? Spain's Experience with Immigration and Integration

*Joaquín Arango*

## Introduction

Spain's experience with immigration attracted international attention in recent years, not only for the level of immigration the country sustained over a very short period of time, but also for how it dealt with this incoming population. Surprisingly, Spain's wave of immigration has not led to the public and political backlash that has been characteristic of other immigrant-receiving countries in Europe. On a continent that is increasingly becoming known for rising anti-immigrant sentiment and restrictive policies, Spain appears to be an outlier.

This chapter examines why Spain, one of the countries hit hardest by the economic crisis and with some of Europe's highest levels of unemployment, has not seen a wave of anti-immigrant sentiment among either the general populace or the political class. The first section describes how Spain has dealt with the recent rise in immigration, as well as how government and society viewed immigration and immigrant integration before and after the onset of the economic crisis. The second section seeks to explain why Spain has reacted in a way that is so distinct from its European neighbors. Finally, the conclusion discusses prospects for the future, analyzing whether the current stance on immigration will be maintained or whether a change in the government's political orientation, prolonged unemployment, and a shifting demographic profile of immigrants and their children will move attitudes in the direction of the rest of Europe.

## The Facts: Spain, a Peculiar Case?

### Before the Crisis

Despite its severity, the current economic crisis has not led to a backlash against immigration in Spain. This is less surprising when taking into account that the phenomenal increase in the size of the immigrant population in the years that preceded the recession was met with a generally calm, quiet reception. Indeed, between 2000 and 2009, Spain's foreign-born population more than quadrupled, rising from under 1.5 million to over 6.5 million (see OECD 2011a). During this period, the immigrant share of the total population grew from just under 4 percent to almost 14 percent, including more than half a million individuals who were naturalized (ibid.). The average annual net inflow of foreign-born individuals during this time was close to 500,000 people, making Spain the second-largest recipient of immigrants in absolute terms among Organization for Economic Cooperation and Development (OECD) countries, following the United States.[144]

Sustained economic growth between the mid-1990s and 2007, at rates generally above the European Union (EU) average, was the main driver behind the dramatic rise in the number of immigrants. As the native population aged, the increasingly shrinking cohort of Spaniards entering the labor market each year filled only half of the several million new jobs created during this period. As a result, there was high demand for foreign labor, largely to fill low- or semi-skilled jobs. A virtuous circle between economic growth and immigration took place: The former induced the arrival of a large number of immigrants, and the latter decidedly contributed to economic growth.

---

144  For data on migrant inflows, see OECD 2011b; and for information on total populations, OECD 2011d.

**Figure 1: Foreign Population, Municipal Registers, by Region of Origin, 1998–2011[145]**

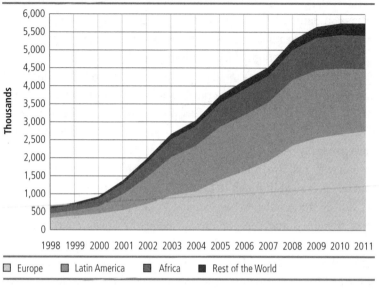

Source: Instituto Nacional de Estadística 2012a

This growth in the immigrant population did not lead to significant anxiety or backlash. Immigration was seen as a requirement of the labor market, an outcome of economic progress, and perhaps even a sign of modernity. Surveys indicated that while some segments of the population were worried about the growing number of immigrants, they accepted that these workers were needed (Cea d'Ancona and Valles 2010). Public concerns about immigration rose in 2006 during the "*cayucos* crisis," the arrival of some 30,000 people from Western African countries to the Canary Islands in small- or medium-sized fishing boats. These clandestine flows, as well as the acute concerns they generated, subsided after 2006, when the Spanish government

---

145 This figure shows Spain's foreign population, not its foreign-born population. The latter was larger by approximately 1 million people in 2009 and included immigrants to Spain who had naturalized.

reached agreements with several governments in West Africa to control the exodus of migrants in exchange for compensation.[146]

Overall, the immigration boom experienced during the 2000s was not accompanied by a surge in public concern, and the migration issue in Spain has not been politicized to any significant degree. There are no populist, xenophobic, right-wing parties that take anti-immigrant positions at the national or regional level, with the exception of a very small party, Plataforma per Catalunya (Platform for Catalonia), which made some strides in a few municipalities in the 2011 local elections in Catalonia.[147] Overall, pro-immigrant, anti-racist groups have generally been more vocal and influential than xenophobic ones. In policy terms, Spain has remained immune to the restrictive drive that has prevailed in much of Europe in recent years.[148]

Immigration policies have tended to be open, and integration efforts sustained and comprehensive. Policy has been concerned not with the size of flows but, rather, with opening or enlarging avenues for legal immigration. High rates of irregularity have been a chronic feature of the immigration landscape in Spain. The number of unauthorized immigrants began increasing rapidly in 2000, and despite efforts to curtail irregular migration, it had reached a sizeable proportion by 2004. The most reliable estimates for that year put the number at around 1 million people (Cebolla and Ferrer 2008). Until then, im-

---

146  Spain's relative success in stemming clandestine crossings from Morocco across the Strait of Gibraltar, through a combination of high-tech devices and cooperation with the Moroccan government, had caused a shift in departure points, this time toward the Canary Islands, from far-away countries such as Mauritania and Senegal. Spain signed bilateral agreements for cooperation on matters of migration with Cape Verde, Gambia, Guinea-Conakry, Mali, and Niger, and memoranda of understanding with Senegal, Mauritania, and Nigeria. Spain also opened new embassies in six of these countries. Compensation included work visas, vocational training programs, equipment, training for the control of migration flows, and foreign aid. See Gobierno de España 2009.

147  In the local election held in May 2011, Plataforma per Catalunya received 65,905 votes (2.3 percent of the total of Catalonia) and obtained 67 council positions.

148  The exception to this is the period between 2000 and 2004, when the government was headed by the center-right Partido Popular (PP), whose stance on immigration became more restrictive following its first term (1996–2000). The nature of PP's second term will be discussed later in the chapter.

migration policies had attempted to address irregular immigration through different admission schemes, several regularization processes, and efforts to improve control of who enters and stays in the country. The 2004–2005 immigration policy reform, implemented shortly after a new center-left government took office in 2004 following eight years of center-right PP rule, clearly intended both to curtail irregularity and to make it easier for employers to hire foreign workers. Its cornerstone was a "shortage" list known as the "catalog of hard-to-fill occupations."[149] Companion reform measures included increased work-site inspections, harsher sanctions on employers for hiring unauthorized workers, the regularization of more than 570,000 unauthorized immigrants in 2005, and a greater emphasis on integration.[150] The 2005 regularization was the largest and most efficient of Spain's previous extraordinary regularization programs (which occurred in 1986, 1991, 1996, and 2000–2001).[151] The new policy increased the number of immigrants allowed to enter legally and contributed to lowering the proportion of unauthorized immigrants. As of 2009, the unauthorized population had fallen to an estimated 300,000 to 390,000 people (González-Enríquez 2009).

The Spanish government has shown a strong commitment to immigrant integration, which has been a central component of immigra-

---

149 The catalog is a list of occupations for which there are usually few or no native or European Union (EU) workers available. Based on the information provided by the official employment offices, the catalog is published by the government every three months, after negotiation with trade unions and employers' confederations. Foreign workers can be hired to fill vacant jobs within the listed occupations without going through the so-called labor-market test – that is, without employers needing to obtain certification that shows there are no native or EU candidates to occupy the position.

150 The legal instrument for the reform was a bill, a royal decree, which amended the immigration law known as 4/2000. All the elements of the new policy were contained in the new bill, except the decision to increase the number of work-site inspections, which was announced by the minister of labor.

151 Arango and Jachimowicz 2005. This regularization was harshly criticized by a few representatives of other European countries. Northern European countries, in particular, have tended to judge the Spanish stance toward immigration as too soft and have voiced irritation that Spain's actions might have consequences for other EU member states in the long run in light of EU free-movement provisions.

tion policy since the 1990s. A national integration plan was adopted by the central government in 1994, which, alongside a catalog of principles and good intentions, included the establishment in the same year of valuable instruments, such as the Permanent Observatory for Immigration and the Forum for the Social Integration of Immigrants. The forum is a tripartite consultative body made up of representatives of major nongovernmental organizations (NGOs), immigrant associations, employers' federations, and trade unions; regional and municipal governments; and a number of national government ministries. Its voice must be heard before any bill on immigration or integration can be adopted by the government or sent to parliament. Similar bodies have been created in several regions. In 2007, the central government adopted a more ambitious triennial *Plan for Citizenship* and Integration (PECI), now in its second term. Integration plans also exist in regions and some cities. In addition, a national fund to support municipal integration efforts and foster coordination across all levels of government was established by the central government in 2007.

Spanish integration policies have ranked high in all three editions of the Migrant Integration Policy Index (MIPEX). Unlike other European states, Spain's integration policies have not been characterized by requirements to pass tests on language or civic knowledge. Since 2008, the conservative government in the Valencia region has promoted the idea that immigrants should be required to sign an integration contract, but this has not been implemented as it lacks the necessary legal basis.

In 2003, a bill by the then conservative majority in parliament authorized the police to use information contained in the municipal registers to detect unauthorized immigrants, but this was met with widespread protest, and there is no evidence that the plan was ever implemented. Indeed, appeals from authorities to identify and bring unauthorized immigrants to the police, common in other countries, would be unacceptable in Spain.

Furthermore, a legal reform passed in 2000 extended welfare benefits – health, education, and sometimes other social benefits, such as a basic income for needy families – to unauthorized immigrants. The only requirement is that they be listed in the municipal population register, or *padrón municipal*. Registration, or *empadronamiento*, is mandatory for all residents in the municipality, regardless of their legal status. By enrolling, all immigrants receive a health card that entitles them to full health coverage and access to education for their children. Even unregistered immigrants who do not have a health card are treated in hospitals without being reported to the police. This exceptional feature of the Spanish system has seldom been questioned. Only a few municipalities with conservative governments attempted to do so in 2008, but they soon withdrew their claims when the central government made it clear that such exclusion was against the law.

Yet, this peculiar feature, seen by many as a cornerstone of the Spanish integration model, will soon disappear. A legislative decree adopted by the PP government in April 2012 amended the law, making the health card contingent as of September 2012 upon legal residence and affiliation in the social security program, thus limiting health care for irregular immigrants to minors below 18, pregnant women, and people in emergency situations. This announcement has sparked intense debate. Opponents claim that the decision is contrary to human rights, inefficient in terms of cost savings, dangerous on public health grounds, and possibly unconstitutional. The regional governments of Catalonia, Navarre, Andalusia, and the Basque Country announced their refusal to comply, as did a number of medical associations.

Civil society also plays a critical role in immigrant integration, and many civil society organizations (CSOs) work in close partnership with local and regional governments (as well as the central government) to assist public powers in the integration process. The regions (*comunidades autónomas*) and municipalities assume the lion's share of responsibility for immigrant integration in Spain's semi-federal state – including health, education, housing, social services, and the promotion of cultural activities. The partnerships between subnational governments and NGOs constitute a very valuable asset in Spain's integration strategy.

## Under the Spell of the Crisis

It was widely believed that Spain's general acceptance of immigrants would change when the long period of sustained economic growth finally came to an end, as happened in the summer of 2007. The construction sector was the first and hardest hit by the crisis, as Spain's building boom had been larger than those of Germany, France, and Italy combined. The burst of the construction bubble severely affected banks, which had borrowed heavily from abroad. A credit crunch followed, and with it came stagnation. Government spending to create jobs and foster activity increased the public debt; then budget cuts were implemented to keep the deficit from spiraling out of control. As the crisis deepened, many worried about the potential rise of xenophobic impulses and aggravated social tensions.

Circumstances for immigrants have indeed been dire, not due to social tensions, but because of the way the crisis has impacted the job market and the construction sector, in particular. In 2005, just before the peak of Spain's economic boom, about 36 percent of male immigrants were employed in the construction sector (see European Working Conditions Observatory 2007). These men, and some in manufacturing, were far more likely to have lost their job during the crisis than their female counterparts, predominantly employed in the services sector. Not that this industry has been spared: As a result of the credit crunch and the contraction of household consumption and public spending, the services industry – a sector that employed close to 60 percent of Spain's foreign-born population in 2005 and nearly 90 percent of female immigrants – has also shrunk (ibid.).

As a result of these changes, there has been an astronomical increase in immigrant unemployment, which averaged over 36 percent during the first quarter of 2012 (Instituto Nacional de Estadística 2012b). Because it took time for the severity of the crisis to fully manifest itself, substantial immigrant flows persisted until the last part of 2008, thus aggravating unemployment. In 2009, a deceleration of incoming immigrant flows was clearly under way, pointing toward the stabilization of the size of the immigrant population that was noted in

2010. While more than the usual proportion of immigrants have returned home in the face of such high unemployment, there is no doubt that the majority have decided to stay.[152]

Interestingly, the crisis has not significantly altered social attitudes toward immigration, and immigration and integration policies have remained basically unchanged until now. This is all the more remarkable given that unemployment, while especially high among immigrants, has deeply affected native workers, as well. As of June 2012, overall unemployment in Spain stood at 24.8 percent (US Bureau of Labor Statistics 2012, Table 2).

Five years after the start of the crisis, the rather liberal admission policies adopted at the end of 2004 remain in force. The marked decline in the number of immigrants admitted yearly for employment purposes since 2009 is not explained by more restrictive admission criteria but, rather, by the self-adjusting nature of admission mechanisms in a context of shrinking demand. The plan for voluntary return put in place by the government in 2008 (*Plan de retorno voluntario*) was criticized by observers who interpreted it as a sign of change in policy, but it could also be seen as a step forward in the portability of social rights, as it offered unemployed immigrants the possibility of receiving 40 percent of their accumulated unemployment benefits when leaving Spain and the remaining 60 percent within a month of their return home. More significantly, the immigration bill passed by Congress in 2009 at the government's behest did not imply any significant change in the orientation of immigration policy. Its main aim was to bring immigration legislation in line with some rulings by the Constitutional Court and to introduce recent EU directives.[153]

Furthermore, the crisis has not eroded the strong commitment to integration that prevails in Spanish society. The strategic PECI

---

152  See Instituto Nacional de Estadística, "Padrón Continuo" and "Estimaciones de la población actual" for data for various years before and during the crisis. Since 2009, around 30,000 migrants have participated in the three programs for voluntary assisted return put forth by the Spanish government (www.ine.es).

153  Directives 2001/51/EC of June 28, 2001; 2001/40/EC of May 28, 2001; and 2002/90/EC of November 28, 2002. See *Ley Orgánica 2/2009*.

adopted in 2007 ran its course without setbacks, and its successor, PECI II, approved in 2011, maintained its spirit and goals. Central government funding to support municipal and regional integration programs has not been immune to the drastic budget cuts required by fiscal consolidation. The budget for the General Directorate for the Integration of Immigrants totaled more than 300 million euros in 2009, of which 200 million euros was allocated to support municipal and regional programs. For 2011, the directorate's budget was 140 million euros, of which 70 million went toward municipal and regional programs (Ministry of Labor and Immigration 2010). No allocation for such support appears in the 2012 budget (Ministry of Employment and Social Security 2012).

In addition to providing integration funding, in recent years, the Spanish government has made efforts to extend voting rights to immigrants from countries outside the European Union. To make this possible, Spain had to appeal to foreign governments to sign bilateral diplomatic agreements, as a provision of the Spanish Constitution states that voting rights may be extended to non-EU foreign citizens only on the basis of reciprocity. At Spain's initiative, a number of such agreements were signed before local elections in May 2011, and others are being negotiated.

No major social disruptions have been reported since the onset of the crisis, and politicization of immigration has not significantly increased. According to surveys regularly conducted by the Centro de Investigaciones Sociológicas (CIS), public worry about immigration has remained roughly the same, while concern about unemployment and the economy has soared.[154] In the years since the onset of the fiscal crisis, both tolerant and adverse attitudes toward immigrants have

154 The monthly public opinion surveys of the Centro de Investigaciones Sociológicas (CIS) include a question about the three major problems facing Spain as perceived by respondents. In December 2011, immigration ranked fifth in popularity, with slightly over 7 percent of respondents mentioning it. The monthly average for 2011 was 10.8 percent, well below the averages in the years preceding the economic crisis. Immigration had ranked third on a number of occasions, such as during the 2006 *cayucos* crisis, when there was a surge in irregular migrants from sub-Saharan countries attempting to reach the Canary Islands by boat.

**Figure 2: Attitudes Toward Migrants in Spain, 1993–2009**

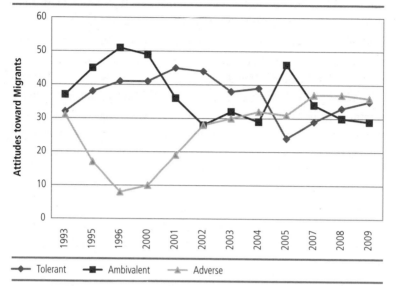

Source: Cea d'Ancona and Valles 2010

increased slightly, while ambivalent ones have tended to decline (Cea d'Ancona and Valles 2010). More significant changes took place between the mid-1990s and 2002, when a proportion of ambivalent attitudes turned adverse.

On the other hand, qualitative surveys suggest that the reason cited by many citizens to justify immigration – that the labor market needs immigrant workers – may be losing ground due to the high levels of joblessness (see Rinken 2011). This may explain the decline in the proportion of citizens harboring ambivalent attitudes toward immigration and suggest why some of them may have turned adverse.

## The Case of Catalonia

While there has not been significant backlash at the national level, the regional story is a bit different. Catalonia's populist, openly xenophobic party, Plataforma per Catalunya, has had only meager electoral success, but support for it is increasing. It received more than 75,000 votes in the 2010 Catalan regional elections, or about 2.4 percent of all votes cast – not enough to enter the regional parliament (for election results, see Generalitat de Catalunya 2010). Concern about immigration has also fueled the success of a conservative PP candidate who ran for mayor in 2011 on an anti-immigrant, xenophobic platform in Badalona, a sizeable city near Barcelona. In May 2012, a tough immigration platform authored by this same mayor was approved by an overwhelming majority at the regional conference of the Catalan branch of the Popular Party.

In the case of Catalonia, the crisis may have exacerbated anti-immigrant sentiments that were previously latent. Immigrants and natives have always competed for scarce social resources in disadvantaged neighborhoods, but the economic crisis has led to greater grievances. Beyond the emergence of the Plataforma per Catalunya, the Catalan branch of the Partido Popular has been more daring in its critique of immigration. At the same time, a number of local governments, with the cooperation of NGOs, have launched initiatives to improve public perception of immigrants, including a program in Barcelona to counter popular rumors that may tarnish the image of immigrants or generate negative attitudes toward them.

## Searching for an Explanation: Some Possible Clues

What explains the overall lack of negative reaction to immigration in Spain? Why have policies tended to favor immigration more than those in most surrounding countries? Why has there not been a strong rejection of diversity or multiculturalism? What factors have made Spain different from most of the rest of Europe in this regard? Answers to these questions do not come easily and cannot be found in the existing literature. Spain's exceptionalism is probably not the result of a single factor but, rather, of a handful of contextual dynamics, from the recent legacy of immigration to Spanish political history and culture.

## Immigrant Demographics and Labor Force Participation

Demographics are central to understanding Spain's stance toward immigration. Contemporary immigrant flows to Spain date back to around 1980 and did not reach sizeable proportions until the turn of the century; the majority of immigrants arrived in recent years. As a result, young adults of prime working age are preponderant. At the beginning of 2012, 55.9 percent of immigrants were in the 20–44 age group compared with 34.7 percent of the general population. As a result, the labor-force participation rates of immigrants are higher than those of the rest of the population.[155] Compared to natives, these young working immigrants also have more geographic mobility, consume fewer public services (especially in the areas of health, pensions, and welfare benefits), and contribute significantly to the growth of gross domestic product (GDP). A second generation is in the making, but it is not yet as large as in more mature receiving countries.[156] It remains to be seen how the Spanish populace will respond as immigrants fall into more established patterns of settlement and achieve more social visibility.

Immigration to Spain is, above all, for the sake of jobs. Most immigrants have come in search of employment or to accompany relatives who are migrant workers; and filling vacancies in the labor market has been the government's foremost justification for admitting immigrants. Asylum-seekers and refugees have represented a very

---

155 Immigrant labor force participation rates in the third quarter of 2010 were approximately 8 percent higher than those among natives, for both men and women (87.7 percent for male immigrants compared to 79.5 percent for native men, and 77.8 percent compared to 69.6 percent for women). In the years before the crisis, the differences were larger. See OECD 2011c.

156 In 2010, youth under 20 years of age represented 19.9 percent of the foreign population, a proportion similar to the rate for the total population of Spain (19.6 percent), a rapidly aging population in which the weight of the youngest age groups has been shrinking since the 1980s. While 19 percent of Spain's general population is 65 or older, the corresponding proportion among immigrants is only 12.2 percent. One of five births in Spain is to mothers of foreign nationality.

minor percentage of immigrant flows.[157] This implies that most immigrants are economically active and are therefore perceived as necessary, productive, and even beneficial. The belief that immigrants in Spain have made a highly positive contribution to economic growth has been supported by a number of studies and has been held by the majority of the Spanish populace, at least until the start of the recession (see Fundación Ideas 2011; Izquierdo, Jimeno, and Rojas 2007). Since then, high unemployment rates may be reducing immigrants' positive contributions in aggregate terms and are certainly eroding, though not erasing, the belief that the labor market needs immigrants and that they take jobs that Spaniards disdain (Rinken 2011).

## Political Culture

Turning to the social and political context, a decisive factor behind the calm reception of large-scale immigration to Spain has been the predominantly pro-immigrant orientation of public powers and political actors across all levels of government and society (with some differences among them). Beyond economics and the obvious mutual influence of social perceptions and institutional attitudes, why are Spain's public powers generally pro-immigrant? The answer lies in the elusive territory of culture and, more precisely, of political culture. The contemporary political culture of Spain was refashioned in the transition years between the end of the Franco dictatorship and the full recovery of democracy in the 1970s. During this climactic time, as they became more attuned than before to political developments, the majority of Spanish citizens underwent a process of political resocialization that left an enduring mark upon the political culture. The values associated with democracy were idealized, while those associated with dictatorship fell into disrepute. As a result, democratic, egalitarian, and universalistic values became the paradigm of social desirability.

---

157  In 2010, the number of asylum requests amounted only to 2,744. In the preceding decade, that number oscillated between 3,000 and 9,000 per year; OECD 2011a.

The core of this revitalized political culture formed the basis for attitudes toward immigration – a social phenomenon that came about just as the elevation of democratic values was predominant. Indeed, it can be reckoned that, by its very nature, immigration provides a privileged field for the expression and exercise of equality, solidarity, and cosmopolitanism. The fact that the number of immigrants remained small for years – not surpassing the 1 million mark until the end of the 1990s – and that their impacts were perceived as positive facilitated the favorable attitudes observed into the 21st century. The passage of time and a changing reality have somehow weakened popular support for immigration, but the thrust of the political culture still remains strong at a normative level.

Needless to say, all of this does not imply that immigration has no opposition. As anywhere else, immigrants have friends and foes. Indeed, according to several surveys, a slim majority of the populace now perceives that there are too many immigrants on Spanish soil (see CIS, various dates). That said, opposition toward immigration is more understated in Spain than perhaps anywhere else on the continent. This is due to three factors: (1) The expression and manifestation of anti-immigrant attitudes are restrained by cultural norms; (2) Groups favorable to immigration are large, active, and vocal against any statement or practice that can be seen as racist, xenophobic or simply hostile to immigrants; (3) There is a widespread consensus that immigrants are entitled to the same endowment of rights as the other members of society.

The wide acceptance of the extension of *empadronamiento* to "illegal" immigrants – an adjective often contested in Spain, where the alternative irregular is preferred – and its implications in terms of rights is one example of the ongoing influence of egalitarian values. In fact, as a recent analysis of surveys puts it, Spaniards tend to favor expanding the rights and benefits granted to immigrants: "[T]he majority of respondents support offering the maximum number of welfare benefits (health and education) and social and political rights (e.g., voting in elections, right to practice their religion, etc.) to immigrants" (Martinez i Coma and Duval-Hernández 2009: 29). Obviously, the decision by the PP government in April 2012 to withdraw health care benefits for most irregular immigrants marks a departure from the consensus that existed until then

The reaction to the Madrid terrorist bombings of March 2004, which left nearly 200 dead and almost 2,000 injured, is a striking example of how predominantly favorable attitudes toward immigration have been maintained. The fact that such a tragedy, carried out by mostly Moroccan Islamist militants, did not result in a drive toward the securitization of immigration policy, as seen in the United States and at the EU level, attests to the influence of the political culture. Polls conducted in the aftermath suggest that the majority of Spaniards did not blame immigrants for the terrorist act. Fewer than one in four expressed "little sympathy" for Moroccan immigrants – a figure similar to that for Romanians, another group that scores relatively low on the sympathy scale but that had nothing to do with the attack (ibid.: 20).

Although the political culture described above influences all political actors, differences among these actors are far from negligible. Especially relevant are the differences in orientation between the two major political parties, the center-left PSOE (Socialist Party) and the center-right PP. The former has been responsible for the openly pro-immigrant stance that has characterized Spanish immigration and integration policies, especially during the party's years in government (1982–1996 and 2004–2011). The PP was in government between 1996 and 2004, and started a new four-year term at the end of 2011. During its first four-year term, its policies followed along the same lines as the PSOE administration before it. However, the PP turned toward more restrictive policies during its second term (2000–2004), when the number of immigrants, including those in irregular condition, started to increase rapidly. Admission channels for labor migration were made narrower despite increased demand from employers, and the "fight against illegal migration" became the foremost policy priority. Since 2004, the PP has criticized the immigration policies of the PSOE government, above all by blaming the 2005 regularization for the rapid increase in immigration despite the fact that the PP government had legalized some 468,000 unauthorized immigrants in three regularization processes carried out in 2000–2001. In the 2008 general election, the PP announced that it would require immigrants to sign an integration contract very similar to the one advocated by French President Nicolas Sarkozy. A similar integration contract was proposed by the PP to the Parliament of Catalonia in the lead-up to the November 2011 general election. The approval of such a contract on the regional or national level – neither of which seemed likely at the time – would have implied that immigrants would be obliged to learn the official language (two, in the case of Catalonia), respect Spain's customs and habits, and return home if they are unemployed for a long period. No similar proposal had been put forth by the new Spanish government as of May 2012.

## National Identity

Finally, concerns over national identity seem less relevant for attitudes toward immigration in Spain than in other countries, at least so far. With the partial exception of Catalonia, where prominent political leaders have sometimes voiced such concern, immigration is not perceived as a threat to national identity. Identifying the underlying reasons is, again, far from easy. It is likely that immigrants' relatively recent arrival and lack of visibility play a role.

It could also be surmised that Spanish nationalism is, in itself, under question. Spain's recent history – from the loss of the empire to the restoration of democracy – is judged by many as far from brilliant, both in economic and political terms. Meanwhile, the Spanish state faces vigorous calls for a higher degree of self-government – even independence – from nationalist movements in Catalonia and the Basque Country. The widespread perception in the final years of the Franco dictatorship that these claims had been forcibly repressed lent mass support to demands for devolution, decentralization, and their practical implementation in Spain as a whole. All of this may have prevented the rise of a militant national identity that could otherwise feel threatened by immigration. In recent years, however, the support for decentralization and regional self-government has cooled as conservative segments of the polity have reacted against the claims of Basque and, especially, Catalan nationalists.

## Conclusions

Is Spain's relative egalitarianism likely to persist into the foreseeable future, or will attitudes and policies toward immigration and integration increasingly mirror those that prevail across much of Europe? While arguments can be found for both, the second option appears most likely.

To start, the job market looks to be getting worse. Signs indicate that the prolonged economic crisis and high unemployment rates will continue for years. Meanwhile, immigrants' visibility will increase with time, as a large second generation comes of age and the population becomes multigenerational. This evolution is bound to result in a different perception and a less-favorable evaluation of the impacts of immigration.

As for the likely influence of political and cultural factors, the picture is less clear. The political orientation of the central government shifted in 2011. With the popularity of the incumbent PSOE government eroded by both the social impacts of the economic crisis and the fiscal austerity measures used to contain them, the conservative PP won a majority of regional and municipal elections in May. Then, in the general election on November 20, 2011, the PP won a landslide victory at the federal level.

Although the PP's electoral platform did not say much about immigration, significant changes can be expected. Party members have called for tests of "Spanishness" to acquire citizenship and have promoted the idea of "circular migration," meaning that immigrants are welcome when the economy requires their labor but should leave when this need is absent. Other legal changes have been announced, including the suppression of the figure of *arraigo* or *rootedness*, i.e., the possibility of applying for individual legalization after three years of irregular stay in the country provided that certain conditions are met.

As of May 2012, no policy changes had taken place, with the exception of the announced withdrawal of health care rights to the majority of irregular migrants. This, together with the fact that the new government has downgraded the institutional locus of immigration within the government structure, may point toward a different orientation and a new, less prominent stance for immigration and integration. The rank of the highest officer responsible for immigration and integration has ceased to be that of a junior minister, devolving instead to a general secretary, and the three general directorates that were responsible for managing immigration and integration have been reduced to just one. The former Ministry of Labor and Immigration has seen its name changed to the Ministry of Employment and Social Security.

Beyond the symbolic message these changes convey, there are implications for intragovernmental cooperation on the topic of immigration, especially as far as the usually delicate balance with the Interior Ministry is concerned. It also implies that the only Spanish voice in the EU councils on immigration will be that of the Interior Ministry, whose focus is more on national security and policing than integration. All in all, it can be expected that, with the PP at the helm, Spain's immigration policies will fall more in line with the dominant paradigm in Europe.

Yet if restrictionist policies come to the fore, it is likely they will meet resistance from both political opposition parties and civil-society groups. This resistance is likely to limit the policy changes that a conservative government might want to promote. A certain balance between the new spirit and the preceding orientation might be the end result. But all of this is, of course, sheer speculation.

## Recommendations

Economic growth is expected to be sluggish, a fact that will not facilitate the re-absorption of the large numbers of immigrants left jobless by the economic crisis. The likely persistence of high overall unemployment will impair the job opportunities of immigrant youth, especially the less skilled. Meanwhile, financial cuts to lower the fiscal deficit are bound to seriously curtail social benefits and welfare provisions. This, in turn, may intensify the competition between immigrants and disfavored segments of the receiving society for scarce social resources, aggravating animosity and grievances.

In such a context, government action at the federal, regional, and local levels, in close cooperation with CSOs, will be necessary to maintain immigrant integration efforts and prevent the deterioration of general attitudes toward immigrants. If anything, the decided commitment that a host of institutions has shown to maintain integration efforts – from the federal to the local level – must be maintained or reinforced. The maintenance of the plethora of programs and policies that currently exist will aid in preventing and managing social tensions and conflicts that may occur. Unfortunately, fiscal austerity will not allow for the desirable expansion of public expenditure in important areas, such as vocational training and proactive job training programs to aid immigrant access to employment. Ideally, and despite the hardships imposed by the adverse economic environment, these areas should be made a high priority, or at least protected from financial cuts.

The tremendous difficulties that public administrations are likely to face in funding integration programs and policies might be balanced by renewed focus on those policies and programs that do not require heavy expenditure. This includes programs that foster social communication, the acceptance of diversity in the receiving society, civic participation, and the interaction of people of different origins. In the same vein, the new government should push the parliamentary approval of anti-discrimination legislation providing for equality of treatment and opposition to all forms of discrimination that the preceding government was about to send to parliament in late 2011. Given the influence that politicians tend to have on the formation of societal attitudes, it would be highly desirable that the new government be perceived as no less favorable to immigrant integration than the previous administration was.

## Works Cited

Arango, Joaquín, and Maia Jachimowicz. Regularizing Immigrants in Spain: A New Approach. *Migration Information Source, Special Issue: The Unauthorized,* September 2005. www.migrationinfor mation.org/Feature/display.cfm?id=331.

Cea d'Ancona, M. Ángeles, and Miguel Valles. *Evolución del racismo y la xenofobia en España [Informe 2010].* Madrid: Ministerio de Trabajo e Inmigración, 2010. www.oberaxe.es/files/datos/4e202300 88dc8/INFORME%20RACISMO%202010.pdf.

Cebolla, Héctor, and Amparo González Ferrer. *La inmigración en España (2000–2007): Del control de flujos a la integración de los inmigrantes.* Madrid: Centro de Estudios Políticos y Constitucionales, 2008.

CIS – Centro de Investigaciones Sociológicas. *Barómetros de Opinión.* Various dates. www.cis.es/cis/opencm/ES/11_barometros/index.jsp.

European Working Conditions Observatory. Employment and Working Conditions of Migrant Workers – Spain, 2007. www.euro found.europa.eu/ewco/studies/tn0701038s/es0701039q.htm.

Fundación Ideas. *La contribución de la inmigración a la economía española. Evidencias y perspectivas de future.* Madrid: Fundación Ideas, 2011. www.fundacionideas.es/sites/default/files/pdf/I-La_contri bucion_de_la_inmigracion-Ec_0.pdf.

Generalitat de Catalunya. Resultats Definitius. 2010. www.gencat.cat/ governacio/eleccions/eleccions2010/resultats2010/09AU/ DAU09999CM_L2.htm.

Gobierno de España. *Plan Africa 2009–2012.* Madrid: Agencia Española de Cooperación Internacional para el Desarrollo, 2009. www. maec.es/es/Home/Documents/PLANAFRICA09_12EN.pdf.

González-Enríquez, Carmen. *Update Report Spain: Estimate on Irregular Migration for Spain in 2009.* Hamburg: Hamburg Institute of International Economics, 2009 http://irregular-migration.hwwi. net.

Instituto Nacional de Estadística. *Population Register.* Madrid: Instituto Nacional de Estadística, 2012a.

Instituto Nacional de Estadística. Encuesta de Población Activa, primer trimestre 2012. Notas de prensa, April 27, 2012b. www.ine.es/ daco/daco42/daco4211/epa0112.pdf.

Izquierdo, Mario, Juan F. Jimeno, and Juan A. Rojas. On the Aggregate Effects of Immigration in Spain. Documentos de Trabajo 0714, Banco de España, 2007. www.bde.es/webbde/SES/Secciones/ Publicaciones/PublicacionesSeriadas/DocumentosTrabajo/07/Fic/ dt0714e.pdf.

*Ley Orgánica 2/2009. Boletín Oficial del Estado núm 299, December 12, 2009.* www.boe.es/boe/dias/2009/12/12/index.php.

Martinez i Coma, Ferran, and Robert Duval-Hernández. Hostility toward Immigration in Spain. Discussion Paper No. 4109. Bonn: IZA, April 2009. http://ftp.iza.org/dp4109.pdf.

Ministry of Employment and Social Security. *General Budget 2012.* Madrid: Ministry of Employment and Social Security, 2012.

Ministry of Labor and Immigration. *General Budget 2011.* Madrid: Ministry of Labor and Integration, 2010.

OECD – Organization for Economic Cooperation and Development. *International Migration Outlook 2011.* Paris: OECD, 2011a. www. oecd.org/migration/imo.

OECD – Organization for Economic Cooperation and Development. Key Statistics on Migration in OECD Countries: Inflows of Foreign Population 2000–2009. 2011b. www.oecd.org/document/30/ 0,3746,en_2649_37415_48326878_1_1_1_37415,00.html.

OECD – Organization for Economic Cooperation and Development. Key Statistics on Migration in OECD Countries: Labor Market Outcomes of Immigrants 2008–2010. 2011c. www.oecd.org/docu ment/30/0,3746,en_2649_37415_48326878_1_1_1_37415,00.html.

OECD – Organization for Economic Cooperation and Development. ALFS Summary Tables: Population. 2011d. http://stats.oecd.org/index.aspx?queryid=254.

Rinken, Sebastian. La evolución de las actitudes ante la inmigración en tiempos de crisis eonómica: un análisis cualitativo. In *Inmigración y crisis económica: Impactos actuales y perspectivas de futuro*, edited by Eliseo Aja, Joaquín Arango, and Josep Oliver Alonso. Barcelona: Cidob Edicions, 2011: 24–47.

US Bureau of Labor Statistics. *International Unemployment Rates and Employment Indexes, Seasonally Adjusted, 2008–2012.* Washington, DC: BLS, Division of International Labor Comparisons, 2012. www.bls.gov/fls/intl_unemployment_rates_monthly.pdf.

# Immigration and National Identity in Norway

*Thomas Hylland Eriksen*

## Introduction

The terrorist attacks of July 22, 2011[158] revealed a dimension of Norwegian society that was scarcely known outside of the country, and was poorly understood within it. After that terrible day, no one could deny the existence of an active, militantly anti-immigrant, notably anti-Muslim, network loosely connected through websites and social media,[159] as will be discussed at greater length further in this chapter. Adherents posted online messages attacking the government as treacherous and the national elites as spineless for accepting cultural pluralism and continued immigration into the country. While the most vociferous, they are not the only ones to hold such views. Associated with the right-wing populist Progress Party (PP), anti-immigrant sentiments can be found across the political spectrum. One opinion poll indicates that 25 percent of the population thinks that "there are

---

158 Anders Behring Breivik acknowledged killing 77 people and injuring more than 200 others in a bombing and shooting rampage in Oslo and a summer youth camp on Utøya island on July 22, 2011. Breivik, a right-wing extremist, said he acted in defense of Norway and to protect the country from multiculturalism and Islamic "colonization" of Europe.

159 Although Breivik claimed membership in a shadowy pan-European militant nationalist organization known as the Knights Templar, Norwegian police testified at trial that Breivik acted alone and that there was no evidence of the existence of the group. See Criscione 2012.

too many Muslims in the country";[160] of these, many state that their voice is not being heard. Indeed, a possibly deepening rift in Norwegian society divides the defenders of diversity from those who fear encroachment on Norwegian culture by immigrants, in particular Muslims, who represent values that are ostensibly incompatible with the liberal individualism and democratic ideals prized by the majority. This chapter assesses the connection between the recent rise of resentment against immigration (particularly against Muslims) and broader trends in Norwegian nationalism, and proposes a few policy recommendations with the aim of minimizing this rift in Norwegian society.

## The Norwegian Context

Unlike nearly all other Organization for Economic Cooperation and Development (OECD) countries, Norway was scarcely affected by the financial crisis that began in 2008. Its petroleum wealth and the fact that it is not part of the European Union have effectively insulated it from the effects of the euro crisis and other signs of economic instability, and have contributed to keeping unemployment very low. In March 2012, the official unemployment level was only 3 percent (Statistics Norway 2011b). It is important to keep this economic context in mind when analyzing the circumstances surrounding immigration to Norway and society's reaction to it.

### National Identity and Ethnic Minorities

Like most national identities in the modern world, the Norwegian one claims an ancient ancestry (Gellner 1983; Eriksen 2010). Viking my-

---

160 It should be noted that the public survey figures for Oslo, where more than half of the Muslims live, is only 16 percent. See Norwegian Broadcasting Corporation (NRK) 2011. The survey was carried out by Norstat on behalf of NRK.

thology became a prominent element of the mainstream Norwegian self-understanding during the final decades of the 19th century.[161] Growing out of the Romantic movement of the time, Norwegian nationalism has historically been based on ethnicity, while also being influenced by Enlightenment concepts of human rights (it should nonetheless be noted that rights were initially accorded only to men with property and that minority rights were not on the agenda) and the failed 1848 democratic revolutions in continental Europe. Because of its historical homogeneity, and because Norwegian society has always been relatively small (there were 0.9 million inhabitants in 1814, 3 million in 1945, and 5 million in 2012) (Statistics Norway 2012b), the institutions of the modern state, from mass media to the educational system and the labor market, have been capable of building, and making credible, an image of the nation as a family. In addition, the perceived vulnerability of Norwegian nationhood – full independence from Sweden was achieved only in 1905, and the country was under German occupation from 1940 to 1945 – contributes to a sense that today's Norway, distant from an aggressor Viking past, might again be besieged by foreigners.

Ethnic minorities in Norway have historically been few in number, with the exception of the Sami (Lapps)[162] of the far north. "National minorities" include Jews, Romani (a mixed, "travelling" group of partly Gypsy origin), Roma and Kvens (long-established groups of Finnish origin). Numbers are uncertain since "national minorities" are not registered statistically by ethnicity. An estimate is that there

---

161  Before this, after a mass conversion to Christianity in the 11th century, the pagan Vikings had not been a significant element of Norwegian self-understanding. Following the emergence of a Romantic nationalist ideology in the mid-19th century, the heroism and boldness that characterized the warlike Vikings were largely seen as positive expressions of Norwegian national spirit (*Volksgeist*).

162  The indigenous people of northern Scandinavia, the Sami, speak a Finno-Ugric language and are associated with reindeer herding, which is still the main source of livelihood for a minority of the Sami. In Norway, they number about 40,000 and are fully integrated into the modern Norwegian state, but they maintain special linguistic and cultural rights and, since 1989, have had their own parliament with legislative power over cultural and regional issues.

are 15,000 Kvens, 1,500–2,000 Jews, 2,000–3,000 Romani, and around 400 Roma.[163] Despite these relatively small numbers, there has been considerable animosity toward minority groups. In the Norwegian Constitution of 1814, Jews were not even allowed into the country. Groups of itinerant Roma from Southeast Europe are even today associated with begging and petty crime (a phenomenon not unique to Norway). "Norwegianification" (*fornorskning*) was the official policy well into the 1970s toward the Sami, once a largely nomadic group of reindeer herders.

During the German occupation, resistance was widespread, and the Germans enjoyed limited legitimacy. However, the resistance movement was mainly nationalist in character and did not visibly engage with the issue of the genocide against Jews and other minorities. In other words, unlike in Germany, but not entirely unlike in Austria, the ethnic undercurrents that formed part of Norwegian nationalism before the war were not dealt with critically in the aftermath of the war and were allowed to continue to thrive.

### Immigration to the Welfare State

Throughout the 19th century and well into the 20th, Norway was a net exporter of people. About one-third of the population emigrated before World War I, mostly to North America – at a rate among the highest in Europe. After 1945, this flow reduced to a trickle, and since the late 1960s, Norway has been a net importer of people.

Before 1975, most non-Western immigrants to Norway, largely from Pakistan and Turkey, came for jobs. In 1975, the government imposed a general ban on immigration (with exceptions for the neighboring Nordic countries), leaving only two ways for third-country nationals to legally enter Norway: through family reunification or as

---

163　See the Norwegian government's white paper on legal protection against ethnic discrimination (Arbeidsdepartementet 2002).

refugees. This finally changed with the European Union's 2004 enlargement, when migration from the new member states of the European Union grew significantly. Although Norway is not an EU member state, it has signed the Schengen free movement agreement and coordinates many of its policies with the European Union, including policy on labor migration. The number of first- and second-generation immigrants nearly tripled in the 16 years from 1995 to 2011, rising from 215,000 to 600,000 (Statistics Norway 2012c). Of this population, 500,000 are first-generation immigrants and 100,000 are Norwegians born to immigrant parents. A further 210,000 people were Norwegian born with one foreign-born and one Norwegian-born parent (Statistics Norway 2012a). These numbers are considerable in a population of 5 million.

Norway's stability, safety, wealth, and welfare system make it an attractive destination for migrants from many backgrounds in spite of its cold climate and peripheral location. The fast growth in immigrant numbers must chiefly be understood in this context, rather than as something encouraged by state policy. In actual immigration policy, Norwegian governments, whether majority Labour or Conservative, have on the whole been neither more nor less liberal than other governments in Western Europe.

The largest national groups of immigrants are currently Swedes and Poles. Official records indicate that about 60,000 Poles and 34,000 Swedes live in the country (Statistics Norway 2012c); the actual numbers are higher, although many are temporary residents. As EU citizens, Swedes and Poles are not registered as labor migrants. They live and work in Norway periodically without settling permanently, and there is no perceptible resentment against them. In contemporary discourse, both private and public, the word "immigrant" (*innvandrer*) does not apply to Swedes and Poles but, rather, connotes non-Europeans, usually Muslim. Slightly less than one-third of the total immigrant population – about 180,000 people – comes from a predominantly Muslim country; membership in Muslim congregations is fewer than 100,000 (or less than one-sixth of the total immigrant population) (Statistics Norway 2010).

**Figure 1: Immigrants and Norwegian-Born Children of Immigrant Parents, by Country Background, 1970–2011**

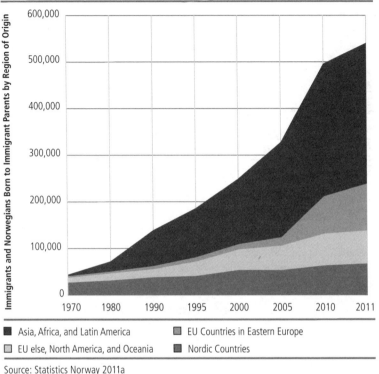

Source: Statistics Norway 2011a

Non-European migrants tend to have lower labor force participation rates than ethnic Norwegians and European immigrants, and tend to retire earlier (see Aalandslid 2009). There are notable differences between nationalities: Sri Lankans (70 percent), for example, are closer to the majority pattern than Somalis (30 percent). Generally, participation in the labor market increases with the length of residence in Norway. Gender also plays a role, as men tend to work more than women. These discrepancies are cause for concern in the Norwegian bureaucracy and public sphere (Brochmann et al. 2011).

**Figure 2: Registered Unemployed (Ages 16–74) as Share of Labor Force by Country Background, 1989–2010**

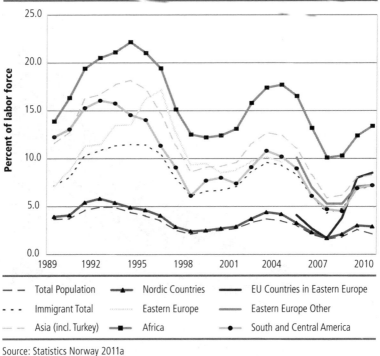

Source: Statistics Norway 2011a

## Immigrant Integration: Government Policies and Social Reactions

Alongside the rapid growth of the ethnic minority population, debates about integration, immigration policy, multiculturalism, and national identity have flourished in Norway and have, as in many other European countries, become a central political issue since the end of the Cold War. Norway's success in maintaining high levels of welfare, security, and employment – in the midst of global economic turmoil – also may contribute to the rise of xenophobic views. The notion that "we Norwegians" are a vulnerable island of prosperous stability in a rough sea may be seen as reason to close ranks and restrict flows across borders.

## Integration: Multiculturalism versus Assimilation

As do all Western European countries, Norway – especially as it diversifies – has a pressing need to strike a balance between equality and difference, between unity and diversity, as the government attempts to foster a fair and just society that includes both old and new Norwegians. Throughout Norway's postwar history and especially under the leadership of the Labour Party (in power since 2005), inclusion and the values associated with equality have been seen as paramount.

One primary objective of the Norwegian government is to ensure high participation by inhabitants in the labor market. To this end, ethnic discrimination in the labor market is illegal. The main organization for employers, the Confederation of Norwegian Enterprises (NHO), has run campaigns encouraging its members to employ people of minority backgrounds. It should be noted, however, that discrimination has been documented (Craig 2007), although convictions have not followed.

When it comes to social integration, the term *multiculturalism* is increasingly shunned for connoting segregation and misguided tolerance. Few politicians today would describe themselves as multiculturalists. Instead of *multicultural*, the word *diverse* is more often used to describe the composition of the population of Oslo (where 29.6 percent of residents have an immigration background) (Statistics Norway 2012a). Politicians emphasize that diversity presupposes equal participation in shared institutions, such as the educational system and the labor market. Policies that could be deemed multiculturalist with a view to according special treatment for Muslims nevertheless exist, for instance, in health services (where Muslim women can choose to be examined by female doctors), in prisons and hospitals (where halal food is an option), and in some schools (where girls can seek exemption from showering after gym class, an issue that is decided at the local level).

The thrust of Norwegian policies toward immigrants has nevertheless trended in the direction of equality, sometimes understood as assimilation. One reason may be that the same word, *likhet*, means both "equality" and "similarity" in Norwegian. In other words, no terminological distinction is made between equal rights and cultural similarity. Claiming equality, therefore, is an understandable and laudable thing to do in Norway, while claiming the right to difference is more difficult to handle ideologically. This is partly a result of the history of Norwegian nationalism (dealt with above) and also partly an indirect outcome of the Labour-led construction of the welfare state, where equality has always been associated with cultural homogeneity.

In academic parlance, a distinction between *integration, assimilation,* and *segregation* is often made. Assimilation entails the eventual disappearance of any difference between groups, leading to one group "swallowing" another. Segregation takes many forms, including "malign" forms, such as apartheid, and "benign" forms, such as strong forms of multiculturalism that encourage cultural autonomy among the constituent groups of society. Segregation implies internal self-governance on the part of minorities and highly regulated, restricted contact across ethnic boundaries. In social science literature on ethnicity and cultural pluralism, integration refers to the maintenance of a distinctive cultural identity while simultaneously participating as equals in greater society (see Eriksen 2010). While integration in this sense has been the goal of successive Norwegian governments, it has proved elusive.

While, over the past 20 years, the Norwegian government has largely succeeded in setting policies to foster equal opportunities for its increasingly diverse population, policy is not necessarily practice. This is evident, for example, in the continued existence of ethnic discrimination in the labor market. Yet it is undeniable that Norwegian policymakers have been determined in their efforts to foster social well-being for the entire population. On the other hand, they have dealt with minorities' claims to the right of difference in less consistent and, arguably, less satisfactory ways. For example, religious organizations automatically receive substantial state support, while other minority organizations and nongovernmental organizations (NGOs) do not. As a result, the state indirectly encourages immigrants to identify along religious lines, which may not have been the intention in the first place. Moreover, language policy in schools has been inconsistent. There is no national policy concerning instruction in minority languages versus Norwegian in the first years of primary school, where decisions are taken at the municipal level.

In conclusion, Norwegian governments have been skilled in legislating equality but less skilled in dealing with diversity. Partly, this is a result of the history of the Norwegian welfare state, where cultural diversity was not an issue, but it should also be pointed out that diversity today is associated with national or ethnic groups, not individuals; people are treated as Tamils, Vietnamese, etc., and not in accordance with their basic, individual human concerns and needs. Regardless, ethnic discrimination (although illegal) continues to exist, and the promise of equal treatment is often not fulfilled, be it in the labor market, the housing market, or education.


**Areas of Tension**


In the aftermath of the 1970s oil shock, the main criticism of immigration (from the left and right alike) was that it would lead to unemployment and depress wages for natives. Since the mid-1980s, however, when Norway began to enjoy very substantial oil revenues, the arguments around immigration shifted in nature. While one argument against immigration continues to be economic, the other centers on the perceived cultural "otherness" of immigrants. Since Norway has a comprehensive welfare state that relies largely on a high level of taxation, there is some concern across the political spectrum about immigrants contributing less and taking relatively more from the welfare state than the majority. Meanwhile, contemporary public debates do not reference the competition for jobs or the economic crisis. On the contrary, many immigrants are welcomed by large segments of the population precisely because they are viewed as carrying out the work that Norwegians would be loathe to take. Resentment, where it exists, is largely associated with the perceived cultural otherness of immigrants, but the suspicion that many arrive as "welfare tourists" is also still very much alive.

Public discontent over the level of immigrant integration can be analyzed within a number of different policy areas, including housing, crime, gender equality, and religion. First, there is a broad and increasing concern around "ghettoization." In the greater Oslo area, home to nearly a quarter of the country's overall population and more than half of the immigrant minority population,[164] there is a tendency toward territorial ethnic segregation. Always a deeply class-divided city along east-west lines, class is now being supplemented by ethnicity. The majority of non-Western immigrants live in the eastern parts of the city, where ethnic Norwegians form a diminishing minority. The tendency of "white flight" from the most immigrant-dense suburbs in the outer suburbs of Grorud Valley (*Groruddalen*) has been documented and caught the attention of the media in the summer of 2011 (City Council of Oslo 2010). Today, there are several primary and lower-secondary schools in the area where the proportion of children of non-European immigrants ranges from 60 to over 90 percent (City Council of Oslo, Board of Education 2011). For the city as a whole, the number of non-European immigrant children rose from 31 to 40 percent between 2000 and 2010, and in 51 of the 125 primary/lower-secondary schools, minority children are the majority. It is often argued that these children are being poorly integrated, and that the communities in which they live are hotbeds of crime and religious fundamentalism.[165] However, this latter allegation has not been documented.

Second, the link between migration and crime is frequently made in the press and by certain politicians. Immigrants are overrepresented in crime statistics (Skarðhamar, Thorsen, and Henriksen 2011), most involving young men from low socioeconomic backgrounds. Nearly all rapes in public spaces in Oslo have in recent years been committed by immigrants (see, e.g., Oslo police quoted in Net-

---

164 Statistics Norway 2012a. Immigrants and their descendants represent 12 percent of the national population, but 28 percent of the city's population.
165 See, e.g., Human Rights Service and Document.no for influential websites where this view is frequently presented.

tavisen.no 2011). This contributes to growing resentment within Norwegian society.

Third, issues concerning gender equality are central to the Norwegian debates on minorities and integration. When the Muslim headscarf is discussed in Norway, it is not with reference to secular values (as in France), nor to notions of "common values" (as in the Netherlands), but exclusively as a question of women's rights. Gender equality has recently become a value central to Norwegian self-understanding; even the PP, which in the past defended traditional gender roles, now represents itself as favorable to gender equality. Within this context, opposition to the headscarf has almost exclusively been framed within a feminist discourse, where the argument has been that women who wear the hijab must necessarily be oppressed by their husbands, brothers, or fathers. When it comes to marriage, there are fundamental differences between mainstream Norwegian culture's focus on individualism and the cultures of many immigrant communities, where family and kinship are seen as paramount to well-being. It is important to note here that a number of first- and second-generation Norwegian Muslims have defended the ideal of gender equality that is prevalent in Norwegian society, criticizing their cobelievers for lagging behind in their cultural adaptation to modernity.[166]

Fourth, the role of religion in public life has been widely debated for years, particularly as it pertains to freedom of expression. The issue of how to balance freedom of expression and respect for religion reached a climax during the Danish cartoon controversy of 2005–2006,[167] which spilled into Norway when a small Norwegian magazine reprinted the Danish cartoons. There is a belief voiced in certain segments of the Norwegian blogosphere that the media consists solely

---

166 Among the most outspoken public intellectuals on this issue are the writer-comedian Shabana Rehman and the politician-lawyer Abid Raja.

167 On September 30, 2005, the Danish newspaper *Jyllands-Posten* published an editorial with caricatures of what the Prophet Mohammed might have looked like, using illustrations from 12 different political cartoonists. This sparked outrage among many religious Muslims who viewed the drawings as offensive; defenders of the cartoons said the newspaper was simply exercising its right to free speech.

of leftist multiculturalists who practice self-censorship and refuse to criticize Islam and Muslims. Conversely, others argue that one can hardly open a newspaper without finding an article that criticizes this group. Such arguments point to the existence of a deepening rift within Norwegian society about issues of cultural diversity and, in particular, Muslims. Those who defend diversity and certain multiculturalist policies (such as supporting religious minorities as well as non-religious minority organizations financially) argue that it is possible to be a good Norwegian citizen who is committed to the democratic values of society without sharing the majority's way of life in every respect. They also do not see a possibly irreconcilable conflict between the Muslim faith and Norwegian identity. Foreign Minister Jonas Gahr Støre illustrated this point in 2008 when he gave a much-cited speech titled "A New and Larger 'We'" in an Oslo mosque, where he emphasized the need to expand the conceptualization of what it meant to be Norwegian. Those of this view are characterized as a "multiculturalist elite" by the anti-immigration lobby and consist of politicians, editors and journalists, intellectuals, and academics.

Finally, as mentioned above, when it comes to debates on diversity and multiculturalism, it is really one group that is the center of discussion: Muslims. Concerns about migration, which had once largely been on economic grounds, took on a cultural and religious focus following the Salman Rushdie affair in 1988[168] and the end of the Cold War. This was exacerbated after the 9/11 attacks on the United States. Today, it can be said that Norwegian xenophobia and racism are no longer centered on "visibly different" people, previously the main target of ethnic discrimination (see Gullestad 2006), or Jews (anti-Semitism is not very visible, although criticism of Israel is), but Muslims, regardless of their origins. Generalizing statements about Muslims have become common in the media, even if frequently countered

168  Salman Rushdie's controversial novel *The Satanic Verses* was partly inspired by the life of Mohammed and refers to an alleged part of the Quran. While well-received in some Western countries, the book provoked widespread protests (some violent) from Muslims who accused it of mocking their faith, and Rushdie faced death threats.

by more nuanced or opposing views. In contemporary Norway, "the other" is now a Muslim – if a man, a possible perpetrator; if a woman, a potential victim.

Other visible minorities in Norway have not provoked negative reactions from the native population. For example, there is no controversy around the religious practices of Tamils, the dietary habits of Hindus in general, or the wearing of the Sikh turban. Although forced marriages (as opposed to arranged marriages) occur among several immigrant groups (Bredal 2011), the practice is associated with Islam. Similarly, female circumcision is believed by many to be a Muslim custom (which it essentially is not).

Criticism of Muslims and Islam takes many forms, from the reformist ("Make Islam conform with modern life") to the Manichaean ("Islam represents absolute evil and must be fought at any cost"). Differentiating between these positions is important lest one lose the ability to distinguish between a concern to strengthen social cohesion in the country through common values, at one end of the spectrum, and calls for civil war and the dehumanization of the "other," at the other. To this we now turn.

## Islamophobia in Norway

Classic right-wing extremist groups (notably neo-Nazis and skinheads) have been visible but never prominent in Norway, and are certainly more marginal today than they were 20 or 30 years ago. However, the development of resentment and militant contempt toward Muslims had not been mapped by the police, partly because such sentiments were not considered a major security risk before the mass killings that shocked the world on July 22, 2011, and partly because these ideological tendencies were not anchored in organizations and were therefore difficult to gauge and observe.

That said, *Fremskrittspartiet* (the Progress Party, or PP) is a well-established formal political party that shares many right-wing views. The party was founded in 1975 as a libertarian, anti-establishment voice; beginning in the mid-1980s, it oriented its identity around an anti-immigrant platform. Its leadership has openly argued against "the dream from Disneyland" (of multiculturalism), and its legendary leader, Carl I. Hagen, said in 2007 that "not all Muslims are terrorists, but all terrorists are Muslims." In 2009, this party received 22.9 percent of the votes in the parliamentary elections. Its performance in the local elections of 2011 was much weaker, with a national average of 11.4 percent. The decline, which may have been temporary, is likely to be connected to the fact that Anders Behring Breivik, the perpetrator of the July 2011 terrorist attacks, had been a member of the party for a decade.

## The Extremists

The new Islamophobic right is not formally associated with any political organizations (though the PP shares some of its views); instead, Islamophobia can be found among adherents of many different political parties. It is therefore impossible to measure how widespread the ideology is. What is clear is that, after the 2011 attacks, the Norwegian authorities have (belatedly) discovered that it may represent a security threat. However, anyone who has followed the discourse on the more popular anti-Islamist websites,[169] which between them have tens of thousands of unique visitors every week, would have expected violence to erupt, although not on this scale and in this form.[170]

The anti-diversity discourse on the Internet has two salient characteristics: First, contributors cannot easily be identified; most write under assumed names and form a loosely knit network. Also, they are ordinary citizens, often with middle-class jobs (albeit often somewhat downwardly mobile) – not tattooed, leather-wearing skinheads (Strøm-

---

169  These include sites such as: www.rights.no ; www.document.no; and www.honestthinking.org.

170  Most of the 77 fatalities were white Norwegian members of the Labour Party's youth wing.

men 2008). Many feel that the Norway they love is being transformed into a culturally diverse society where one is discouraged from speaking one's mind because of the predominance of "politically correct" tolerance. Second, the discourse on these websites creates self-confirming, closed circuits where the reality check that would have been offered by broader and more nuanced access to information is absent. One may spend one's days perusing selected websites without once being exposed to a counterexample or counterargument. Breivik would not necessarily have been exposed to the fact that most Muslims in Norway are Democrats, and that many are not practicing the religion of their ancestors. Instead, his preferred sources of information warned him about the weak and spineless "multiculturalist elite," the fanaticism (and evil) of Islam, and secret deals made with Muslim states by the politically correct government.

It is within this camp that we see routine attacks on the "multiculturalist elite" and politicians who support multicultural policies, delivered in often extremely violent language; the one-sided depiction of ethnic relations in Norway (Muslims are always medieval, brutal, and wrong; Norwegians are gullible and naïve); and the open flirtation with paranoid "Eurabia" thinking (according to which European political elites are complicit in conspiracies aiming to Islamicize Europe) (an oft-mentioned book on this is Ye'or 2005). Online posts commonly express doubt about the fundamental legitimacy of the democratically elected and about the possibility of getting the media to present the "truth," and they voice the belief that the country's cultural and intellectual elites are unprincipled, anti-national, relativist, and treacherous. Experience from elsewhere indicates that such strong expressions of religious and racial prejudice are a recipe for violence.

Such conspiratorial and paranoid views represent a dark undercurrent of Norwegian nationalism – marked by racial supremacism and a complex moral superiority harking back to Protestantism and the early days of social democracy – that has never been addressed critically in this country. Although rare, traces of this outlook can easily be found in mainstream Norwegian society, where "Islam" is sometimes depicted as a festering boil on European culture and identity.[171] These expressions are not only dangerous in that they call into question the legitimacy of the democratic process, but also in that they see the presence of certain cultural minorities in the country as impossible to reconcile with nationhood. Anti-defamation laws notwithstanding, in practice, it is impossible to stop this kind of discourse as it unfolds on the Internet.

### The Rest of the Spectrum

While those who subscribe to the beliefs previously mentioned may be seen as extreme, not all who are skeptical of the Muslim presence in Norway fit under the heading "extreme right." Many gravitate toward the PP, but many are disillusioned Social Democrats, self-designated feminists, and political centrists. One member of the fiercely anti-Muslim organization SIAN (Stop the Islamification of Norway) was also a member of the Socialist Left party. Many Islamophobes are far from identifying with the PP politically and would probably have voted for an anti-immigration social democratic party, if possible. In other words, anti-Muslim sentiment is spread across most of the political spectrum, if not evenly.

The most important view shared by all who associate with these loosely knit networks is the belief that Muslims cannot become good Europeans, or good Norwegians, until they cease to be Muslims. This view has not only been voiced by members of parliament (MPs) from the PP, but also by various commentators and intellectuals who do not identify with the right wing. Historian Nils Rune Langeland, in an interview with influential left-of-center newspaper *Dagbladet* only days before the terrorist attacks, spoke of a coming *reconquista* (referring to the fall of Granada and the expulsion of the Moors in 1492),

---

171  For example, a recent headline from the country's largest and most influential newspaper, *Aftenposten*, read "Islam ulmer i Paris' forsteder" (Islam Smouldering in Paris Suburbs). Of course, religions do not "smoulder."

raised the possibility that the "Germanic peoples of the North may yet rise" and concluded by stating that Muslim girls may get good grades at university but "they will never crack the European code" (Hobbelstad 2011). With the hindsight of the terrorist attack, Dr. Langeland's analysis reads almost like a recipe for armed revolt against creeping "Islamification by stealth" (a PP term) and the loss of honor and masculine strength among mainstream Norwegians.[172] However, the interview was published without much initial controversy, which illustrates that this perception of Muslims has become so commonplace that Norwegians today hardly raise an eyebrow when they read statements like those made by Langeland. What is interesting, in other words, is the ordinariness of his generalizations and the trivialization of his contempt.

## Looking Ahead: Conclusions and Recommendations

Contemporary Norway is divided when it comes to questions of cultural diversity and immigration. For at least a decade, the main focus has been on Islam and Muslims, but this may shift with changes in the international political and economic scene and migration patterns to Norway. With the current economic crisis in large parts of Western Europe, increased migration from the European Union, particularly Southern Europe, may be envisioned in the near term. It should also be kept in mind that, even today, arguably the most stigmatized and excluded minority in the country are Roma, who are not Muslim. Today, the Roma minority is minuscule and itinerant, but this may also change.

The problem facing Norway and its national identity in this century is the fact that the country was founded on the premise of ethnic homogeneity (and a considerable degree of cultural homogeneity), while contemporary Norway displays increasing diversity. In other words, the old map does not fit the new territory. The 2011 terrorist

---

172  For an analysis of masculinity in this context, see Kimmel 2011.

attacks were intended by Breivik as a first step toward cultural and ethnic purification of the country, although the targets were Norwegian "traitors" and not immigrants.

In order for the nation to instill solidarity and cohesion among its diverse inhabitants, a number of steps need to be taken. These include:

*Strengthen unity and citizenship.* The government should make efforts to ensure that all members of society are treated fairly and justly, and to create symbolic events with a strong ritual content in order to strengthen the sense of belonging. Citizenship ceremonies for new Norwegians may be a step in the right direction in this respect, as would public rituals celebrating the "unity in diversity" of the new Norway. The significance of emotionally charged rituals outside of sport (winter sports, hugely popular among ethnic Norwegians, do not necessarily help integrate newcomers) has probably been underestimated by leading politicians.

*Promote diversity within a framework of Norwegian values.* It is important to make a sharp distinction between social integration and cultural assimilation in order for a national identity not based on ethnic identity to appear credible, not least to minorities. This would allow cultural and religious diversity to coexist with a cohesive society based on fundamental values associated with Norway, such as trust, accountability, democracy, informality, egalitarianism, and gender equality. First and foremost – and this may be the most urgent task – national leaders must state, in no uncertain terms, that being Norwegian is not a question of racial or ethnic origin, but of citizenship and commitment to the common good.

*Ensure representation of diversity.* The country will need to deemphasize ethnicity and religion in the public sphere, while simultaneously ensuring that minorities are represented in key positions in politics, the bureaucracy, the media, and academia, as well as socially important institutions, such as the health service, educational sector, and police force. Meanwhile, immigrants and their descendants must be encouraged to show their adherence and loyalty to their new country by taking part in all aspects of public life, ranging from participation in the labor market, public celebrations, and civil society, on par with the majority.

*Prevent discrimination.* Tendencies toward ethnic segregation in the labor market must be addressed. Minority youth are already well-represented in higher education; anti-discrimination laws should be effectively implemented across job sectors.

*Diversity should once and for all replace multiculturalism as a descriptive term.* Diversity may or may not refer to differences between groups, and this makes it possible to reconceptualize Norway as a country where individuals may be diverse, and not just groups. It is true that, in the 20th century, the project of nation-building and of developing a welfare state entailed policies aimed at creating a stable, homogeneous national identity. In the 21st century, this must be supplemented with legal and factual recognition of diversity and a full acknowledgement of the compatibility between a cohesive society and cultural diversity.

## Works Cited

Aalandslid, Vebjørn. 2009. *A Comparison of the Labour Market Integration of Immigrants and Refugees in Canada and Norway.* Oslo: Statistics Norway, 2009. www.ssb.no/english/subjects/06/01/rapp_200931_en/rapp_200931_en.pdf.

*Aftenposten.* Islam ulmer i Paris' forsteder (Islam Smouldering in Paris Suburbs). *Aftenposten* October 17, 2011.

Arbeidsdepartementet. *Rettslig vern mot etnisk diskriminering.* Oslo: Arbeidsdepartementet 2002. www.regjeringen.no/nb/dep/ad/dok/nouer/2002/nou-2002-12/27.html?id=145445.

Bredal, Anja. *Mellom makt og avmakt* (Between Power and Powerlessness). Oslo: Institutt for samfunnsforskning, 2011.

Brochmann, Grete, Torben M. Andersen, Anne Britt Djuve, Einar Niemi, Knut Røed, Inge Skeie, and Sverre Try. *Velferd og migrasjon: Den norske modellens framtid* (*Welfare and Migration: The Future of the Norwegian Model*). Report for the Ministry of Children, Equality, and Social Inclusion, 2011. www.regjeringen.no/en/dep/bld/dok/nouer/2011/nou-2011-07.html?id=642496.

City Council of Oslo. Flyttestatistikk for Oslo 2010 (Demographic Mobility in Oslo 2010). 2010. www.utviklings-og-kompetanseetaten.oslo.kommune.no/oslostatistikken/flytting.

City Council of Oslo, Board of Education. Elever med et annet morsmål enn norsk og samisk i Oslo – skoleåret 2010–2011 (Pupils with Another Mother Tongue than Norwegian or Sami in Oslo – the School Year of 2010–2011). December 16, 2011. www.utdanningse taten.oslo.kommune.no/category.php?categoryID=10160.

Craig, Ronald. *Systemic Discrimination in Employment and the Promotion of Ethnic Equality*. Leiden, Netherlands: Martinus Nijhoff, 2007.

Criscione, Valeria. Oslo police refute Breivik's claim of terrorist network, saying he acted alone. *Christian Science Monitor* May 30, 2012. www.csmonitor.com/World/Europe/2012/0530/Oslo-police-refute-Breivik-s-claim-of-terrorist-network-saying-he-acted-alone.

Document.no. www.document.no.

Eriksen, Thomas Hylland. *Ethnicity and Nationalism*, 3rd edition. London: Pluto, 2010.

Gellner, Ernest. *Nations and Nationalism*. Oxford: Blackwell, 1983.

Gullestad, Marianne. *Plausible Prejudice*. Oslo: Universitetsforlaget, 2006.

Hobbelstad, Inger Merete. På sporet av det krigerske. *Dagbladet* July 15, 2011, www.dagbladet.no/2011/07/15/kultur/nils_rune_lange-land/europa/islam/velferdsstaten/17321062.

Human Rights Service. www.rights.no.

Kimmel, Michael. A Tale of Two Terrorists Redux. *Sociological Images* July 27, 2011. http://thesocietypages.org/socimages/2011/07/27/a-tale-of-two-terrorists-redux/.

Nettavisen.no. 45 av 48 voldtekts-mistenkte er utlendinger. *Nettavisen.no* October 27, 2011. www.nettavisen.no/nyheter/article 3260189.ece.

Norwegian Broadcasting Corporation. En av fire nordmenn ser på islam som en trussel. *NRK.com* October 26, 2011. www.nrk.no/nyheter/norge/1.7847186.

Skarðhamar, Torbjørn, Lotte Thorsen, and Kristin Henriksen. *Kriminalitet og straff blant innvandrere og øvrig befolkning* (Crime and Punishment among Immigrants and the Rest of the Population). Oslo: Statistics Norway, 2011. www.ssb.no/emner/03/05/rapp_201121/rapp_201121.pdf.

Statistics Norway. Medlemmer i Den norske kirke og i tros-og livssynssamfunn utenfor Den norske Kirke 2010 (Members of the Church of Norway and of Religious Associations Outside of The Church of Norway, 2010). www.ssb.no/minifakta/main_08.html #tab0808.

Statistics Norway. Focus on: Immigration and Immigrants. 2011a. www.ssb.no/innvandring_en/.

Statistics Norway. Focus on: Labour. 2011b. www.ssb.no/arbeid_en/.

Statistics Norway. Immigrants and Norwegian-Born to Immigrant Parents. 2011c. www.ssb.no/innvbef_en/.

Statistics Norway. Immigrants and Norwegian-born to immigrant parents, by country background and municipality. January 1, 2012. Absolute numbers and per cent. 2012a. www.ssb.no/english/subjects/02/01/10/innvbef_en/tab-2012-04-26-09-en.html.

Statistics Norway. Focus on: Population. 2012b. www.ssb.no/befolkning_en/.

Statistics Norway. Population, immigrants and Norwegian-born to immigrants by country background. 1970–2012. Absolute numbers and per cent. 2012c. www.ssb.no/english/subjects/02/01/10/innvbef_en/tab-2012-04-26-06-en.html.

Strømmen, Øyvind. *Eurofascism.* Lulu.com, 2008.

Ye'or, Bat. *Eurabia: The Euro-Arab Axis.* Madison, NJ: Fairleigh Dickinson University Press, 2005.

# Immigration Resources

More details about the Transatlantic Council on Migration, convened by the Migration Policy Institute and supported by its policy partners, the Bertelsmann Stiftung and Barrow Cadbury Trust (UK policy partner), can be found at their websites:
- The Transatlantic Council on Migration: www.migrationpolicy. org/transatlantic
- The Migration Policy Institute: www.migrationpolicy.org
- The Bertelsmann Stiftung: www.en.bertelsmann-stiftung.de
- The Barrow Cadbury Trust: www.bctrust.org.uk.

## The Transatlantic Council on Migration's Published Volumes

This book is the sixth Transatlantic Council on Migration volume published with the Bertelsmann Stiftung. The earlier works:
- *Delivering Citizenship* examines how citizenship has become a dynamic policy vehicle for promoting the political incorporation of immigrants and, by extension, their more complete integration.
- *Talent, Competitiveness and Migration* analyzes two opposing policy pressures confronting policymakers: While there is strong popular and political outcry to protect jobs at home as a result of the economic crisis, policymakers also face mid-term demographic challenges. The volume maps how profound demographic change is likely to affect the size and character of global migration flows,

and how governments can shape immigration policy in a world increasingly attuned to the hunt for talent.

- *Migration, Public Opinion and Politics* analyzes how media coverage, public opinion, and political rhetoric can play an important role in advancing – or impeding – immigration policy reforms. The volume examines what publics across the Atlantic think about immigrants and immigration. It also asks: What effect does media coverage have on the prospects for changing the laws and practices that shape immigration and immigrant integration? And how should politicians and others who champion reform speak about immigration?

- *Prioritizing Integration* takes stock of the impact of the global economic crisis on immigrant integration in Europe and the United States and assesses where immigrants have lost ground, using evidence such as employment rates, levels of funding for educational programs, trends toward protectionism, and public opinion. The volume details how governments can use the recovery period as an opportunity for more meaningful and targeted investments in integration – ones that will boost economic competitiveness and improve social cohesion.

- *Improving the Governance of International Migration* examines the key steps to building a better, more cooperative system for governance of migration amid ambivalence by contemporary states about such a model. States desire a more global governance framework because they know they cannot reach their goals by acting alone, yet they fear the necessary compromise on terms they may not be able to control and regarding an issue that is politically charged. The volume provides a persuasive analysis of what form greater international cooperation on migration should take, as well as the goals it should aim to achieve.

To learn more about these publications or to purchase them in hardcopy or e-book format, please visit: www.bertelsmann-stiftung.org/publications.

## Other Related MPI Resources

Migration Policy Institute Europe, a nonprofit, independent research institute established in Brussels in 2011 that builds upon the experience and resources of the Migration Policy Institute: www.mpieurope.org.

MPI's Program on European Migration: www.migrationpolicy.org/research/europe.php.

# About the Transatlantic Council on Migration

The Transatlantic Council on Migration – formally launched in the beginning of 2008 as an initiative of the Migration Policy Institute (MPI) – is a unique deliberative and advisory body that aims to have a tangible, measurable impact on migration and immigrant integration policy on both sides of the Atlantic. As such, it provides a mechanism for forward-looking, sustained discussions among four groups – senior policymakers, leading global migration experts, political leaders, and civil-society/private-sector stakeholders – who would not otherwise come together to deliberate on policy.

The Council has a dual mission:

- To help inform the transatlantic immigration and integration agenda and promote better-informed policymaking by proactively identifying critical policy issues, analyzing them in light of the best research, and bringing them to public attention.
- To serve as a resource for governments as they grapple with the challenges and opportunities associated with international migration. Council members representing governments (and other governments, as appropriate) are encouraged to bring policy initiatives to the Council so that they can be analyzed, vetted, and improved before implementation – and/or evaluated after they have been executed.

The Council has pursued evidence-based policy recommendations on migration and integration primarily through the following three vehicles: 1) formal meetings designed to foster forward-looking discussions among policymakers, opinion leaders, and experts; 2) direct consultations with governments and government institutions to manage migration more effectively, including informal discussions with key decision makers; 3) publications and the public dissemination of Council conclusions.

## Support and Membership

The Council's work is generously supported by the following foundations and governments: Carnegie Corporation of New York, Open Society Foundations, Bertelsmann Stiftung (Policy Partner), the Barrow Cadbury Trust (UK Policy Partner), the Luso-American Development Foundation, the Calouste Gulbenkian Foundation, and the governments of Germany, the Netherlands, Norway, and Sweden.

The permanent Council members are: Giuliano Amato, former Prime Minister and Minister of the Interior in Italy; Michael Chertoff, former US Secretary of Homeland Security and now senior of counsel at Covington & Burling LLP; the Rt. Hon. Charles Clarke, former member of the British Parliament (1997–2010) and former Home Secretary (2004–2006); Ana Palacio, founding partner of Palacio y Asociados and formerly Parliamentarian of the European Union, Foreign Minister of Spain, and Senior Vice President and General Counsel of the World Bank; Trevor Phillips, Chairman of the UK Commission on Equality and Human Rights; Rita Süssmuth, former President (Speaker) of the German Bundestag (1988–1998) and twice leader of Germany's Independent Commissions on Immigration and on Integration in the first half of the last decade; and Antonio Vitorino, partner in the international law firm Gonçalves Pereira, Castelo Branco & Associados, former European Commissioner for Justice and Home Affairs (1999–2004) and former Deputy Prime Minister of Portugal.

The Council is convened by MPI President Demetrios G. Papademetriou.

## Council Meetings

The full Council meets twice annually, and all meetings are held under the Chatham House Rule. Smaller preparatory and expert sessions are held prior to each meeting.

Extraordinary meetings of interested Council members are convened in the capital of the country that is consulting the Council at any one time. Such meetings focus on issues of particular concern to the host country and/or are in response to an immigration crisis.

Papers commissioned for the November 2011 Council meeting, which was held in Berlin, are presented in this volume.

More information about the Council and its membership, operations, and publications can be found at: www.migrationpolicy.org/transatlantic.

# About the Authors

*Joaquín Arango* is Professor of Sociology at the Complutense University of Madrid and Director of the Center for the Study of Migration and Citizenship at the Ortega y Gasset Research Institute. Until May 2012, he was President of Spain's National Forum for the Social Integration of Immigrants.

He is Co-Editor of the *Spanish Immigration and Immigration Policies Yearbook* and serves on the editorial boards of several scientific journals and a number of advisory committees. He is presently involved in European research projects dealing with irregular migration, the impact of admission policies on immigrant integration, attitudes toward immigration and diversity, and domestic migrant workers. He has worked as an expert for the European Commission, the Council of Europe, the Organization for Economic Cooperation and Development, the International Labour Organization, the United Nations Economic Commission for Europe, Eurostat, and other international institutions.

Trained as a demographer and economic historian at the University of California, Berkeley, and as a sociologist at the Complutense University, his scientific interests include migration theories, migration systems and regimes, immigration and integration policies, labor migration, and the impacts of the economic crisis.

*Irene Bloemraad* is Associate Professor in Sociology and the Thomas Garden Barnes Chair of Canadian Studies at the University of California, Berkeley, as well as a Scholar with the Canadian Institute for Advanced Research. Her work examines the intersection of immigration and politics, with emphasis on citizenship, immigrants' political and civic participation, and multiculturalism.

Her research has appeared in academic journals spanning the fields of sociology, political science, history, and ethnic/migration studies. Her books include the recently published *Rallying for Immigrant Rights: The Fight for Inclusion in 21st Century America* (edited with Kim Voss, University of California Press, 2011), *Civic Hopes and Political Realities: Immigrants, Community Organizations, and Political Engagement* (edited with Karthick Ramakrishnan, Russell Sage Foundation Press, 2008), and *Becoming a Citizen: Incorporating Immigrants and Refugees in the United States and Canada* (University of California Press, 2006), which won an honorable mention for the Thomas and Znaniecki Award for best book published in the previous two years from the American Sociological Association's International Migration section.

*Jörg Dräger,* born in 1968, Jörg Dräger studied physics and business administration at the University of Hamburg before transferring to Cornell University in New York State, where he received his M.Sc. and Ph.D. in theoretical physics. During his time in Cornell (1991–1996), he served as an academic assistant while completing his studies and doctoral thesis.

He began his professional career 1996 at the management consulting firm Roland Berger in Frankfurt/Main. In 1998, he returned to Hamburg to become executive director of the newly founded Northern Institute of Technology, a private institute of higher education that focuses on international MBA programs.

From 2001 to 2008, he served as Hamburg's (politically independent) Minister of Science and Research and was a member of Germany's Permanent Conference of Educational Ministers as well as deputy representative to the Bundesrat, the federal body that represents the German states at the national level. From 2004 to 2006, he also held the office of Minister of Health and Consumer Protection in Hamburg.

Since July 1, 2008, he has been a member of the Bertelsmann Stiftung Executive Board where he is responsible for the program areas of education, integration and democracy. He also serves as Executive Director of the CHE Centre for Higher Education. In January 2012, Dräger was appointed Adjunct Professor for Public Management at the Hertie School of Governance in Berlin.

*Thomas Hylland Eriksen* is Professor of Social Anthropology at the University of Oslo and was Research Manager of Cultural Complexity in the New Norway (CULCOM), a major interdisciplinary research program, from 2004 to 2010.

His research has mainly dealt with the cultural implications of globalization, ethnicity, nationalism, and identity politics more broadly conceived. His most recent books in English are *Ethnicity and Nationalism*, 3rd edition (2010); *Small Places, Large Issues*, 3rd edition (2010); *Globalization: The Key Concepts* (2007); and the co-edited volumes *A World of Insecurity: Anthropology and Human Security* (2010) and *Paradoxes of Cultural Recognition* (2009).

*Naika Foroutan* is Assistant Professor of Social Sciences at Humboldt University Berlin, where she heads the Volkswagen research project "Hybrid European-Muslim Identity-Models" (HEYMAT). She also works as a freelance analyst for radio and television on topics such as political Islam, politics in the Middle East, migration, integration, hybridity, and anti-Muslim racism.

Dr. Foroutan currently also heads a project entitled "The Young Islam Conference" (JIK). A mixture of lectures, workshops, and a simulation game that enables around 50 students to get to know the German Islam Conference, the most important forum between the German state and Muslims living in Germany. This project is being conducted in cooperation with the Mercator Foundation and with support from the Federal Ministry of the Interior.

In the past, she has taught seminars at the universities of Berlin and Göttingen in different disciplines, including international relations, political systems, political theory, and the politics of identity.

She wrote her dissertation on intercultural dialogues between the West and the Islamic world. Her current work focuses on nation-states transforming into countries of immigration as well as their migration and integration policies, with a particular focus on people with a Muslim background as agents of change and on the politics of identity around the topic of hybridity.

*Michael Jones-Correa* is Professor of Government at Cornell University and is team leader for the 2010–2013 theme project "Immigration: Settlement, Immigration and Membership" at the Institute for the Social Sciences at Cornell.

Professor Jones-Correa is co-author of *Latinos in the New Millennium* (Cambridge, 2012) and *Latino Lives in America: Making It Home* (Temple, 2010); author of *Between Two Nations: The Political Predicament of Latinos in New York City* (Cornell, 1998); editor of *Governing American Cities: Inter-Ethnic Coalitions, Competition and Conflict* (Russell Sage Foundation, 2001); a co-principal investigator for the 2006 Latino National Survey; as well as author of more than two dozen articles and chapters on immigration, race, ethnicity, and citizenship in the United States.

He was a Visiting Fellow at the Russell Sage Foundation in 1998–1999, the Woodrow Wilson International Center for Scholars in 2003–2004, and the Center for the Study of Democratic Politics at Princeton University in 2009–2010. In 2004–2005, he served on the Committee on the Redesign of US Naturalization Test for the National Academy of Sciences. In 2009, he was elected Vice President of the American Political Science Association and, in 2010–2012, he was appointed to the American National Election Studies (ANES) Board of Overseers.

*Christian Joppke* holds a Chair in Sociology at the University of Bern, Switzerland. He received a PhD in sociology from the University of California, Berkeley, in 1989. Previously, he taught at the University of Southern California, European University Institute, University of British Columbia, International University Bremen (since renamed

Jacobs University), and the American University of Paris. He has also held research fellowships at Georgetown University and the Russell Sage Foundation, New York.

Among his recent books are *Citizenship and Immigration* (Cambridge, UK: Polity, 2010), *Veil: Mirror of Identity* (Cambridge, UK: Polity, 2009), and *Selecting by Origin: Ethnic Migration in the Liberal State* (Cambridge, Mass.: Harvard University Press, 2005).

*Ulrich Kober* is Program Director in the area of Integration and Education at the Bertelsmann Stiftung's headquarters in Germany. He has been with the Bertelsmann Stiftung since 2000. One of the most prominent projects for which Mr. Kober has been responsible was a federal competition on innovative integration projects. This competition was initiated by the then President of Germany, Johannes Rau. It resulted in the identification and dissemination of best practice on integration. It also promoted the positive aspects of integration and social cohesion in Germany. He was responsible for the 2008 Carl Bertelsmann Prize, which was awarded to the Toronto District School Board for its excellence and equity policy.

Mr. Kober was a member of the Catholic Jesuit order and has worked in various fields of education and integration. From 1991 to 2000, he was a Research Assistant for European migration policy at the Jesuit European Office in Brussels, Director of a civic education center in Dresden, and a secondary-school teacher in Berlin and Medellín, Colombia. He held study grants from the Studienstiftung des deutschen Volkes (1983–1991) and of the German Academic Exchange Service/DAAD (1995–1996). He has a master's in theology from the University of Munich and a master's in sociology from the London School of Economics.

*Monique Kremer* is a Research Fellow at the Dutch Scientific Council for Government Policy (Wetenschappelijke Raad voor het Regeringsbeleid) and the University of Amsterdam. She published extensively on comparative welfare states before becoming interested in issues of integration, migration, and development policy. Currently, she is working on the paradoxical relationship between migration and the welfare state. She is also an editor of "Policy and Society" (*Beleid en Maatschappij*) and of the series *Care and Welfare* of Amsterdam University Press.

*Will Kymlicka* is the Canada Research Chair in Political Philosophy in the Philosophy Department at Queen's University in Kingston, Canada, where he has taught since 1998. His research interests focus on issues of democracy and diversity and, in particular, on models of citizenship and social justice within multicultural societies. He has published eight books and over 200 articles, which have been translated into 32 languages, and has received several awards, most recently the 2009 Premier's Discovery Award in the Social Sciences.

He is Co-Director, along with Keith Banting, of the Multiculturalism Policy Index project, which monitors the evolution of MCPs across the Western democracies. The MCP Index project is designed to provide information about MCPs in a standardized format that aids comparative research and contributes to the understanding of state-minority relations.

Born and raised in Canada, he was educated at Queen's and Oxford University, and held positions at various Canadian, American, and European universities before moving to Queen's. He is also a recurrent visiting professor in the Nationalism Studies program at the Central European University in Budapest.

*Cas Mudde* is Assistant Professor in the Department of International Affairs at the University of Georgia. Previously, he taught at DePauw University, Central European University in Budapest, the University of Edinburgh, and the University of Antwerp. He has also been a Visiting Scholar at Universita Karlova (Czech Republic), Academia Istrapolitana Nova (Slovakia), University Jaume I (Spain) and, in the United States, at New York University, the University of California Santa Barbara, the University of Oregon, and the University of Notre Dame.

The bulk of his academic work has been in the broad field of extremism and democracy, and he is involved in various projects on populism, focusing particularly on the relationship between various types of populism and liberal democracy worldwide. He has started a research project that examines how liberal democracies can defend themselves against extremist challenges without undermining their core values.

Dr. Mudde is the author of *The Ideology of the Extreme Right* (Manchester University Press, 2000) and *Populist Radical Right Parties in Europe* (Cambridge University Press, 2007). He has edited or co-edited five volumes, including *Racist Extremism in Central and Eastern Europe* (Routledge, 2005), *Western Democracies and the New Extreme Right Challenge* (Routledge, 2004), and *Uncivil Society? Contentious Politics in Post-Communist Europe* (Routledge, 2003). His co-edited volume *Populism in Europe and the Americas: Corrective or Threat to Democracy?* will be published by Cambridge University Press in 2012.

He received his master's degree and PhD from Leiden University in the Netherlands.

*Demetrios G. Papademetriou* is President and Co-Founder of the Migration Policy Institute (MPI), a think tank dedicated exclusively to the study of international migration. He is also President of the Migration Policy Institute Europe, a nonprofit, independent research institute in Brussels that aims to promote a better understanding of migration trends and effects within Europe. He is also the convener of the Transatlantic Council on Migration, which is composed of senior public figures, business leaders, and public intellectuals from Europe, the United States, and Canada.

Dr. Papademetriou has served as Chair of the World Economic Forum's Global Agenda Council on Migration (2009–2011); Chair of the Migration Committee of the Organization for Economic Cooperation and Development (OECD); Director for Immigration Policy and Research at the US Department of Labor; Chair of the Secretary of Labor's Immigration Policy Task Force; and Executive Editor of the *International Migration Review.*

He has published more than 250 books, articles, monographs, and research reports on migration topics and advises senior government and political party officials in more than 20 countries (including numerous European Union member states while they hold the rotating EU presidency).

His most recent books include *Migration and the Great Recession: The Transatlantic Experience* (co-author and co-editor, 2011); *Immigration Policy in the Federal Republic of Germany: Negotiating Membership and Remaking the Nation* (co-author, 2010); and *Europe and its Immigrants in the 21st Century: A New Deal or a Continuing Dialogue of the Deaf?* (2006, editor and author).

He holds a PhD in comparative public policy and international relations (1976) and has taught at the universities of Maryland, Duke, American, and the New School for Social Research.

*Shamit Saggar* has been Professor of Political Science at the University of Sussex since 2004 and a board member of the Solicitors Regulation Authority (SRA).

After earning a PhD in government from the University of Essex, Dr. Saggar's academic career has spanned the University of Liverpool, Queen Mary – University of London, and the University of Sussex. He was a Harkness Fellow at UCLA, 1993–1994; a Yale World Fellow, 2003–2004; and a Visiting Professor of Public Policy at the University of Toronto, 2008–2009.

Between 2001 and 2003, Dr. Saggar was Senior Policy Advisor within the Prime Minister's Strategy Unit in the Cabinet Office.

He has held a number of nonexecutive and board membership posts, including with the Financial Services Authority, the Association of British Insurers, the Accountancy Foundation, the Peabody Trust, the National Consumer Council, and the Better Regulation Commission.

*Patrick Simon* is Director of Research at the Institut national d'études démographiques (INED) and is a fellow researcher at the Center for European Studies (CEE) at Sciences Po. He was a Visiting Scholar at the Russell Sage Foundation and a Fulbright Fellow in 2010–2011.

Trained as a sociodemographer at L'École des hautes études en sciences sociales (EHESS), where he carned a doctoral degree in 1994, he has studied social and ethnic segregation in French cities, antidiscrimination policies, and the integration of ethnic minorities in European countries. He is one of the principal investigators of a large survey *Trajectories and Origins: The Diversity of Population in France*, conducted by INED and the Institut national de la statistique et des études économiques (INSEE).

He teaches political science at Sciences Po, with a focus on ethnic minorities, integration, and discrimination. He has worked as an expert for the European Commission, Eurostat, the Council of Europe, and the Human Rights Commission of the United Nations.

*Will Somerville* is a Senior Policy Analyst at the Migration Policy Institute (MPI) in the international program. He is also the UK Director for Unbound Philanthropy, a global grant-making foundation, and advises several international and UK-based philanthropic foundations.

Prior to joining MPI in 2006, Mr. Somerville worked at the Commission for Racial Equality, the Centre for Economic and Social Inclusion, the UK Prime Minister's Strategy Unit, Cabinet Office, and the Institute for Public Policy Research.

He has authored over 60 policy papers, chapters, and journal articles. His most recent book is *Immigration under New Labour* (Policy Press, 2007). He is also a contributor to *The Guardian*.

He holds a first-class degree from Leeds University and a master's, with distinction, in social policy from the London School of Economics. He is a Fellow of the Royal Society of Arts (RSA).

# Acknowledgments

This book would not have been possible without the unwavering support and active contributions of the partners and funders of the Transatlantic Council on Migration: the governments of Germany, the Netherlands, Norway, and Sweden; the Carnegie Corporation of New York; the Open Society Foundations; the Bertelsmann Stiftung (the Council's policy partner); the Barrow Cadbury Trust (the Council's UK policy partner); the Luso-American Development Foundation; and the Calouste Gulbenkian Foundation.

We would like to give special thanks to the Members of the Council, who are the soul of this endeavor: Peter Altmaier, Giuliano Amato, Michael Chertoff, Charles Clarke, Ana Palacio, Trevor Phillips, Rita Süssmuth, and Antonio Vitorino. Their dedication to the Council's mission of having a tangible, measurable impact on migration and immigrant integration policy on both sides of the Atlantic is what makes our work possible.

Finally, the editors would like to acknowledge the work of several Council staff members who helped conceptualize this book and offered thoughtful comments on the individual chapters during each stage of editing: Natalia Banulescu-Bogdan, Kate Brick, Elizabeth Collett, and Michelle Mittelstadt. Thanks also are owed to the Bertelsmann Stiftung and project lead Christal Morehouse for their role in the publication of this volume and prior Council books.

In acknowledgments by individual authors:

Cas Mudde, author of Chapter 2, would like to thank researchers at the Migration Policy Institute, and particularly Anne Nielsen, for their research assistance, as well as Shayna Alexander for suggesting various useful websites.

Naíka Foroutan, author of Chapter 7, thanks Sina Arnold and Benjamin Schwarze for their research, edits, and comments.

The authors of Chapter 9, Shamit Saggar and Will Somerville, would like to thank Meghan Benton, James Hampshire, Michelle Mittelstadt, Beryl Randall, and Trevor Phillips for their comments and suggestions.